From the Parent Stem

FROM THE PARENT STEM

ENGLAND *and the* MAKING *of* AMERICA

A TIMELINE

PART II
1700–1773

Raymond M. Brown

ISBN: 979-8-9922161-5-8 (Paperback)
ISBN: 979-8-9922161-1-0 (Hardcover)

Library of Congress Control Number: 2025908413

Printed by Raymond M. Brown in the United States of America.

First printing edition 2025.

Author's Contact: sonoflibertywalk@gmail.com

Book cover background: Union Flag, aka King's Colors

On August 12, 1819, seventy-six-year-old Thomas Jefferson would write his reflections on the June 1776 debates in Congress concerning the vote for independence: "It appearing in the course of these debates that the colonies of N. York, New Jersey, Pennsylvania, Delaware, Maryland, and South Carolina were not yet matured for falling from the parent stem, but that they were fast advancing to that state, it was thought most prudent to wait a while for them, and to postpone the final decision to July 1, but, that this might occasion as little delay as possible a committee was appointed to prepare a declaration of independence."

INTRODUCTION

There was once an aged king who wished to have a tapestry made of his life and approached an Owl with his request. The Owl, a master tailor, replied he would be most happy to oblige and asked only that the king bring him the pieces.

The king complied and eagerly awaited its completion.

But returning on the appointed day, the king was incensed to find that the project had never begun. He angrily approached the Owl who calmly replied, "The task has been impossible. You have brought me but a part of your life when you need to bring it all."

Thus, the king went home and reluctantly returned with those pieces he had formerly left behind, and the Owl was able to weave the most beautiful tapestry in the kingdom.

From the Parent Stem is a tapestry of the many events leading to the creation of the United States of America. Beginning in early Britain and ending in Philadelphia on July 4, 1776, this timeline tells a story so important that it will have a profound impact on the reader's understanding of our nation's origins as historical injustices are laid bare, cherished myths are set aside, and seldom-told tales are told.

From the Parent Stem: England and the Making of America is divided into four books:

Book I   The Beginning to 1699

Book II   1700 – 1773

Book III   1774 – 1775

Book IV   1776 – July 4, 1776

In addition to the many significant historical events, *From the Parent Stem* also includes correspondences of George Washington, daily entries from the Congressional Journals, and the important proclamations and petitions of Great Britain's Parliament and the two Continental Congresses, as all are intertwined with the social and military events of the day to provide the reader a new historical perspective.

While *From the Parent Stem* is a story meant to be read from start to finish, the timeline can also be used as a reference. To keep the text easy to understand and not overwhelm the reader, most entries are divided into three parts: the heading; supportive information; and additional notes designed to provide clarification, commentary, or interesting facts to enhance the reader's comprehension.

As the book's author, I sincerely believe all American history teachers, all American history students, and all Americans who wish to learn a more honest tale of the founding of the United States should own a copy. In addition, it is my sincere hope that *From the Parent Stem* will be appreciated by international readers—particularly those in the United Kingdom.

I present to you, *From the Parent Stem: England and the Making of America.*

Most sincerely offered,

Raymond M. Brown

A Common Bond: The Lucrative Fur Trade

PART TWO

1700 – 1773

1700s

White immigration to England's colonies becomes more diverse as Scots, Irish, Germans, and French Huguenots begin arriving in greater numbers.

As the transatlantic shipping industry expands in the 1700s, so too does the number of arriving non-English as the North American colonies become more multinational.

Note: Immigration to the colonies during the first 100 years had been mostly English. Now, during the 1700s, it would become a more mixed group, including European foreigners and Africans imported as slave workers.

These arriving Whites were Protestants, for Catholic immigration to most of the colonies continued to be discouraged or legally barred.

The importation of Africans to North America increases dramatically.

During the 1600s, fewer than 21,000 Africans were transported to England's mainland colonies, and the majority of laborers were indentured Whites. But between 1700 and 1776, approximately 250,000 African people will be transported to North America representing an exponential increase.

Note: The African slave trade during the 1700s would be conducted mainly by Portugal, France, and England. For the Portuguese, most Africans were bound for Brazil and the West Indies. For the English slavers, the largest market for slaves was the West Indies sugar islands, including Barbados and Jamaica, with fewer bound for the North American mainland.

By 1700, a full 80 percent of the West Indies islands' population were African.

Religious liberty is in short supply in North America; most colonies have an official Church supported by public taxation.

Massachusetts, Connecticut, and New Hampshire are officially Congregational Church (Puritan) colonies. New York, Virginia, Maryland, Carolina, Barbados, Jamaica, Newfoundland, and Nova Scotia are officially Church of England (Anglican) colonies. All French and Spanish colonies are officially Roman Catholic.

1700

The population in England's North American colonies is approximately 260,000.

The four largest towns are: Boston (6,700 inhabitants); New York (5,000); Philadelphia (4,400); and Charles Town (4,000 Whites plus 3,000 enslaved Africans).

Quaker migration to Barbados and Jamaica has grown considerably.

Note:	Many Quakers were involved in the slave trade, but during the next fifty years the religious sect's views on slavery would evolve as they begin the work of abolition.

The *Piracy Act* of 1698: Trials are no longer required to be held in England.

To expedite the prosecution of pirates, Parliament passes a statute allowing trials for all *piracies, felonies, and robberies* committed upon the seas to be held in any of the kingdom's newly formed Admiralty Courts.

Note:	The 1696 Navigation Act had established a system of seven regional Vice Admiralty Courts to deal with smuggling and other nautical crimes. Now, instead of transporting the defendants to London for trial, the accused could be tried in one of the regional sites such as Boston, Jamaica, or Barbados. The law called for those accused of pirating to be tried swiftly, and if convicted, to suffer capital punishment.
	To deter piracy, Charles Town, South Carolina, would hang convicted pirates from oak trees at the edge of town at a site today known as the White Point Garden, or *Pirates' Sway*. Facing the bay, these executions were to be a visible warning to others.
	England would reward privateers who sought out and attacked known pirates.
	Despite the title, the Piracy Act of 1698 was passed in 1700.

March 1700

***An Act to Prevent the Further Growth of Popery*, aka the *Popery Act* of 1698, is passed by Parliament.**

The Popery Act is designed to stamp out any growing Catholicism in England by calling for stronger application and enforcement of existing laws against the religion.

Note:	The law offered a £100 reward to anyone who apprehended a priest guilty of conducting an illegal mass.
	Any priest running a school educating youth in the Catholic faith could be subject to perpetual imprisonment.
	Catholic parents were not permitted to withdraw *a fitting maintenance* (parental support) due to a child adopting the Protestant religion.
	The titles of Acts and the dates they were enacted were often different. The Popery Act of 1698 was enacted in 1700.

1700   **Massachusetts orders Catholic priests to leave the colony within three months or suffer imprisonment or execution.**

> Note: This was mainly a warning to those French Jesuits missionizing among the Indians in the frontier regions of Maine, for few Catholics dared reside in the populated regions of Massachusetts.

North Carolina receives its first Anglican minister.

The Church of England sends Reverend Daniel Brett to minister to the people and counter the growing Quaker influence.

> Note: Reverend Brett's disorderly behavior would soon earn him the nickname "the Monster of the Age."

The South Carolina rice industry continues to rapidly accelerate.

More than 300 tons of *Carolina Gold* rice are exported from Charles Town to England as the colony is now producing more rice than there are ships to carry it.

> Note: Rice cultivation had increased the need for laborers, particularly in Carolina's southern regions, resulting in an increased number of African slaves. The Carolina rice producers would seek slaves from Senegal and other rice-growing African regions for their expertise.

June 24, 1700   **The first North American anti-slavery tract, *The Selling of Joseph*, is printed in Boston.**

Due to Massachusetts's increasing number of slaves and the corresponding unease many Whites felt concerning the Africans living amongst them, Samuel Sewall writes the first anti-slavery tract published in North America, *The Selling of Joseph*, based on an incident in Boston. In his tract Sewall refutes the common rationalizations for the enslavement of Africans and decries the practice of man-stealing, including the following arguments against it:

- "For As Much as Liberty is in real value next unto Life: None ought to part with it themselves, or deprive others of it, but upon the most mature Consideration."

- "The numerousness of Slaves at this day in the Province, and the Uneasiness of them under their Slavery, hath put many upon thinking whether the Foundation of it be firmly and well laid; so as to sustain the Vast Weight that is built upon it. It is most certain that all Men, as they are the sons of Adam, are Coheirs; and have equal Rights unto Liberty, and all other Comforts of Life."

- "Yet through the indulgence of GOD to our First Parents after the Fall, the outward Estate of all and every of the Children, remains the same, as to one another. So that Originally, and Naturally, there is no such thing as Slavery."

- "He that Stealeth a Man and Selleth him, or if he be found in his hand, he shall surely be put to Death. Exod. 12.16. This Law being of Everlasting Equity, wherein Man Stealing is ranked amongst the most atrocious of Capital Crimes: What louder Cry can there be made of the Celebrated Warning, *Caveat Emptor!*"

- "And all thing considered, it would conduce more to the Welfare of the Province, to have White Servants for a Term of Years, than to have Slaves for Life. Few can endure to hear of a Negro's being made free; and indeed they can seldom use their freedom well; yet their continual aspiring after their forbidden Liberty, renders them Unwilling Servants. And there is such a disparity in their Conditions, Color & Hair, that they can never embody with us, and grow up into orderly Families, to the Peopling of the Land; but still remain in our Body Politick as a kind of extra-vasat Blood. As many Negro men as there are amongst us … might make Husbands for our Daughters. And the Sons and Daughters of *New England* would become more like *Jacob*, and *Rachel*, if this Slavery were thrust quite out of doors. Moreover it is too well known what Temptations Masters are under, to connive at the Fornification of their Slaves; lest they should be obliged to find them Wives, or Pay their Fines."

- "It is likewise most lamentable to think, how in taking Negros out of *Africa,* and Selling of them here, That which GOD ha's joyned together men do boldly rend asunder, Men from their Country, Husbands from their Wives, Parents from their Children. How horrible is the Uncleanness, Morality, if not Murder, that the Ships are guilty of that bring great Crouds of these miserable Men, and Women."

Note:	Sewall's tract went on to refute the four main rationalizations Massachusetts Puritans used for their enslavement of Africans: "These Blackamores are of the Posterity of Cham, and therefore are under the Curse of Slavery"; "The Nigers are brought out of a pagan country, into places where the Gospel is Preached"; "The Africans have Wars with one another: our Ships bring lawful Captives taken in those Wars"; "Abraham had servants bought with his Money, and born in his House".

Aug. 1700 **Frustrated with the English, the Iroquois plan to make peace with the French.**

In Albany, the Iroquois complain about their losses due to warring against the French and their Indian allies. The Iroquois tell the English it is their plan to attend a large intertribal peace conference to be hosted by the French the following summer in Montreal. Alarmed by this announcement, the English begin waging an unsuccessful attempt to prevent the Iroquois from attending.

Note:	England and France were locked in relentless competition for the wealth generated by the Indian trade and acquisitions of tribal lands. In addition, both countries actively courted the tribes as vital military allies, and neither France nor England intended to yield to the other.

Oct. 1700 **Four Hundred *Choctaws* arrive at the Louisiana Colony's *Fort Biloxi* seeking French aid against their *Chickasaw* enemies.**

The French have allied themselves with the Choctaw Nation, whereas the Chickasaw have allied themselves with the English. Egged on by the Europeans, the two powerful tribes will be greatly reduced by the wars between them over the coming years.

1701 **At Albany, New York, females serve on a jury for the first time in North America.**

Pennsylvania begins an armed watch for pirates on the Delaware River.

Yale University is founded in Connecticut to train Congregationalist (Puritan) ministers.

Originally called the *Collegiate School*, it will be renamed *Yale* in 1718 to honor a wealthy donor, Elihu Yale, governor of the East India Company.

African slaves arriving in England from the colonies are not to be considered property but are instead declared to have the *limited rights of villeins*.

In the case *Smith v. Brown and Cooper*, a plaintiff has brought suit for £20 owed by the defendant for the sale of a slave purchased in Virginia. During the case, Chief Justice John Holt avers, "As soon as a negro comes to England, he becomes free. One may be a villein in England, but not a slave." Justice Holt continues, "Though the sale of Negroes is supported by Virginia law, there are no such laws in England."

> Note: Villeins had limited rights and could therefore be legally compelled to servitude.

April 1701   **William Penn meets with Indians to secure additional lands and treaty rights.**

William Penn meets tribal representatives, including the Conestoga, Shawnee, Susquehanna, Delaware, and North Patomick at *Conestoga Indiantown* alongside the Susquehanna River. The Pennsylvania proprietor hopes to gain trade routes into the interior regions, reinforce previous land allotments, and obtain additional lands and treaty rights. In return for promises of protection and trade annuities, Penn secures an agreement that the tribes will trade only with the Pennsylvania Colony.

> Note: The lucrative Indian trade was important for Penn to secure as Pennsylvania was in competition with its neighbors—New York to the north and Maryland to the south.
>
> This would be the last treaty agreement brokered by Penn himself.

May 1701   **King Louis XIV begins to consolidate France's North American holdings.**

French plans are underway to assert control over its vast territories by establishing forts, settlements, and trade posts throughout the western regions of the Great Lakes, the Mississippi River Valley, and the Gulf Coast as France expands its North American presence.

> Note: The 1697 *Treaty of Ryswick* had confirmed France's territorial rights in North America and returned French lands captured during King William's War.

May 23, 1701   **In London, the Scottish pirate Captain Kidd is hanged.**

Found guilty of piracy and murder, Kidd is hanged twice. The rope breaks the first time and the pirate is hauled up the gallows and hanged a second time.

> Note: Kidd's body would be gibbeted at Tilbury, England, for three years as a warning to others.
>
> Captain Kidd's claim to have buried treasures in various locations contributed greatly to the *buried treasure* lore so often associated with pirating. Modern hunters continue to search for Kidd's *hidden loot*.

June 1701   **The *Act of Settlement* opens England's monarchy to Germany's royal *House of Hanover*.**

The Act of Settlement names Princess Anne—the deposed James II's second Protestant daughter—to be England's next monarch after King William III's death. But as Anne has no surviving children, following her reign: the role of queen is to pass to her Protestant cousin, *Electress Sophia,* of Hanover, Germany; and from thence to Sophia's Protestant offspring.

> Note: The seventy-year-old Sophia (Stuart) of Hanover was: a daughter of England's King James I; a niece of the executed King Charles I; a first cousin to the Stuart brothers, Kings James II and Charles II; and a second cousin to future Queen Anne.
>
> Still today, Catholics are barred from Great Britain's monarchy by the 1701 Act of Settlement.

The Act of Settlement strengthens England's Bill of Rights by further restricting the powers and prerogatives of the Crown.

The restrictions include:

- England's monarch is required to take communion in the Church of England.

- Parliamentary consent must now be given before the monarch engages in war or leaves the country.

- If the monarch is foreign-born, England is not responsible for going to war to save territories that are not its own.

- Judges are to hold office on good conduct rather than being dependent on royal pleasure.

- Impeachments by the House of Commons are not pardonable by the sovereign.

- Foreign-born persons, except those born of English parents, are barred from serving: in the Privy Council; as members of either of the Houses of Parliament; or from enjoying any office or place of trust, either civil or military; nor are they entitled to receive land grants from the Crown.

July 19, 1701   **The Iroquois grant their western hunting grounds to the king of England in the *Nanfan Treaty*.**

Meeting in Albany, New York, English authorities and Iroquois leaders agree to grant title of their western lands to King William III in gratitude for the many royal favors bestowed upon them, and in appreciation of eighty years of peace.

Note:	Known as the *Iroquois Beaver Hunting Grounds*, the lands included those north of the Ohio River extending to the Mississippi River.
	As France had claimed rights to the region since the 1680s, the Treaty of Nanfan gave England a counterclaim setting up inevitable conflicts between the two nations.

July 24, 1701   **France establishes *Fort Detroit* under the leadership of Antoine de la Mothe Cadillac.**

Fort Detroit is founded to serve as a base for the French fur-trading operations in the Great Lakes region and to help strengthen France's territorial claims.

Note:	Fort Detroit's founder would lend his name to the modern Cadillac car—originally made in Detroit, Michigan.

Aug. 4, 1701   **The Iroquois and Great Lakes tribes meet with the French in Montreal and agree to a historic peace known as the *Great Peace,* or the *Grand Settlement*.**

The numerous tribes attending the large conference agree to *bury the tomahawk* and allow the French to settle future disputes between them. This will permit a peaceful flow of French trade goods into and out of the interior regions to the benefit of all.

The Iroquois—suffering from the deadly effects of smallpox and war during the past decade—pledge to remain neutral in any future conflicts between the Whites rather than to ally themselves with the English as in the past. In return, the French open their trading posts to the Iroquois and allow them access to trade routes of the Great Lakes region.

Note:	More than thirty tribes were represented from far and wide—many were former enemies. Eyewitnesses counted more than 1,500 canoes beached on Montreal Island.
	The successful peace treaty at Montreal represented a major coup for France. With an Indian peace established, France would further its claims to the western lands of North America by building forts and trade posts throughout the region.

Sept. 16, 1701   **The exiled King James II—England's last Catholic monarch—dies in France.**

Upon James's death, both Spain and France declare his Catholic son, James Francis Edward Stuart, to be England's King James III; thus provoking hostilities amongst the countries once again.

Oct. 28, 1701	**William Penn's *Charter of Privileges* is adopted for the residents of Pennsylvania.**

To quiet colonial dissatisfactions, the Quaker proprietor issues the Charter of Privileges to serve as the colony's new constitution.

The charter bans taxes for the support of religious institutions and guarantees religious freedom, stating, "That no Person or Persons, inhabiting in this Province or Territories, who shall confess and acknowledge One almighty God, the Creator, Upholder and Ruler of the World; and professes him or themselves obliged to live quietly under the Civil Government, shall be in any Case molested or prejudiced, in his or her Person or Estate, because of his or their conscientious Persuasion or Practice, nor be compelled to frequent or maintain any religious Worship, Place, or Ministry, contrary to his or their Mind, or to do or suffer any other Act or Thing, contrary to their religious Persuasion."

The charter also grants the Pennsylvania Assembly power to introduce or amend laws instead of merely voting on those proposed by the Governor's Council. In addition, the right to public office—previously permitted only to freeholders (landowners)—is opened to all Christian males.

Note:	Not all colonial assemblies would be empowered to introduce law. Many royal governors believed that yielding this power to the popularly elected legislators would engender mob rule.
	Overall, the Charter of Privileges would strengthen Pennsylvania's separation of Church and State and help balance the powers between the executive, legislative, and judiciary.
	Pennsylvania's religious tolerance and fertile soils would make the colony a destination for Protestant immigration from Germany.

Pennsylvania's Charter of Privileges permits the three *Lower Counties on the Delaware* to form a political assembly separate from Pennsylvania.

Note:	This would result in Delaware's separation from Pennsylvania in 1704.

Nov. 1701	**William Penn sails to England and never returns to North America.**

Penn learned in August that certain factions in England were once again working to wrest Pennsylvania from his proprietorship and make Pennsylvania a royal colony. Determined to prevent it, Penn returns to England.

Note:	William Penn had visited Pennsylvania only twice; spending less than four years total in the colony.

Feb. 21, 1702	**England's King William suffers injury when his horse stumbles on a molehill.**

The king's collarbone is broken, and as a result, William will catch pneumonia and die within a fortnight.

March 2, 1702	**Parliament charges James Francis Edward Stuart with treason.**

Learning of King William's death, James Francis Edward Stuart has declared himself to be England's king. For this, Parliament charges the thirteen-year-old son of former King James II with treason; though it matters little for the adolescent James lives in French exile.

> Note: James Francis Edward Stuart would become known to England's Protestants as *James the Pretender*, and later as the *Old Pretender*.
>
> In all, three failed attempts would be made to place James Francis Edward Stuart on Britain's throne. James himself would lead two rather weak campaigns in 1708 and 1715. In addition, his son Charles Edward Stuart would lead Jacobite forces in a final attempt to return his father and the Stuart family to Britain's monarchy in 1745.

March 8, 1702   **King William III dies and Princess Anne Stuart is proclaimed Queen of England.**

King William and Queen Mary have provided no heirs. Therefore, as stipulated by the 1701 Act of Settlement, the Protestant Princess Anne is declared queen.

> Note: Parliament, determined never to again have a Catholic monarch, had prepared for this moment by passing the Act of Settlement nearly a year before. As such, many Catholic claimants were passed over, including Queen Anne's half-brother James Francis Edward Stuart—twenty-three years her junior.
>
> The Jacobites would react with glee when it was learned the king's death was caused by his horse tripping on nothing but a small molehill.

The Catholic nations of Europe refuse to acknowledge Anne Stuart as England's queen.

> Note: Both France and Spain considered King William III's death an opportunity for intrigue against their common enemy, England. As such, Queen Anne would soon declare war against both nations.

The Massachusetts General Court declares the witchcraft trials of 1692–1693 to have been unlawful.

> Note: In 1711, hoping to close a sad chapter, the General Court would grant a restitution of £578 to the victims' heirs.

April 15, 1702   **East Jersey and West Jersey are returned to the Crown by their proprietors and merged.**

The two Jersey colonies, divided from each other in 1674, are reunited. Now a royal colony, New Jersey is to share a governor with New York.

> Note: As the various colonies of England grew in wealth and power, most proprietary colonies would be confiscated by the Crown and declared to be royal colonies.
>
> In 1688, both East Jersey and West Jersey had been forced to merge with New York and the New England colonies into the Dominion of New England, but the political union was dissolved in 1691 during England's Glorious Revolution.

May 1702   *Queen Anne's War* begins as England declares war on France and Spain.

Queen Anne's War, a part of the larger European *War of Spanish Succession*, becomes another forest war in North America involving the English colonials and their Indian allies against the Spanish, French, and their tribal allies.

> Note: Queen Anne's War, to last until 1713, would be also referred to as New England's *Third Indian War* having followed King Philip's War (1675–1676) and King William's War (1689–1697).

June 11, 1702   **The detested Joseph Dudley arrives to serve as the royal governor of Massachusetts.**

The native-born Dudley is well known, having had a long history of acrimony with his fellow New Englanders. Dudley has served as acting governor of the despised Dominion of New England; was arrested in the Puritan revolt of 1689; held captive for ten months in Boston; and sent to London for trial. Dudley later served as chief magistrate in the New York trial of the popular rebel Jacob Leisler. Now, stepping ashore in Boston, the new governor of Massachusetts and New Hampshire arrives to a cool reception.

> Note: Former Governor William Phips, having constantly clashed with the colony's Puritan leaders, had sailed to England on November 17, 1694, to answer charges levied against him. While in London, Phips had died of a fever and Joseph Dudley was appointed to replace him.

The North American colonists learn that England is once again at war.

Along with his royal commission, Governor Dudley arrives with the alarming news that England has declared war against France and Spain.

1702   **France establishes settlements on the Mississippi Gulf coast as the development of the Louisiana Colony gets underway.**

The French soon build forts in Mobile, Biloxi, and on Dauphin Island as they expand their presence in the region.

> Note: Mobile would serve as the administrative capital of the Louisiana Colony until 1722.
>
> With the French in Alabama, the Spanish in Florida, and the English in Carolina; future conflicts would be unavoidable. In a pattern already well established, the three European powers would use the Native American tribes as allied proxies in their struggle for control over North American lands and the Indian trade.

July 15–16, 1702 **In Boston, rebellion stirs against the English Navy over impressment.**

Before returning to England, Captain Robert Jackson of the HBS *Swift* sends naval press-gangs ashore in search of men to press into service; but Jackson has not first consulted with the royal governor as required by law. Captain Jackson's men target sailors from docked merchant ships angering both the seamen and their employers who protest Jackson's actions to the new Lieutenant Governor, Thomas Povey. Povey orders the *Swift* not to leave the harbor; threatening to fire upon the ship if it passes the cannons of Fort Castle William.

> Note: At the time, the new royal governor, Joseph Dudley, was away in Portsmouth, New Hampshire, presenting his commission and establishing his governance.

Captain Jackson ignores the orders of Lieutenant Governor Povey and the *Swift* is fired upon by Bostonians manning the fort. Five sailors aboard the *Swift* are injured and one of the impressed men dies. Captain Jackson is arrested by the colonial authorities, jailed, and sent to England to face charges levied against him.

> Note: The charges against Captain Jackson would be dismissed, angering the Massachusetts authorities.
>
> The Royal Navy's press-gangs were seen as threats, not only by the civilian seamen, but also by their employers—the monied and influential men of the American seaports. When possible, the colonials would share information as to where and when the impressments were being conducted, causing merchant ships to sail an alternative route or to a different port to avoid them. This was bad for colonial commerce and represented lost revenue to the ship owners. Boston—being the largest North American seaport at that time—was a particular target for the press-gangs.

The term *Royal Navy* had begun being used in 1660 following the Restoration of the Crown. For much of the eighteenth century a British warship would be referred as *HBMS* (His/Her Britannic Majesty's Ship), or simply *HBS* (His/Her Britannic Majesty), eventually referring generally to all British naval vessels. At some point around the American War for Independence, *HMS* (His/Her Majesty's Ship) would become the dominant prefix for all British naval ships.

1702   **England's newly established Admiralty Courts become operational.**

As a result, the English Admiralty removes the royal governors' jurisdictions over Royal ships operating in the colony's territorial waters but retains the governors' commissions as vice admirals.

Sept. 10, 1702   **The Carolina General Assembly authorizes a military campaign into Florida.**

With England and Spain at war, an attack is planned against St. Augustine—only 275 miles south of Charles Town.

Nov.–Dec. 1702   **North America's Queen Anne's War begins in Florida.**

Aboard fourteen ships, Carolina Governor James Moore sails with 1,000 militiamen and Yamasee warriors into northern Florida to seize St. Augustine. Expecting assistance by English naval forces from Jamaica, Governor Moore arrives but finds no sign of his expected support. Undeterred, the disappointed governor and his men proceed to launch the attack alone.

Laying siege to St. Augustine while waiting for reinforcement that never arrives, Moore fails to capture the Spanish bastion, and in frustration, orders the town burned before quitting the attack.

Unable to return by sea due to Spanish naval threats, Governor Moore orders his vessels destroyed as his mixed militia force begins an overland march to Charles Town, destroying Indian villages and Spanish missions along the way.

Note:	A forest war now began in the southern frontier region as English and Spanish authorities each urged the Indians to attack the other.
	Governor Moore's Florida campaign was considered a failure; he would resign as Carolina's governor the following year.

Aug. 10, 1703   **Queen Anne's War arrives in New England.**

A strike force of 500 French and Abenaki successfully attacks Wells, Maine, and the surrounding Casco Bay region as more than 150 English are killed, tortured, or marched away as captives to Montreal.

Sept. 1703   **Massachusetts offers bounties for Indian scalps in retaliation for the frontier raids.**

The assembly offers citizens a £40 bounty for each scalp of the hostiles, essentially opening a hunting season on all Indians.

Note:	Some examples of bounties for Indian scalps over the years are:
	In 1637, Massachusetts Bay and Connecticut paid the Mohawk bounties for Pequot heads, and later scalps.
	In 1641, New Amsterdam paid "ten fathoms of wampum" to friendly Indians for the heads of their Raritan enemies.

In 1675, for the first time, Massachusetts paid bounties to Whites for Indian scalps during King Philip's War.

In 1689, Massachusetts offered scalp bounties to Whites and the Narragansett.

In 1692, authorities in New France offered the Indians bounties for English scalps.

In 1696, Massachusetts offered £50 for adult Indian scalps, £25 for females, and £10 for children.

In 1722, Massachusetts would offer scalp bounties on Indian families.

In 1724, New Hampshire would offer £100 for each scalp. Connecticut would offer militiamen a choice: wages plus £20 for every Indian scalp or prisoner; or no wages and £40 for each scalp.

In the 1730s, the French in Louisiana would offer bounties to Choctaw for Chickasaw scalps.

In 1746, Massachusetts would offer Indian scalp bounties.

In 1747, New York would pass a Scalp Act.

In 1755, Massachusetts would offer £40 for males, and £20 for each Penobscot woman and child under the age of twelve.

In 1756, Pennsylvania Governor Robert Morris would declare war against the Delaware and offer 130 Spanish pieces of eight (Spanish dollars) for the scalps of Delaware males above the age of twelve, and 50 for women.

In 1764, Pennsylvania would offer scalp bounties for those of warring Indians: 134 Spanish pieces of eight for males and 50 for females.

Dec. 7, 1703   **The worst recorded storm in British history kills thousands.**

England is struck by an unprecedented catastrophic cyclone which kills 11,000 people. Houses and chimneys are toppled, woods and forest trees are uprooted, ships are destroyed, and whole towns are laid waste. The Royal Navy loses thirteen ships as more than 1,500 sailors drown.

Note: Most English could agree that the storm was God's punishment upon them, but they disagreed over what they were being punished for.

1704   **Delaware separates from Pennsylvania due to differences and political divisions.**

The Three Lower Counties are to have their own assembly but will continue to share a common governor with Pennsylvania.

Note: Delaware would formally declare itself independent of both Pennsylvania and Great Britain on June 15, 1776.

Delaware is often listed as being the first state of the United States. Though a bit of a misnomer, Delaware would receive this honor due to having been the first state to ratify the United States Constitution on December 7, 1787.

In Europe, English forces capture Gibraltar.

Note: The rocky fortress guarding the entrance to the Mediterranean Sea—today a part of the United Kingdom—continues to be a political irritant between Spain and Great Britain.

Gibraltar is not an island as many believe it to be, but rather a small peninsula.

In northern Florida, Indian warriors led by Colonel James Moore, destroy Spanish missions and attack the *Apalachee* as Queen Anne's War continues.

Attempting to end the threat posed by the Spanish and their allied tribes in the region, former Carolina Governor James Moore leads another assault into Florida. Moore's army consists of 50 Carolinians and nearly 1,000 mostly *Creek* and *Yamasee* warriors—traditional enemies of the Apalachee. Sparing few, Moore's Indian army attacks the Apalachee villages and destroys ten of the eleven mission towns.

Colonel Moore states in his report that the expedition killed more than 1,100 Indians and captured 4,300 as slaves—many being Christian converts.

Note:	Moore gave permission for two Catholic priests and five Spaniards to be tortured and burned at the stake by his Indian allies.
	These cross-border raids into Florida would continue for the next two years, ending the Spanish mission system in the region as thousands of Spanish-allied Indians were sold into slavery and others were driven out.
	The Apalachee—for whom the Appalachian Mountains were named—would never recover from the depredations against them.

In Maryland, Catholics are barred from political office to prevent the "growth of Popery in this Province."

A royal colony under Protestant control since 1692, Maryland's Catholics continue to suffer discrimination.

Note:	The Anglicans and Puritans in Maryland were emulating events in England.

Feb. 28, 1704   **Deerfield, Massachusetts, is attacked and overwhelmed by 250–300 French and Indians.**

In the predawn darkness, Deerfield, an outlying frontier community on the Connecticut River, presents an easy target as snowdrifts against the fort allow the Abenaki warriors to silently scale the walls and open the gate to their comrades eagerly waiting to begin the attack.

Totally staggered by the onslaught, 56 Deerfield residents of all ages are slaughtered and more than 100 are taken captive to be tortured, exchanged for ransom, or kept by the Indians as slaves. For six weeks the captives are force-marched through 300 miles of snowy wilderness, arriving at Montreal in mid-April. Of the original 109 captives, only 88 will survive as the Indians kill many along the way.

Note:	French Jesuit missionaries had successfully converted many Indians to a hybrid form of Catholicism by mixing the Native beliefs with their own. Exerting considerable influence over the Wabanaki tribes, the Jesuits encouraged their attacks upon the New Englanders and often accompanied the Indians to help direct their military campaigns.

Feb. 1704   **Massachusetts requests that England send military assistance.**

The New Englanders ask Queen Anne to send armed troops, but the request is denied for England is focused on the European theater of the *War of Spanish Succession.* However, the queen and her ministry support the colonists *going it alone* and urge them to use their militias as best they can.

Note:	In addition, most in England believed the purpose of Royal troops was to counter the professional armies of Europe—not to be parading among America's vast forests chasing savages.
	The denial would cause much New England resentment.

April 24, 1704	**The *Boston News-Letter* begins publication; the first continuously printed newspaper in North America.**

The newspaper will be published for nearly seventy-five years until shutting down on February 29, 1776, over issues concerning the American War for Independence.

May 1704	**A New England militia assaults Port Royal, Acadia, in retaliation for the attacks on Deerfield and other settlements.**

Led by Colonel Benjamin Church, the New England militiamen attack Port Royal but are unable to capture the town. In frustration, the militia forces attack and destroy other French coastal settlements in the region taking prisoners to be used in exchange for English prisoners held by the French.

The Carolina Colony requires its general assembly to be members of the Anglican Church.

The assembly passes a law requiring reception of the Holy Eucharist to be in accordance with the Church of England.

Note:	The law was designed to reduce the political power of the large number of Quakers from northern Carolina elected to the assembly at Charles Town.

July 1704	**At Port Royal, the New Englanders issue dire warnings to the governor of New France.**

Before retreating from Acadia, Colonel Benjamin Church sends a letter to Governor Vaudreuil warning him that if the frontier barbarities against the English continue, they will resort in kind against the French settlers. In addition, Church demands that all French priests residing among the Indians in Maine's frontier be removed.

1705	**Though Queen Anne's War continues, 1705 brings a lull in the fighting as the French and New Englanders agree to exchange prisoners.**

Captives are exchanged following negotiations, with many of the Deerfield survivors among them.

***An Act concerning Servants and Slaves* legalizes slavery in Virginia.**

"All servants imported and brought into the Country … who were not Christians in their native Country … shall be accounted and be slaves. All Negro, mulatto and Indian slaves within this dominion … shall be held to be real estate."

Note:	With the rising number of Africans in Virginia, the House of Burgesses passed the 1705 slave code to remove all doubt concerning their legal status in the colony. Based loosely on the Barbadian slave codes, the Act placed restrictions on slave behaviors and included severe punishments for violators.
	Also known as the *Virginia Slave Codes of 1705*, the Act would be the most draconian of the various slave laws established in England's mainland North America until the passage of South Carolina's Negro Act of 1740.
	The Virginia Slave Codes represented a shift from Virginia's economic dependence on indentured labor to African slavery.

Jan. 17, 1706	**Benjamin Franklin is born in Boston.**

Franklin is the tenth child born to Josiah Franklin, a maker of candles and soaps, and his wife Abiah.

1706 **French privateers continue to attack English fishing vessels and merchant ships operating in the North Atlantic.**

In the Bahamas, *Eleuthera Island* is nearly abandoned as most settlers flee the threat of Spanish raids.

Summer 1706 **Anger rises in New York over naval impressments.**

Needing sailors to man ships, the Royal Navy impresses New York seamen, infuriating the citizens and Royal Governor Edward Hyde.

Note:	Captain Niles of the HBS *Triton's Prize* made profits by the dishonest means of impressing more men than necessary and then *selling them off* to other ships.

A confrontational standoff between Niles and the New York authorities develops, and Governor Hyde threatens to fire upon the *Triton's Prize* if it is moved. Captain Niles falls ill during the ensuing impasse and dies four days later, thus averting the crisis.

Note:	Once on American shores, disgruntled British sailors would often simply disappear into the vastness or secure employment for higher wages on one of the many merchant ships. British naval officers complained that the colonists regularly encouraged their crews to desert.

Virginia's most sensational witchcraft trial takes place.

Grace Sherwood of Prince William County has been ordered tried by the *water test*. Brought from her cell to face a crowd chanting "Duck the witch!" the forty-six-year-old Sherwood is bound and tossed into the Lynnhaven River. Sherwood floats and is therefore declared guilty and forced to spend nearly eight years in jail before being released.

July 22, 1706 **The *Treaty of Union*: A plan to unite England and Scotland into a common kingdom.**

Though Scotland and England have intermittently shared a common monarch since the death of Elizabeth I in 1603, both countries have retained their own Parliaments and national independence. Now, a political union is agreed to.

The following are among the terms:

- The Union is to begin on May 1, 1707.

- The Union shall be known as the Kingdom of Great Britain.

- The Union is to be a Protestant kingdom.

- The line of succession to the throne will be from Germany's House of Hanover (thus eliminating James Francis Edward Stuart and all future Stuart heirs).

- Scotland's Parliament is to be dissolved as the two nations form a new *British* Parliament. The Scots are guaranteed forty-five seats in the House of Commons and sixteen in the House of Lords.

- Scotland is to retain its own legal and religious system.

- The two countries are to share a common currency and flag.

- Both Scotland and England's Parliaments must approve the treaty.

> Note: Throughout the years, many in England had wished to conquer Scotland but the fiercely independent Scots had always successfully resisted. Scotland, now in economic straits, would gain access to England's expanding trade and navigation empire as the two nations enjoyed the rights and benefits of common citizenship. In addition, by this political union, England removed the historical threat Scotland represented and severed Scotland's close alliance with France.

Sept. 1706

Charles Town, South Carolina, is attacked by French and Spanish naval forces.

Five French warships arrive carrying 1,000 French, Spanish, and Indians hoping to destroy Charles Town and drive the English from the Spanish-claimed lands. Sanctioned by France's King Louis XIV, the invaders battle the Carolina defenders intermittently over a two-week period before finally retreating.

> Note: England's North American colonists were fighting Queen Anne's War on two fronts: against the Spanish and their Indian allies in Carolina and Florida; and against the French and their Indian allies in upper New England and Canada.

Nov. 30, 1706

The Anglican Church of England becomes Carolina's established church.

The *Church Act* allows dissenters to practice their faiths and participate in politics, but only the Anglican Church is to be supported by public funds and have the power to perform marriages, upsetting the colony's Quakers.

> Note: The Anglicans tried to stymie the increasing Quaker influences in Carolina. Six years earlier, Reverend Daniel Brett had been sent from England as the first Anglican minister in Carolina; since May 1704, all assembly members were required to take communion in the Church of England. With the passage of the 1706 Church Act, the Anglican Church now becomes the official religion of Carolina.
>
> The Anglican Church in the United States would break from the Church of England in 1789 due to American independence. No longer able to recognize the British monarch as the head of the Church and wanting to show complete separation, the Church of England in the United States would become today's Episcopal Church.

March 1707

A New England army attacks Port Royal, Acadia (Nova Scotia).

Led by Colonel John March, the militiamen are too few to overcome the French fortress with its cannons and superior number of defenders. Though they fail to take the fort, Colonel March's men satisfy themselves by laying waste to Port Royal's outlying buildings.

As the army begins the trek homeward, reinforcements arrive with orders from Massachusetts Governor Dudley directing Colonel March to make a second attempt. Hence, the militiamen return to Port Royal, but the French have also been reinforced and again resist the onslaught. Unable to capture the fort, the New Englanders turn homeward once again.

May 1, 1707

The *Kingdom of Great Britain* is formed as England and Scotland unite.

Scotland's Parliament is dissolved, and the two countries are united under one Crown and one Parliament, known as the *Parliament of Great Britain*.

> Note: The term *British* would, over time, replace *English* and *Scottish* to describe citizens of this newly expanded political entity, but unofficially, both groups would continue a separate nationalist identity.
>
> Many English and Scots were opposed to the Union and actively worked against it.

Most English, both in England and North America, would continue to view the Scots as pugnacious foreigners.

Scottish Jacobites believed their true king to be King James II's son, James Francis Edward Stuart, then living in French exile. Hence, England would struggle to keep Scotland in the British Empire over the coming years, with many Scots yet today yearning for total independence.

The Red Ensign flag, flown on Britain's commercial ships since 1674, would be redesigned to represent the new political union. Formerly the flags' cantons had contained either St. George's Cross or St. Andrew's Cross to identify the vessel's country of origin. The new design replaces both cantons with Britain's Union flag.

The Kingdom of Great Britain would be renamed the *United Kingdom of Great Britain* in 1801, representing the addition of Ireland to the kingdom.

Scottish immigration to North America will now increase.

Though a smattering of Scots already resides in England's colonies, a Scottish influx is about to begin, particularly in Nova Scotia and the frontier regions of Pennsylvania, North Carolina, Georgia, and New York.

Note: Protestant Scots living in Ireland, dubbed *Scotch-Irish* by the American colonials, would also begin to arrive.

The Scots—England's long historical enemies—were not particularly welcomed when arriving in Britain's colonies, especially in Puritan New England. Famed for their military prowess, these Scottish newcomers tended to settle collectively in the more remote and dangerous frontier regions, serving somewhat as a buffer between the Indian tribes and the more settled Eastern regions.

1707   **Indian scalp bounties are reinstated by the Massachusetts General Court, as Queen Anne's War continues.**

Early 1708   **Massachusetts officials arrive in London to lobby for military assistance.**

With the support of Queen Anne, Parliament agrees to eliminate the French threat against New England by authorizing the capture of New France and removal of its French citizens. The Massachusetts agents are assured that British military assistance will be forthcoming.

March 11, 1708   **A veto is exercised by a British monarch over Parliament for the last time.**

Queen Anne, not totally trusting of the Scots, withholds her assent to the *Scottish Militia Act*; an Act passed by Parliament to reorganize and arm Scottish militia units.

Note: Today, the British monarchy no longer has the power to veto legislation.

March 23, 1708   **James Francis Edward Stuart, hoping to seize Britain's throne from his half-sister Anne, attempts to land in Scotland.**

Nineteen-year-old James Stuart arrives with nearly 5,000 French and Irish troops to begin a military campaign against England, but foul weather and a lack of French naval support due to interception by the British fleet, force James to return to France.

April 1708   **The Massachusetts agents return from London with good news.**

Arriving in Boston, the agents carry assurances of military assistance from Queen Anne and a proclamation calling for the New Englanders to organize their militias in preparation for a joint campaign against New France.

With this positive news, the colonial officials begin soliciting support and organizing their militia armies for an expected summer or autumn campaign.

> Note: The plan called for New England militias to march northward and attack Montreal while a British naval support force sailed up the St. Lawrence River to attack Quebec in a coordinated two-pronged offensive.

1708 **Press-gang operations in Britain's colonies are banned.**

In response to pressure from commercial interests, Great Britain passes *An Act for the Encouragement of Trade to America*, also known as the *American Act*. The statute bans naval press-gangs in the Western Hemisphere except to recover deserters; and the colonials finally seem to have protection from this hated practice. Yet an unresolved question remains: Are press-gangs required to obtain the colonial governor's approval before seeking sailors to impress?

> Note: When in need of seamen, the Royal Navy was often little concerned whether the impressed men were deserters.

June 8, 1708 **One of the most treasure-laden ships in history is sunk by British forces in Colombia.**

Returning to Spain with gold to help finance the war against Britain, the *San Jose* is downed at Cartagena, Colombia.

> Note: The *San Jose* was discovered by treasure seekers from the United States in 1981, but the Colombian government refused to permit the ship to be salvaged. Having lain on the ocean floor for over 300 years, the *San Jose* is today estimated to be worth many billions of dollars.

June 1708 **In Massachusetts, preparations continue for the upcoming campaign against New France.**

Awaiting the arrival of British military forces, the majority of the New England militiamen continue to train at Boston, while others are sent north to the Lake Champlain transportation corridor to clear the frontier route leading to Canada.

Aug. 29, 1708 **Haverhill, Massachusetts, is attacked by the French, and Abenaki and Nipissing warriors.**

In a predawn strike, nearly forty residents are killed or captured, but the attackers are quickly pursued. Forced to abandon their cached baggage, the mixed force of French and Indians must endure a return to Montreal without supplies, causing some of the French troops to surrender.

Oct. 1708 **The joint military campaign to capture New France ends with a fizzle as Britain backs out.**

Massachusetts authorities receive official notification of what they have suspected for the past month: the anticipated British assistance will not be forthcoming. Though disappointed, the New Englanders decide they will go ahead with the campaign if the Royal Navy at Boston will agree to support them.

The navy does not agree, and the campaign against New France is considered over.

> Note: Britain's government had prioritized national needs and chosen instead to send the promised military forces to fight in Portugal, thus leaving the colonials on their own.

Jan. 1, 1709   **French forces capture Britain's St. John's, Newfoundland.**

> Note: St. John's, with its sheltered bay facing east to the Atlantic, was the closest North
> American seaport to Europe, at less than 2,000 miles from Ireland.

March 23, 1709   **The *Foreign Protestants Naturalization Act* of 1708 allows Protestant foreigners to become
citizens of the Kingdom of Great Britain.**

The Act is passed to allow citizenship for the large number of Huguenots that have arrived in
England fleeing religious persecution in France. The Act requires the foreigners to swear an oath
of allegiance and take communion in a Protestant church.

> Note: So many would take advantage of the Naturalization Act that it would be repealed in
> 1711.
>
> Before 1708, those not born subjects of England, could only become citizens by an
> Act of Parliament.

1709   **Queen Anne invites *Palatine Germans* to migrate, and England is quickly overwhelmed.**

Wracked by war and a severe winter, the Protestant Germans have heard rumors of free land in
Britain's North America; in response, 10,000 arrive in England between May and November. The
great numbers cause a proclamation to be issued stating: all who arrive after October 1709 will be
sent back to Germany—yet the immigrants continue to arrive.

Queen Anne approves a scaled-down military campaign against New France.

The previous year's plan had been to capture Quebec and Montreal, whereas Britain now decides
to attack and capture Port Royal, Acadia.

> Note: Disappointed once before, many New Englanders doubted the promised assistance
> would be forthcoming and were thus hesitant to reorganize their militias.

1710   **Britain begins a *Blue Water Policy* to build and expand its naval strength.**

> Note: Great Britain would become the world's No.1 sea power by the mid-1700s and
> continued its domination until being surpassed by the United States during World
> War II. Ruling the oceans for 200 years would give rise to the expression "Britannia
> rules the waves."

In South Carolina, the African population now exceeds the White population.

The demand for laborers continues to keep pace with the ever-expanding agricultural industry of
the colony.

> Note: In 1710, South Carolina had 5,000 Whites (mostly English) and 6,783 enslaved
> Africans. The Black majority in South Carolina would continue until the 1920s.

April 1710   **The poor riot over a lack of food in Boston's first *Bread Riot*.**

Many of Boston's impoverished citizens are hungry due to food scarcity and high prices. Though
wheat is available, the owners are shipping it abroad to be sold for handsome profits rather than
distributing it to the local poor.

A ship containing wheat attempts to leave the harbor, but the vessel is boarded by men who break
its rudder and refuse to let it sail. The following day, fifty Bostonians unsuccessfully attempt to

bring the rudderless ship to shore. The culprits are arrested but soon released without charge due to public support.

April 10, 1710   **The *Statute of Anne*: The first copyright law in Great Britain is now in force.**

A fourteen-year copyright protection is granted to works of literature. If the author is still alive at the end of the protected period, the copyright can be renewed for another fourteen years.

> Note: Passed by Parliament the previous year, the law was designed to protect authors from others publishing their works and to promote education.
>
> Copyright is addressed in Article 1, Section 8 of the United States Constitution, which states that the Congress shall have power "To promote the progress of science and useful arts, by securing for limited times to authors and inventors the exclusive right to their respective writings and discoveries."

July 1, 1710   **Additional British naval forces arrive in Boston to lead the assault against French Acadia.**

> Note: In 1708, the New Englanders had prepared for a military campaign against New France that had been called off. Therefore, they were astonished when British warships arrived to begin the campaign.

Summer 1710   **In London, Indian chiefs arrive from New York and create a public sensation.**

Seeking military assistance against their French enemies, the four sachems—three Mohawk and one Mohican—have been sent by Albany Mayor Pieter Schuyler to meet with Queen Anne. The chiefs are treated as dignitaries by the royals and public alike as they are transported around London by carriage to visit various sites.

Pledges of friendship are exchanged, and the chiefs are sent home with gifts, promises of military support, and assurances of English missionaries being established among their people to counter the religious gains made in the region by the French Jesuits.

> Note: While in London, the Mohawk leaders: *Sa Ga Yeath Qua Pieth Tow; Ho Nee Yeathe Taw No Ro; Tee Yee Ho Ga Row*; and the Mohican: *Etow Oh Koam;* would have their portraits painted. Known as the *Four Indian Kings,* these portraits hang today in Canada's National Archives in Ottawa, Ontario.

Sept. 18, 1710   **The British–New England campaign to capture France's Port Royal begins.**

Thirty-four ships carrying 400 British marines and 1,500 New England militiamen sail northward from Boston to begin the attack.

Oct. 5, 1710   **Port Royal surrenders, completing Great Britain's control of Acadia.**

The Royal Navy transport the French soldiers and government officials back to France, but French citizens (Acadians) may remain if they swear an oath of allegiance to Britain's Queen Anne.

> Note: Acadian resentment of the soon-to-arrive Scot and English settlers would be reciprocated, resulting in continued wars between the groups in future years.
>
> Port Royal had been the capital of Acadia. Now under British control, Port Royal would be renamed *Annapolis Royal* after Queen Anne and made the capital of Nova Scotia.

1710   **Thousands of Germans crowding London are sent to Ireland and North America.**

With Germans continuing to arrive, Queen Anne encourages the immigrants to resettle in Britain's colonies. Approximately 3,000 Germans move to Pennsylvania, Carolina, New York, and Virginia; 4,000 are sent to Ireland.

Britain's *Post Office Act* establishes a postal system in the North American colonies.

The post is to be controlled by a postmaster general in London and his deputy in New York City.

1711	**The 1711 *White Pines Act* is passed.**

The Act extends the 1691 prohibition on the harvesting of large white pines in New Hampshire and Massachusetts to include the entire region from New Jersey to Maine, reserving all trees larger than two feet in diameter for use by the Royal Navy.

> Note: Difficult to enforce, the White Pines Act would often be ignored.

Jan. 1711	**Edward Hyde arrives to govern North Carolina as a distinct and separate colony from South Carolina but faces resistance.**

The deputy governor of Carolina's northern region, Thomas Cary, is reluctant to cede power to the arriving governor for Hyde doesn't have proper commission papers. Cary continues to believe himself to be North Carolina's legitimate executive.

> Note: Hyde, appointed by the colony's Proprietor's Council in London, had arrived in Virginia to assume the North Carolina governorship. But unfortunately for Hyde, the man from whom he was to receive his commission, Carolina Governor Edward Tynte, had died six months earlier in Charles Town.
>
> Edward Hyde was the first distinct governor of North Carolina. Previously, the northern region of Carolina had been served by a deputy governor appointed by the Carolina governor in Charles Town.

April–May 1711	**A massive military force sails from England to capture New France.**

With Port Royal already under British control, Great Britain now plans to capture Quebec and Montreal as the largest British force up to that time, led by Sir Hovenden Walker, sets sail for Boston. There, Admiral Walker is to obtain New England troops and additional supplies before launching a surprise attack against the French.

> Note: The 1711 campaign against Quebec would be known as the *Walker expedition*.

May 1711	**North Carolina Governor Edward Hyde declares Thomas Cary to be in open rebellion and attempts to have him arrested.**

The former deputy governor, Thomas Cary, has taken refuge in a neighbor's fortified plantation house at Bath Creek armed with a cannon and forty supporters. Governor Hyde, accompanied by 150 armed men, decides against attacking Cary and retreats.

June 1711	**British naval forces arrive in Boston, and the people rejoice at such a show of strength.**

The Royal fleet arrives to launch an invasion against New France. The two-pronged offensive calls for New England militia forces to attack Montreal by land, while the British Navy attacks Quebec after sailing up the St. Lawrence River.

Mid-July 1711 **British marines arrive in North Carolina to rescue the embattled Governor Hyde.**

Hoping to overthrow the new governor, an emboldened Thomas Cary and his supporters sail to attack Hyde at the fortified river-plantation home of Thomas Pollock by firing cannons from their ship. Governor Hyde requests military assistance from Virginia's Lieutenant Governor Alexander Spotswood, who readies a militia and sends a Royal ship from Chesapeake Bay. Realizing it would be treason to fire on the King's forces, Cary flees to Virginia where he is apprehended and sent in chains to England for trial. There, by the influence of friends, Cary is not charged and will instead be sent back to North Carolina in 1713.

Note:	Though readied, the Virginia militia was not ordered to North Carolina.
	This episode of North Carolina history is often referred to as *Cary's Rebellion*.

July 30, 1711 **The British fleet sails from Boston to begin the long-awaited attack on Quebec.**

The large armada is a mix of colonial and British vessels, including nine ships of war, two bomb vessels, and sixty transports and tenders carrying 7,500 troops and 6,000 sailors—all with high confidence of victory over the French.

Note:	The second arm of the campaign—2,300 New England troops and Iroquois warriors commanded by Francis Nicholson—was already en route up the Hudson River corridor with plans to attack Montreal.

Aug. 22, 1711 **En route to Quebec, the British fleet suffers a historic disaster.**

The Royal fleet and New England vessels are driven into rocks by storm winds and tidal forces in the mouth of the St. Lawrence River causing one of the largest disasters in Britain's naval history. Seven transport ships, one supply ship, and nearly 900 lives are lost.

Great Britain's campaign to capture New France ends abruptly.

Following the naval disaster, the campaign against Quebec is called off as the New England army and their Indian allies en route to attack Montreal, are ordered to return to Albany.

Note:	Upon hearing the news, New England commander Francis Nicholson would throw his wig upon the ground and stomped on it in contemptible disappointment.
	The disappointed Mohawk warriors accompanying the colonials stated they were so ashamed they felt the need to cover their faces.

In North America, Queen Anne's War is now primarily over.

With the campaign against New France now ended, Queen Anne's War will come to a close for the New Englanders other than suffering sporadic Indian raids in the isolated frontier regions.

Note:	Saved from losing New France only by British misfortune, France would formulate plans to construct a mighty fortress at the mouth of the St. Lawrence to safeguard French Canada from future invasions.

During the campaign, much disdain had been displayed by the British military toward the New Englanders—whom they viewed as bumpkins. This attitude would continue to be a source of friction between the two groups into future years.

Sept. 10, 1711 **The *South Sea Company* is chartered in London.**

The company is to be a trading and finance joint-stock company created to help reduce Britain's national debt. In return, the company receives a monopoly over British trade with the South Seas region (Polynesia and the South Pacific).

Note: In 1713, the South Sea Company would receive exclusive rights to import Africans as slaves to Spain's New World empire.

The South Sea Company, England's first public–private partnership company, would collapse in 1721, hurting many monetarily, including the British government.

Sept. 22, 1711 **The *Tuscarora War* begins in North Carolina, to last until 1715.**

After suffering years of land encroachments; being regularly cheated in trade; the threat of the Indian slave market; and abuse by the White settlers; the Indians go to war in what becomes known as the Tuscarora War—the largest Indian war in North Carolina's history.

The war ignites when Swiss colonists run the Tuscarora off their lands without payment and the Indians retaliate. For a three-day period, the aggrieved Tuscarora kill nearly 150 settlers in horrific manners and take thirty prisoners. In response, panicked frontier refugees, mostly women and children, flee into the larger communities en mass as hasty garrisons are built for protection throughout the region.

Note: The North Carolina government would have to deal with the warring Indians in a more weakened state due to the division and disarray caused by Cary's Rebellion.

Both the Yamasee and Cherokee would ally themselves with North Carolina to help defeat the Tuscarora.

In New York, colonial officials would urge the Iroquois Five Nations—relatives of the warring Tuscarora—to intervene and bring the Tuscarora to peace. Should that fail, they wanted the Iroquois to attack the Tuscarora.

The Europeans continue to create and foster Native American dependencies on trade goods—guns in particular—in hopes that the Indians will use them against tribal enemies.

It is in the interest of the Europeans to *keep the Indian knives at each other's throats* rather than pointed at theirs. As such, long-held tribal animosities are regularly manipulated by the Whites in hopes that the Indians might destroy each other. This also makes the Indians dependent on ammunition, powder, and colonial gunsmithing; thus, helping to secure the tribes' cooperation and loyalty.

Note: In the Carolinas, like elsewhere, alcohol was used to take advantage of the Native American people. Traders often reported that the Indians would arrive with trade goods on their backs and leave with the profits in their stomachs. Another observer reported that the Indians were never "contented with a little, but when once begun, they must make themselves quite drunk; otherwise, they will never rest, but sell all they have in the World, rather than not have their full dose."

In the Carolinas, a thriving Native American slave trade has developed.

The English encourage the Indians to raid their enemies for captives to be traded as slaves, with most being shipped to Barbados or Jamaica.

> Note: The Carolina traders encouraged their Native allies to raid the Spanish missions in Florida to secure Indians for the slave market and help drive Spain from the region.
>
> Serving as a missionary to the Carolina tribes from 1706 to 1717, the Anglican minister Dr. Francis Le Jau had written in his 1708 report to London, "I perceive dayly more and more that our manner of giving Liberty to some very idle and dissolute Men to go and Trade in the Indian Settlements 600 or 800 miles from us where they commit many Enormities and Injustices is a great Obstruction to our best designs. I have tried to get some free Indians to live with me and wou'd Cloath them but they will not consent to it, nor part with their Children tho' they lead miserable poor lives. It is reported by some of our Inhabitants lately gone on Indian Trading that they excite them to make War amongst themselves to get Slaves which they give for our European Goods … The Indian Traders have always discouraged me by raising a world of Difficultyes when I proposed any thing to them relating to the Conversion of the Indians. It appears they do not care to have Clergymen so near them who doubtless would never approve those perpetual warrs they promote amongst the Indians … poor women and children, for the men taken prisoners are burnt most barbarously. I am informed it was done So this last year & the women and children were brought among us to be sold."

The Europeans encourage alienation between the Native Americans and Africans.

The Whites do not want the Africans and Indians forming alliances, nor for the tribes to permit the Africans to dwell among them. Rightly concerned that their slaves will simply flee into the forest, the English provide bounties to the Indians for catching and returning runaways.

Oct. 2, 1711   **The first *Great Fire of Boston* destroys 100 buildings, leading to another bread riot.**

The second Boston bread riot takes place after a large fire destroys 110 homes, displacing hundreds of the poor.

> Note: Fires in Boston, like in all North American colonial towns, were semi-regular occurrences always resulting in terror.
>
> A bread riot is a rather benign term to denote civil unrest by the poor seeking relief from their sufferings—usually the lack of food or shelter.

Oct. 1711   **The Tuscarora repulse a North Carolina militia sent against them.**

Under the command of Captain William Brice, the militiamen are repulsed by hundreds of Tuscarora warriors and forced to retreat to the safety of fortifications.

> Note: Receiving a request for assistance, South Carolina would send militia forces to aid the panicked North Carolina settlers, but Virginia refused.

Dec. 20, 1711   **The British Parliament passes the *Occasional Conformity Act*.**

For any public office requiring membership and communion in the Church of England, if any officeholder attends "any conventicle, assembly or meeting" of any other religion—a fine shall be levied, and they shall be barred from office.

> Note: The Act was one more attempt to keep Roman Catholics and Nonconformists out of Parliament and offices of public trust by reserving the positions for members of the Church of England.

Jan. 24, 1712   **Carolina is formally divided into the separate colonies of *North Carolina* and *South Carolina*.**

Differences between the two regions have led to the governmental division of the Carolina Colony. Southern Carolina, including Charles Town, has been developed by settlers from Barbados and retains those influences with a growing planter aristocracy. The mountainous northern region of Carolina has been settled by migrating Virginians, Quakers from England, and arriving French Huguenots. Added to the political and economic differences between them, a long and difficult transport between northern Carolina and the capital at Charles Town has made an eventual separation inevitable.

> Note: Though independent from each other, North and South Carolina would remain proprietary colonies until 1729, when the Lords Proprietors would sell their interests to the British Crown.

Jan. 29, 1712   **The Tuscarora fortress town of *Narhantes* is destroyed.**

A South Carolina militia consisting of 32 Whites and 500 Yamasee warriors arrives in North Carolina to assist in the campaign against the Tuscarora. Led by Captain John Barnwell, the mixed army attacks Narhantes and takes the town within hours. After the carnage is complete, Barnwell's forces move on to attack additional Tuscarora towns.

> Note: The attack against Narhantes was a killing spree as 300 Tuscarora were massacred and another 100 taken captive to be sold as slaves among the English or kept by the Yamasee to be tortured or enslaved.

Feb. 27, 1712   **The Tuscarora halt an attack against *Catechna* by torturing their prisoners.**

Barnwell's army of Yamasee and South Carolinians, now augmented by North Carolina militiamen, attack the Tuscarora town of *King Hancock,* aka *Hancock's Town* or Catechna. To stop the onslaught against them, the Tuscarora begin torturing their English captives. Hearing their cries, Captain Barnwell agrees to quit the attack if the Indians will release all prisoners and agree to meet in one month to discuss terms.

In agreement, the Tuscarora free twelve captives and promise to bring twenty others to the proposed meeting.

> Note: The Tuscarora would not show at the appointed time, and the Carolinians would again move against them.

April 7, 1712   **North and South Carolina militiamen accompanied by Yamasee allies attack Catechna a second time.**

Led by South Carolina Captain John Barnwell, the mixed-militia army returns to Catechna and lays siege for ten days before the town finally falls to the attackers. Following the surrender, Tuscarora leader King Hancock is taken prisoner and executed by another Tuscarora chief, *Tom Blount,* who has agreed to help the English.

> Note: Unrewarded for his efforts by North Carolina, Captain Barnwell would return to South Carolina with many Tuscarora prisoners. There, Barnwell would sell his captives for profit in return for his military ventures, causing violence to flare again.

April 7–8, 1712   **The *New York Slave Revolt* of 1712.**

> Note: Comprising 20 percent of the city's population, New York had one of the largest numbers of Africans in North America, and all—whether free or enslaved—were severely restricted by law and social custom. In consequence, a group of Africans hoping to ignite a city-wide rebellion, hatched a plan to revolt against the Whites.

The riot begins when slaves armed with knives and swords set fire to a small outbuilding and attack the Whites who come to extinguish it. The Africans kill nine and wound others before fleeing as additional townsmen approach, but they are soon captured by militia groups.

In the resulting panic, more than seventy Africans are arrested, jailed, quickly tried, and sentenced to suffer draconian punishments and executions as a horrid warning to others. Twenty Africans are publicly executed—four by burning; one on the breaking wheel; one suspended in chains and starved; and the others hanged. Six additional Africans choose to commit suicide rather than submit.

Note:	A pregnant woman indicted in the plot would be spared hanging only until she gave birth.
	As a result of the revolt, New York would pass more severe measures and legal restrictions against the Africans.

May 1712
The *Fox Indian Massacre*: One thousand Fox are brutally slaughtered near modern-day Detroit, Michigan.

Accompanied by *Mascouten* and *Kickapoo* allies, the Fox besiege the newly constructed French frontier fort, *Fort Pontchartrain,* at a time of perceived vulnerability.

Note:	Fort Pontchartrain's commander, Jacques Dubuisson, was temporarily away and the French-allied tribes of the region had not yet returned from their winter hunts.

Under attack and nearly overwhelmed, Fort Pontchartrain's acting commander sends urgent appeals to his Indian allies for help, and they reply en mass as *Ottawa, Huron, Illiniwek, Osage,* and others soon arrive to save the French and to exact revenge on their traditional tribal enemies.

After an initial battle, the Fox escape during a night's rainfall and fortify themselves at Presque Isle, today known as Windmill Point. The fleeing Indians are pursued and attacked for the next five days. Finally overcome, the Fox are offered no mercy by their French and Indian attackers, resulting in 1,000 Fox, Mascouten, and Kickapoo losing their lives.

Note:	Michigan farmers ploughing the area would turn up bones from the massacre until the late 1800s.
	Fighting between the Fox and the French would continue until 1726.

1712
Britain's Parliament passes the 1712 *Stamp Act.*

Parliament imposes a domestic stamp tax on paper used for newspapers, legal documents, and other official purposes.

Note:	Britain's internal domestic taxes did not apply to its colonies.

Living in England and suffering from major debts, William Penn unsuccessfully attempts to sell the Pennsylvania Colony to Queen Anne.

June 7, 1712
The first slave importation ban is applied in Britain's North America.

Although slavery is permitted to continue, Pennsylvania bans further importations of African slaves, becoming the first British colony to do so.

Early Dec. 1712
A large army of Native Americans arrives in North Carolina to fight the Tuscarora.

Arriving under the command of South Carolina Colonel James Moore II, the army consists of 33 Whites and 900 Yamasee, Catawba, Cherokee, and Apalachee warriors.

> **Note:** In a state of desperation, most of Moore's Indian allies had arrived to fight for food and supplies.
>
> Colonel James Moore was the son of former Carolina Governor James Moore, who led military campaigns into Florida against the Spanish in 1702 and 1706. Colonel Moore, like his father, would also become a governor of South Carolina.

1713

The problem of naval impressments in Britain's colonies remains unsettled.

Now that Queen Anne's War has ended, certain questions remain. Is the 1708 ban forbidding colonial impressments still in effect? If not, does a British naval captain need to first seek approval from the colony's royal governor before acting?

Differing interpretations will make future conflicts unavoidable.

> **Note:** The colonists in North America believed the 1708 impressment ban was still in effect, whereas many British naval officers would choose to return to past practices and again began impressments in the colonial seaports.

Jamaica overtakes Barbados as Britain's largest producer of sugar—and profits.

> **Note:** The African slave trade would continue to increase with the rise of sugar production. The sugar industry, considered the hardest work with a correspondingly high mortality rate, had a near insatiable need for new slaves.

A profitable rum industry develops in colonial New England.

Large amounts of molasses are produced as a by-product of the West Indian sugar industry, much of which is shipped to New England to be distilled into rum.

> **Note:** Rum would become the primary alcoholic drink for the North Americans in the 1700s.

March 1–23, '13

In North Carolina, the Tuscarora suffer irreparable defeat.

South Carolina Colonel James Moore's Indian army lays siege to the fortified Tuscarora town of *Neoheroka* for nearly a month before the town is finally overwhelmed. The victory crushes the Indians as 400 Tuscarora are burned to death inside Neoheroka; 160 are killed outside the fortification; and 400 are taken away as prisoners.

> **Note:** The Tuscarora prisoners would be sold as slaves to help defray the cost of the military campaign.

April 11, 1713

The *Treaty of Utrecht* officially ends Queen Anne's War, which has run since 1702.

The terms include:

- The Catholic monarchs of France and Spain agree to recognize Queen Anne as Britain's rightful monarch, thereby recognizing the Protestant succession to the British throne.

- Britain agrees to recognize Philip V as the king of Spain.

- France and Spain agree to remain separate countries rather than unifying.

- France and Spain recognize Britain's possession of Gibraltar.

> **Note:** Spain would unsuccessfully attempt to recapture Gibraltar from Britain in 1727.

- France retains Cape Breton; site of the future French fortress of Louisbourg.

- Britain receives most of French Acadia and Newfoundland, and recognition of territorial rights to the Hudson Bay region known as *Rupert's Land*.

> Note: The French government would force its subjects to move from Newfoundland.
>
> France also wanted its subjects in Acadia to relocate to Cape Breton Island, but most would refuse to leave, and Britain agreed to let them stay. This decision would create continued conflict between the region's Catholic French and the Protestant English and Scots.

- France acknowledges British rights to rule the Iroquois as subjects and recognizes Britain's sole trading rights with the Iroquois League.

- Britain receives the right to import African slaves to the Spanish Indies in a long-sought contract known as the *Asiento de Negros*.

| 1713 | **Britain's South Sea Company contracts to supply African slaves to Spain's New World empire.** |

The exclusive agreement, purchased from the Spanish government for £7.5 million, calls for the South Sea Company to import 144,000 Africans over the next thirty years, with 4,800 slave *units* to be shipped annually to the Spanish colonies.

> Note: A male slave equaled one unit; women and children would be counted as fractional units.

In addition, Britain could send one—but only one—merchant ship per year into Spain's New World colonies for trade purposes.

> Note: This profitable agreement for Great Britain represented a crack in the *Spanish wall*— a ban that had been used for centuries to prevent foreign interlopers into Spain's lucrative colonial trade. Now, though illegal, other English merchants would begin to make inroads as well.
>
> Britain's Royal African Company and independent traders would continue to supply slaves to the British West Indies and North America.

| May 7, 1713 | **North Carolina Governor Thomas Pollock writes to New York Governor Robert Hunter asking him to deny succor to Tuscarora refugees.** |

Many of the now-defeated Tuscarora flee northward in search of protection from the Iroquois, and Governor Pollock wishes to deny them sanctuary.

| May 1713 | **In Boston, hundreds riot over the price of wheat and bread.** |

Protesting food prices and wanting to prevent the exportation of essential wheat to the West Indies, hungry citizens break into a merchant's ship searching for grain, and a warehouse seeking corn. When Massachusetts Lieutenant Governor William Tailer tries to intervene, he is shot and wounded by the mob.

> Note: New emergency laws would be passed because of the unrest, including: a prohibition on the export of grain in times of food shortage; the requirement that ships docking in Boston sell their grain to one of fifteen identified bakers for a set price; standardization of the price of a loaf of bread; and the establishment of a public granary selling grain at below market value.

| June 1713 | **Hoping to stave off total defeat, the Tuscarora retreat to the dense North Carolina swamps.** |

| | Note: | Marauding bands of Tuscarora would continue to roam the countryside for the next year and a half conducting guerrilla warfare and keeping the settlers in a panic. |

July 13, 1713   **With Britain and France no longer at war, the French-aligned Wabanaki Confederacy makes peace with Massachusetts and New Hampshire in the *Treaty of Portsmouth*.**

In a peace conference at Portsmouth, the Wabanaki pledge their loyalty to Queen Anne and agree to trade only at government trade posts that the Indians shall allow to be built in their lands. The tribes also agree to permit the English refugees dislocated by the war to return to their former homes, and consent to settle all future grievances between the two groups in English courts rather than by private revenge.

| | Note: | Wabanaki lands formerly claimed by France were now under the control of Great Britain by terms of the European *Treaty of Utrech*, and the Wabanaki were begrudgingly forced to adapt to the new situation. |

1714   **New Hampshire recognizes the legal status of slavery, already existing within its borders.**

| | Note: | By this time, Africans were a part of the social fabric of North America, living in every colony from Maine to the Carolinas. |

June 8, 1714   **Sophia of Hanover—the heir presumptive to the throne of Great Britain—dies in Germany.**

The 1701 Act of Settlement bars Catholics from England's monarchy and names the Protestant Sophia of Hanover as heir to the British throne following Princess Anne. According to the Act, if Sophia is deceased at the time of Anne's death, the monarchy is to be offered to Sophia's next-in-line Protestant offspring. Thus, Sophia's death now places her son, fifty-four-year-old *George Ludwig,* next in line to Britain's throne.

| | Note: | George Ludwig was the great-grandson of England's King James I. |
| | | The 1701 Act of Settlement had been passed following the death of Queen Anne's last surviving child—eleven-year-old William, Duke of Gloucester, on July 11, 1700. At that time, with neither King William III nor Princess Anne having any living progeny, Britain's Parliament had felt it paramount to establish a Protestant line of succession. |

Aug. 1, 1714   **George Ludwig of Hanover, Germany, is proclaimed to be king of Great Britain.**

| | Note: | Living in French exile, George Ludwig's twenty-six-year-old cousin, James Francis Edward Stuart, would continue to claim his right to the British throne. To help bolster James Stuart's claim, some suggested he renounce his Catholicism and convert to Protestantism, but James would refuse. |
| | | George Ludwig was unable to speak English. |

Oct. 20, 1714   **In London, George Ludwig is crowned King George I and begins Britain's *House of Hanover*.**

The Protestant prince-elector of Hanover (formerly known as the Electorate of Brunswick-Lüneburg) becomes the first king of the *United Kingdom of Great Britain* as riots break out by those in opposition.

| | Note: | Many Jacobites in England, Scotland, and Ireland opposed the *German foreigner*, instead preferring Queen Anne's Catholic half-brother, James Francis Edward Stuart. |

Though nearly fifty English Catholic royals had more legitimate claims, Parliament would not allow a Catholic to assume the throne—forbidden by England's 1701 Act of Settlement.

King George I and his heirs would concurrently rule Great Britain and the Kingdom of Hanover until Queen Victoria assumed Britain's throne in 1837. As a female, Victoria was forbidden from leading Hanover by *Semi-Salic Law*. Instead, Queen Victoria's uncle, Ernest Augustus, became the King of Hanover—thus ending one hundred twenty-three years of sharing a common monarch between the two kingdoms.

Feb. 11, 1715 **The Tuscarora War of North Carolina ends, leaving much of the colony in ruins.**

Though the Carolinians have suffered 200 killed, the Tuscarora Nation has been nearly decimated, with more than 1,000 killed, another 1,000 sold into slavery, and 3,000 others forced from their homes and living as forest refugees. However, with a peace treaty now signed, North Carolina's dispossessed White settlers begin returning to rebuild their former homes and to occupy the vacated Tuscarora lands.

Note: Tuscarora villages and towns had been destroyed, and their power had been forever broken by the North and South Carolina militia forces and their Indian allies.

The Tuscarora would be invited to reside on land reserved for them near Lake Mattamuskeet, but most would leave North Carolina permanently, choosing to move northward to resettle in Pennsylvania, and later, eastern Ohio under the protection of their Iroquois relatives.

In 1722, the Tuscarora would become the *Sixth Nation* of the Iroquois Confederacy but were not to be equal members with the other five tribes. Henceforth, having lost their independence, the Tuscarora would: be considered as adopted children; be subordinate to the League; no longer be able to declare war; and need to secure Iroquois permission for a great many things as the price for the League's protection.

April 15, 1715 **South Carolina's *Yamasee War* begins with the *Pocotaligo Massacre*.**

Reports of Yamasee unrest cause South Carolina officials to send an eight-member delegation to conference with the Indians. Hoping to avert the looming troubles, the delegates meet with the Yamasee, listen to their grievances, and make favorable promises in return. Yet, despite the progress made, while overnighting, the Carolinians are attacked by the Indians; two manage to escape and spread the alarm of the hostilities.

Note: A witness to the event, Indian agent Charles Rodd would later describe the initial attack: "But next morning at dawn their terrible war-whoop was heard and a great multitude was seen whose faces and several other parts of their bodies were painted with red and black streaks, resembling devils come out of Hell…"

The South Carolina delegation leader, Captain Thomas Naine, was tied to a stake and slowly burned to death over several days.

Yamasee warriors attack English traders living in the Indian towns and surrounding areas, including Port Royal, South Carolina, killing nearly 100.

Many settlers become refugees in the ensuing panic, fleeing to the safety of Charles Town or neighboring North Carolina and Virginia. In Charles Town, panicked people arrive by the hundreds creating food shortages as the Yamasee War continues to spread.

> Note: The Yamasee had originally resided in the Florida regions, but being enemies of the Spanish, the tribe had moved northward to ally themselves with the English and conduct trade, which included providing captives for the Indian slave trade.
>
> Yamasee warriors had only recently helped the Carolina militia armies defeat the Tuscarora Nation. Yet the relationship deteriorated due to grievances shared by nearly all Indians against the Whites, among them: continued land encroachments; the Indian slave trade; the depletion of deer and elk due to the robust hide trade; debts owed to the traders (the Yamasee were in debt to South Carolina traders worth 100,000 deerskins); the introduction of alcohol; and a general lack of respect shown toward the Indian people. In addition, intrigues by the Spanish in Florida and French in Louisiana helped lead to the outbreak of war between these former allies.
>
> Participating tribes would include the *Catawba, Apalachee, Shawnee, Creek, Ochese, Choctaw, Yuchi, Savannah River Shawnee, and Apalachicola.* Though some Cherokee would join the war, overall, the Cherokee Nation would refrain from the conflict until eventually aligning itself with the Carolinians.

South Carolina calls for the formation of regional militias to attack the warring Indians as many fear a pan-Indian revolt.

Both North Carolina and Virginia will respond accordingly.

> Note: Although the colonies were normally very competitive, intercolonial cooperation was usually displayed during military campaigns against the Native Americans for all saw the Indians as a common threat, particularly those colonies closest to the conflicts.
>
> South Carolina had helped North Carolina in its recent war against the Tuscarora and now North Carolina militias would help the sister colony in return.

Late April 1715   **Yamasee warriors attack a South Carolina militia sent against them in the *Sadkeche Fight*.**

South Carolina Governor Charles Craven leads a militia force to punish the Yamasee, but the Carolinians are surprised by the Indians in a dawn attack. The governor and his 250-man army awaken to a volley of shots from 500 Yamasee who lay ambuscaded in the surrounding woods. After a forty-five-minute battle, the Indians withdraw.

May 1715   **The Catawba have joined the Yamasee in their war against the English.**

Throughout the summer and into the next year, hundreds of Carolina settlers and Indian people are killed as the fighting continues to spread.

May 17, 1715   **A South Carolina militia is overwhelmed by Indian warriors in the *Barker Ambush*.**

Colonel Thomas Barker's 90-man army, riding horseback and guided by a former Indian slave, falls into an ambush by 400 Yamasee, Catawba, and other Indians. Colonel Barker and 26 of his men are killed.

Late May 1715   **South Carolina militiamen suffer additional losses at *Schenkingh's Cowpen*.**

The survivors of the Barker expedition have continued their offensive against the Yamasee and now pay dearly as they are attacked after permitting a group of unarmed warriors to enter their defensive palisade. In a ruse, the Yamasee had expressed a wish to surrender, but once inside the compound, the Indians pull out hidden weapons and manage to kill twenty-two of the Carolinians.

June 13, 1715   **The Catawba are defeated at the *Battle of the Ponds*.**

Led by Captain George Chicken, South Carolina forces launch an assault against the main body of Catawba, killing forty and wounding many more whom the Indians manage to carry away during their retreat.

> Note: The loss would cause the Catawba to seek peace.
>
>   The Carolina militias usually included a number of enslaved Africans.

July 1715   **Announcing they are ready for peace, a Catawba delegation visits Virginia and offers to help fight the Yamasee.**

Mid-July 1715   **In North Carolina, Yamasee-allied warriors numbering 500–700, attack the settlement of New London and plantations in St. Paul's Parish.**

> Note: Though the Yamasee War would continue, these attacks represent the last major Indian offenses of the war.

Aug. 1, 1715   **In Britain, the *Riot Act* of 1714 goes into effect.**

The Riot Act applies only to gatherings of persons numbering twelve or more whom the authorities consider threatening. The sheriff has authority to disperse such groups by reading them the Riot Act. After having read the Act aloud, such groups have one hour to disband or be arrested to face felony charges, including possible death without benefit of clergy.

> Note: The Riot Act of 1714 did not apply to Britain's colonies.
>
>   The law would remain on Britain's legal books until 1967.
>
>   The expression "read the Riot Act" refers to this law.

Aug. 1715   **The South Carolina Assembly allocates funds for the construction of ten new protective forts due to hostilities with the Yamasee.**

In addition, the assembly authorizes funding for a provisional militia numbering 1,200 men.

Hoping to evade the South Carolina militias, the Yamasee retreat to the safety of Spanish Florida.

Sept. 1, 1715   **France's long-reigning King Louis XIV, known favorably as the *Sun King*, dies.**

For seventy-two years, the popular Louis XIV has ruled France as an absolute monarch. Now, the king's parentless five-year-old great-grandson becomes King Louis XV.

> Note: The power of the French monarchy would decline during the reign of Louis XV as France would lose much of its colonial empire, including New France, to Britain.
>
>   King Louis XV's failures would help lead to the French Revolution in 1789 and the execution of his grandson, King Louis XVI, in 1793.

Autumn 1715   **In Scotland, Jacobites ready a revolt against Britain's new monarch, King George I.**

Once preparations are complete, James Francis Edward Stuart is to arrive from France to lead a military campaign to secure the throne.

North Carolina enacts legislation legally recognizing and defining slavery: the 1715 *North Carolina Slave Code.*

The law's overall purpose is to police the behaviors of the colony's Africans. Among the restrictions imposed: to leave a plantation to which a slave belongs requires a ticket from the overseer; slaves are forbidden to gather in groups, including religious worship; and slaves are forbidden from striking a White person, even in self-defense. In addition, the law requires Whites to help capture runaways, and perhaps the most punishing aspect—slavery shall be considered permanent and hereditary.

Approximately 2,500 Africans are now annually imported into North America as slaves.

Note: Though the enslavement of Africans was permitted in all the colonies, the need for laborers was greatest in the ever-expanding agricultural industries of the Carolinas, Virginia, and Maryland. As a result, it was there that the merchants and transporters of slaves, often New Englanders, looked to sell their human cargo.

Carolina traders urge the Cherokee to war against the Yamasee.

Hoping to solicit Cherokee aid, the traders encourage tribal hostilities in an attempt to defeat the warring Indian alliance. The Cherokee are promised great rewards, including firearms, if they agree to fight the Yamasee and their tribal allies.

Dec. 22, 1715   **James Francis Edward Stuart arrives in Scotland, hoping to become the king of Great Britain.**

With Scottish Jacobites rising in his support, twenty-six-year-old James Stuart believes that the time is right to assert his claim against the German imposter, George Ludwig. Landing at Peterhead, James's supporters recognize him as Scotland's king.

Note: If successful, James Stuart would rule as King James III of England; and King James VIII of Scotland.

Jan. 27, 1716   **The Cherokee kill Creek warriors arriving to conference and the tribes go to war.**

Suspecting a plot, the Cherokee attack and kill twelve Creek arriving for talks at the Cherokee town of *Tugaloo*. Later, when a party of Carolinians arrive, the Cherokee tell them the Creek delegation had really been a war party ready to attack and were thus killed.

Note: Now at war with the Yamasee-allied Creek, the Cherokee would align themselves with South Carolina.

Feb. 1716	**James Francis Edward Stuart flees Scotland.**

Though having managed to set up a Royal court at Scone Palace, James Francis Edward Stuart absconds to France due to the approach of government troops and never again returns to Britain.

> Note: In France, James Stuart would find himself an unwelcome guest for his former supporter, King Louis XIV, had died. Seeking a permanent exile, the following year James and his family would receive and accept an invitation from Pope Clement XI to live in Rome. Retiring to Italy, James Stuart would keep his hope alive of an eventual return of the Stuarts to Britain's monarchy.
>
> Twenty-nine years into the future, James Stuart's son, Charles Edward Stuart, would make a final attempt to secure the British throne for his father in the *Jacobite Rising* of 1745.
>
> As a result of the Jacobite rebellions, Britain would build northern military outposts in England and Scotland to more easily suppress the Scottish insurrections.

Maryland is restored to the Calvert family by the new administration of King George I.

The Calverts lost control of Maryland in the Protestant Revolt of 1689 during England's Glorious Revolution; and now, after twenty-seven years, the colony is finally returned.

> Note: Maryland would remain under Calvert proprietorship until the American War for Independence.

May 1716	**Britain's *Septennial Act* extends the maximum length of Parliament from three to seven years.**

This longer period between Parliamentary elections hinders the ability to quickly remove Members of Parliament.

> Note: The seven-year limitation would last until 2011; replaced by the *Fixed-term Parliaments Act* requiring Parliamentary elections at least once every five-years.

June 6, 1716	**African slavery is established in France's Louisiana.**

The Africans arrive with French colonists from the West Indian island, Saint-Domingue.

> Note: Before the introduction of the Africans, the French in Louisiana had been using Native Americans as slaves.
>
> During the next four years, the French Mississippi Company would bring nearly 3,000 Africans to Louisiana as France sought to develop the region.

1716	**Anti-slavery tracts printed in Massachusetts argue that competition with the labor of slaves slows the potential importation of Whites.**

Summer 1716	**Frontier raids continue in South Carolina as the Yamasee War continues.**

1717	**Criminal transports to Britain's colonies increase after Parliament passes laws collectively known as the *Transportation Act* of 1717.**

Convicted felons—ranging from murderers to petty street criminals—are all liable to be sent to North America in lieu of harsh sentences or executions in England. This enables Britain to *empty its jails* and helps relieve the constant labor shortage in the colonies. Bonded merchants guaranteeing the transportation and service of the convicts are to profit by receiving property interests, and many in Parliament see this as a win-win situation. The Act is beneficial for:

- England, by helping rid the country of criminals and vagabonds.

- The British government, which need not pay for their transportation to North America.

- The transporters, who profit from selling the convicts' service contracts.

- The convicts, who can live a life of sorts while serving out their term of indenture.

Note:	Prisons, as such, did not exist in Britain at the time. Jails were primarily used for people awaiting trial. The use of prisons to house large numbers of convicts would begin when Britain could no longer exile them by simply *sending them away*.

Sentences range from seven years for lesser crimes to fourteen years for more serious crimes; and oft include a lifetime banishment. To return to Britain before one's term is completed could result in execution. An estimated 50,000 people will be sent to the colonies under this Act.

Note:	The 1717 Transportation Act would be amended several times to allow for the exile and transportation of persons convicted of lesser crimes, including political opposition.
	The transportation of convicts to North America and the West Indies would continue for the next six decades. The last ship to bring British convicts to North America would land in Virginia in April 1776.
	In 1785, New South Wales in Australia would be made a penal colony for Britain's criminals and political enemies. The first ship of convicts would arrive two years later, in 1787.

In Maine, the Wabanaki Confederacy protests the English invasion and construction of frontier forts.

Attending a peace conference at Arrowsic, Maine, the Wabanaki claim sovereignty over their lands and the trading posts located upon them. Negotiating with the Indians, Governor Shute offends the sachem *Wiwurna* with constant interruptions and claims of Massachusetts's rights to the region. Wiwurna demands a clear border between the English and the Indians, but the Massachusetts officials are ambiguous, and the two groups will again go to war.

French traders establish *Fort des Sables* at Irondequoit Bay, New York, as an Indian trade post.

Having enjoyed a quasi-peace with the Iroquois since 1701, the French build a trade post at the site of present-day Rochester hoping to conduct trade with the Seneca.

Note:	The Nanfan Treaty of 1701 had granted England proprietorship of Iroquois lands, and the 1713 Treaty of Utrecht had acknowledged the Iroquois to be trade partners with and under the protections of the British sovereign. Thus, the British and colonial officials would view Fort des Sables, located on the southern shore of Lake Ontario, as a French intrusion.

The Cherokee, armed with guns and supplies provided by South Carolina, help bring the Yamasee War to an end.

South Carolina's Yamasee War has had catastrophic outcomes.

The war's effects include:

- Seven percent of the South Carolina colonists have been killed – 400 Whites and Africans.

- Twenty-five percent of the Yamasee have been killed.

- The countryside is left vacant as the White refugees have streamed into Charles Town, as well as North Carolina and Virginia.

- Most of the Yamasee have become war refugees: some push west and join with the *Lower Creek*, aka *Muscogee*; others head south to Florida, eventually joining with other Indians and escaped African slaves to form the *Seminole Tribe*; yet others will form the *Yamacraw Tribe* in 1728.

- The Southeast tribes are left further divided following the war and are thus less able to resist the ever-steady migrations of Whites onto Indian lands.

- The war has helped to end the Indian slave trade as the Carolina planters now turn solely to the usage of enslaved Africans.

Note:	Preceding the Yamasee War, approximately 25 percent of the slaves in South Carolina were Native Americans.
	In 1708, the Spanish governor of Florida estimated that 12,000 Florida Indians had been captured and sold into slavery by the English and their Indian allies. Many were Christianized Indians residing at the Spanish missions.
	Carolina's Lords Proprietors, living in England, had shown little concern for the colony's Indian problems. This, combined with other grievances, had furthered dissatisfaction with the absentee overseers and would result in North and South Carolina being returned to the Crown in 1729.
	Ten years would pass before South Carolina fully recovered from the Yamasee War.
	The last distinctive Yamasee village—near St. Augustine, Florida—would be decimated by smallpox and measles in 1727.

Scottish immigration to North America begins to increase.

With Scotland and England united by the 1707 Act of Union, Scottish immigration to Britain's colonies increases.

Note:	During the next sixty years, 250,000 Scots would arrive in North America.

May 1717   **Maryland passes laws forbidding marriage between Whites and Mulattos.**

Aug. 1717   **The French *Mississippi Company* is organized to develop the vast Mississippi region of North America.**

Expecting to find an abundance of gold, silver, and other wealth, the company is: granted control over the entire Mississippi region; given a monopoly on the expected trade; and charged with establishing a new Louisiana capital at the Mississippi River's mouth.

Note:	The Mississippi Company agreed to transport 6,000 French colonists and 3,000 African slaves to help develop Louisiana.
	The Mississippi Company, to be run by a Scottish economist and friend of the French Court, John Law, would see quick growth. The company's meteoric rise would make many French shareholders rich as the French word *millionaire* became used for the

first time. To the ruin of many investors, the Mississippi Company's financial bubble would burst in 1720.

The Illinois Country becomes a part of French Louisiana, to be known as *Upper Louisiana*.

The Illinois region, formerly administered as a part of Canada's New France, will now be governed from New Orleans to the south.

> Note: Upper Louisiana would include the modern states of Illinois, Indiana, and Missouri.

1718

New Orleans **is founded by the French Mississippi Company.**

Like two geographical bookends, New Orleans is to serve as the southern base of New France, at the mouth of the Mississippi River, while Fort Louisbourg—to be constructed nearly 4,000 miles away at the mouth of the St. Lawrence River—is to serve as a northern base and guardian fortress of French Canada.

The Mississippi Company is granted a monopoly on France's tobacco and slave trade.

The Bahamas becomes a royal colony as Great Britain attempts to suppress pirating in the West Indies.

Known as the *Republic of Pirates*, the Bahama Islands serve as a stronghold for many pirates of the region, and Britain wishes to end the trade disruptions caused by it. Therefore, Woodes Rogers, a former pirate himself, is appointed as the new royal governor. Governor Rogers immediately offers a king's pardon to all pirates willing to end the practice as Britain asserts control over the island group, which has formerly been run by the Lords Proprietors of the Carolinas.

The Spanish establish the Indian mission of *San Antonio de Valeron*, located today in modern Texas.

> Note: The San Antonio mission would later enter American folklore after the *Battle of the Alamo* on March 6, 1836.

May 1718

Charles Town, South Carolina, is terrorized by the pirate Edward Teach, aka *Blackbeard*.

Using several ships, Teach blockades Charles Town's bay and searches any vessel attempting to depart. In need of medicine for his crew, the notorious pirate seizes the *Crowley* and holds the passengers ransom. Threatening death to the captives, Teach's demands are met, and after releasing his prisoners, the pirates sail north along the Carolina coast.

July 30, 1718

Pennsylvania is inherited by William Penn's sons.

William Penn dies in England, and his three sons inherit the Pennsylvania Colony.

> Note: The Penn family would control Pennsylvania until the American War for Independence.

Sept. 17–24, '18

In Nova Scotia, the French settlement of *Canso* is attacked and taken by the British Navy.

Believing the French Acadians to be responsible for a *Mi'kmaq* raid upon a British station at Shelbourne, Nova Scotia, Captain Cyprian Southack leads an attack against the Acadians.

Defended by 300 French, Canso's *Fort St. Louis* sustains bombardment for three days before finally being overrun. The British then proceed to burn and pillage the settlement; execute some of the Acadians; and place others on the barren Canso Islands without supplies.

> Note: An ongoing guerrilla war would continue in Nova Scotia for many years between the French Acadians and their Mi'kmaq allies against the Scot and English setlers.
>
> The attack against Canso would be called the *Squirrel Affair*, receiving its name from Captain Southack's ship, the HBS *Squirrel*.

Nov. 22, 1718   **The pirate Blackbeard is killed off the North Carolina coast.**

Edward Teach is killed near the Outer Banks at Ocracoke Inlet in an engagement with the British Navy at the request of Virginia Governor Alexander Spotswood. To collect the bounty, Teach's head is removed and taken to Virginia where it is placed atop a pole at Hampton River as a warning to others and to serve as *food for the birds*. The spot is today referred to as *Blackbeard's Point*.

> Note: Edward Teach captured more than forty vessels during his two-year reign.
>
> Teach's death represents the end of the often-romanticized Golden Age of Piracy of 1689–1718.

1719   **South Carolinians revolt against their English proprietors.**

Unhappy with the colony's proprietors, South Carolinians wanting military protection from the Indians seize the militia and request the Crown take control of the colony. As a result, the British Board of Trade will appoint Francis Nicholson as governor.

> Note: Among his many colonial administrative positions, the veteran Nicholson had served as lieutenant governor of the Dominion of New England and royal governor of Virginia, Maryland, and Nova Scotia before being appointed South Carolina's first royal governor.
>
> The Carolinians would be given more control over their affairs with the charge of making wealth—for both themselves and the Crown. To assist the colonists, the royal government would increase the number of African slaves imported to South Carolina and provide additional military support.

Maryland's assembly hopes to stimulate iron production by passing an *Act for the Encouragement of an Iron Manufacture within this Province.*

> Note: English manufacturers would oppose the Act, for Britain was to produce the kingdom's necessary iron—not the colonists of North America.

The first Philadelphia newspaper is published: *American Weekly Mercury*.

Rhode Island passes laws restricting Catholics from public office.

The colony's general assembly passes laws guaranteeing that all men professing Christianity are available for public office and the military—excepting Catholics.

April 1719   **Potatoes are planted in North America for the first time.**

The potato—native to South America and introduced to Ireland in 1589 by Sir Walter Raleigh—is brought to New Hampshire by Scotch-Irish immigrants.

April 25, 1719	***Robinson Crusoe* is published in London, claimed to be the first novel written in English.**

The novel by Daniel Defoe will become one of the most widely published books in Britain's history.

1719	**France begins construction of the *Fortress of Louisbourg* to serve as the guardian of New France.**

Located at the mouth of the St. Lawrence River on the eastern tip of Acadia's Cape Breton Island, the massive fortress is to serve as a military base of operations to defend against intrusions into New France and the North Atlantic.

> Note: Louisbourg would take twenty-four years to complete.
>
> When finished, Fortress Louisbourg, with stone walls eleven meters thick in some places; emplacements for 148 cannons; surrounded by a deep ditch; and facing the sea on three sides—would be considered impregnable by the French.

Summer 1719	**France begins building *Fort Niagara* to stem the Indian fur trade flowing into New York.**

The French wish to stop the tribes of the Great Lakes region from trading furs at Albany by blocking their access routes.

> Note: Located at the Niagara Falls portage connecting Lake Erie with Lake Ontario, Fort Niagara's placement would give the French a major strategic advantage over their English rivals.

1720s	**German immigration to North America increases, particularly to Pennsylvania.**

With King George I now on the throne, the migration of Protestant Germans to Britain's colonies continues to grow.

> Note: Though each colony controlled its own qualifications for land ownership, nearly all required British citizenship. With Pennsylvania's liberal attitude toward religion and property ownership—the Quaker colony was an ideal destination.
>
> In the future, the Pennsylvania Germans would become known as *Pennsylvania Dutch*. The bestowed name came from the language they spoke, *Deitsch* or *Deutsch*.

Virginia encourages new immigration in hopes of populating its Piedmont region east of the Blue Ridge Mountains.

New immigrants will create profits for Virginia through increased land sales while also serving as a buffer between the Western Indians and the colony's coastal plain.

> Note: Many of the Scotch-Irish and Germans arriving in Pennsylvania would later migrate southward and westward into Virginia.
>
> Britain's colonies in North America competed for new immigrants to develop their western frontier lands.

Tea consumption has become popular.

No longer a drink consumed solely by the wealthy—tea is now enjoyed by the masses in Britain and the North American colonies.

1720   **Fort Niagara is visited during its construction by a delegation of Seneca warriors, who order the French to abandon the site.**

Accompanied by British agents, the Seneca declare Fort Niagara to be a French intrusion upon Iroquois lands—representing a grave threat to the tribe's control over much of the Western Indian trade.

> Note: The French were building Fort Niagara to control access to the Great Lakes and the continent's remote interior regions. As such, they considered the fort's construction vital to their own interests. Consequently, they would refuse the Seneca demands.
>
> Iroquois opposition to Fort Niagara had been encouraged by the British traders.
>
> Today, Fort Niagara represents the oldest continuously occupied military site in North America, with the United States Coast Guard still retaining a presence.

Britain's Board of Trade forbids the New Yorkers from trading with the French.

The *First Chickasaw War* erupts in the Mississippi Region, to last until 1725.

> Note: The French had allied themselves with the Choctaw, whereas the more powerful and warlike Chickasaw were in alliance with the British. This set the stage for an inevitable conflict as the European powers would compete for the Indian trade and resources of North America.

The war begins when Chickasaw warriors kill a French trader they believe to be spying on them and the French respond by providing firearms to the Choctaw, urging attacks upon the Chickasaw. In retaliation, the Chickasaw stem the flow of French traffic on the Mississippi River connecting Louisiana to Canada.

Aug. 7, 1720   **At Canso, Nova Scotia, French fishermen and Mi'kmaq warriors attack the unfinished *Fort William Augustus*.**

Still seething over the loss of Canso two years earlier, the French want to drive the English out.

> Note: The French and Mi'kmaq attack on Canso would help lead to another New England war with the Wabanaki Confederacy in 1722.
>
> Canso, as well as other settlements of the North Atlantic, was important to the fishing industry as a site to process catch, repair ships and nettings, and conduct trade.

1721   **Massachusetts minister Cotton Mather encourages the slaves to accept their fate.**

In Boston, Mather preaches that slaves should "not long for freedom as they have an easy servitude."

> Note: Unruly slaves in New England were often threatened with being sent to the West Indies.
>
> New England had both Indians and Africans serving as slaves and servants.

Philadelphia's *American Weekly Mercury* publishes one of the first criticisms of Britain's practice of sending convicts to the colonies to fill labor shortages.

The article states that despite the money earned and the needed labor they provide, shipowners are becoming more reluctant to transport convicts to the American shores due to colonial complaints concerning the corrupting influences they have on society.

April 22, 1721   **Boston's largest smallpox epidemic begins, affecting nearly half of the town's 12,000 residents.**

Beginning on a ship in the harbor, the disease spreads throughout the town leaving 850 dead over the next year. The Puritan minister Cotton Mather encourages inoculation by administering a small dose of the disease, but it is a process that has not yet caught on with the public.

> Note: Reverend Mather had learned of smallpox inoculation from his West African slave, who had been inoculated in Africa.
>
> According to Mather's description of the dreaded disease, "I never saw the Devil so let loose upon any occasion. The people who made the loudest Cry … had a very Satanic Fury acting them … Their common Way was to rail and rave, and wish Death or other Mischiefs, to them that practis'd, or favour'd this devilish Invention."

Britain continues to fortify its anti-piracy laws in an ongoing attempt to curtail the practice.

Now, anyone who knowingly conducts trade with pirates is to be considered guilty of pirating, and if convicted, shall suffer the same punishments.

Summer 1721   **The Cherokee sign their first formal peace treaty with the English.**

Delegates from thirty-seven Cherokee towns meet with South Carolina officials at the invitation of Royal Governor Francis Nicholson. Leading the conference, former Governor James Moore, Jr. addresses issues including trade, French encroachments, and general grievances between South Carolina and the Cherokee. Beginning the conference, a peace is established by the smoking of the pipe and a distribution of presents to the Indian delegates. During negotiations, the Cherokee agree to cede their lands between the Santee, Saluda, and Edisto Rivers to South Carolina; and to help keep the peace, an Indian agent is appointed to superintend Cherokee affairs.

> Note: The Cherokee would remain allies of Great Britain (the *English*) until the Cherokee *War against the Redcoats* in 1758.

1721   **In South Carolina, Britain builds *Fort King George* 116 miles north of St. Augustine, threatening Spain's La Florida.**

Fort King George—the southernmost outpost for Britain's mainland colonies of North America—is to help protect South Carolina from Spanish and Indian threats; thereby encouraging settlement to the region.

> Note: Threatened by the British military presence, Florida Governor Antonio de Benavides would organize formerly enslaved Africans from South Carolina into a militia unit as a part of his defensive strategies. In addition, Governor Benavides would encourage the Yamasee and Creek to attack the British fort—considered to be on Spanish lands.
>
> In 1727, Fort King George would be relocated 100 miles northward to a more secure position near Port Royal, South Carolina.

1722   **France transfers the capital of Louisiana from Mobile, Alabama, to New Orleans.**

Jan. 1722   **In central Maine, a Massachusetts militia attempts to capture French priest Father Sebastién Rale at the Abenaki town of *Norridgewock*.**

The New Englanders consider Rale to be a French agent stirring the Indians to war and a 300-man army has been sent to capture him. Forewarned, Father Rale manages to escape, but the Massachusetts men find the priest's personal belongings containing papers proving their suspicions to be accurate.

Early 1722   **Massachusetts demands the Indians deliver up all Catholic priests residing among them.**

Massachusetts officials believe the French priests are encouraging and directing the Abenaki in their attacks against New England. The Indians refuse.

April 16, 1722   **The *Boston News-Letter* republishes a London article regarding the shipping of felons to North America.**

"Eighty five Felons have been lately ship'd off for our Colonies in America. Tho' we abound with those Vermin such Numbers of them are order'd for Transportation every Sessions, it is hoped in a little Time the Plantations there will be pretty well stock'd, tho' it were to be wish'd with honester People."

April 20, 1722   **Parliament passes the 1722 *White Pines Act*, prohibiting the harvest of white pine trees.**

The cutting down and use of white pines located outside the boundaries of the colonial boroughs is prohibited, as all are reserved for the king.

> Note: White pine lumber was valued by the colonials for all sorts of general purposes, including the building of houses, ships, wagons, and barns. To skirt the law, the New Englanders would greatly expand the boundaries of their boroughs to incorporate the valued trees.

June 13, 1722   **Abenaki warriors raid Brunswick, Maine.**

In response to the Massachusetts raid on Norridgewock six months earlier, the Abenaki burn the settlement of Brunswick and take sixty English captive, most of whom will be used in exchange for French and Indian prisoners being held in Boston.

July 1722   **In Nova Scotia, Annapolis Royal is under siege by the Mi'kmaq.**

The French-allied Mi'kmaq attempt to blockade Annapolis Royal by cutting off supplies, capturing fishing vessels, and taking prisoners. The Indians burn fisheries, capture fishing boats, and hold eighty New England fishermen prisoner aboard vessels as Massachusetts Governor Samuel Shute demands retaliation.

> Note: To quell the attack and secure a release of the English captives, Annapolis Royal's Lieutenant Governor John Doucett would order twenty-two Mi'kmaq held as hostages.
>
> Under British control since 1710, Annapolis Royal was the former French capital of Acadia—Port Royal.

July 15–27, 1722 **Maine's Fort George comes under attack from Penobscot and *Medunic* warriors.**

Led by French priest Father Lauverjat, a 600-strong Indian strike force lays siege to Fort George for twelve days while burning houses and barns and killing cattle. During the siege, five English are killed and seven are taken prisoner.

July 25, 1722   **Massachusetts Governor Shute declares war against the Wabanaki Confederacy.**

The *Second Wabanaki–New England War* begins, representing a peak in Indian warfare in northern New England.

The boundaries separating the French and British in Canada—reset by the 1713 Treaty of Utrecht—have caused confusion, animosity, and additional conflicts in the region. Britain claims Maine, Nova Scotia, New Brunswick, and Newfoundland, but the Wabanaki tribes—allies of the French—had not been consulted in the European negotiations that established the new boundaries. All the while, settlers from New England continue to migrate northward into Wabanaki lands, particularly in Maine's Kennebec River area and Nova Scotia, with little regard for the Indians' sentiments.

The Wabanaki Confederacy—mostly Mi'kmaq, *Maliseet,* and Abenaki—consider the hated English to be encroachers upon their lands. Egged on by the influential Catholic priest Father Rale with promises of French support and arms, the Indians go to war, attacking settlers in Nova Scotia, Maine, Vermont, New Hampshire, and Massachusetts. The New Englanders enlist the aid of their Mohawk allies, and both attack the Wabanaki in retaliatory raids for the next three years.

> Note: The Wabanaki had gone to great lengths to protest the encroachments; including the presentation of a document showing the proper borders—but the Indians were ignored by Massachusetts Governor Shute.
>
> The French priest Father Rale lived among the Abenaki at Norridgewock in central Maine and urged them to attack the English. In response, Massachusetts had offered a reward for Rale's head.
>
> The three-year Indian war would be known by various names, including the *Second Wabanaki–New England War, Father Rale's War, Grey Lock's War,* and *Dummer's War.*

July 1722   **Annapolis Royal, Nova Scotia, is blockaded by Mi'Kmaq warriors.**

The Mi'Kmaq—skilled in amphibious warfare—prowl Nova Scotia's coast while attempting to starve the English at Annapolis Royal. Managing to capture many English fishing vessels, the Indians hold the fishermen captive on their own boats. Combined with Abenaki and Maliseet warriors, the Mi'Kmaq plan a direct attack against Annapolis Royal by land and sea.

> Note: The Wabanaki, especially the Mi'kmaq, conducted a skilled naval war of sorts, capturing English vessels and more than eighty prisoners during the three-year war.

The *Battle of Winnepang*, Nova Scotia.

A New England militia attacks the Mi'kmaq near present day Jeddore Harbor, hoping to free English captives held on boats in the harbor. Storming the vessels in a surprise attack, the militiamen quickly overwhelm the Indians, killing thirty-five of the thirty-nine Mi'kmaq guards and freeing fifteen prisoners.

> Note: The New Englanders would remove the heads of five Indians and place them on pike poles above the fort at Canso—serving both as war trophies and as a grisly warning to the Mi'kmaq.

Aug.–Sept. 1722 **At Albany, New York, the Iroquois and British officials sign a treaty to** *Renew the Covenant Chain* **"to polish it and make it shine brightly."**

The 1722 Albany Indian Conference recognizes the Tuscarora as a member of the Iroquois League.

Note:	The Tuscarora, defeated in the recent war with North Carolina, joined the Five-Nation Iroquois League. From now on, the Iroquois Confederation would be known as the *Six Nations*. The Tuscarora adoption would bolster Iroquois power, which had been waning since the 1680s due to: European intrusions; wars with French and Indian enemies; and various introduced diseases.
	The Iroquois, like most Native American tribes at the time, practiced the adoption of conquered people of their choosing—both White and Indian captives alike—assimilating them into the tribe to increase their numbers.

The Iroquois:

- Agree to stay west of the Blue Ridge Mountains and to no longer attack the Powhatan to the south.

Note:	The once powerful Powhatan Confederation, which had ruled over much of Virginia, had been destroyed by years of war with the English and now practically ceased to exist.

- Agree to treat (make treaties) with the English and not the French. If they travel to Canada to deal with the French, then they are not to return.

- Agree to permit the distant tribes to safely pass through Iroquois lands for purposes of trade with the British.

- Agree to only war against the French Indians of Canada if they invade Iroquois lands.

The British:

- Advise the Iroquois to stay sober, away from the destructiveness of rum, and to not trade their necessary corn for it.

- Warn the Iroquois that God will severely punish those that say one thing and do the contrary.

- Request that Iroquois emissaries be sent to the Eastern Tribes warring against Massachusetts and require that they cease such actions.

Note:	To ensure the emissaries' safety, a Christian would accompany them, and each Indian would receive a passport so as not to be molested during their journey.

- Offer rewards to the Iroquois for confiscating French goods destined to Canada in order to stop the French trade, thus forcing the Indians to trade with the English.

The Iroquois:

- Complain that English traders are illegally selling goods to the French traders, who then sell them to France's Indian allies.

Note:	As it was often easier for French traders to obtain goods from their English rivals rather than from distant France, an illicit trade had developed between them.

- Complain that the price of goods is much higher than it used to be, and that they are cheated with inferior products, including powder (gunpowder).

The British:

- Tell the Iroquois that they may not pass into eastern Virginia unless they have a passport from the governor of New York, with the penalty being death or slavery.

Note:	This was an attempt to set bounds between the Indians of Virginia and the Iroquois.
	Virginia offered a reward of one gun and two blankets for the capture of any runaway African the Indians should meet in the woods.

To renew the Covenant Chain of friendship, wampum belts are exchanged accompanied by the delivery of presents by the British to their Indian *children*: "That the Covenant Chain which is hereby renewed & brightened may be recorded in everlasting remembrance to be sent down to your & our children & to our Children's Children, to last as long as the mountains & Rivers & the sun & moon shall endure."

Note:	The Covenant Chain metaphor connecting the English and Iroquois in trade and friendship was first used in 1677 between the Mohawk and New York Governor Andros. Now the chain had been expanded to include Pennsylvania and Virginia, whose governors were in attendance to represent their colony's interests with the powerful Iroquois League.
	The Iroquois explained the Covenant Chain concept thus: "When the Christians first came to this Country our Ancestors fastened the ship that brought them behind a Great Mountain with a Chain in order to secure the same which mountain lyes behind the Sinnekees Country, so that the one end of the Chain, being fastened there and the other end at ye Ship, if anybody would steal away & molest this ship the chain will jingle & make a noise & so alarm all the 5 Nations who are bound to defend this ship & this is the foundation & original of the Covenant Chain among the 5 Nations, which our ancestors made, which was to preserve this ship from any harm gave a Belt of Wampum."
	The Iroquois met annually in Albany to have the chain *polished* with presents; to conference and air grievances; and to renew treaties making Albany the fulcrum in British–Iroquois affairs.

Sept. 10, 1722 **Arrowsic, Maine, is overwhelmed by nearly 500 Abenaki and *St. Francis* warriors.**

Arrowsic's fort and its defenders can do little against the onslaught, even after the arrival of militia reinforcements. The Indians conduct a firefight and roam the surrounding countryside killing cattle and burning dwellings before deciding to carry their attacks to other English settlements located along their return route to the Abenaki town of Norridgewock.

March 9, 1723 **In Maine, New England militiamen locate and destroy a large Penobscot village.**

A recently vacated village containing twenty-three wigwams and surrounded by a fourteen-feett high protective wall is destroyed by 230 militiamen led by Colonel Thomas Westbrook as the New Englanders continue a campaign of attrition against the Wabanaki.

Aug. 13, 1723 **The Wabanaki–New England War expands as Northfield, Massachusetts, comes under attack.**

Thus far, the conflict has been fought primarily in Maine and Nova Scotia, but it now expands southward as Abenaki Chief *Grey Lock* joins the war against the English. For the next two years Grey Lock attacks western Massachusetts settlements and isolated cabins, causing frontier disruptions. Chief Grey Lock's successful raids and elusive escapes will cause Massachusetts to construct *Fort Dummer* (in present-day Vermont) to be used as a base of military operations against the Indians.

Aug.–Sept. 1723 **At the annual Albany Conference, New England representatives continue to seek Iroquois assistance against the Wabanaki Tribes.**

Massachusetts Lieutenant Governor William Dummer requests that the Iroquois join the English in the war, but the Iroquois refuse, stating that the war holds no purpose for them. Dummer then requests that the Iroquois use their influence by attending a council fire at Boston for the purpose of negotiations. The Iroquois agree.

> Note: During Indian councils, a central fire known as a council fire would be lit and kept burning throughout the conference. In addition, the term was also a metaphor for the conference itself.

Autumn 1723 **Iroquois emissaries travel to Boston to attend a council fire.**

The Iroquois threaten the warring tribes to make peace with the English, or the Iroquois will join the war against them.

1724 **King George I attempts to settle border issues between Pennsylvania and Maryland.**

Disputes and bad relations have developed due to an undefined border between the two colonies. A Royal Proclamation of 1724 is issued to resolve the controversy, barring both colonies from building new settlements in the disputed territory until an official border can be surveyed.

Spring 1724 **Maine settlers are ordered to the frontier blockhouses for safety.**

Massachusetts's acting governor, Lieutenant Governor William Dummer, issues the orders as the Wabanaki begin their spring offensives in the ongoing war.

April 30, 1724 **Abenaki warriors overpower whale boats near Fort George, Maine.**

Paddling large canoes, hundreds of Abenaki warriors attack two boats containing New England militiamen, killing seventeen.

Aug. 24, 1724 **The Abenaki town of Norridgewock is destroyed, and Father Rale is killed.**

Two hundred New England militiamen accompanied by Mohawk allies surprise Norridgewock while most of the warriors are away. The attackers kill fifty Abenaki men, women, and children—including the French priest Father Rale—and then proceed to plunder the church and village, followed by destruction of the settlement's crops and fields.

> Note: The notorious *Father Sébastien Rale*, responsible for many of the Indian atrocities committed against the English, was shot and scalped. With a bounty offered on his head by Massachusetts, Father Rale's scalp would be taken to Boston for reward.

Sept. 1724 **At the annual Albany Conference, the Iroquois are again courted to help end the ongoing war with the Wabanaki Confederacy.**

The Iroquois report the warring tribes' response to peace overtures: "they replied that they could not lay down the hatchet against New England, because New England had taken their land and still held their people prisoner. They said that they would make peace when New England restored the land and freed the prisoners."

The New Englanders remind the Iroquois that they have promised to make war against the warring Wabanaki, but the Iroquois deny making such promises and reply, "If we should make war it would not end in a few days as yours doth but it must last till one nation or the other is destroyed as it has been heretofore with us."

The Iroquois also blame the French governor of Canada for keeping the war going and suggest that the English return their Indian captives if they wish for peace. The New England delegates request that if the Iroquois do not join the war, they at least permit their young men to fight with the English militias.

Nov. 1724   **Massachusetts authorizes a scalp-hunting expedition against the warring tribes.**

The General Court agrees to sponsor John Lovewell and forty to fifty accomplices to "kill and destroy" the colony's Indian enemies. Lovewell's men agree to range the woods for several months if the assembly will pay them a daily salary and provide bonuses of £100 for every male scalp and £50 for all others.

> Note: Lovewell's Rangers would return to Boston the following month with only one scalp and a fifteen-year-old Abenaki boy.

Dec. 24, 1724   **Eighteen-year-old Benjamin Franklin arrives in London to purchase a printing press.**

Having worked as a printer's apprentice in Boston for his older brother James before running away to Philadelphia, the young Franklin now goes to work in London print shops for the next year and a half to secure the funds to buy a press.

1725   **The population of African slaves reaches 75,000 in Britain's North American colonies.**

Jan. 29, 1725   **John Lovewell and his Rangers—known as *snowshoe men*—set out once again into New England's cold winter woods to hunt and kill Indians.**

1725   **Britain grows concerned over French activity in the interior regions of North America.**

Since making peace with the Iroquois in 1701, the French have steadily gained the upper hand in the Indian trade as they continue to settle along the Mississippi River, using its waterway as a trade and transportation route connecting Canada to Louisiana.

March 1725   **Massachusetts authorities award Lovewell's Rangers £1,000 for Indian scalps.**

John Lovewell and his men return to Boston and parade through the streets, with Lovewell showing off by wearing a wig made of the scalps they have taken.

April 16, 1725   **Buoyed by their success, Lovewell's scalp hunters again set out in search of Indians.**

May 9, 1725   **Lovewell's Rangers are annihilated during the *Battle of Lovewell's Pond*.**

Deceived by an Abenaki ruse, John Lovewell and his men fruitlessly chase an Indian warrior and are ambushed upon returning to retrieve their cache of packs and baggage. Nineteen of the thirty-six men are killed, including Lovewell.

1725   **The Indian war in New England and Nova Scotia begins to wind down.**

Massachusetts Lieutenant Governor Dummer and the Wabanaki begin a peace process as wampum belts are passed among the warring tribes for their deliberations.

Dec. 15, 1725   **The Second Wabanaki-New England War ends after three years of fighting.**

In Boston, the *Treaty of Peace and Friendship* peace is signed by Wabanaki sachems and New England officials. Among the treaty's terms, the tribes agree:

- Not to molest or interfere with colonial traffic or affairs.

- That all misunderstandings, quarrels, and injuries between the Indians and Whites are to be settled in the English courts.

- That the tribes are responsible for any restitutions required by crimes of their members.

- To release any remaining White prisoners among them.

In return, the British officials agree to:

- Cease hostilities against the Indians.

- Release Indian captives.

- Not interfere with the Indian's hunting and fishing.

- Consult with the tribes as the first owners of the land in future negotiations with France.

> Note: Not all the warring Wabanaki attended the treaty negotiations.

1726   **In Philadelphia, rioting poor are forcefully suppressed after tearing down the public pillories and breaking out in general disorder.**

South Carolina is exporting 4,500 metric tons of rice annually from Charles Town.

Sept. 14, 1726   **At the annual Indian Conference in Albany, the 1701 Nanfan Treaty is renegotiated.**

The British reserve to the Iroquois a sixty-mile-wide strip of land along the south shore of Lake Ontario and Lake Erie.

> Note: The lands had been a part of the enormous region granted to the English in 1701 located north of the Ohio River and extending from New York to the Mississippi River. With the French now building western forts along the shores of the Great Lakes, returning control to the Iroquois would strengthen Britain's hold on the region by incorporating the Six Nations in British designs against the French.

1726   **For a second time, the Iroquois visit Fort Niagara and demand the fort be abandoned.**

As before, the French refuse.

Oct. 11, 1726   **Benjamin Franklin returns to North America after practicing the printing trade in London.**

The twenty-year-old Franklin begins working in the Philadelphia shop of Thomas Denham.

1727   **The last execution in Great Britain for witchcraft takes place.**

Janet Horne is paraded through her Scottish town and swabbed with tar before being publicly burned for practicing witchcraft. Horne's deformed daughter is also sentenced but manages to escape.

Feb. 11, 1727   **The *Anglo-Spanish War* of 1727 breaks out, to last until 1729.**

The war begins when Spain's forces launch a five-month siege of Gibraltar in an unsuccessful attempt to seize the rocky fortress, held by Britain since 1704.

May 27, 1727   **The Abenaki complain about the low prices paid by the English for pelts.**

Massachusetts's acting governor, William Dummer, receives a letter dictated by the Abenaki complaining of the fall in prices paid to them for beaver pelts and the corresponding increase in prices for English goods the Indians must purchase. Dummer invites the Abenaki to visit the Boston merchants to see for themselves that they are paid the best price possible and the value of the pelts is not fixed but instead fluctuates with market conditions.

June 22, 1727   **Britain's King George I dies in Germany of a stroke.**

Note:	The visit to Germany had been the king's sixth since his coronation in 1714.
	George I was entombed at the *Leine Palace* in his German homeland of Hanover. In a bit of irony, the king's remains would be removed to the chapel at *Herrenhausen Gardens* during World War II due to British bombing.
	Unable to speak English and considered a foreigner by many, George I was never popular with the British public.

The Iroquois League forces the Shawnee to abandon Pennsylvania.

Both the Shawnee and Delaware (Lenape) reside upon Iroquois lands by permission that is now revoked due to Shawnee attacks against the English in violation of Iroquois prohibitions. Consequently, the powerful Six Nation League orders the Shawnee to move westward and declares that due to their actions, both the Shawnee and Delaware are to be henceforth considered women and no longer looked upon as men.

Note:	Many Shawnee would move west to the Ohio Country, while others moved northward to Canada.

July 1727   **The governor of New France demands that the British abandon Fort Oswego.**

Located on Lake Ontario's southern shore, the newly constructed fort represents a major threat to the French, as their main transportation route connecting Canada with France's interior lands and Louisiana runs practically under Fort Oswego's nose. Hence, Oswego's ability to menace or possibly sever this important French link means the British fort must go.

Note:	In addition, Fort Oswego represented a major intrusion into the profitable Great Lakes Indian trade—long considered by the French to be their own.

Summer 1727   **The *Meskwaki*, more commonly known as the *Fox*, go to war against the French.**

The Fox, living in the region of modern Illinois and Wisconsin, are located between the French and the Western Sioux with whom the French desire to establish trade. As such, the Fox, never friends with the French, wish to use their position to become middlemen between the two groups. The French reject this arrangement, and the Fox declare war.

> Note: The Fox and the Choctaw Tribes were the two major impediments to the free flow of French traffic and correspondence along the Mississippi waterway and France wanted them out of the way.
>
> Of Algonquian origins, the Fox had been originally located in the St. Lawrence River Valley, but had been forced westward, settling in the central Wisconsin region.

Oct. 4, 1727   **In London, German-born *George Augustus* is crowned King George II of Great Britain.**

Having returned from attending his father's funeral in Germany, forty-three-year-old George Augustus is crowned at Westminster Abbey.

> Note: George II would be nicknamed "the king who wasn't there" due to his long absences to Germany—the land of his birth and upbringing.
>
> King George II would be the last foreign-born British monarch, and like his father, the king was unable to speak English.

Spring 1728   **South Carolina militia forces venture into northern Florida to attack Spain's Indian allies.**

Three hundred militiamen led by Colonel John Palmer lay waste to Indian villages of the region as they push forward to the gates of St. Augustine. Showing themselves, but lacking the necessary strength to breach the gates, the South Carolinians retreat toward home while continuing their campaign against the Indians.

1728   **In Georgia, the *Yamacraw Tribe* is formed by Chief *Tomochichi*.**

Consisting of 200 remaining members of the Yamasee and Lower Creek, the newly created Yamacraw settle on the banks of the Savannah River desiring to be close to the British traders and to reside on their ancestral homelands.

> Note: Chief Tomochichi, originally a member of the Creek Tribe, aka Muscogee, would prove a loyal friend to the English; an enemy to the Spanish; and would help mediate relations between the Whites in Georgia and the neighboring Native American tribes.

French King Louis XV orders the Fox Nation to be destroyed.

At war with the French, the Fox are disruptive to French trade and are impediments to France's goal of establishing a corridor running from New France to Louisiana.

> Note: By 1733, fewer than 500 Fox would be alive—a near extermination that would shock even their tribal enemies.

New Jersey petitions the Crown for independence from New York.

Though permitted its own assembly, New Jersey is currently headed by New York's royal governor and a twelve-member governor's council.

> Note: Ten years would pass before New Jersey received its own royal governor.
>
> Similarly, Delaware had a general assembly but shared a governor with Pennsylvania; and New Hampshire shared a royal governor with Massachusetts.

1729   **Britain's Parliament passes the *White Pines Act* of 1729.**

The Act places additional restrictions on the use of the New England tree—prized by the colonists and the British Crown alike. The Crown wishes to reserve the trees for naval ships but the colonists value them for their lumber, thus the illegal harvestings continue.

Note:	The white pine was considered so important a resource that harvest restrictions had been placed on the tree in 1691, 1711, 1722, and 1729.

North Carolina and South Carolina become royal colonies.

Separated in 1712, the two colonies now become royal colonies after seven of the eight Lords Proprietors sell their interests to King George II. As property of the Crown, each colony is to receive a royal governor appointed by the Board of Trade.

Note:	One proprietor, Earl Granville, refused to sell his interests. Granville's family would retain ownership of a sixty-mile-wide strip along the Virginia border known as the *Granville District* until its confiscation by North Carolina during the American War for Independence.
	As royal colonies, Carolinians were granted more control over their affairs with the charge of generating wealth, both for themselves and the Crown. To assist this goal, the British government would provide the Carolinians with an increased number of African slaves and military support.
	At this time, North Carolina had a population of approximately 24,000 Whites and 6,000 enslaved Africans. In South Carolina, there were approximately 10,000 Whites and 20,000 enslaved Africans.

Benjamin Franklin purchases the *Pennsylvania Gazette* in Philadelphia.

The young Franklin will do most of the work of writing and printing the paper.

The Shawnee request the French provide lands upon which the tribe might settle.

Ordered out of Pennsylvania by the Iroquois two years earlier, the Shawnee request French permission to relocate to New France. The French agree, believing the Shawnee will serve as a protective buffer between them and the Iroquois.

The *Yorke-Talbot Opinion*: British merchants and plantation owners seek legal clarification regarding Christianized slaves.

In England, the legal question arises: "Is an African slave who becomes a Christian still considered a slave?"

Note:	The justification used by Europeans for enslavement of the Africans had been based on considering the Africans heathens. Thus, the question: Is the continued enslavement of an African converted to Christianity and baptized legal? Many colonial laws had been passed against manumission of Christianized slaves, but what about in England? The laws were still unclear, and many wished for legal clarification.

In 1729, London Attorney General Philip Yorke and Solicitor General Charles Talbot issue the following, "We are of the opinion, that:

1. A slave, by coming from the West Indies, either with or without his master, to Great Britain or Ireland, doth not become free;

2. And that his master's property or right in him is not thereby determined or varied;

3. And baptism doth not bestow freedom on him, nor make any alteration to his temporal condition in these kingdoms.

4. We are also of opinion, that the master may legally compel him to return to the plantations."

Note:	The opinion was not a court decision but rather the opinion of the government's two most senior officers, the attorney general and solicitor general. Thus, the legality of slavery in Britain would continue to remain somewhat murky.
	In 1807, Great Britain would prohibit all further slave trade within the British Empire.
	In 1833, slavery would be prohibited in Great Britain and most of Britain's colonies by the *Slavery Abolition Act*.

Nov. 9, 1729 **The *Treaty of Seville* ends the Anglo-Spanish War of 1727.**

The treaty fails to end the tensions and issues between Spain and Britain; hostilities will reignite in 1739.

Nov. 29, 1729 **The *Natchez* massacre the French in Louisiana as the two groups go to war.**

The Natchez have long been allies of the French, having welcomed Robert de La Salle in 1682. Through the years the tribe's population has much declined due to disease, and now, after decades of grievances and land loss, Natchez warriors execute a surprise attack against *Fort Rosalie* and the surrounding region. The Natchez kill 230 French soldiers and male settlers but spare the women and African slaves.

Note:	Many of the soldiers were decapitated in revenge for similar atrocities committed by the French against the Natchez.
	Fort Rosalie's commander, Sieur de Chépart, was taken prisoner and killed.
	Fort Rosalie was located at the site of modern Natchez, Mississippi.

The French, assisted by their Choctaw allies, begin a campaign of retaliation against the Natchez resulting in the tribe's destruction by 1736.

Seeking refuge, many Natchez flee to the Chickasaw Nation, trade allies of the British, thus increasing French hostility toward the Chickasaw.

Note:	The French would sell many of the Natchez into slavery.

1730 **In England, cotton is spun into cloth by machine for the first time.**

This technological advance will bring about a seemingly insatiable British demand for cotton and further increase the numbers of Africans imported into the colonies to produce it.

Note:	Cotton still required the painstakingly slow process of removing seeds by hand. This problem would finally be solved in 1793 by Eli Whitney's invention of the *cotton engine*, more commonly known as the *cotton gin*.

The Mohawk request that the New York governor prohibit the Christians from purchasing their lands, since they have so little remaining.

The last witchcraft trial in colonial North America?

For using sorcery to find lost items and treasures, a Virginia woman known only to history as Mary is sentenced without a formal trial to be lashed thirty-nine times, ending a long chapter in North American colonial history.

> Note: The last witchcraft trial in the United States would take place in Salem, Massachusetts, on May 14, 1878. Charges of witchcraft were brought against Daniel Spofford of Newburyport by Lucretia Brown, who believed "the defendant practices the art of mesmerism and by his said art and power of his mind influences and controls the minds and bodies of others." The case was quickly dismissed due to defects in the writ.

Britain's Board of Trade approves a *township system* for South Carolina to encourage the colony's development by increasing the number of White immigrants.

Eleven 20,000-acre townships are to be created and located at least sixty miles from Charles Town, with the promise of fifty acres to each new family willing to settle in the more remote regions.

> Note: South Carolina's African slave numbers were rapidly increasing, but the colony's White population was not. In addition, most of the colony's settlers hugged the coastal areas, leaving the interior regions largely unsettled and undeveloped. Thus, the Township System was intended to rectify the situation.
>
> An influx of White immigrants would provide additional protections from the Spanish and the hostile Indians and counterbalance the increasing number of Africans. As Governor Robert Johnson wrote, "Nothing is so much wanted in Carolina as white Inhabitants."

In England, James Oglethorpe and associates petition Britain's government to establish a new colony in North America.

Thirty-six-year-old Oglethorpe believes that a new British colony established south of South Carolina would be an ideal place for England's unemployed poor and those in debtors' prison to begin life anew. More convincingly to Britain, the new colony would serve as a protective buffer between Spanish Florida and South Carolina.

> Note: The influential James Oglethorpe was an Oxford graduate, military officer, and Member of Parliament.
>
> As the new colony would be located in Spanish-claimed La Florida, some Members of Parliament were unsupportive, believing it would push things too far with Spain.

April 18, 1730   **The first synagogue to be built in North America is consecrated in New York City.**

In 1654, a number of Dutch Jews fleeing the Portuguese Inquisition in Brazil arrived in New Amsterdam. Over the years, the congregation rented quarters for religious services, and now finally have a synagogue of their own—*Congregation Shearith Israel.*

> Note: This was the first building constructed exclusively to be used as a synagogue in Britain's mainland North American colonies (Barbados had a synagogue built in 1654). Often called the *Spanish and Portuguese Synagogue* or *Mill Street Synagogue,* the building was torn down in the 1820s, though the congregation still exists.

Late July 1730   **In the Illinois frontier, 900 Fox are surrounded by their Indian enemies and French troops.**

The Meskwaki, more commonly known as the Fox, have been fighting a war with the French and French-allied tribes in the southern Wisconsin area and now flee eastward seeking the protection of the Iroquois. Pursued by their enemies, the Fox take refuge in a wooded grove surrounded by open prairie in today's McLean County, Illinois. As their Indian enemies continue to increase in number, the Fox busily build protective fortifications as they prepare for a siege against them. Meanwhile, French military authorities in the region are notified of the situation and respond with troops as the Fox, in a dire situation, are encircled by 1,400 *Potawatomi*, Illiniwek, Kickapoo, and Mascouten warriors, and professional French soldiers.

Sept. 7, 1730   **In London, the *Whitehall Treaty* is proposed to a visiting delegation of Cherokee leaders.**

> Note: Believing England's king would protect their lands from further encroachments, Cherokee chief *Attakullakulla* and six others had accompanied Scotsman Sir Alexander Cuming from Charles Town to meet with King George II. During that meeting, the king had expressed his love for his Cherokee children and claimed a chain of friendship existed between the two nations. The Cherokee then met with officials of the Board of Trade to listen to the proposed treaty terms presented on the king's behalf.

"Hear then the words of the Great King whom you have seen and who has commanded us to tell you

"That the English everywhere on all sides of the Great Mountains and Lakes are his people and his children whom he loves That their Friends are his Friends and their Enemies are his Enemies That he takes it kindly that the Great Nation of Cherokees have sent you hither a great way to brighten the chain of friendship between him and them & between your people and his people That the chain of friendship between him & the Cherokee Indians is like the sun which both shines here and also upon the great Mountains where they live and equally warms the hearts of the Indians and of the English That as there are no spots or blackness in the sun so is there not any rust or foulness in this chain and as the Great King has fastened one end of it to his own breast he desires you will carry the other end of the chain and fasten it well to the breast of your Nation and to the breasts of your old wise men your Captains and all your people never more to be broken or made loose And hereupon we give four pieces of white cloth to be dyed blue.

"The Great King and the Cherokee Indians being thus fastened together by the chain of friendship he has ordered his people and children the English in Carolina to trade with the Indians and to furnish them with all manner of goods that they want and to make haste to build houses and to plant corn from Charles Town towards the Town of the Cherokees behind the great Mountains for he desires that the English and the Indians may live together as the children of one Family whereof the Great King is a kind & loving Father. And as the King has given his land on both sides of the Great Mountains to his own children the English so he now gives to the Cherokee Indians the privilege of living where they please and he has order'd his Governor to forbid the English from building houses or planting corn near any Indian Town for fear that your young people should kill the cattle and young lambs and so quarrel with the English and hurt them And hereupon we give two other pieces of white cloth to be dyed red.

"The Great Nation of the Cherokees being now the children of the Great King of Great Britain and he their Father the Cherokees must treat the English as brethren of the same family and must be always ready at the Governor's command to fight against any Nation whether they be white men or Indians who shall dare to molest or hurt the English and hereupon we give Twenty guns.

"The Nation of The Cherokees shall on their part take care to keep the trading path clean and that there be no blood in the path where the English white men tread even though they should be accompanied by any other people with whom the Cherokees are at war Whereupon we give four hundred pounds weight of gunpowder.

"That the Cherokees shall not suffer their people to trade with the white men of any other Nation but the English nor permit white men of any other Nation to build any Forts Cabins or plant corn amongst them or near to any of the Indian Towns or upon the land which belong to the Great King and if any such attempt should be made you must acquaint the English Governor therewith and do whatever he directs in order to maintain & defend the Great King's right to the Country of Carolina Whereupon we give five hundred pounds weight of swan shot and five hundred pounds weight of bullets.

"That if any Negro slaves shall run away into the woods from their English masters the Cherokee Indians shall endeavour to apprehend them and either bring them back to the Plantation from whence they run away or to the Governor and for every Negro so apprehended and brought back the Indian who brings him shall receive a gun and a match coat Whereupon we give a box of vermillion ten thousand of gun flints and six dozen of hatchets.

"That if by any accidental misfortune it should happen that an Englishman should kill an Indian The King or Great Man of the Cherokees shall first complain to the English Governor and the man who did it shall be punished by the English laws as if he had killed an Englishman and in like manner if an Indian kills an Englishman the Indian who did it shall be delivered up to the Governor & be punished by the same English law as if he was an Englishman Whereupon we give twelve dozen of spring knives four dozen of brass kettles and ten dozen of belts.

"You are to understand all we have now said to be the words of the Great King whom you have seen and as a token that his heart is open and true to his children and friends the Cherokees & to all their people he gives his hand in this Belt which he desires may be kept and shown to all your people and to their children and children's children to confirm what is now spoken and to bind this Treaty of Peace and Friendship betwixt the English and the Cherokees as long as the Mountains and Rivers shall last or the sun shine Whereupon we give this Belt of Wampum."

Concluding the meeting, the Cherokee are told that, "their Lordships desired they would give their answers thereto on Wednesday morning next," and were then shown samples of the presents they would receive if they agreed to the treaty.

| Sept. 9, 1730 | **The Cherokee give their answer, and the Whitehall Treaty is approved.** |

Having listened to the proposed treaty terms two days earlier, the Cherokee delegates meet again with representatives of the Board of Trade to deliver their answer. Speaking for the group, *Scalilosken Ket-agusta* delivers the following words:

"We are come hither from a dark mountainous place where nothing but darkness is to be found but are now in a place where there is light. There was a person in our Country with us he gave us a yellow token of warlike Honour that is left with Moyitchoy of Telloqua And as Warriors we received it He came to us like a Warrior from you a Man he was his talk was upright and the token he left preserves his memory amongst us.

| Note: | This was referring to Sir Alexander Cuming, who accompanied the Cherokee to England. Cuming, an audacious Scotsman, had arrived in North America to visit the Cherokee supposedly due to a dream. While traveling among the tribe, Cuming had made such an impression on the Cherokee that they declared him to be a Cherokee chief. At Cuming's encouragement, seven Cherokee chiefs agreed to sail to London and meet with the king; however, once in England, Cuming had said goodbye to the chiefs, to their great disappointment. |

"We look upon you as if the Great King George was present and we love you as representing the Great King and shall dye in the same way of thinking.

"The Crown of our Nation is different from that which the Great King George wears and from that which we saw in the Tower But to us it is all one and the chain of friendship shall be carried to our people.

"We look upon the Great King George as the Sun and as our Father and upon ourselves as his children For tho' we are red and you white yet our hands and hearts are join'd together.

"When we shall have acquainted our people with what we have seen our children from generation to generation will always remember it.

"In war we shall always be as one with you The Great King George's enemies shall be our enemies his people and ours shall be always one and dye together.

"We came hither naked and poor as the worm out of the earth but you have everything and we that have nothing must love you and can never break the chain of friendship that is between us.

"Here stands the Govr of Carolina whom we know This small rope which we show you is all we have to bind our slaves with and may be broken but you have iron chains for yours However if we catch your slaves we shall bind them as well as we can and deliver them to our friends again and have no pay for it.

"We have look'd round for the person that was in our Country he is not here however we must say that he talk'd uprightly to us & we shall never forget him

"Your white people may very safely build houses near us We shall hurt nothing that belongs to them for we are the children of one Father the Great King and shall live and dye together."

Then laying down his Feathers upon the table headed, "This is our way of talking which is the same to us as your letters in the Book are to you And to you Beloved Men we deliver these feathers in confirmation of all we have said and of our Agreement to your Articles."

Note:	Dressed in traditional Cherokee attire, the chiefs had proudly carried with them the crown of the Cherokee nation, consisting of five eagle tails and four scalps.
	As British allies, the Cherokee Nation would serve as a barrier between the French in Louisiana, and the British in Virginia and the Carolinas. In addition, the treaty would help pave the way for the founding of the Georgia Colony in 1732.

Sept. 9, 1730   **The Fox are horrifically massacred in the Illinois frontier.**

Surrounded for nearly a month, the fortified Fox have grown desperate and use the opportunity of a night rainstorm on September 8 to escape. In the morning, they are pursued and attacked by the French and Indian forces. Though the Fox make a valiant resistance, in the end they are overwhelmed and slaughtered suffering the deaths of 200 men and 300 women and children. In addition, 300 others are taken prisoner and forty Fox warriors are "burned."

Note:	Most of the captive Fox women and children would be sold as slaves.
	Following the massacre, the Fox would avoid complete annihilation only by the refuge provided to their remaining members by the *Sauk* tribe, aka *Sac*.
	In May 1712, nearly 1,000 Fox, Mascouten, and Kickapoo warriors were massacred by their French and Indian enemies near present-day Detroit, Michigan.
	In 1728, King Louis XV had ordered the Fox Tribe to be destroyed due to being impediments to France's North American trade goals.
	From this point forward, the Fox and Sauk would ally themselves with Great Britain.

Oct. 1730   *Cresap's War*: **Violence begins over the unresolved Pennsylvania–Maryland border issue.**

The boundary separating the two colonies has always been in dispute. A 1724 proclamation by King George I had supposedly quieted the disagreement, but small-scale hostilities now break out between colonial settlers living in the border region in what is today Pennsylvania's York County.

Note:	The dispute between the two colonies would not be finally resolved until the Mason-Dixon survey line in 1767.
	Philadelphia, according to the original colonial charters, was founded and located on lands designated as Maryland's.

April 1731 **British shipping merchant Captain Robert Jenkins is stopped by a Spanish fleet, who slice off his ear.**

Suspected of smuggling, Captain Jenkins is arrested in the West Indies. While under interrogation, a Spanish officer cuts off Jenkins' ear, and according to Jenkins, tells him to "carry it to his Majesty King George."

Note:	The incident would give the next war between Britain and Spain its name: *War of Jenkins' Ear*.
	The 1729 Treaty of Seville ending the 1727 Anglo-Spanish War had given Spain permission to stop and inspect British ships trading with Spain's colonies.

1731 **The Royal African Company abandons its involvement in the African slave trade.**

The slave trade is left to other British and North American suppliers as the company focuses on other African commodities, in particular, ivory and gold.

The Mississippi Company relinquishes control of Louisiana to the French Crown.

The company's assignment has been to make Louisiana a financial success by developing the region's natural wealth, including an expected discovery of gold and silver. Now, after fourteen years, the French company is bankrupt, and Louisiana, isolated and far from France, will be turned into a plantation colony. To accomplish this, Louisiana will soon receive an influx of French settlers and African slaves.

Massachusetts minister Jonathan Edwards begins preaching a series of sermons that help lead to a new religious movement known as the *Great Awakening*.

Many Congregationalist Puritans believe in a spiritual predestination that can be revealed by works, whereas Edwards believes in *justification by faith alone*. Preaching with passion and energy at his church in Northampton, Reverend Edwards tells the people they are all sinners before an angry God in need of forgiveness and redemption. To obtain ultimate felicity, one must convert and live a holy life.

Note:	Edwards, an intellectual Puritan minister, believed all humans had an inner light in need of spiritual revival or religious acceptance, writing, "Unless a man is united with Christ, he is wicked and therefore has no shred of righteousness to endear him to God. It is the belief in Christ that justifies the ungodly." Therefore, Reverend Edwards would emphasize that man only becomes worthy of God's love after justification. According to Edwards, the key to a unified understanding of Salvation was the believer's *new sense* of divine and spiritual realities.
	Credited with hundreds of religious conversions, Jonathan Edwards is often called *the Father of America's Great Awakening*.
	Reverend Edwards was a slave owner.

Nov. 1731 **The first public lending library in British North America is established in Philadelphia.**

The *Library Company of Philadelphia* is begun by Benjamin Franklin and fifty members of the Junto Club. The library is to be a subscription library supported by its members.

Note:	The Junto Club, formed by Franklin and his friends in 1727, was a group of learned men who met Friday evenings in Philadelphia to discuss issues of morals, politics, or natural philosophy.

| Feb. 22, 1732 | **George Washington is born a fourth-generation Virginian.** |

Washington's great-grandfather, John Washington, had settled in Virginia in 1657.

| 1732 | **Construction of Pennsylvania's state house—the future *Independence Hall*—begins in Philadelphia.** |

| June 9, 1732 | **The Georgia Colony is established by royal charter as a proprietary colony.** |

Carved from the southern region of South Carolina and named in honor of King George II, Britain's newest colony is founded to:

- Provide an opportunity for those in England's debtors' prisons and workhouses who are worthy of relief and rehabilitation and are willing to move to North America to begin life anew.

- Generate profits for Great Britain and Georgia's proprietors.

- Serve as a safety buffer for South Carolina by helping to keep foreign competitors from the region.

In addition, it is hoped that the proposed settlement of Savannah will be used by those British privateers preying on Spanish ships and thus contribute to the settlement's financial success.

Note:	Spain had long claimed the entire Carolina territory as a part of La Florida; the founding of Georgia was to be Britain's counterclaim.
	No Catholics or Jews would be permitted to settle in Georgia. The religious ban would help keep out the Spanish and the French.
	Georgia would ban slavery in 1735 as it was expected that the poor Whites would provide cheap labor for the colony's development instead of Africans slaves.
	Alcohol would be prohibited.

| 1732 | **Parliament passes the 1732 *Hat Act* to stem the colonial production of hats.** |

Entitled *An Act To Prevent The Exportation Of Hats Out Of Any Of His Majesty's Colonies Or Plantations In America And to restrain the number of apprentices taken by the hat-makers in the said colonies or plantations, and for the better encouraging the making hats in Great Britain,* the law is designed to protect Britain's hat manufacturers from competing with a growing hat industry in North America. Among its provisions, the law requires that all colonial hat makers to have first served a seven-year apprenticeship and prohibits all American colonies from exporting finished hats from the colony in which they are produced. Thus, for example, a hat made in New York could be only sold in New York, and not in neighboring Pennsylvania or New Jersey.

| Note: | The overall goal of Parliament was to restrain the budding American manufacturing industry, for the colonies were expected to support the mother country—not to compete with it. |

Parliament passes the *Debt Recovery Act* of 1732.

The law enables British merchants owed payment by Virginia planters to seize property, including lands and slaves to satisfy debt.

Violence between the frontier settlers of Maryland and Pennsylvania increases.

Without a clearly defined border, some of the region's settlers are unsure in which colony they reside. The situation has created land disputes and other issues as the people's divided loyalties help propel violence amongst them.

The proprietors of Maryland and Pennsylvania attempt to solve their border dispute.

Charles Calvert and the Penns sign an agreement designating a boundary between their colonies; however, Calvert, the 3rd Lord Baltimore, soon backs out, claiming ambiguities and changes in the document to which he has not agreed.

Dec. 19, 1732   **In Philadelphia, twenty-six-year-old Benjamin Franklin begins publishing *Poor Richard's Almanack*.**

The popular almanac will be published annually until Franklin returns to London as an agent for the Pennsylvania Colony in 1757.

Feb. 12, 1733   **The first British colonists arrive on Georgia's coast.**

Arriving from England aboard the *Anne*, James Oglethorpe disembarks at Yamacraw Bluff with 114 settlers to found the settlement of Savannah.

Note:	Georgia would be administered from England by the *Trustees for the Establishment of the Colony of Georgia in America,* but the colony would be directly run by Oglethorpe.

April 1733   **In London, the *Excise Bill* of 1733 is withdrawn due to opposition.**

Introduced to Parliament in 1732 by Sir Robert Walpole, the Excise Bill proposes duties on salt, tobacco, and wine to maximize revenue to relieve the taxes paid by wealthy estate owners in England. To discourage smuggling, Walpole's bill also proposes that customs officers may search private dwellings to look for untaxed goods. After intense protests and widespread opposition, Walpole withdraws the bill.

Note:	In the future, many Americans would co-opt the arguments used by the British against the tax.

May 20, 1733   **James Oglethorpe signs an agreement with Yamacraw Chief Tomochichi.**

Oglethorpe presents Tomochichi with gifts of clothing, pipes, tobacco, gunpowder, and cloth. In return, Chief Tomochichi gives Oglethorpe some buffalo skins painted with images of eagles and buffalos and asks that the English protect his people.

Note:	Tomochichi explained that to the Yamacraw, the eagle represented speed and the buffalo represented strength. The English, like birds, had flown across the sea and were strong as beasts since nothing could withstand them.

June 9, 1733   **James Oglethorpe writes his opinions of the Indians to a British official in London.**

The following are among Oglethorpe's descriptions:

- The Indians are wanting of conversion to Christianity, only needing an interpreter to instruct them.

- They are as moral as Christians. They do not commit adultery or the plurality of wives, nor do they support murder.

- Their two biggest obstacles to Christianity are their desire for revenge, which they call honor, and alcohol, introduced to them by the traders. Revenge is necessary to bring about justice for an injustice since they have no courts. In cases of murder, it is the next-of-kin that is obliged to exact satisfaction or suffer shame.

- The chiefs have no real power except to call together old men and their captains to propound to them, without interruption, the measures they think proper. When the chief is finished, all others have a right to be heard and then come to some unanimous resolution. The meetings can last for two days. They then recommend to the young men the agreed resolution of action. They are very eloquent in speech, with many attributes that the British admire in Greek and Roman writings. Lots of similes and metaphors are used in their speech. To the young men, they speak to their passions; to the old men, they speak to reason only.

1733–1743 **In Louisiana, the French and Chickasaw Nation again go to war.**

The French wish for the western waterway anchoring Canada and Louisiana to remain open as a corridor for trade and communications between the two distant colonies. Most tribes of the Mississippi region have aligned themselves with the French, excepting the powerful Chickasaw. As the Chickasaw Nation controls the river's upper regions, these allies of the British are able to close France's vital interior river routes. Therefore, the French want the Chickasaw destroyed and offer the Choctaw—tribal enemies of the Chickasaw—a reward of one gun, two pounds of lead, and one pound of gunpowder for each Chickasaw scalp.

> Note: When the hostilities break out, the French would use both military troops and their Choctaw allies in attempts to crush the Chickasaw.
>
> Until recently, the Fox, aka Meskwaki, in the Illinois region had also threatened France's western trade corridor, but the Fox had been nearly exterminated by their French and Indian enemies.

Sept. 1733 **At the annual Albany meeting, British officials tell the Iroquois to forbid French intrusions.**

The Iroquois are reminded by New York Governor William Cosby that they had formerly submitted themselves and their lands to the king's protection. As such, the royal governor forbids the Iroquois to permit any French settlement upon their lands as the struggle continues between France and Great Britain for control of the vast interior lands and forest resources of North America.

> Note: The Iroquois had been at peace with the French since the Great Peace of 1701.

Nov. 23, 1733 **African slaves take control of Denmark's West Indian island of St. John.**

In a planned attack, 150 Akwamu Africans revolt in one of the earliest and longest-lasting slave rebellions in the Americas. The rebellion will not be suppressed until the following spring by French and Swiss troops arriving from Martinique.

> Note: St. John is part of today's Virgin Islands, controlled by the United States.

Dec. 1733 **Britain's *Molasses and Sugar Act of 1733* goes into effect, *For the better securing and encouraging the trade of his Majesty's sugar colonies in America.***

Both Great Britain and the North American colonies regularly buy and consume French sugar, molasses, and rum; as a result, the influential British West Indian planters believe they are losing profits.

> Note: Rum, a profitable by-product of sugar production, had been banned in France due to pressures from the French brandy industry which did not wish to compete with the inexpensive colonial import. Therefore, the French producers were forced to export much of their rum to foreign markets.

The Molasses Act of 1733 is designed to increase the sale and consumption of sugar and molasses produced by Barbados, Jamaica, and Britain's other sugar-producing colonies. The Act's overall purpose is more about regulation and control over the lucrative sugar trade rather than raising governmental revenue. By increasing the cost of French sugar and its byproducts through taxation, Parliament is attempting to steer consumer purchases to British produced sugar, molasses, and rum.

The tax to be placed on foreign sugar products imported into England, Ireland, or the North American colonies is: 6 pence on each gallon of foreign molasses; 9 pence on each gallon of foreign rum; and 5 shillings on every 100-weight of foreign sugar. The tax/duty must be paid before the cargo is unloaded.

> Note: Most American rum producers believed the French molasses to be superior and without it they would be unable to meet their needs. Import duties would not be high enough nor well enough enforced to keep the French molasses and rum out of Great Britain or its North American colonies.
>
> A result of these and other Acts restricting British trade was the creation of a prolific number of smugglers, particularly in North America, with its long and untenable coastline. Though smuggling was criminal in the eyes of the law, enforcement would be lax, and smuggled goods from foreign countries would continue to be regularly consumed throughout the colonies. When a lone smuggler might be apprehended, sympathetic jurors would often set him free, to the chagrin of the British magistrate.

March–Dec. '34 **Tomochichi and other Yamacraw leaders visit London accompanied by James Oglethorpe.**

Meeting with King George II and Georgia's trustees, Chief Tomochichi advocates for trade agreements and education for his people.

April 23, 1734 **The *Mast Tree Riot* erupts in Exeter, New Hampshire.**

> Note: White pines larger than twenty-four inches in diameter were reserved for the Royal Navy, but local people had conducted various schemes over the years to illegally harvest the trees.

New Hampshire Lieutenant Governor David Dunbar suspects that an illegal lumber operation is being conducted in Exeter, but when he seeks to investigate, Dunbar is turned around by threats and gunshots. Not to be deterred, Dunbar sends a team of ten men to investigate in his stead. When the agents overnight at a tavern, they are set upon and violently beaten by locals dressed as Indians. As the battered men flee for their lives into the dark countryside, they are cursed and threatened with murder should they ever return.

1734 **The French construct *Fort Saint-Frédéric* at Crown Point in upper New York.**

Located in the Champlain Valley halfway between Montreal and Albany, Fort Saint-Frédéric is built to protect New France from British and Mohawk raids, while conversely providing the French a base for launching raids against the colonists of New York and New England. Built four stories high with stone walls twelve feet thick, the octagon-shaped fort has cannons installed on every floor.

> Note: The Champlain Valley—the major transportation route connecting Canada and New York—gave Fort Saint-Frédéric an advantageous strategic position for the French. As

such, the British and New England colonials would make several attempts to capture the French fortress before finally succeeding in 1759.

Nov. 17, 1734   **New York publisher John Peter Zenger is arrested for his works.**

John Peter Zenger, a German immigrant and publisher of the *New York Weekly Journal*, is arrested and hauled to jail after publishing severe criticisms of New York Governor William Cosby. Written under the pseudonym *Cato,* the articles concern Cosby's corruptions in office and the incensed Governor Cosby orders the newspapers publicly burned. Though Zenger is charged with seditious libel, he refuses to name the anonymous authors and is forced to sit in jail nine months until receiving a trial the following August.

Jan. 1, 1735   **Georgia bans slavery, believing it unnecessary for the colony's economic success.**

Note: The ban on slavery would last only sixteen years.

1735   **Parliament's *Witchcraft Act* of 1735 ends the long history of witchcraft prosecutions in Great Britain and the North American colonies.**

To believe people possess magical powers is now illegal, for such thought is merely illusionary. To claim such powers or to believe others hold such powers can send a person to jail for a year.

The British establish a naval station at Port Royal, Jamaica, in hopes of playing a greater role in the West Indies.

Among the many benefits of establishing a naval presence in the West Indies, Britain hopes to better compete with its commercial rivals and to suppress the ongoing privateering and pirating in the region.

Georgia seeks Scottish immigrants to help defend the colony.

Desperate for settlers to populate Georgia and help defend the fledgling colony against Spanish and Indian threats, Georgia's trustees seek the fiery Scots as immigrants. Known for their legendary bravery and martial prowess, Georgia's London trustees hire Lieutenant Hugh Mackay and Captain George Dunbar to travel to Scotland to secure those willing to migrate.

Note: For twenty-eight years, England and Scotland had been united by the 1707 Act of Union. But though politically united as *Britons*, a long history of conflict had left each somewhat distrustful of the other. Most English still self-identified as English and most Scots remained Scots.

Aug. 4–5, 1735   **In New York, the trial of John Peter Zenger establishes the legal principle that "Truth is the defense against libel."**

Arrested and jailed the previous November for his publications criticizing Governor William Cosby, Zenger's lawyers argue during the two-day trial that though Zenger does not deny printing the articles, the prosecution cannot charge them false. Therefore, attorney Andrew Hamilton tells the jury that truth is the defense against libel and a verdict of *not guilty* is a true cause for liberty.

After only ten minutes of jury deliberation, Zenger is declared innocent.

Note: The trial of John Peter Zenger would help lead to the First Amendment of the United States Constitution guaranteeing freedom of the press.

Jan. 10, 1736   **In Georgia, Scottish immigrants occupy the southernmost British outpost in North America.**

At the direction of Georgia's trustees, the Scots found their settlement of *New Inverness* on the site of Britain's former Fort King George.

Note:	Built in 1721, Fort King George had been relocated northward to Port Royal, South Carolina in 1727 due to its vulnerable location. This abandonment had left Georgia with no protection on its southern flank. As such, James Oglethorpe had recruited Scotsmen and their families to help create a new southern defense for the colony.
	Twenty miles to the south of New Inverness, the Scots would build *Fort Frederica* on St. Simon Island. Located a mere 100 miles north of St. Augustine, Fort Frederica represented the southern extent of British settlements on mainland North America.
	Spain would consider both New Inverness and Fort Frederica as intrusions into La Florida; thus, Spanish forces would invade Georgia in 1742.
	The settlement of New Inverness is today's Darien, Georgia.

Feb. 1736   **English minister John Wesley visits Georgia.**

Wesley, an Anglican clergyman, has been invited to Savannah by James Oglethorpe to minister in Georgia and to spread Christianity among the Indians. Reverend Wesley stays for two years before returning to England and there founds a religious movement called *Methodism*.

Note:	Yamacraw Chief Tomochichi would meet with Reverend Wesley and his brother Charles, requesting an Indian school be built in Savannah so his people might receive a Christian education.
	Charles Wesley, often referred to as the forgotten Wesley brother, was a prolific writer of Christian songs, including the hymns "Hark the Herald Angels Sing" and "Christ the Lord Has Risen Today."

Early May 1736   **A Maryland militia crosses into Pennsylvania as the frontier border disputes continue.**

The militiamen are spotted near Wrightsville, Pennsylvania, thirty miles north of the border.

1736   **Savannah, Georgia, prepares for an expected attack by Spanish forces from St. Augustine.**

Spain considers Georgia to be an illegal intrusion into La Florida and demands the British vacate Savannah and retreat north of the 33rd parallel. Instead, James Oglethorpe orders protective forts to be built as the Georgia colonists prepare for war.

Note:	The thirty-third parallel is located forty miles north of modern Charleston, South Carolina.
	Despite the numerous threats, immigration to Georgia—particularly by Scots and Germans—would continue to grow due to promises of free land.

Aug. 8, 1736   **In London, a Mohegan chief dies while waiting to address King George II.**

Mohegan sachem *Mahomet Weyonomon* dies of smallpox while waiting for an audience with the king and is buried in an unmarked grave in a South London churchyard.

Note:	Mahomet Weyonomon had traveled to England to protest Connecticut encroachments upon Mohegan lands directly to the king.
	King George II was in Hanover, Germany, and would not return until January 1737.

Sept. 1736	**Maryland militiamen make a second incursion into Pennsylvania.**

Once again, Maryland flexes its muscle in the ongoing dispute between the two colonies as an armed militia force brazenly crosses the border.

An Indian school is opened in Savannah, Georgia, for the Yamacraw.

At the request of Chief Tomochichi, the Indian school has been established to provide the Yamacraw youth with a Christian education. The short-lived school is supervised by Benjamin Ingham, a friend of John and Charles Wesley.

Nov. 1736	**In a turnabout, Pennsylvania militiamen cross into Maryland and arrest Thomas Cresap—a border ruffian and agitator.**

Cresap, a violent frontier settler from England, has been a big part of the border violence between the two colonies. Wanted for murder by Pennsylvania, the Marylander is taken to Philadelphia and paraded through the streets in chains before being placed in the city jail. Cresap will be held in custody until 1738.

Aug. 18, 1737	**King George II issues a proclamation ordering Maryland and Pennsylvania to cease hostilities.**

1737	**The Boston *Brothel Riot* erupts.**

Religious Puritans attack the town's brothels and bawdy houses.

Sept. 19, 1737	**The *Walking Purchase*: Pennsylvania's proprietors defraud the Delaware Tribe.**

To secure the acquisition of coveted Delaware lands, William Penn's son, Thomas Penn, presents the Delaware (Lenape) with an unsigned draft of a deed dated 1686. The deed (since deemed a forgery) grants the Penn family the right to buy Delaware lands roughly from south of Easton northward for "the distance a man could walk in a day."

Presented to the Indians as a legally binding contract agreed to by their predecessors fifty years earlier, the suspicious Delaware reluctantly agree, believing the distance measured will be a normal day's walk through the woods. It will not.

To prepare for marking the lands for Pennsylvania, Thomas Penn:

- Selects the three fastest runners in the colony and has them train for months for the event.

- Has a straight path cleared for the runners to follow, heading in a northwesterly direction rather than northerly.

- Has supplies placed along the way for the runners.

- Has ferries standing by to carry the runners across the Lehigh River.

- Offers a prize of £5 and 500 acres of land to the runner who runs the farthest.

The race continues into a second day, and after eighteen hours of running covering sixty-five miles, Edward Marshall earns the prize.

As a result, the Delaware lose 1,200 square miles of land, cry foul, and appeal to the Penn authorities, King George II, and the Iroquois Nation—all to no avail. As such, the Delaware are forced to relocate to western Pennsylvania or the Ohio region, taking with them bitter feelings as a cheated people. Many Lenape will exact their revenge on Pennsylvania settlers in coming years.

> Note: The victorious runner, Edward Marshall, would never receive his promised prize of 500 acres. In addition, the runner's family would be singled out for vengeance by the Delaware, who attack Marshall's farm killing his wife and son and wounding his teen-age daughter. In revenge, Edward Marshall would allegedly kill twenty Delaware.

Dec. 7, 1737   **Philadelphia experiences a violent nighttime earthquake.**

The quake strikes at 11 p.m. and is so severe that people believe their houses will surely fall upon them. Felt 100 miles away, the earthquake is followed by several days of an unusual red sky, which many believe to be a sign from God to always be prepared for their deaths.

> Note: Benjamin Franklin would report on the quake in his *Pennsylvania Gazette* and was so intrigued that he printed two additional articles about the causes of earthquakes for his readers.

1738   **New Jersey becomes completely independent from New York.**

Though New Jersey has had its own assembly, the government has been overseen by New York's royal governor and a twelve-member governor's council since 1702. Lewis Morris is appointed as the colony's first governor.

> Note: Two of Governor Morris's grandsons would make their mark on the history of the United States. As a delegate from New York, Lewis Morris III would be a signer of the Declaration of Independence; and his half-brother, Gouverneur Morris, would be a Pennsylvania delegate to the Constitutional Convention of 1787 and author the U.S. Constitution's Preamble.

Fort Mose, Florida, becomes the first free African settlement in what is now the United States.

La Florida Governor Manuel de Montiano establishes the settlement of Fort Mose several miles north of St. Augustine for Florida's free Africans and the runaway slaves arriving from South Carolina. Wishing to disrupt the ever-encroaching British settlement in the region, Governor Montiano encourages British-held Africans to flee to the sanctuary offered in Florida.

> Note: Fort Mose would be destroyed in 1740 during the War of Jenkins' Ear but would be rebuilt and reoccupied in 1752. In 1763, Great Britain would take control of Florida causing many of the Fort Mose residents to leave with the departing Spanish rather than risk re-enslavement or punishment under British rule.

English minister George Whitefield arrives in Savannah, Georgia.

Like John Wesley, Whitefield has been invited to Savannah by James Oglethorpe to serve as a parish priest. During his stay, Whitefield decides his *calling* is to start a Georgia orphan house and returns to England to raise funds.

> Note: Whitefield's *Bethesda Orphanage* in Savannah yet exists as the modern *Bethesda Academy,* though it is no longer an orphanage.
>
> While in England, Reverend Whitefield would experience a *religious awakening* and return to North America to preach, becoming the most singular influence in America's First Great Awakening—a profound religious movement that would sweep Britain's mainland colonies during the 1740s.

May 25, 1738   **In London, a peace agreement is signed between Maryland and Pennsylvania.**

King George II has compelled the two colonies to send representatives to London in order to negotiate a settlement between them. As part of the agreement, each colony is to release all prisoners; hence, Thomas Cresap will be released from his Philadelphia jail and return to the Maryland frontier.

June 15, 1738   **James Oglethorpe reports that the Spanish in Florida are encouraging the Creek Nation to attack the Georgia settlers.**

> Note: Savannah was only 175 miles north of La Florida's capital, St. Augustine, and the Spanish wanted these British trespassers out.

Aug. 1738   ***All Slave-Keepers That Keep the Innocent in Bondage, Apostates*, is published in Philadelphia.**

Written by the eccentric radical Quaker abolitionist Benjamin Lay and published by Benjamin Franklin, the book is a condemnation of slavery and does much to further the abolitionist cause.

> Note: The following month during a Quaker meeting, Lay—only four feet tall—would stab a hollow book filled with red berry juice and purposefully splash the onlookers, stating, "Thus shall God shed the blood of those persons who enslave their fellow creatures."
>
> Known as *Little Benjamin*, Lay compared himself to the biblical David who slew Goliath.

1739   **Frenchmen Pierre and Paul Mallet are the first French to sight the Rocky Mountains.**

> Note: In 1540, Spanish conquistadors under Francisco Coronado had first sighted the Rocky Mountains in present-day New Mexico, but this was not communicated to France or England.
>
> The Rocky Mountains received their name from the Cree Nation.

Aug. 21, 1739   **Georgia's James Oglethorpe meets with Creek leaders to reinforce relations and settle understandings of the boundaries between the Indians and Whites.**

Sept. 1739   **The *Stono Rebellion*: The largest slave revolt in British North America takes place in South Carolina.**

From the Stono River region of South Carolina, twenty-one native-born Africans led by a slave named *Cato* escape and begin a flight to Florida, 150 miles to the south. Carrying a banner proclaiming *Liberty*, the group's numbers soon grow to over eighty. The fleeing slaves commit violence and murder along the way but are eventually defeated by well-armed militia forces.

> Note: The violence left thirty Whites and forty Africans dead in its wake. Most of the captured slaves were executed; some were sent to the West Indies; and others who managed to escape were hunted down by Carolina militias and their Indian allies to prevent them from reaching sanctuary.

Oct. 5, 1739   **Yamacraw Chief Tomochichi dies—a great friend to Oglethorpe and the English people.**

Always a welcoming friend to the English, Tomochichi is given a funeral complete with military honors by the people of Savannah to show their gratitude and appreciation to the great chief.

Oct.10, 1739   **The obituary of Chief Tomochichi is published in Savannah, Georgia:**

"Savannah in Georgia Oct. 10, 1739

King Tomo Chichi died at his own town, 4 miles from hence, of a lingering illness, being aged about 97. He was sensible to the last minutes, and when he was persuaded his Death was near, he showed the greatest Magnanimity and Sedateness, and exhorted his People never to forget the Favors he had received from the King when in England, but to persevere in their Friendship with the English. He expressed the greatest Tenderness for General Oglethorpe and seemed to have no Concern at dying but it's being at a Time when his Life might be useful against the Spaniards. He desired his Body might be buried among the English in the Town of Savannah, since it was he that had prevailed with the Creek Indians to give the Land, and had assisted in the founding of the Town. The Corps was brought down by Water. The General, attended by the Magistrates and People of the Town, met it upon the Water's Edge. The Corps was carried into Provincial Square; The Pall was supported by the General, Col. Stephens, Col. Montaigut, Mr. Carteret, Mr. Lemon, and Mr. Maxwell. It was followed by the Indians, and Magistrates, and People of the Town. There was the respect paid of firing Minute Guns from the Battery all the Time from the Burial, and funeral firing with small Arms by the Militia, who were under Arms. The General has ordered a Pyramid of Stone which is dug in this Neighborhood, to be crested over the Grave, which being in the Center of Town, will be a great Ornament to it, as well as Testimony of Gratitude.

Tomo Chichi was a Creek Indian and in his Youth was a great Warrior. He had excellent Judgement, and a very ready Wit, which shewed itself in his Answers upon all Occasions. He was very generous, giving away all the rich Presents he received, remaining himself in a willful Poverty, being more pleased in giving to others than possessing himself, and was very mild and good natured."

Note:	Chief Tomochichi's obituary closed with a news update concerning Georgia's preparations for the expected military campaign to be launched against Spanish Florida. The addendum expressed hope that privateers would use Savannah as a base of operations for attacking the Spanish to the south, and thereby help protect Savannah from counterattack.

"General Oglethorpe has ordered 400 Creeks, and 600 Cherokee Indians, to march down to the Southern Frontiers, and is arming our several Boats. All the Arms of the Militia have been view'd, and Powder had been issued to them out of the Magazine. Twenty Voluntiers, who find themselves Horse and Arms, have desired to Leave to go against the Spaniards, no Purchase, no Pay. An Express arrived last Night from Frederica, that a Privateer Sloop from New York put in there for Refreshments, and then failed to cruize off Augustine. We expect most of the North America Privateers will make this Province their Rendezvous, near it is the best Station for cruizing upon the homeward bound Spanish Trade, and Provisions are plentiful upon this River.

There is one Privateer of 24 Pieces of Cannon fitted out from this Town, at the Charge of Capt. Davis, one of the Freeholders here, the Spaniards having seized Effects of his to the Value of 40,000 Pieces of Eight. We have taken a Spanish Spy."

Note:	In March 1740, Chief Tomochichi's obituary would be republished in the *Gentlemen's Magazine* in London for the British public.

Oct. 22, 1739   **Britain launches an attack on Venezuela, beginning the War of Jenkins' Ear.**

Trade disagreements, territorial disputes, and other issues between Spain and Great Britain have led once again to fighting as British ships launch a surprise attack against Venezuela's main port, La Guaira, but are repulsed.

> Note: Part of a wider Anglo-Spanish War that would last until 1748, the War of Jenkins' Ear would be primarily a maritime war fought in the West Indies.
>
> The war would usher in four years of military conflict between the British in Georgia and the Spanish in Florida.
>
> Privateers would wreak havoc on the shipping trade of each nation.
>
> According to legend, Captain Robert Jenkins—having had his ear severed by the Spanish authorities in 1731—would present a jar containing his pickled ear to a committee of Parliament's House of Commons, thus giving the war its name.

Nov. 20, 1739 **British forces attack and overwhelm Porto Bello, New Granada.**

Naval Admiral Edward Vernon successfully attacks the Spanish fortress, gaining Britain an early victory in the war against Spain.

> Note: The fall of Porto Bello (located on the east coast of modern Panama) gave Britain a false sense of early victory in a war that would continue until 1748.
>
> *New Granada* was the name given to Spain's lands in northern South America, including modern Colombia, Venezuela, Ecuador, and Panama.

1740s **The growing of indigo in South Carolina begins to expand.**

Though introduced to South Carolina in the 1670s, the colony's indigo production has been rather anemic due to competition with a superior indigo grown in the West Indies. But with the War of Jenkins' Ear interrupting South Carolina's rice trade and making the West Indian indigo difficult to obtain, the colony's indigo production greatly increases.

> Note: Though indigo would become a commercial success in South Carolina, it would always remain second in value to the colony's production of rice.
>
> The growing of indigo, like the region's other agricultural crops, increased the demand for labor to produce it.

English and Scottish youths continue to be sent against their will to Britain's colonies.

1740 **The Chickasaw Nation agrees to permit the French to use the Mississippi River.**

French use of the western waterway anchoring New France to Louisiana has long been thwarted by the British-allied Chickasaw. After warring for years against the French, the Chickasaw now sign a truce granting the French permission to use the Mississippi unmolested, but the bad blood between them continues.

One in every six slaves in Britain's North America is in a northern colony.

Spain continues to encourage British-held Africans to escape to Florida with offers of free land.

At war with Britain in the West Indies, Spain is attempting to create domestic disruptions to the colonists in Georgia and South Carolina, seen as occupiers of Spanish lands.

> Note: The Stono Rebellion was a direct result of Spain's policy, and the Spanish wished to encourage more rebellions.

At this time, Georgia was the only British North American colony not to permit slavery within its borders.

A religious movement dubbed the *Great Awakening* sweeps Britain's North America.

English minister George Whitefield begins a fourteen-month tour preaching nearly every day while traveling from Georgia to Maine and drawing ever-larger crowds of curious people as his reputation spreads before him.

Preaching long sermons without notes, the charismatic Reverend Whitefield emphasizes the need for a personal spiritual conversion while exciting the crowds into such overpowering frenzies that audience members swoon and faint. At the conclusion of each emotional sermon, Whitefield challenges the congregation to accept Jesus Christ, stating, "Come poor, lost, undone sinner, come just as you are to Christ."

Note:	Many would attend Whitefield's services only to participate in the fun and to hear the little man preach, but left the events unexpectedly religiously converted.
	Philadelphia printer and publisher Benjamin Franklin would befriend Whitefield as he traveled thorough Pennsylvania. Attesting to the minister's oratory skills and conversionary prowess, Franklin would publish Whitefield's sermons and sold more newspapers as a result.
	The Great Awakening would establish the tradition of traveling preachers speaking to crowds in outdoor settings and under tents, *taking it to the people*. Previously, highly trained and well-educated ministers had confined themselves within church buildings—not so with the preachers of this new movement.
	Most historians credit the Massachusetts minister Jonathan Edwards as beginning the Great Awakening in the mid-1730s, but credit Reverend Whitefield as having set it afire.

Reverend George Whitefield's North American tour—the biggest intercolonial sensation of the time—leaves a trail of religious upheaval in its wake.

Very much against the norms of the rigid formality of the Anglican Church and Puritan Congregationalism, Whitefield and other traveling Methodist and Baptist ministers of America's Great Awakening period are viewed as threats to the established religious order, resulting in various colonial laws being passed to stem the unconventional religious movement.

Note:	Some historians believe that the Great Awakening helped lead to the American War for Independence as it was a simple matter to move from challenging the authority of the Church—to challenging the authority of the government.
	The great speaker and Virginia statesman Patrick Henry is said to have acquired his oratory skills as a young man by accompanying his mother to religious camp meetings. Although not a convert himself, Henry watched and learned from the powerful preaching that seemed to grip the congregation as the ministers easily moved them to and fro while eliciting emotional outbursts.

Jan. 1, 1740   **Colonel James Oglethorpe launches a military campaign into northern Florida.**

Hoping to drive the Spanish from the region, Oglethorpe leads 200 militiamen aboard fifteen ships southward along the coast, but the Georgia militia manages to only capture two small forts guarding St. Augustine before returning to Savannah.

May 13, 1740   **As a result of the Stono Rebellion, South Carolina passes the *Negro Act* of 1740, *A Bill for the better ordering and governing of Negroes and other slaves in this province.***

The following are among the Act's provisions:

- All Negroes and Indians are declared slaves (except those already free); the offspring are to follow the condition of the mother; and such slaves are deemed human chattel.

- The term Negro is reserved to African slaves.

- A hard (dark-colored) Mulatto or Mestizo is a slave.

- For a Mulatto to be considered White is a question for the solution of a jury.

- Every slave found outside of town or out of the plantation to which such slave belongs "shall be punished with whipping on the bare back, not exceeding twenty lashes."

- Slaves found outside the house or plantation without White accompaniment may be detained and examined by any White person. "If any such slave shall assault and stricke such white person, such slave may be lawfully killed."

- Slaves who willfully destroy produce or manufactures, assist slaves to escape out of South Carolina, or maliciously poison any person (including other slaves) shall suffer death.

- Any slave guilty of a homicide upon any White person, except by misadventure or in defense of his master or other person under whose care and government the slave shall be, shall upon conviction suffer death.

- If several slaves shall receive death sentences at one time for attempting to raise an insurrection or enticing any slave to run away and leave this province, if deserving of mercy determined by the justice, corporal punishment shall be permitted, provided that one or more of the convicted slaves shall be executed, for example, to deter others from offending in the like kind.

- No owner shall permit his slaves to work for another for money without a ticket in writing under pain of forfeiting the sum of current money for every such offense.

- Due care shall be taken to restrain wanderings and meetings of Negroes and other slaves, at all times, and more especially on Saturday nights, Sundays, and other holidays, and the using and carrying of wooden swords, and other mischievous and dangerous weapons, or using and keeping of drums, horns, or other loud instrument, which may call together or give sign or notice to one another of their wicked designs and purposes, is to be prohibited.

- As Christians, it is important to restrain barbarity toward the slaves; therefore, to willfully murder a slave shall lead to a fine of £700 currency, but if it is done in a heat of passion, it is a £350 fine.

- If a slave owner willfully cuts out the tongue, puts out the eye, castrates, or cruelly scalds, burns, or deprives any slave of limb or member, or shall inflict other cruel punishment other than by whipping or beating with a horsewhip, cow-skin, switch, or small stick, or by putting irons on, or confining or imprisoning such slave, there is to be a £100 fine in current money.

- If a slave owner shall neglect or refuse to allow such slave or slaves under his care sufficient clothing, covering, or food, a fine or penalty of £20 current money for each offense may be imposed.

- Slave owners are not allowed to work slaves more than fifteen hours a day from March 25 to September 25, nor more than fourteen hours between September 25 and March 25, subject to a fine of between £5 and £20.

- Every such person and persons found guilty of teaching slaves to write shall, for every such offence, forfeit the sum of £100 current money.

> Note: The colonists blamed the Stono Rebellion and general slave unrest on the native-born Africans, whom they considered the most troublesome. Therefore, prohibitively high tariffs would be imposed on slaves arriving directly from Africa in order to reduce their numbers entering South Carolina. In addition, new efforts would be employed to teach the slaves the concepts of Christianity in the hope that religious instruction would make them less resistant to a life of servitude.
>
> The Stono Rebellion had greatly heightened White fears of additional slave uprisings. Hoping to intimidate those slaves harboring similar ideas, nearly fifty slaves suspected of collusion, support, or with interests of their own were hanged in the Charles Town area.
>
> The South Carolina Negro Act of 1740, based on the slave codes of Barbados, would contain the most restrictive slave laws in mainland British North America. The South Carolina laws would serve a model for other states in the American South.

May 1740

Georgia's James Oglethorpe leads a second military campaign against La Florida.

Along the way, Colonel Oglethorpe's militia forces attack and capture the free African settlement of Fort Mose. Leaving 170 men behind to hold the fort, Oglethorpe's army moves on to attack St. Augustine.

> Note: Accompanying Oglethorpe were Scottish Highlanders and Creek, Chickasaw, and *Uchee* warriors.

June 1, 1740

Britain's *Plantation Act* of 1740 encourages Protestant migration to North America.

An Act for Naturalizing such foreign Protestants and others therein mentioned, as are settled or shall settle in any of his Majesty's Colonies in America goes into effect.

With the French in Canada and Louisiana; the Spanish in Florida; an ever-increasing number of Africans arriving as slaves; and facing hostile Indians on every frontier border; Britain feels it is necessary to encourage an additional influx of Protestant immigrants to its North American colonies.

- Any resident alien living in Britain's colonies for seven years will be considered a natural-born British citizen upon taking a loyalty oath, professing the Christian faith, and receiving communion in a Protestant church.

- Once becoming British citizens, they are permitted to acquire property and to have political rights.

June 13, 1740

Georgia and South Carolina militia forces attack St. Augustine.

Colonel Oglethorpe's 1,000-strong army begins a siege against *Fort Castillo de San Marcos* while a supportive British naval fleet tries to blockade Spanish reinforcements and supplies.

June 26, 1740

Spanish forces, accompanied by Africans and allied Indians, counterattack at Fort Mose.

Taking advantage of the ongoing siege against St. Augustine, the Spaniards lead a surprise counter-offensive against Fort Mose—recently captured by Oglethorpe's men. Arriving well before dawn, the Spanish troops overtake the fort's combatants in heavy hand-to-hand fighting, killing approximately seventy-five of the Georgia and South Carolina militiamen.

July 20, 1740	**The attack against St. Augustine is ended.**

Unable to capture St. Augustine and expecting retaliatory attacks against Savannah, Colonel Oglethorpe orders the two-week siege abandoned and the army sails for home.

> Note: Due to the British assaults, Spain would build a second fort, *Fort Matanzas*, at St. Augustine.
>
> St. Augustine's original fortress, the Castillo de San Marcos, begun in 1682, today remains the oldest masonry fort in the mainland United States.

1741	**New Hampshire permanently separates from Massachusetts Bay Colony.**

New Hampshire formerly shared a common governor with Massachusetts, but the colony now receives its own appointed royal governor, Benning Wentworth.

The *Legend of Plymouth Rock* begins.

In Massachusetts, Thomas Faunce, ninety-five years old and unable to walk, is carried in a chair to the Plymouth shore and points to a large rock, stating it to be the site that the *Mayflower* passengers first stepped ashore in 1620. Thus begins the Legend of Plymouth Rock.

> Note: Faunce's father had arrived aboard the *Anne* three years after the *Mayflower* landing. Growing up in Plymouth, the younger Faunce had been told by his father and others that the rock was where it all began—and to not forget the spot.
>
> Until that time, the Plymouth citizens had either known little or thought nothing of it.
>
> Many historians doubt the story.

The Aleutian Islands are visited by Europeans for the first time.

Hired by the Russian government, Danish explorer Vitus Bering arrives to explore the Alaskan archipelago and the strait that today bears his name.

> Note: The Aleutians would become a major source of furs for the Asian market, particularly the sea otter.

March–April '41	**The *New York Slave Conspiracy* of 1741.**

Fires are being set in New York City, including at the governor's house, and the arson is blamed on a conspiracy of African slaves and poor Whites, many of whom are indentured. Suspecting an insurrection, the authorities set about suppressing it and interrogate hundreds of New York's slaves and servants. Punishment is severe as the officials publicly burn thirteen Africans, hang seventeen, and export seventy others never to return. Two White men and two White women are also hanged.

> Note: The event eerily reflected upon the New York Slave Revolt of April 1712. Then, too, the Africans accused of participation were executed in draconian manners.

March–May '41	**British maritime forces attack Cartagena, Colombia, but fail to take the Spanish fortress.**

Sailing from Port Royal, Jamaica, with one of the largest British fleets ever assembled, Admiral Edward Vernon lays siege to Cartagena. Included with the British forces are 3,600 Virginians led by Lawrence Washington—an older half-brother of George Washington.

After assaulting Cartagena for nearly two months, Admiral Vernon sends false reports of victory to the British naval station in Jamaica which forwards the news to England. Learning of Vernon's success, great celebrations erupt in London only to be cut short when the truth arrives.

June 8, 1741   **Riots erupt in Boston against the British Navy over impressments.**

Captain James Scott of the HBS *Astraea* arrives in Boston and sends press-gangs ashore to replace fifty deserters lost the previous month, but citizens armed with clubs and cutlasses attempt to thwart them. Governor Shirley and the Massachusetts Council order Captain Scott to release the apprehended men or be fired upon. The number of rioters soon swells to more than 300 and the men are eventually released, but resentment only continues to rise over impressment issues.

Note: British naval captains often blamed the colonial shipping merchants for encouraging royal sailors to desert by offering employment and higher wages.

Reverend Johnathan Edwards writes and delivers the sermon "Sinners in the Hands of an Angry God," and affects great multitudes of people.

Written following George Whitefield's religious tour of North America, the emotional work is a rhetorical masterpiece illustrating the uncertainty of earthly existence. In the sermon, Edwards reminds people that: they live only by God's grace and at his pleasure; death is soon; and all will be judged by an angry God with vengeance far more fearful and painful than anyone can comprehend.

Note: Reverend Edwards would be dismissed from his church in 1750. A believer in *civilizing* Indians, Edwards would go to Stockbridge, Massachusetts, to minister to the Mahican and Mohawk, becoming their tireless defender and advocate while also raising funds for their education.

Oct. 13, 1741   **Defiance continues against naval impressment as Boston officials are assaulted.**

Two local officials are beaten severely by a late-night crowd that suspects them to be agents of the hated press-gangs.

Dec. 3, 1741   **In Philadelphia, Benjamin Franklin creates a better heating stove.**

Franklin's improved version of the cast-iron heating stove is advertised for sale in the *Pennsylvania Gazette* for the first time.

Note: Franklin's design—dubbed the *Franklin Stove*—is still sold today.

May 1742   **The *Bethlehem Female Seminary* becomes the first woman's boarding school in North America.**

Note: Established in Bethlehem, Pennsylvania, the school yet exists; becoming the coeducational *Moravian College* in 1954.

July 5, 1742   **Spain attempts to capture Georgia's Fort Frederica.**

At war with Great Britain, Spain sends 2,000 troops ashore under the command of La Florida's governor, Manuel de Montiano, to attack Fort Frederica on St. Simons Island. The Spanish troops engage the Georgia forces, commanded by Colonel James Oglethorpe, in two battles—the *Battle of Bloody Marsh* and the *Battle of Bloody Hole Creek*—but, with help from Native American allies, the Georgians repel the Spanish troops.

> Note: Though future threats remained, this would be Spain's only attack against Georgia.

July 1742   **Pennsylvania's Walking Purchase of 1737 is upheld by the Iroquois against the protesting Delaware, who have thus far refused to relocate.**

Meeting in Philadelphia and accompanied by 300 warriors, the Onondaga chief *Canasatego* declares the treaty to be legitimate, stating that the disputed lands were not Delaware lands to sell in the first place, but were instead lands controlled by the Six Nations.

Canasatego tells the Delaware, "You deserve to be taken by the hair of your heads and shaken till you recover your senses and become sober. We have seen a deed signed by your chiefs above fifty years ago, for this very land. But how came you to take upon yourselves to sell land at all? We conquered you; we made women of you."

The Iroquois chief then orders the Delaware to depart the council, and to evacuate the lands immediately.

> Note: Pennsylvania had solicited help from the Six Nations to force the Delaware removal.
>
> According to the Iroquois, by being designated *women*, the Delaware were without authority to sell the land.
>
> The Delaware would continue to seek justice in this fraudulent loss of lands. In 2006, the case made it to the United States Court of Appeals for the Third Circuit, which ruled against them. The Delaware then appealed to the United States Supreme Court, which refused to hear the case.

1742   **The Cherokee and Iroquois agree to peace.**

Though historical enemies, both tribes are now common allies of the British, and with British encouragement, an uneasy peace is negotiated.

> Note: Peace between the two tribes would last only until 1755, when war would again break out between the British and the French. Though the Iroquois would retain their alliance with the British, the Cherokee would choose to support the French.

Oct. 1, 1742   **Riots break out on election day in Philadelphia.**

Divided politics spill over after the Anglican Proprietary Party threatens the Quakers and their German supporters. The Anglicans use dockside ruffians to intimidate the opposition from voting as fighting erupts and fifty sailors are jailed.

> Note: The Quakers would win the election.

1743   **The American Philosophical Society is founded in Philadelphia to promote the *finer arts and general knowledge.***

Founded by Benjamin Franklin and others, the prestigious organization is still in existence today.

March 1743   **Leading militia forces and allied Indians, Colonel James Oglethorpe again attempts to capture St. Augustine.**

For the third time in three years, Oglethorpe's mixed army advances to the fort's gates but can do little more.

June 22, 1743   **King George II is the last British monarch to lead troops into battle.**

In Bavaria, Germany, George II nominally leads a Hessian calvary charge against the French at the *Battle of Dettingen*, becoming the last British king to command troops during battle.

Note: Many English suspected that the king's true interests were foreign, favoring his German homeland over Great Britain.

1743   **The Iroquois threaten war against Virginia after skirmishing with settlers in the Shenandoah Valley.**

Once again, frontier conflicts have arisen over encroachments into Indian lands. The dispute with the Iroquois will lead to the *Treaty of Lancaster* the following year.

March 15, 1744   **France allies itself with Spain and declares war against Great Britain.**

March 30, 1744   **Great Britain declares war against France and another Anglo-French war begins.**

At war with Spain since 1739, Britain now extends its war to include France as a part of the European *War of Austrian Succession.*

Note: The conflict would soon cross the ocean to include fighting between New France and Britian's North American colonies, in particular—the colonies of New England. There the war would become known as *King George's War*.

May 3, 1744   **In North America, Louisbourg learns that France and Great Britain are at war.**

Knowing that Britain's colonies are unaware that war has broken out, the French forces at Louisbourg ready a pre-emptive attack against Canso, Nova Scotia.

Note: Louisbourg was desperate for supplies and wished to send troops southward to capture them before Britain's colonists learned that war had broken out.

May 13, 1744   **King George's War begins in North America.**

A French strike force numbering 17 vessels carrying 129 French regulars and 212 militiamen launches a dawn attack against British-held Canso. Totally surprised by the assault, the weakly defended settlement surrenders after the town's protective blockhouse is destroyed by French cannons. Pleased with their success, the French load their booty and 100 English prisoners onto the ships, set fire to the buildings at Canso's harbor, and return to Louisbourg.

Note: Britain's American colonials were now fighting in two different theaters: the War of Jenkins' Ear against Spain in Florida and the West Indies; and King George's War against the French in Canada and New England.

Provisions were in such short supply at Louisbourg that the prisoners would become a burden. After terms were agreed to between Massachusetts Governor Shirly and Louisbourg's Commandant Jean-Baptiste Duquesnel, 340 English prisoners would arrive in Boston on October 18, 1744, in exchange for the French prisoners held there.

May 23, 1744   **Boston learns that Great Britain and France are again at war.**

A merchant ship from Glasgow, Scotland, arrives in Boston carrying the news.

1744   **A Native American military unit is created by Massachusetts to protect Annapolis Royal.**

Nova Scotia's small British population is constantly under threat by the French Acadians and their Mi'kmaq allies, and in response, *Gorham's Rangers* is formed as an auxiliary force for protecting British interests. Excepting Commander John Gorham, all sixty members are Native Americans from the Massachusetts Bay Colony including Wampanoag, *Pequawket*, *Nauset*, and *Mashpee* warriors. Specializing in amphibious assaults using whaleboats, the group's swift and brutal guerrilla-style tactics soon earns them a reputation that will strike fear into their Mi'kmaq and French enemies.

> Note: Gorham's Rangers were notorious scalp hunters, seeking the bounties paid by both Massachusetts and Nova Scotia.
>
> Doubled in size in 1747, Gorham's Rangers would be the main defenders of British Nova Scotia from 1744 to 1749.
>
> The Native fighters would gradually be replaced by Scots and Irish, and in 1760, the unit would be adopted into the British Army and deployed in the continued defense of Nova Scotia.
>
> Gorham's Rangers are often seen as a prototype for the famed Rogers' Rangers, formed eleven years later in New Hampshire.

July 4, 1744   **The *Treaty of Lancaster*: A two-week conference between the Six Nations and officials from Maryland and Virginia is concluded at Lancaster, Pennsylvania.**

Lancaster has been abuzz for nearly a month as hundreds of Iroquois and various colonial officials have come together to settle land disputes. With taverns and inns full of colonials and the Indians camped in and around the town, the two groups intermingle while viewing each other with curiosity. As in the past, the two major contentions are boundary clarifications and the continued intrusions of White settlers onto lands controlled by the Six Nations. This time, the encroachments are in Virginia's Shenandoah Valley, and the Iroquois want restitution.

Gifts of rum, pipes, and tobacco accompanied by warm toasts begin the meeting as wampum belts are exchanged. By the conference's conclusion, the Iroquois agree to sell their remaining interests in the Shenandoah region for 200 pounds of gold.

> Note: Future disputes would arise over the boundary agreed to by the *Lancaster Treaty*. The Iroquois believed the western boundary for White settlement was to now be the Ohio River's watershed, but to the colonists it was the actual Ohio River—a major difference on the map.
>
> Many in those days considered the Allegheny River as continuing southward to the confluence with the Great Kanawha River at modern Point Pleasant, West Virginia. Unlike today, it was there that some (particularly land speculators) believed the Ohio River to begin. This point of contention would make a difference in drawing boundary lines regarding the size of the Iroquois land cession.
>
> Onondaga Chief Canasatego addressed the colonial representatives, suggesting the British colonies form a confederacy modeled on the Iroquois League to secure a stronger defense against the French threats. In demonstration, Canasatego took one arrow and easily broke it—but picking up a bundle of six arrows to represent the Six Nations—the chief failed to break them. Benjamin Franklin was there to hear Canasatego speak, and some historians believe his words helped lead Franklin to secure a future congress of the colonies at Albany in 1754.

1744	**William Trent buys vast acreages in the Ohio Country from the Iroquois Six Nations.**

With his partner, George Croghan, Trent hopes to make large amounts of wealth in the Indian trade and speculation in lands.

> Note: Croghan, a wise trader, urged the opening of trading posts in or near the major Indian towns as opposed to forcing the Indians to travel great distances to trade their furs and other forest goods. Croghan believed this practice would wed the Indians and British traders in profitable union.
>
> To capitalize on their economic ventures, the two men planned to establish and operate a major Indian trade post at the confluence of the Allegheny and Monongahela Rivers at present-day Pittsburgh; and a second post 250 miles further west in the French-claimed Ohio Territory.
>
> Trent's father, William Trent, a rich shipping merchant, had founded Trenton, New Jersey, allowing the younger Trent sufficient wealth to begin his frontier ventures.

Early Sept. 1744 **Annapolis Royal, Nova Scotia, is besieged by French and Indian forces.**

Hoping to dislodge the British from Annapolis Royal, French Commander François Dupont Duvivier arrives at *Fort Anne* accompanied by 200 French troops and hundreds of Mi'kmaq and Maliseet warriors. Declaring that French naval reinforcements are soon to arrive, Duvivier demands the fort's commandeer, Nova Scotia Governor Paul Mascarene, to surrender and avoid destruction. Governor Mascarene, with 220 inside Fort Anne, refuses the ultimatum and the assault begins on September 6. Failing to take the British fort after a month-long siege and with no reinforcements in sight, French Commander Duvivier sails away on October 5.

1745	**The charismatic evangelical English minister George Whitefield returns for his third religious tour of North America.**

> Note: Whitefield championed the legalization of slavery in Georgia, believing it would add to the colony's prosperity and allow funds for the orphanage he had established. Like many ministers of that day, Whitefield used scripture and divine will to justify African enslavement.
>
> Reverend Whitefield would leave behind 4,000 acres of Georgia land and fifty slaves upon his death in 1770.
>
> Reverend George Whitefield was America's first national celebrity.

Jan. 1745 **In Boston, plans are prepared to attack Louisbourg.**

Acting independently without authorization from London, the New Englanders decide to raise an army to capture the massive French citadel.

> Note: Located at the mouth of the St. Lawrence River, Louisbourg served as the eastern guardian of New France and as a base for French military operations in North America. Long seen as a thorn to be removed, the New Englanders had decided to do the job themselves.
>
> Though supportive, New York, Pennsylvania, and New Jersey would decline to contribute troops, whereas the New England colonies having more at stake due to their proximity to New France would provide more than 4,000 men.

Britain's naval forces refuse to join the Louisbourg campaign without official orders.

Having decided to go it alone, the New Englanders prepare vessels for the journey north, while the militia army organizes and drills in preparation.

> Note: A British squadron in the West Indies under the command of Vice Admiral Peter Warren had refused to assist the New Englanders in their campaign. Many of Warren's officers held low opinions of the American colonials based on their past experiences fighting together in the 1741 Cartagena campaign.
>
> Benjamin Franklin would write to his brother John Franklin, a participant in the Louisbourg expedition, warning against overconfidence: "Fortified towns are tough nuts to crack."

Mar. 16–22, '45 **New England troops, finally readied, depart Boston aboard ninety ships.**

Numbering 4,200 men, the flotilla staggers its departure for Canso, Nova Scotia, which is to be used as a gathering and launch site for the attack on Louisbourg.

> Note: The fleet would suffer severe storms along the way, sickening most of the New England troops.

April 22, 1745 **In a turn of events, British warships arrive at Canso to assist the New Englanders.**

Arriving from the West Indies, Vice Admiral Peter Warren has been ordered to support the New England assault on Louisbourg with his naval guns. Now, the first of Warren's ships, the HBS *Eltham*, arrives at Canso, soon to be followed by Commodore Warren himself aboard the sixty-gun HBS *Superb*.

> Note: The Royal fleet had been occupied in the West Indies, fighting against Spain in the War of Jenkins' Ear, which had wound down.
>
> If successful, Vice Admiral Warren would be personally entitled to receive one eighth of the French spoils taken by his British squadron, with the remainder to be divided among his ships.

May 11, 1745 **The assault against Louisbourg begins.**

Most of the fighting is borne by the New Englanders, with the British fleet providing little support other than blockading the sea against French reinforcement.

June 16, 1745 **After sustaining a six-week siege, Louisbourg surrenders.**

The 4,000-strong New England army captures the French citadel, once considered impregnable.

> Note: As part of the surrender agreement, the French troops and citizens of Louisbourg were to be safely transported to France.
>
> In an act of duplicity, the French flag continued to be flown over the captured fortress in the hopes of fooling any French reinforcements that might arrive.

At Louisbourg, resentment builds between the British Navy and New England forces.

Naval commander Vice Admiral Peter Warren has taken control of the fort's capitulation and allows the French liberal surrender terms—much to the New Englanders' displeasure. Many of the colonials resent Warren's authority, for British naval forces had not fired a single shot in support.

> Note: In addition, the New England men had volunteered in the expectation of receiving a share of the plunder, but would be denied, causing legal issues over the allotment of

the *spoils of war*. To the angry militiamen—it was British Navy that deserved nothing.

July 3, 1745   **The news of Louisbourg's capitulation reaches Boston and the town celebrates.**

Nearly all in New England wish for the French to be completely expelled from North America and consider the capitulation of Louisbourg to be the beginning of France's ouster.

1745   **The *Jacobite Rising of '45*: The last Scottish revolt against Britain's Hanoverian monarchy.**

Many in Scotland continue to believe James Francis Edward Stuart to be Britain's true sovereign, James III. Highland clans have promised an uprising against the German-born George II if James Stuart's son, Charles Edward Stuart, will come to Scotland and lead them.

> Note: Known as the *Bonnie Prince*, Charles was the twenty-three-year-old Catholic grandson of England's former king, James II. Born in Rome and raised in luxury, Charles Stuart hoped to secure the British throne for his father by armed revolt and had secured the pope's blessing to do so.
>
> Many of Britain's troops were fighting in mainland Europe in the War of Austrian Succession; hence, the Jacobites believed it was time to strike.

July 22, 1745   **Prince Charles Edward Stuart lands in Scotland to begin a military campaign against King George II.**

Aug.–Sept. 1745   **Bonnie Prince Charlie leads 2,000 Scottish Jacobites south toward England.**

Initially enjoying military success, Charles Stuart expects 7,000 French reinforcements that never arrive.

Great Britain attempts to blockade New France, hoping to disrupt the French–Indian trade.

The British wish to enter the rich Indian trade of the Ohio Country and other western areas now dominated by the French. By interrupting the flow of goods destined for French traders in Montreal and Quebec, it is believed that the tribes will turn to the English traders to supply their needs.

1745   **The first trade post in the Ohio region is built by Pennsylvania traders.**

Fort Sandusky is built on Sandusky Bay near the western end of Lake Erie by permission of Wyandot chief, *Nicolas Orontony*. The small fort will last but a few years.

Sept. 19, 1745   **New Jersey's *Horse Neck Riots* break out.**

Land disputes arise between the settlers and proprietors of Horseneck, New Jersey, over legal title of certain lands. The settlers claim ownership by earlier private treaties made directly with the Indians, yet because title to Indian lands could be granted to private citizens only by royal authority, the proprietors view their claims as illegitimate, and the settlers begin to be evicted.

A settler, Samuel Baldwin, is arrested and placed into the Newark prison, but Baldwin's supporters defy authorities by marching to the jail and releasing him. Troubles, arrests, and jailbreaks will continue for several years, leaving most settlers with disputed titles to either buy their land from the legally recognized proprietors, or be evicted.

> Note: These events would lead to anti-British sentiments among many in New Jersey.

Sept. 1745   **"God Save the King" begins its musical journey to becoming Britain's national anthem.**

With Bonnie Prince Charlie enjoying initial military success in Scotland, the rule of King George II is under real threat. As such, the Theatre Royal band performs Henry Carey's "God Save the King" after a play to the audience's delight. The band continues the performances nightly, and the song soon spreads to other venues; eventually rising to become Great Britain's national anthem.

Nov. 20, 1745   **In Boston, civil authorities sentence two British sailors to hang for murder.**

A naval press-gang sent ashore by Captain Arthur Forrest of the HBS *Wager* severely wounds two men resisting impressment. Both men, heroes of the recent Louisbourg campaign, die of their wounds within a week. As a result, the two sailors are arrested, tried, found guilty, and sentenced to hang, but are eventually released due to a legal technicality.

> Note: This event would further galvanize Boston public opinion against impressment and stoke additional resentment against the British Navy.

Early Dec. 1745   **Britain's King George II readies to flee to Hanover if necessary.**

Leading the approaching Jacobite army, Prince Charles Stuart is only 120 miles from London and the city panics. But, heeding his advisors' counsel, the Bonnie Prince turns his forces around and returns to Scotland.

> Note: This would represent the high-water mark for the Jacobites.
>
> In February, 5,100 German troops (Hessians) would arrive in England, hired by King George II to help defeat the Scots.

Jan. 18, 1746   **In New Jersey, Princeton University is established by *New Light* Presbyterians to train ministers.**

> Note: In 1783, the Second Continental Congress would meet at Princeton for four months.

April 2, 1746   **At Louisbourg, British naval forces and New England troops arrive to relieve those guarding the captured French fortress.**

Concerned that France will eventually attempt to repossess Louisbourg, the New Englanders have been guarding the fort since its surrender nine months earlier.

April 16, 1746   **In Scotland, the *Jacobite Rising of '45* is crushed at the *Battle of Culloden*.**

Bonnie Prince Charlie and his Jacobite army are defeated by forces led by King George II's twenty-five-year-old son, William Augustus, Duke of Cumberland. The 5,000-strong Scottish army suffers terrible losses due to English cannon fire near Inverness, Scotland, and the Jacobite rebellion collapses.

> Note: The Battle of Culloden would be the last major pitched battle to take place in Great Britain.
>
> The *Cumberland Gap* leading through the Appalachian Mountains to Kentucky would be named for George II's son, William, the Duke of Cumberland.

Bonnie Prince Charlie goes into hiding and his ordeal becomes the stuff of legend.

The prince, now a fugitive sought by British authorities, moves around Scotland under a series of guises in hopes of escaping to France.

> Note: According to legend, *Drambuie*, a popular liqueur made commercially today in Scotland, was the personal recipe of Bonnie Prince Charlie. The prince is purported to have given it to Captain John McKinnon in gratitude for providing him sanctuary during the 1745 Jacobite uprising. Whether true or not, the distillery continues to tout the legend boasting that *Drambuie* is "A Link to the 45." Included on every bottle is the slogan, "The Spirit Lives On."

England attempts to crush the troublesome Highland clans of Scotland once and for all.

After warring against the Scottish Jacobites, England wishes to permanently end the Highlanders' power and fierce sense of independence. Therefore, severe retaliations are enacted against the Scots, nearly resulting in the loss of Highland culture.

Examples include:

- Many Scots are imprisoned and executed.
- Many suffer the loss of their lands.
- The Scottish clans are outlawed.
- Weapons are forbidden.
- Bagpipes and tartans are no longer allowed.

> Note: The laws against Highland dress and tartans would not be rescinded until 1782.
>
> Large numbers of Scots would migrate to North America to begin life anew, but before emigrating they were required to swear an oath of loyalty to King George II. Hence, many Scots would refuse to support the future American War for Independence, choosing instead to fight for the king.

June 1746

With Louisbourg under British control, New England receives news that Great Britain has decided to conquer New France.

The two-pronged plan is as follows:

1. British Vice Admiral Peter Warren, currently at Louisbourg, is to lead a naval force up the St. Lawrence River and attack Quebec.

2. William Gooch of Virginia is to lead a militia army from Albany, New York, to attack France's Fort Saint-Frédéric at Crown Point, and then continue north to attack Montreal.

> Note: With so many Massachusetts militiamen readying for departure and others away guarding Louisbourg, the colony would grow increasingly alarmed that Boston was vulnerable to attack by French naval forces.

June 20, 1746

A French fleet sails to recapture Louisbourg and attack the New England coast— particularly Boston—but the mission becomes a fiasco.

Sailing from France, the fleet experiences the utmost difficulties during the voyage, including: a hurricane; the death of the admiral; the suicide of the second-in-command (he literally *fell on his sword*); a lack of reinforcement supplies; sickness; and additional mishaps. As a result, the French fleet eventually aborts the campaign and arrives home in December without having met any objectives.

June 1746   **Great Britain renews the ban on naval impressments in its West Indies colonies unless first approved by the royal governor.**

An Act for the Better Encouragement of the Trade with his Majesty's Sugar Colonies in America comes into effect. With press-gangs operating in the West Indies, many trade vessels are hesitant to sail there, for the seamen do not want to chance impressment and the owners do not wish to lose their crews. These fears help create island food shortages as everything in the West Indies depends on the free flow of trade goods; yet the paramount issue remains—impressments are affecting the profits of the lucrative British sugar and molasses industry.

Note: The impressment ban applied only to the British West Indies, causing resentments in Great Britain's North American mainland colonies.

Mid-Aug. 1746   **A New England army sets forth to capture Montreal.**

New England militia forces have continued to gather at Boston and now, numbering more than 5,000 troops, begin their march northward in the assumption that the British Navy will be supporting them by simultaneously sailing to attack Quebec.

Aug. 23, 1746   **Great Britain halts its offensive against New France.**

The British call off the mission to capture French Canada, believing that the campaign could perhaps be better launched the following year.

Sept. 29, 1746   **Charles Edward Stuart arrives safely in France, never to return to Scotland.**

Sought by agents of King George II, Prince Charles has been a fugitive since his defeat.

Note: In the future, Charles Stuart would convert to Protestantism, believing it would enhance his chance of becoming a future king of England. Making little difference, the exiled prince would revert to Catholicism.

         For the rest of his life, Charles Edward Stuart would live in European exile. History would dub Prince Charles, the *Young Pretender*; and his father, James Francis Edward Stuart, the *Old Pretender.*

Oct. 1746   **Learning that the Canada campaign has ended, the New England army returns home.**

En route to Montreal, the army receives word that Britain has called off the military campaign to capture New France. Now, without the expected British naval attack against Quebec, the New Englanders are ordered to return to Albany; they receive this news with utmost disappointment.

Note: As a reward for their participation—if victorious—the militiamen had expected to receive a portion of the enemy's spoils. These New Englanders would return home sourly empty-handed.

1747   **A cure is found for scurvy—the scourge of seafarers and navies.**

Scottish naval surgeon James Lind discovers by experiment that citrus prevents sailors from getting scurvy.

As King George's War continues, the New York Colony passes the *Scalp Act* of 1747.

Feb. 5, 1747   **Massachusetts offers rewards to allied Indians for the scalps of the warring tribes.**

"To Indian allies: £35 for scalps of male over 12, £10 for scalps of males under 12 or females any age; £40 male prisoner over 12, £25 for male prisoners under 12 or female prisoners. English who accompany the Indian parties entitled to share in the bounty."

April 9, 1747   **The last execution by beheading in Great Britain takes place.**

For participating in the Battle of Culloden Moor, Scottish Highlander and clan leader Simon Fraser, aka Lord Lovat, has been found guilty of treason against the Crown and is executed on the chopping block at Tower Hill, becoming the last person to be executed in such a manner in Britain.

Note: A great crowd would gather for Lovat's execution, but tragedy struck when the seating scaffolding collapsed due to the weight of those vying for a view, killing nine spectators and injuring many others. Lovat laughed hilariously at the grisly spectacle before placing his head on the block, allowing the crowd the last laugh.

Lord Lovat's execution would be credited with the phrase, "To laugh one's head off."

Lovat had been condemned to be hanged, drawn and quartered, but King George II, showing mercy, permitted Lord Lovat to be simply beheaded.

Nov. 16, 1747   **British press-gangs seize forty-six men in Boston.**

A British naval squadron under the command of Admiral Charles Knowles is anchored off the Massachusetts shore for repairs and restocking before moving on to fight in the West Indies. In need of men to fill his crews, Admiral Knowles sends press-gangs ashore to secure them.

Nov. 17, 1747   **Boston erupts into three days of rioting over impressments, to be known as the *Knowles Riot*.**

Boston's *lower orders* respond to the previous night's impressment with three days of rioting. An initial crowd of 300 swells to several thousand as they march through the streets seizing British sailors as hostages while demanding the return of the impressed men. The rioters break the windows of Boston's townhouses, threaten Governor Shirley, and then carry a barge from the wharf to Shirley's front yard and proceed to burn it. Though the local militia refuse to appear, the royal governor manages to escape to Fort Castle William while the British naval officers retreat to the safety of their harbored ships.

Boston authorities issue arrest warrants for the rioters' ringleaders, but without the militia they have no enforcement powers, and the unrest continues. British Admiral Charles Knowles refuses to release his captives and instead has his cannons readied, threatening the town with bombardment to quell the rioting.

The crisis finally ends after Governor Shirley persuades Knowles to release the men. Soon afterward, Admiral Knowles, with loathing toward the Bostonians, sails away in anger.

The Knowles Riot would be the largest civil unrest in Boston until the *Stamp Act Riots* of 1765.

1747–1750   **The *Choctaw Civil War* is waged in the western Mississippi region.**

The Choctaw Nation, long a friend and trading partner of the French, descends into bloody civil war when the Western Choctaw wish to begin trade with the British, but the tribe's Eastern division wishes to continue its French alliance. Hundreds of Choctaw will die in the intertribal warfare, encouraged by the Europeans, who provide them the firearms to do so.

Jan. 4, 1748   **In Boston, Sam Adams and others begin publishing the *Independent Advertiser*, stirring dissent and dissatisfaction toward Great Britain.**

Several of the paper's articles and opinion pieces are reprinted in other colonies, including in Benjamin Franklin's influential *Pennsylvania Gazette*.

| | Note: | Twenty-four-year-old Sam Adams, a tough Puritan and a firebrand for independence, had entered Boston politics two years earlier following the failure of his malt business. The energetic Adams would quickly become one of the most influential American colonials working to steer a course toward independence. |

1748   **Rice is the No. 1 commodity in South Carolina, followed by the hide trade and indigo production.**

Rice profits are quickly propelling the South Carolina planters into a powerful class of wealthy and societal elites; yet conversely, the continued need for laborers to produce the rice only increases the number of Africans imported as slaves.

The *Ohio Company of Virginia* is formed by a group of influential Virginia gentlemen.

The Ohio Company's purpose is to make riches by acquiring and selling frontier lands, but Indian ownership and occupation, as well as French claims to the region, are obstacles to the company's designs.

| | Note: | To establish Virginia's claim to the region, the Ohio Company had already begun the work of widening an existing Indian path—the *Nemacolin Trail*—connecting Maryland's *Fort Cumberland* to the *Forks of the Ohio River.* |
| | | The *Ohio River Forks*, aka the *Ohio Forks* or simply the *Forks*, represented the confluence of the Allegheny and Monongahela Rivers at modern Pittsburgh. It is here that the Ohio River begins its western journey into the North American heartland. |

July 12, 1748   **Virginia sets aside 800,000 acres for the proposed *Loyal Company of Virginia*.**

The land company is expected to be readied and organized to compete with the Ohio Company by the end of the year.

1748   **Ignoring French prohibitions, British traders continue to make inroads into the western frontier regions.**

Pennsylvania Irishman George Croghan, a fur trader and frontier land speculator, boldly establishes the trading post of *Pickawillany* deep in the Ohio territory hoping to divert the region's profitable Indian trade from the French. Croghan's actions, combined with the formation of the Virginia land companies, infuriate the French and force them to respond to the trespasses.

Note:	Pickawillany—representing the western-most British trade intrusion into the French-claimed lands—was located near today's Piqua, Ohio.

Oct. 18, 1748 — **The *Treaty of Aix-la-Chapelle* ends Europe's War of Austrian Succession—known as King George's War in Britain's North American colonies.**

The treaty returns most of the territories conquered during the war to the antebellum status quo.

Included among the treaty's terms:

- Britain returns the fortress of Louisbourg to France.

- France returns Fort St. George in Chennai, India, to Britain.

- France returns the conquered provinces of the Spanish Netherlands to Spain.

- France agrees to no longer provide political sanctuary to Charles Edward Stuart.

Note:	This final point would force the Young Pretender and his family to relocate to Rome—the place of his birth and childhood. Upon his death in 1788, Charles Edward Stuart, grandson of the ousted King James II, would be interred in the Vatican's St. Peter's Basilica.

Dec. 1748 — **New Englanders are furious to learn of the return of Louisbourg to France.**

The armies of New England had conquered the mighty fortress three years earlier and now, returned to French control, Louisbourg once again poses a threat. As such, the New Englanders believe that Britain is concerned only with its own needs with little regard for theirs.

Note:	Many continued to believe the long-held rumor that Britain planned to trade the irksome New England colonies to the papist French at some future date.
	The New England colonies would request British reimbursement for the expenses incurred in the campaigns against New France, stating that the loss of funds had hurt their economies.
	New England would continue to slowly drift from the mother country as the "descendants of the *Mayflower*" began to view themselves less as English and more as Americans.

1749 — **France's territorial claims in North America are vast and extensive.**

The French claim lands from the Appalachian Mountains to the Rockies, and from the Gulf of Mexico to the North Pole; except for the British-claimed area around Hudson Bay known as Rupert's Land.

Great Britain establishes a North American naval base in Nova Scotia.

With the British-French rivalry for control of North America intensifying, Halifax is founded as a British military and naval base to counterbalance the fortress of Louisbourg, once again under command of the French.

Note:	Up to this time, Boston had been the main naval rendezvous for Britain to launch military operations in the northern regions of North America.

Halifax would play a significant role in the future American War for Independence.

March 27, 1749 **The British Crown grants the Ohio Company 200,000 acres of western lands, beginning near the Ohio Forks.**

The Ohio Company is promised an additional 300,000 acres without tax or rent for ten years if the company:

- Successfully settles 100 or more families in the region within seven years.

- Constructs a fort and mans it at the company's own expense.

The company's first step to begin selling these newly acquired lands is to have them surveyed. At age seventeen, George Washington is appointed an official surveyor with the company and begins a career that will feed his life-long appetite for accumulating wealth through the acquisition of vast tracts of western frontier lands.

Note: The teenaged Washington's two older half-brothers, Lawrence and Augustine, were investors in the Ohio Company, thus giving him the necessary connections to be employed.

The Indians would soon learn to recognize and hate the survey cuts marked onto remote frontier trees by the surveyors, as the Whites continued to make inroads into Indian lands.

Though the Appalachian Mountains represented a physical barrier, the bigger impediments to the land companies were the French to the north and west; the Spanish to the south; and hostile Indians seemingly in all directions. To the Ohio Company and others—all three represented thorns to be removed if potential fortunes were to be realized.

Summer 1749 **A French expeditionary force travels to the Ohio Region, solidifying tribal alliances and warning the British traders to stay out of the French-claimed territories.**

Traveling from Canada with 250 soldiers and Indian allies, French military leader Céleron de Blainville canoes southward on the Ohio River to cement faltering relationships with the tribes; to promote trade with the French; and to warn the British traders to leave the region. At the junctures of six of the Ohio River's major tributaries, De Blainville nails tin plates onto large trees stating that the Ohio Country is France's domain, and that the British are to stay out. In addition, the expedition buries into the sands inscribed lead plates stating the same.

Continuing onward, the French expedition stops at the *Miami* town of Pickawillany and demands the Indians cease their trade with the British.

Note: The Miami haughtily ignored the French threats.

The practice of burying plates to show land ownership was a common European practice that began in the Middle Ages.

Aug. 1749 **The Iroquois Six Nations grant 200,000 acres of land in western Pennsylvania to the frontier trader George Croghan.**

Croghan seals the deal by supplying the Iroquois with a large number of trade goods out of his private fortune—two and a half tons of merchandise carried by twenty-five pack horses.

Hoping to receive confirmation from Britain's Board of Trade, Croghan writes that the Iroquois have granted him the lands due to his "constant attention to the preservation of peace and as a testimony of the sincerity with which they desired its continuance…"

> Note: This purchase made Croghan the second-largest owner of lands in Pennsylvania, exceeded only by Pennsylvania's proprietors—the Penn Family.
>
> By the mid 1700s, it would be estimated that Pennsylvania had 300 traders working with the Indians of the Ohio Country—one third of them under the direction of George Croghan.

The Pennsylvania Colony acquires additional Delaware tribal lands in eastern Pennsylvania.

Sold by the Iroquois who claimed sovereignty over the Lenape lands, the purchase includes the lands west of the Delaware River and north of the Blue Mountains, and southward to the north bank of the Susquehanna River. In return, Pennsylvania agrees to evict all the Whites living illegally west of the Susquehanna.

Dec. 12, 1749   **The *Loyal Company of Virginia* is formed by a group of Virginia gentlemen.**

The Loyal Company has received an 800,000-acre land grant from Virginia and is required to have it surveyed within four years. The extensive grant includes the Kentucky region, and the company hires Thomas Walker to explore it. While scouting the company's newly acquired lands, Walker discovers the Cumberland Gap leading westward through the mountains.

> Note: The Loyal Company would focus its financial interests in the lands of western Virginia and Kentucky, whereas its rival—the Ohio Company—would become heavily invested in the lands of western Pennsylvania and the region north of the Ohio River.
>
> Thomas Jefferson was an investor in the Loyal Company, among many other wealthy Virginians.
>
> The Loyal Company of Virginia would continue to operate until the American War for Independence.

1750s   **The North American colonial population is approximately 1.2 million.**

German immigration continues in large numbers, particularly to Pennsylvania.

German immigration to Pennsylvania peaks in the 1750s causing many of the English residents, including Benjamin Franklin, to feel overwhelmed by their increasing numbers. Many complain that the Germans are slow to integrate for they form their own communities, continue to speak their own language, and even print their own newspapers.

> Note: The Germans were required to be Protestant and to take oaths of loyalty to the British king in order to emigrate to North America.
>
> Today's Amish and Mennonites of Pennsylvania are descendants of these early German immigrants.

Philadelphia is the No. 1 shipbuilding center in Britain's North American colonies.

French Acadians continue to be a bone of contention between France and Britain.

Each nation claims rights to Nova Scotia, and both have citizens residing there in an uneasy peace punctuated by periodic attacks, each against the other.

> Note: Most of the Acadians had refused to take oaths of loyalty to King George II and the British wanted them ousted and supplanted by Protestant Scots.

June 24, 1750   **Great Britain's *Iron Act* of 1750 goes into effect.**

Britain's domestic iron and steel industry is thriving and needs raw pig iron produced in the North American colonies to help feed it. At the same time, the British steel industry does not wish to compete with the colonies in the production of finished iron products. As such, the Iron Act is designed to benefit both groups by the following:

- The Americans are encouraged to manufacture pig iron for Britain and may ship the iron duty-free.

- Colonial forges for manufacturing *steel* already in existence are permitted to continue, but the construction of new forges for such production is prohibited.

Note:	The royal governors would be required to supply the British Ministry with a *state of affairs*, reporting what American forges already existed.

- The export of pig iron to foreign ports is prohibited.

Note:	Molten iron was poured into small oblong molds roughly resembling pigs in shape to harden into blocks. This crude form of iron, easily bent and shaped, was then used to manufacture wrought iron for such products as chains, nails, musket barrels, railings, lamp posts, and so on. In addition, the iron was used in the manufacture of cast iron and steel.
	The production of pig iron required iron ore and wood for burning—North America had both in abundance.

- The colonial production of finished iron products is prohibited.

The Iron Act benefits the American colonials, as they can ship their pig iron—mostly manufactured in Pennsylvania, New Jersey, Delaware, and New York—to a ready British market without paying a duty.

The Iron Act's benefits to Great Britain include:

- The iron and steel industry receives a cheap source of raw pig iron.

- Manufacturers of finished cast iron and steel products have a protected market to which they can export their products without competition.

The major American resentments over the Act include:

- The manufacturers believe Britain is attempting to tamp down the emerging colonial production of iron and steel.

- The manufacturers are banned from producing finished products, which they are instead forced to buy from Britain.

1750   ***An Act for Extending and Improving the Trade to Africa* opens Great Britain's slave trade to private individuals.**

"Whereas the Trade to and from Africa is very advantageous to Great Britain, and necessary for supplying the Plantations and Colonies thereunto belonging with a sufficient Number of Negroes at reasonable Rates; and for that Purpose the said Trade ought to be free and open to all his Majesty's Subjects: Therefore it be enacted, and it is hereby enacted by the King's most Excellent Majesty, by and with the Advice and Consent of the Lords Spiritual and Temporal, and Commons, in this present Parliament assembled, and by the Authority of the same, That it shall and may be lawful for all his Majesty's Subjects to trade and traffick to and from any Port or Place in Africa, between the Port of Sallee in South Barbary, and the Cape of Good Hope, when, and at such Times, and in such Manner, and in or with such Quantity of Goods, Wares or Mechandizes, as he or they shall think fit, without any Restraint whatsoever."

Enslaved Africans compose 40 percent of the population of Virginia and Maryland.

The Ohio Company employs Christopher Gist to explore its newly acquired lands north of the Ohio River.

A frontiersman and surveyor, Gist is to note the region's particulars and to foster friendly relations with the tribes he should encounter. During his exploration, Gist stops at George Croghan's trade post at the Miami town of Pickawillany and encourages the Indians to trade only with the British and not to ally themselves with the French. Chief *Memeskia,* appropriately nicknamed *Old Britain,* promises he shall keep the French away.

> Note: Christopher Gist would make three explorations of the region for the Ohio Company: 1750–1751; 1751–1752; and 1753–1754.

Jan. 1, 1751   **Georgia legalizes slavery, making the practice unanimous among the North American colonies of the future United States.**

The Georgia planters have demanded slavery be permitted, believing it necessary if they are to compete with the other colonies. Georgia hopes to make profits through rice cultivation and anticipates a large influx of new planters and African slaves; hence, few objections are made.

> Note: Though Rhode Island had supposedly banned African slavery in 1652, the law continued to be ignored.

Sugar cane is introduced to Louisiana by the French.

Though extremely profitable, the backbreaking work required in the production of sugar fuels an increase in African slaves imported to the Louisiana region.

March 31, 1751   **Prince Friedrich Ludwig—heir to the British throne—dies by accident.**

According to the tale, Friedrich (or Frederick), Prince of Wales, the eldest son of King George II, dies after being struck by an errant cricket ball. The death of Prince Frederick places his twelve-year-old son, George William Frederick, in line to inherit the throne as King George III.

> Note: Though history attributes Frederick's death to a cricket accident, many historians believe it was due to a pulmonary embolism.
>
> Prince Frederick, Maryland, was named in his honor.

May 9, 1751   **Benjamin Franklin publishes an article in the *Pennsylvania Gazette* protesting the British practice of sending convicts to the colonies.**

Franklin suggests that perhaps American rattlesnakes be sent to London in exchange and be distributed in St. James's Park and certain other gardens as "Rattle Snakes seem the most suitable Returns for the Human Serpents sent to us by our Mother Country."

May 11, 1751   **The first hospital in North America is built in Philadelphia: The *Pennsylvania Hospital.***

Sept. 29, 1751   **The *Currency Act* of 1751 prohibits the New England colonies from issuing bills of credit.**

> Note: British merchants were frustrated with the practice of the New England colonial assemblies authorizing the creation and issuance of great quantities of paper bills used as tender for payment of debts, dues, and demands. Combined with rising monetary inflation, the practice had caused the merchants to complain of not receiving *just payment* for debts, being paid instead with depreciated colonial paper money (bills of credit). In New England's defense, hard currency was extremely scarce for most available specie (coin money) had already crossed the ocean to pay debts owed to English merchants.

The following are among the Currency Act's restrictions on the New England colonies:

- The making or passing of bills of credit is prohibited.

- Bills of credit already in circulation are to be called in and discharged.

- Colonial bills of credit are to be allowed, if necessary, to pay for extraordinary emergencies of government in case of war and invasion but are to be called in and discharged in a short and reasonable time not to exceed five years.

- Any bills of credit issued to fund colonial government service are to be matched by an equal sum of tax revenue and be retired within two years.

- The further use of bills of credit for private debt is forbidden, but the bills may be used to pay *colonial* public debt.

> Note: This would prevent the New Englanders from forcing British merchants to accept the colonial paper as payment.
>
> The 1751 Currency Act would create a money shortage in Massachusetts, New Hampshire, Connecticut, and Rhode Island.

Oct. 29, 1751   **The *Greenbrier Company* is formed—another Virginia land company.**

The Greenbrier Company is granted and authorized to sell 100,000 acres along the Greenbrier River in western Virginia. Like the Ohio Company and the Loyal Company, the company's goal is to promote land sales and encourage migration into the western frontier regions.

> Note: The Greenbrier proprietors were offered 1,000 acres of land for every family that settled in the region.
>
> Though the company would begin surveying the territory, its efforts would be halted by the coming Seven Years' War, aka the French and Indian War.

Nov. 1, 1751   **A large bell is ordered from London for the nearly completed Pennsylvania State House.**

The Pennsylvania Assembly orders a bell to be cast and inscribed with part of the biblical verse, Leviticus 25:10, "Proclaim LIBERTY throughout all the Land unto all the Inhabitants thereof."

> Note: The bell would become the famous *Liberty Bell* of the future United States.
>
> The name Liberty Bell would be first used during the 1830s by abolitionists, who used the bell as a powerful symbol as they strove to emancipate America's slaves.

Nov. 2, 1751   **Nineteen-year-old George Washington sails to Barbados with one of his older brothers.**

The trip to the tropics has been recommended for Washington's half-brother Lawrence, who is suffering with tuberculosis. As Lawrence's wife has a wealthy uncle living there, the Washington brothers travel to Barbados to spend the winter.

	Note:	Anne Fairfax's uncle, Gedney Clarke—as an investor in North American frontier lands—could offer the Washington brothers sound advice, and perhaps funding for the newly formed Ohio Company of Virginia.
		Washington would spend part of his first weeks touring the island's defenses and discovered Barbados to be heavily fortified. It was in Barbados that Washington was introduced to the British military and its officers, influencing the young man's future aspirations to seek a commission in the regular British Army.
		While in Barbados, Washington would contract smallpox from his host's wife but successfully suffered through the dreaded disease. This would give Washington a lifetime immunity but left his face with permanent pox scars.
		George Washington would return to Virginia, but Lawrence instead sailed to Bermuda, hoping to find medical relief. Following a short stay, Lawrence Washington would return to his Mount Vernon estate and died on July 26, 1752.
		The trip to Barbados would be George Washington's only trip outside of the bounds of the future United States.

1752   **Great Britain adopts the *Gregorian calendar* after resisting for many years.**

	Note:	The Gregorian calendar had been introduced by the Catholic Church in 1582 as a correction to the older *Julian calendar.* Named after the pope who introduced it, Pope Gregory, the Gregorian calendar contained the world's first leap years in order to synchronize the calendar with the natural year.
		Due to its introduction by the Catholic Church, the Protestant countries of Europe, including England, had refused to use it.

Georgia applies to become a royal colony.

The colony's twenty-one-year charter is expiring, and Georgia's trustees request the British government assume responsibility for the colony. Though the king and Parliament approve the request, it will be two years before it becomes official in 1754.

As a royal colony:

- The people will be given the right to elect an assembly.

- The British Board of Trade shall recommend a governor for the colony, subject to the king's approval.

- Freemen in Georgia (except Catholics) are to be granted the right to vote.

- The Church of England (the Anglican Church) is to be the official Church of Georgia.

	Note:	Georgia's governing trustees, numbering twenty-one in 1732, had now grown to more than fifty, and nearly all lived in England.
		Georgia, unlike the other colonies of British North America, had received Parliamentary funds for its original founding and operations.

May 28, 1752   **The *Treaty of Logstown*: The Iroquois Six Nations cede additional lands.**

The Iroquois, Shawnee, and Delaware meet at Logstown—an Indian town on the banks of the Ohio River in western Pennsylvania—to settle land issues with representatives of Virginia and the Ohio Land Company.

The Virginians assert that the Lancaster Treaty of 1744 had granted rights for White settlement westward to the Ohio River, whereas the Iroquois counterclaim that the treaty had only granted the lands extending to the river's eastern watershed—a very big difference.

By the end of the conference, the Iroquois begrudgingly recognize Virginia's claims to lands reaching west to the Ohio River.

> Note: As a result, the Iroquois would feel cheated as the eager Virginia speculators pushed to begin the sales and development of their newly acquired frontier lands.

June 1752   **Benjamin Franklin flies a kite during a thunderstorm to conduct electrical experiments and suggests that lightning and electricity are one and the same.**

Assisting Franklin in the experiment is his twenty-two-year-old son, William.

June 21, 1752   **Pickawillany—an important Indian town and British trade center in the western Ohio territory—is destroyed.**

The Miami town is attacked and set aflame by 30 French soldiers and 230 Ottawa warriors as France continues efforts to keep the British traders out of the western frontier regions.

> Note: Three years earlier, Miami Chief Memeskia—nicknamed Old Britain—had insultingly rebuffed French and Ottawa overtures by threatening to personally eat their hearts should they ever return to Pickawillany. Now, killed by one of the Ottawa he had threatened, Memeskia's heart was quickly eaten as the rest of the chief was placed into a boiling pot.

Sept. 1, 1752   **The Pennsylvania State House bell arrives in Philadelphia but soon cracks.**

The bell will be repaired locally by recasting and installed the following year.

> Note: This original crack is not the bell's renowned crack of today. The Liberty Bell's more famous crack would occur in 1843, when rung to commemorate George Washington's birthday.

May 15, 1753   **The French begin building *Fort Presque Isle* in western Pennsylvania.**

From British traders trespassing into French-claimed lands the French learned that the Ohio Company soon plans to build a fort at the Forks of the Ohio River. The news begins a French race to beat them to it—beginning with the construction of Fort Presque Isle. Fort Presque Isle, located on Lake Erie's southern shore at present-day Erie, Pennsylvania, is to be the northern post of a four-fort link anchored at the south by a major fortification to be constructed at the Ohio Forks, *Fort Duquesne*.

> Note: For at least sixty years, France had been winning influence and making gains with the Western Tribes. French Jesuits were running missions and conducting religious work among the Indians; trade posts were being established; and new French forts continued to form a western barrier to the ever-increasing British intrusions into the French-claimed lands—lands also claimed by Great Britain and its colonies of Pennsylvania and Virginia.
>
> These new French fortifications would represent a major threat to the British traders and influential speculators in frontier lands. The Ohio Company and others expected to reap large profits by the sales of western lands—but the French were in the way.

Pennsylvania's State House is completed after twenty-one years of construction.

The Pennsylvania State House—later dubbed *Independence Hall* by the American public—is finally finished as the building's repaired bell is hung in place.

> Note: The United States Declaration of Independence would be approved in this building in 1776, and it would host the Constitutional Convention of 1787.

June 1753   **Mohawk Chief *Hendrick Theyanoguin*, aka *King Hendrick*, declares that the Covenant Chain joining the Iroquois and the English in friendship is now broken due to grievances.**

This news alarms London's Board of Trade, for Britain and France are locked into fierce competition for the Indian trade. In addition, the British do not wish to lose the Iroquois as allies, and the *broken chain* metaphor represents a major setback in relations with the powerful league.

In response, a large conference is scheduled at Albany for the following summer to cement the faltering Indian alliance. Each of the colonies holding treaties with the Iroquois is asked to attend in order to coordinate all the various agreements into one great treaty.

> Note: Despite his threats, King Hendrick would remain a loyal friend to the English and died fighting alongside them at the Battle of Lake George in 1755.

June 7, 1753   **The *Jewish Naturalization Act* of 1753: Great Britain permits Jews an avenue to citizenship.**

Designed primarily to enable wealthy and enterprising foreign-born Jews to settle in England, Parliament passes the Jewish Naturalization Act, allowing citizenship if:

- An application is made to and approved by Parliament.

- The applicant has lived in England for seven years.

- The applicant takes the required oath (minus participation in the Sacrament).

> Note: Parliament believed that the wealthy Jewish foreigners would contribute to Britain's prosperity and wished to encourage their settlement there.
>
> Though the Act represented a *crack in the door*, few of England's 8,000 natural-born Jews could take advantage of it due to the cost and influence required.
>
> The law would be repealed the following year due to public opposition.
>
> In the British Empire, practicing Jews, like Catholics, would not receive political emancipation until the first half of the nineteenth century.

July 11, 1753   **The French begin construction of a second fort in northwest Pennsylvania, *Fort Le Boeuf*.**

Located fifteen miles south of Fort Presque Isle at the Seneca town of *Venango*, Fort Le Boeuf has been strategically placed along an Indian portage trail connecting Lake Erie to the Allegheny River known as the *Venango Path*.

> Note: The French had already widened the ancient path into a wagon road from Fort Presque Isle to Venango Town.
>
> Located at present-day Waterford, Pennsylvania, Venango Town was an important French transfer site, for it was there that the navigable river system began leading southward to Louisiana—and the French meant to protect it.

Aug. 10, 1753   **Benjamin Franklin and William Hunter are appointed as postmasters general for the North American colonies.**

> Note: Franklin, formerly the postmaster for Philadelphia, had lobbied for the job.

As joint commissioners, Franklin would be responsible for British mail routes north of Annapolis, Maryland; Hunter would be responsible for the same from Annapolis southward.

Benjamin Franklin would be the postmaster general for North America for the next twenty-one years—a plum position. In 1774, Franklin would be removed from his post for certain misdeeds and being too sympathetic to the American rebellion.

Aug. 1753 **The French begin constructing a third fort in Pennsylvania's western frontier, *Fort Machault.***

Note: Due to the priority of first completing Fort Presque Isle and Fort Le Boeuf, Fort Machault would not be finished until the following April.

Sept. 10, 1753 **In Virginia, Great Britain's Indian allies from the Ohio Region gather for the *Winchester Conference.***

Accompanied by the influential trader and land speculator George Croghan, ninety-two Indian delegates including chiefs representing the Oneida, Wyandot, Delaware, *Twightwee* (Miami), and Shawnee meet with Virginia authorities and Ohio Company officials at Winchester to receive presents and munitions as inducements to war against the French.

Meeting for a week, the Indians complain of White intrusions and the building of *strong houses* (forts) on Indian lands, but in the end agree to "turn their hatchets against the French" if their English friends will provide them weapons. The Virginians, having already sent a great quantity of weapons to the Ohio tribes in the spring, now agree to provide a suitable quantity of ammunition for the Indians to be stored and distributed at three particular sites. In addition, Virginia agrees to provide the tribes money for their use in case they should be distressed by their enemies and their hunting and planting prevented.

At the end of the conference, rather than returning home, the Indians travel onward to Carlisle to meet with the Pennsylvania authorities there.

Note: With tensions growing between Great Britain and France over North American land claims and the Indian trade, the western frontier region has become embroiled in a *forest arms race* as both the French and the British set about arming their tribal allies for use as proxies if war should break out between the two European nations.

Alcohol—one of the regularly expected gifts—caused such a problem that the conference had to be temporarily halted.

The presents were distributed among the tribal delegates, but one fifth was specially reserved for the Twightwee as restitution for the deaths of many of their *influential men*; the destruction of Pickawillany; and the loss of Croghan's trade post formerly located among them—all due to the tribe's support of the English.

Sept. 26, 1753 **Indian tribal delegates arrive at Carlisle to conference with the Pennsylvania commissioners and other officials.**

Fresh from conferencing with the Virginia authorities, the Indians arrive to share their sentiments and intelligence regarding the French activities in Ohio. In addition, the Indians hope to receive additional compensation from Pennsylvania for their losses sustained at the hands of their French and Indian enemies.

Though given a hearty welcome by the commissioners, including Benjamin Franklin, the expected presents have not yet arrived, and the Indians refuse to conference. The Pennsylvanians assure them that the gifts are forthcoming and insist that negotiations begin, causing Oneida Chief *Scarrooyady* to declare that the Indians, "could not proceed to Business while the Blood remained on their Garments, and that the Condolences could not be accepted unless the Goods, intended to cover the Graves, were actually spread on the Ground before them."

Therefore, they choose to wait.

> Note: The Indians were well aware of the critical position they held in the British–French forest wars and therefore wished to maximize the benefits received for assisting one side or the other as allies. Using the situation to their advantage, the delegates would demand that more weapons be provided to them, as well as other goods. As such, the Indians would continue to complain, and the officials would be forced to order more presents "to wipe away their tears."
>
> While waiting days for the presents to arrive and the conference to begin, the Indians would protest the prohibition of rum, but the commissioners assured them that if they stayed sober during the treaty negotiations, they would get plenty of rum afterwards.

Oct. 1, 1753   **The *Carlisle Conference* begins after presents are distributed.**

The Indians—ever concerned about the Whites invading their country—are very much against the British plans to construct a fort at the Ohio Forks to counter French inroads in the region. The Indians declare that instead of building the fort, the English should provide them with powder and lead and they will drive the French out themselves. Yet Pennsylvania's officials are reluctant to supply the tribes with munitions, choosing instead to provide other necessities.

During negotiations, the Indians:

- Object to the White settlers crossing the Allegheny Mountains into Indian country.

- Protest the many unlicensed traders entering their lands without authority. The tribes request that the traders be removed and replaced by establishing three specific trading sites at the edge of Indian country—at the Ohio Forks, at Logstown, and a third at the mouth of the Kanawha River.

- Complain of the high prices charged for goods.

- Complain that the traders only seem to offer flour and rum and not enough powder and lead.

- Request that horses are provided to transport their presents home.

- Request that the Shawnee prisoners at Charles Town be released.

- Request that the Iroquois be informed of the conference transactions, for "we do not wish to conceal from them what we do."

In return, the tribes agree to ally themselves with the British; to provide intelligence of French activities in the Ohio Region; and to order the French to leave.

At Carlisle, the Indians complain of the effects of rum on their people.

Speaking to the subject, Chief Scarrooyady states that the traders bring rum in such quantities and get the Indians so addicted that it ruins them by making the Indians sell their very clothes from their backs. Scarrooyady tells the Whites, "We will be ruined if continued."

> Note: Following the treaty's conclusion, the Indians claimed and received their liquor. As reported, "That night they were all drunk; they quarreled and fought, built a great bonfire in the town square, and chased one another with lighted firebrands, yelling hideously. At midnight a number burst into the commissioners' rooms, demanding more rum. Next day three of their old men apologized but justified the conduct by saying that the Great Spirit, who made all things for a purpose, had made rum for Indians to get drunk on."

Benjamin Franklin would recommend the discontinuation of gifts of rum to the Indians, as they were being ruined by it. In creating a report to the Pennsylvania governor concerning the conference, the commissioners would conclude with a warning, stating, "in Justice to these Indians, and the Promises we made them, we cannot close our Report, without taking Notice, That the Quantities of strong Liquors sold to these Indians in the Places of their Residence, and during their Hunting Seasons, from all Parts of the Counties over Sasquehannah, have encreased of late to an inconceivable Degree, so as to keep these poor Indians continually under the Force of Liquor, that they are hereby become dissolute, enfeebled and indolent when sober, and untractable and mischievous in their Liquor, always quarrelling, and often murdering one another: That the Traders are under no Bonds, nor give any Security for their Observance of the Laws, and their good Behaviour; and by their own Intemperance, unfair Dealings, and Irregularities, will, it is to be feared, entirely estrange the Affections of the Indians from the English; deprive them of their natural Strength and Activity, and oblige them either to abandon their Country, or submit to any Terms, be they ever so unreasonable, from the French. These Truths, may it please the Governor, are of so interesting a Nature, that we shall stand excused in recommending in the most earnest Manner, the deplorable State of these Indians, and the heavy Discouragements under which our Commerce with them at present labours, to the Governor's most serious Consideration, that some good and speedy Remedies may be provided, before it be too late."

Oct. 1753 — **George Washington volunteers to deliver a letter from Virginia's Governor Dinwiddie to the French in western Pennsylvania.**

Men of means on both sides of the Atlantic are heavily invested in the western lands, and the French presence threatens potential profits; thus, both the land speculators and traders want them removed.

Note: The Ohio Company's influential investors included Virginia Governor Dinwiddie and George Washington's brother Augustus. As such, George Washington—young, brave, robust in health, and a surveyor with company connections—had an edge in being appointed to lead the mission. Along his journey, Washington would *keep an eye out* for the choicest properties, giving him an advantage over others in the business.

Oct. 31, 1753 — **Departing Williamsburg, George Washington begins a wilderness reconnaissance mission.**

Washington, age twenty-one, is to find the newly constructed French forts and deliver a letter from Governor Dinwiddie declaring the French to be trespassers and warning them to leave the British-claimed lands. Washington's group will eventually include others who join him along the way to assist: Christopher Gist, an Ohio Company explorer and surveyor; Jacob van Braam, a French interpreter; four Indian traders; baggage men; and four Seneca to serve as guides and accomplices, including *Tanacharison*, commonly known as the *Half-King*.

Note: Washington was to note the size and strength of the French forts and garrisons should a military campaign against them become necessary. In addition, he was to make special note of the Ohio Forks to determine the site's feasibility for the construction of a fort.

Washington's round trip of 1,000 miles would take approximately ten weeks.

Dec. 12, 1753 — **Washington arrives at Fort Le Boeuf and delivers Governor Dinwiddie's message to the French commandant.**

Washington is treated well but rebuffed by the French commander, Captain Jacques Legardeur de Saint-Pierre. The captain pens a letter of reply to the Virginia governor stating that he, as a French officer, is merely following orders, but that he will forward Dinwiddie's letter to his superior in Canada, the Marquis Duquesne.

> Note: The French dismissal of Governor Dinwiddie's demands would set the stage for inevitable conflict between the two groups.
>
> Though Robert Dinwiddie was Virginia's lieutenant governor, he was usually referred to as the *governor* due the colony's absentee royal governor, Willem Anne van Keppel, who lived in England and never visited North America.

Dec. 23, 1753   **Forced to deal with winter's cold and ice, Washington begins his arduous journey back to Williamsburg.**

1754   ***King's College* is established in New York City, named in honor of King George II.**

> Note: King's College would be renamed *Columbia* in 1784, after American independence.

Jan. 16, 1754   **George Washington arrives at Williamsburg to report his findings to Governor Dinwiddie.**

> Note: For his efforts, Washington would be appointed a lieutenant colonel in the Virginia militia.

Jan. 1754   **The Virginia House of Burgesses authorizes a fort to be built at the Ohio Forks.**

Virginians under the direction and authority of Governor Dinwiddie begin preparations to construct a fort at the Ohio Forks to assert Virginia's claim to the region. Dinwiddie—an investor in the Ohio Company—easily convinces the assembly to authorize the fort's construction and appoints William Trent to supervise the project.

> Note: Though William Trent had been operating a trading post at the Forks since 1748, with the French now asserting themselves in the region, the Indian trade and schemes of the Virginia land speculators were at risk.
>
> Virginia's claim to the Ohio Forks would be contested by the Pennsylvania Colony, which viewed the region as its own and considered the Virginians trespassers.

Feb. 17, 1754   **The construction of *Fort Prince George* begins in earnest as the Virginians race the French for control of the Ohio Valley.**

> Note: A stipulation of the Ohio Company's land grant had called for the company to construct a fort in the region. Fort Prince George was to be it.

Feb. 1754   **George Washington experiences his first celebrity status after his journal is published on both sides of the Atlantic.**

Washington's official report of his mission to the French at Fort Le Boeuf is presented to Virginia's House of Burgesses and published in Williamsburg's *Virginia Gazette*. The report is then republished in other colonial papers, as well as in those in London.

April 2, 1754   **Leading a militia-work force, Washington once again sets out for the Ohio River Forks.**

Now a Virginia lieutenant colonel, Washington's mission is to travel to the Forks of the Ohio to protect the workmen hurriedly constructing Fort Prince George, and to improve the Nemacolin Trail leading to the Monongahela River into a passable roadway.

April 1754   **The French complete Fort Machault in western Pennsylvania.**

Located halfway between Lake Erie and the Ohio Forks, the French finish the third of four forts planned for the region. Sitting strategically at the conflux of the Allegheny River and French Creek, Fort Machault, like the others, is to protect the Venango Path and help create a western wall against further British encroachments.

Now, having finished Fort Presque Isle, Fort Le Boeuf, and Fort Machault, the French turn their attention to the Ohio Forks and the construction of *Fort Duquesne*. But as the site is presently occupied by Virginia workers they must first evict—the French set out to do it.

April 16, 1754   **The Virginians abandon the strategic Ohio Forks to approaching French troops.**

A force of 500 French and Indians easily run off the Virginia workers who leave their unfinished works behind in their flight. With plans of their own, the French begin constructing Fort Duquesne, named after the governor of New France, Michel-Ange Du Quesne de Menneville, more commonly known as the Marquis Duquesne.

May 9, 1754   **The first political cartoon is published in Britain's American colonies.**

The *Pennsylvania Gazette* publishes a political cartoon of a segmented rattlesnake with the words "Join or Die" to enlist support for the upcoming colonial congress to be held at Albany, New York.

Late May 1754   **Washington establishes a camp only sixty-five miles south of the French at the Ohio Forks.**

En route to protect the Virginia workers building Fort Prince George, Washington learns that the project has been abandoned and the strategic site is now occupied by French troops and their Indian allies. Due to this turn of events, Washington pauses to establish a camp at *Great Meadows*, Pennsylvania, and anxiously awaits reinforcements scheduled to soon arrive.

Note: With Virginia Colonel Joshua Fry fifty miles away at Wills Creek, the young Washington would be in charge at Great Meadows while Fry remained absent.

George Washington had no military experience.

May 28, 1754   **Virginia Lieutenant Colonel George Washington leads an attack against the French, igniting frontier warfare between France and Great Britain.**

The Iroquois accompanying Washington inform the Virginians that a group of French are encamped only eight miles away and urge an attack against them. Hearing this news, Washington decides to launch a dawn attack. Accompanied by forty militiamen and twelve Seneca warriors, Washington soon disappears into the night woods to locate the sleeping French.

In the morning, encircled and unsuspecting, the French troops are attacked and quickly overwhelmed by Washington's force in a fifteen-minute battle.

Note: Following the surrender, the Seneca Half-King would kill French ensign Joseph Coulon de Jumonville with a single blow from his war club. The killing of Jumonville would cause a future diplomatic row.

Of the thirty-two French: ten were killed; twenty-one were captured; and one escaped to make his way back to the Ohio Forks to report the attack, stating that only the intervention of the Indians prevented all the French soldiers from being killed by the Virginians.

The dead French were scalped by the Seneca and left unburied, whereas the prisoners would be sent to Williamsburg.

Fearing a counterattack by the French and Indians encamped at the Ohio Forks, Washington's small group quickly retreats to the Great Meadows camp.

Note: Washington's men suffered one man killed and two wounded.

The French would claim that Jumonville had been on a diplomatic mission to seek out the Virginians and protested that Washington had fired on them without provocation or cause.

Three days after the attack, George Washington would pen a letter to his brother Augustine, stating, "I can with truth assure you, I heard Bulletts whistle and believe me there was something charming in the sound."

The site of the *Battle of Jumonville Glen* is located near present-day Farmington, Pennsylvania.

The *Seven Year's War*, aka the *French and Indian War,* begins in North America.

British–French tensions have been growing for years as both nations vie for control of the Indian trade and the rich lands west of the Appalachian Mountains. As such, Washington's killing of the French troops will provide the spark for igniting another North American forest war involving France, Great Britain, American and Canadian colonials, and the Native Americans.

Note: Americans usually refer to this war as the French and Indian War of 1754 – 1763, beginning on the date of Washington's fight. Yet the British and most historians refer to the French and Indian War as but one theatre of larger European Seven Years' War, thus making the matter a bit confusing. Though military hostilities did break out following Washington's actions, Britain and France would not officially declare war until 1756, making it a seven-year war.

May 30, 1754 **Believing the French troops and their Indian allies to soon be upon them, Washington's men hastily construct defensive works at the Great Meadows camp.**

The men earnestly work for five days to build the aptly named *Fort Necessity*.

Note: An entire month would pass before the French would arrive to do battle.

June 9, 1754 **Virginia reinforcements arrive at Great Meadows.**

Colonel Fry's men arrive from Wills Creek bringing much-needed supplies and nine swivel guns (small cannons). Though their arrival boosts Washington's force to 300 Virginians, Washington learns that his superior officer, Colonel Josh Fry, has died after falling from his horse. Thus, Lieutenant Colonel Washington assumes Fry's command.

June 12, 1754 **One hundred British troops arrive at Great Meadows from South Carolina.**

Captain James Mackay's Independent Company arrives, bringing Washington's combined force to nearly 400 men.

Note: Though Lieutenant Colonel Washington outranked the arriving Captain Mackay, as a regular British Army officer, Mackay would remain in charge of his troops. Thus, Washington and Mackay would work together in a joint-command situation.

> The British soldiers camped separately from the Virginians.
>
> Though Washington had received military reinforcements, his Seneca allies had deserted him.

June 16, 1754	**George Washington supervises the Virginians as they return to the task of roadbuilding.**

The British troops guard the Great Meadows camp, allowing the nearly 300 Virginians to move forward and continue widening the Nemacolin Trail leading to the Ohio Forks.

June 19, 1754	**The *Albany Congress* begins in Albany, New York.**

Common concerns over threats posed by the French and their Indian allies have led six colonies—Rhode Island, Connecticut, Massachusetts, Pennsylvania, New Hampshire, and Maryland—to send representatives to Albany to coordinate military operations by uniting the colonial defenses; settle issues over the Indian trade; and secure Iroquois support against the French.

> Note: The meeting, or *congress*, had been proposed by Pennsylvania's Benjamin Franklin, Thomas Hutchinson of Massachusetts, and other New Englanders to form a *plan of union* by which Britain's North American colonies would come together under one general government.

Held in conjunction with the annual Albany Indian Conference, this year's event is quite different due to the many colonial representatives attending. Concerned about a possible war with France, the Iroquois are courted and plied to strengthen faltering British alliances and to use their influence over the other regional tribes as well. There is a lot of speechmaking by both sides. The British pledge to stop incursions into Iroquois lands as thirty wagons of trinkets, trade goods, and rum are given to the Indians. The Albany Conference will last three weeks, concluding on July 11.

The Iroquois sell large tracts of Pennsylvania land to Connecticut's *Susquehanna Company*.

The Connecticut Colony is feeling *boxed in* and wishes to expand its colonial landholdings, believing its original charter to have included all land extending westward to the Pacific Ocean. Therefore, Connecticut's Susquehanna Company purchases the Wyoming Valley area from the Iroquois for £2,000.

This purchase will create future problems for the following reasons:

- Other tribes, including the Delaware, do not recognize the Iroquois claims to the Wyoming Valley region and deny their right to sell it. This will result in the Delaware waging war to keep the White settlers out.

- Pennsylvania disputes Connecticut's purchase, for the claim runs across the northern portion of Pennsylvania and would greatly reduce its size. As a result, settlers from both colonies will arrive in the Wyoming Valley and become embroiled in violent skirmishes to be later known collectively as the *Pennamite–Yankee War*. Unable to settle their differences, the dispute will continue, threatening the unity of the future Second Continental Congress as it attempts to project a united front against Britain.

June 28, 1754	**Fearing a French attack, Washington and his workers retreat southward to the protection of Fort Necessity.**

The Virginia roadbuilders and militiamen, learning of approaching French soldiers, abandon much of their supplies in a hurried return arriving at Great Meadows to rejoin the British troops. Anticipating the arrival of the French and their Indian allies at any moment, Washington and British Captain James Mackay set their men to work strengthening fortifications.

<table>
<tr><td>Note:</td><td>Washington and his men had been working at Redstone Creek, twenty miles forward from the Great Meadows camp and within forty miles of the French at the Ohio Forks.</td></tr>
</table>

July 3, 1754

The *Battle of Fort Necessity*: French and Indian forces arrive at Great Meadows.

Nearly 600 French and 100 Indian warriors arrive to attack the English and drive them from the region. The French commander Louis Coulon de Villiers is the brother of the slain ensign, Joseph Coulon de Jumonville—and Villiers wants revenge.

Rain falls throughout the day, and Fort Necessity becomes a swampy mess. After trying a failed frontal assault, the Virginians and British troops retreat to the fort and hunker down while trying to keep their powder dry. The French, with the advantage of a slight high ground protected by trees, snipe into the vulnerable fort, and many of the Virginians break into the rum and become intoxicated.

<table>
<tr><td>Note:</td><td>Located in an open meadow and close to the surrounding woodline, the French troops and their Indian allies could shoot with near impunity at the Virginians and British soldiers hunkered down inside Fort Necessity.

The French commander had stopped en route at Jumonville Glen and buried the mutilated French dead.</td></tr>
</table>

The British troops and Virginians surrender to the French.

After sporadic fighting throughout the day, Commander de Villiers calls for a truce to discuss surrender terms. With little hope, British Captain James Mackay and Virginia Lieutenant Colonel George Washington agree, but negotiations are slow due to language difficulties. Finally completed around midnight, the terms allow the men safe passage to Virginia.

<table>
<tr><td>Note:</td><td>The surrender terms permitted the British troops and Virginians to return with their baggage and firearms, but they were required to abandon their nine swivel guns.

The surrender terms, written in French, described the killing of Joseph Coulon de Jumonville as an *assassination*. Though Mackay and Washington both signed the agreement, Washington would later claim the interpreter had mistranslated it.</td></tr>
</table>

July 4, 1754

Fort Necessity is abandoned and destroyed.

In the early morning, the Virginians and the British troops vacate Fort Necessity and begin their journey to Williamsburg to report the situation to authorities. As they march away, the French set fire to the fort and return to the Ohio Forks and the construction of Fort Duquesne.

<table>
<tr><td>Note:</td><td>When news of the defeat would reach London, Great Britain would resolve to capture Fort Duquesne by sending a large military force to North America under the command of Major General Edward Braddock.

Following the battle, Washington would be promoted to the rank of colonel in Virginia's militia forces.</td></tr>
</table>

July 10, 1754

In New York, the Albany Congress agrees to a *plan of union*.

The proposed plan for the colonial confederation is as follows:

- A grand council is to be elected by the colonial assemblies to work with a single president general appointed by the Crown.

- The confederation is to be responsible for regulating westward expansions and defenses, including Indian negotiations; overseeing the building of forts; and raising necessary armies.

- Each colony is to retain its own identity and handle its own internal affairs.

- The necessary funds are to be raised by imposing some taxes.

The agreement is to be presented for sanction to Parliament and the various colonial assemblies for their approval. However, it will be rejected by all groups, mainly for the following reasons:

- The colonial governments refuse to relinquish power to a central authority.

- The British Ministry believes the American colonists have overstepped their bounds. In addition, the ministry finds the agreement somewhat confusing and does not forward it to Parliament.

> Note: Although the plan would be rejected, the British Ministry did like the idea of centralizing its North American Indian policy. Therefore, in 1756, two governmental divisions would be created to better deal with the tribes—a Southern Department and a Northern Department—each with an appointed British superintendent.

Was the Albany Congress the first intercolonial meeting in Britain's North American colonies?

Though many historians consider the Albany Congress to be the first such meeting, others disagree, citing such examples as:

- May 19, 1643: The New England colonies joined in a common confederation called the United Colonies of New England, or the Confederation of New England; including Massachusetts Bay, Plymouth Bay, Connecticut, and New Haven. The union's purpose was to form a mutual defense force to oppose the French and Indian threats. The Confederation of New England lasted until 1686.

- 1686: King James II forced the colonies of Plymouth Bay, Rhode Island, Massachusetts, and New Hampshire into a single political union called the Dominion of New England. Within two years, Connecticut, New York, East Jersey, and West Jersey were also forced to join the short-lived union, dissolved in 1689 after the Dominion's royal governor was overthrown by revolting Massachusetts Puritans.

- May 1, 1690: With the collapse of the royal government of King James II, Protestant rebels took control of New York and formed an insurgent government with the rebel leader Jacob Leisler taking control. Leisler called for and held an intercolonial meeting in New York City with representatives from Massachusetts, Connecticut, Plymouth, and New York to plan a united military campaign against New France.

Oct. 2, 1754 **Georgia's first royal governor arrives from England.**

Administered since its 1732 founding by distant London trustees, Georgia, now a royal colony, receives its first royal governor, John Reynolds.

1755 **The British population of North America is nearly 1.5 million, whereas there are only 75,000–90,000 French.**

Feb. 20, 1755 **Preparing for war, thousands of British troops begin arriving in Hampton, Virginia.**

Leading the troops is Major General Edward Braddock, whose first goal is to drive the French from Fort Duquesne and take possession of the strategic Ohio Forks.

Note:	This was the first time many of the American colonials had ever seen the King's troops.
	With the arrival of such numbers of British soldiers, problems would arise over their support and quartering. How would they be housed and who should pay the cost of doing so? These and other questions would become an ongoing source of irritation between the American colonists and the British Ministry. Yet conversely, the large influx of British military forces in North America would boost the local economies as the colonists scrambled to help provide for their needs.
	Colonial militias, often shoddily dressed and ill-supplied, would fight alongside the King's troops during the various campaigns, causing many of the British regulars to look down their noses at their American cousins. Many more felt contempt toward North America's Indian *savages*—whether allies or enemies. The haughty British, including General Braddock, held little respect for the Indians as a military threat.

Spring 1755 **In Virginia, British military forces begin the urgent task of constructing forts and access routes to the interior regions of North America.**

Note:	These constructions and the corresponding military campaigns would soon make the western frontier regions much more accessible to the American colonials, resulting in an accelerated loss of Indian lands.

The powerful Cherokee Nation is solicited by British and colonial officials as an ally in the fight against the French.

May 29, 1755 **General Braddock departs Fort Cumberland, Maryland, to begin a military campaign against the French—beginning with Fort Duquesne.**

Building a wilderness road as he goes, Braddock heads into the forest with 2,100 fighting men; a large number of camp followers; a herd of cattle; and no Indian support excepting eight Seneca scouts.

Note:	At this moment, several hundred French-allied Indians were encamped near and around Fort Duquesne.
	Several future American notables accompanied the Braddock campaign: George Washington, Daniel Boone, and Daniel Morgan; and though not present, Benjamin Franklin had helped procure the necessary wagons.

June 12, 1755 **Massachusetts Bay Colony offers bounties for Indian scalps.**

The authorities will pay £40 for males over twelve years old and £20 for women and children.

July 9, 1755 **The *Battle of the Monongahela*: General Braddock is mortally wounded as his troops are routed near present-day Pittsburgh.**

Nearing Fort Duquesne, Braddock's large army of 1,400 regulars and 700 colonials is attacked after fording the Monongahela River by thirty French troops and 300 to 600 Indians in a pre-emptive strike. While marching in a long column through a ravine with dense undergrowth, the unsuspecting British troops panic after the forest calm is suddenly shattered by the sounds of gunfire and Indian war cries. As panicked soldiers in the front tumble rearward, those in the rear rush forward, causing the men to collide and bunch together while being shot by enemies hidden behind trees and brush. As the troops retreat in panic, both the British and colonial officers, including George Washington, try to regain military order while facing a withering fire. During the fighting, Braddock has four mounts shot from under him, and while on a fifth, the general is mortally wounded by a shot to his chest, which only adds to the overall sense of doom.

Once regrouped, the British and colonial forces abandon their objective and begin retracing the route to Fort Cumberland while trying to maintain proper order. Along the way, General Braddock succumbs to his wound. To keep the Indians from finding his corpse, the general is buried in the forest roadway and trod over by the retreating troops and wagons. Abandoning the Pennsylvania frontier to the French, Braddock's army arrives at Fort Cumberland eight days later, and after regrouping, continues to Philadelphia.

> Note: Benjamin Franklin and others had warned the self-confident General Braddock of the Indians' fighting prowess, but as a veteran of European military campaigns, Braddock held little respect for the savages' ability to effectively challenge the King's troops. Thus, Braddock had paid for ignoring this advice with his life, along with 450 fellow soldiers killed and another 400 wounded.
>
> Colonel George Washington suffered many close calls during the battle—two horses were shot from under him, and according to his account, four bullets grazed his coat.
>
> Many of the British and Americans taken captive would be tortured to death in the numerous camps surrounding the walls of Fort Duquesne, as joyous Indian warriors held several long nights of wild celebration. The more fortunate captives, at least for the moment, would be force-marched to their captors' villages to suffer whatever fate awaited them.
>
> The Indians saw the British defeat as a great victory and the event greatly influenced their sentiments in favor of the French. As such, the French would encourage the tribes to *take up the hatchet* and be supplied with guns and other weapons of war. Both the Delaware and Shawnee, having been forced from their eastern lands by the English, now sided with the French, seeing the war as an opportunity to exact revenge.
>
> The French attempted to enlist the Cherokee, tentatively supportive of the British. If the tribe should join the French as allies, the Cherokee would represent a serious threat to Virginia and the Carolinas by opening a southern fighting front.

Summer 1755   **The frontier regions of Pennsylvania and Virginia become engulfed in Indian wars.**

The defeat of General Braddock's army has given the Western Tribes a bolstered confidence, and with French support and encouragement, the Indians carry out an offensive to drive the *English* settlers and traders from the region.

> Note: Most of the Indian warriors fighting at the Battle of the Monongahela represented French-allied tribes from the western regions, including the Ottawa, *Ojibwe,* Miami, *Mingo,* Wyandot, *Mississaugua,* Potawatomi, Shawnee, and Delaware. As such, all would carry the news of the English defeat to their distant villages and beyond in great excitement.
>
> The Pennsylvania Assembly was hesitant to provide the necessary funds to defeat the Indians causing many frontier residents to wonder aloud if the Quaker government, secure in Philadelphia, even cared about their plight.

1755   ***Rogers' Rangers*** **is formed in New Hampshire and helps serve as** *eyes and ears* **for the British forces in frontier New York and upper New England.**

The daring company of green-clad men is created by Robert Rogers to be an elite fighting force specializing in reconnaissance and intelligence gathering.

> Note: Trained in woodland tactics and guerrilla fighting, Rogers' Rangers would be considered a forerunner of the United States Army's special forces—the Green Berets.
>
> Many historians believe that Gorham's Rangers, an Indian ranger force developed in Massachusetts to defend Nova Scotia in 1744, was a prototype for Rogers' Rangers.

July 30, 1755 **Virginia suffers the *Draper's Meadow Massacre* and the capture of Mary Ingles.**

Shawnee warriors raid Draper's Meadow in western Virginia killing five and taking others as prisoners, including the then-pregnant Mary Ingles. The captives are force-marched to the Kentucky region where Mary eventually makes an escape, leaving her infant behind. For the next two and a half months, Ingles and another woman struggle 800 miles through the forest wilderness, with Mary eventually returning to her Virginia home and entering the lore of early American history.

> Note: Draper's Meadow is located at present-day Blacksburg, Virginia.
>
> We do not know about Mary Ingles's companion. She was referred to as the old Dutch woman from Pennsylvania but may have been German—*Deutsch*.
>
> Mary's husband, Virginia Captain William Ingles, would approach Virginia's Governor Robert Dinwiddie to urge a punishing expedition against the Shawnee towns along the Ohio River based on intelligence gained from his wife's captivity. This would result in the Sandy Creek expedition against the Shawnee in February 1756.

Aug. 1755–1756 *The Great Upheaval*: **The French are expelled from Nova Scotia.**

The Acadians, located on New England's northern border, have long been enemies of the English. Now, with Britain facing a wider war with France, 7,000 French Acadians are rounded up and relocated to Britain's other North American colonies. Unwanted, unwelcome, and untrusted, the Acadians are separated and widely dispersed in order to cut ties among families and social groups, thus preventing *mischief*, with the most troublesome being sent the furthest south—far from their homeland in Canada.

> Note: Many Acadian parents would spend years trying to reassemble their families, seeking the children who had been separated from them.
>
> The Acadians created refugee crises wherever they arrived. The Protestant colonists of British North America—long enemies of the French—did not particularly wish to receive these Catholic transplants from New France.
>
> The wealthy and influential Marylander Charles Carroll, himself a Catholic, would complain about the arrival of 900 Acadians to Maryland.
>
> Massachusetts Bay Colony would begrudgingly receive 2,000 Acadians.
>
> Initially, Virginia would refuse to accept any Acadians but eventually received 1,100.
>
> Savannah, Georgia would receive 600 Acadians in December 1755.
>
> In Nova Scotia, the exiled French Acadians would be replaced by arriving New Englanders and immigrants from Scotland.

Generally speaking, the Acadians are unwelcome everywhere, with many colonists believing these French cannot be trusted and will only set fire to the towns. As a result, many Acadians die while waiting aboard ships as legal wranglings take place. Others, once settled, choose to return to their former homes in Nova Scotia or sail to France.

Sept. 8, 1755 **The French are defeated at the *Battle of Lake George* in New York.**

New England, New York, and Mohawk forces led by Major General William Johnson march north along the Lake Champlain corridor to attack Fort Saint-Frédéric at Crown Point. Aware of Johnson's plans, French commander Baron Dieskau decides to launch a preemptive strike against the approaching army in what becomes a three-part battle and an eventual victory for the American colonials and the Mohawk.

> Note: The two sides were fairly even in number. The New Englanders had 1,500 men and 200 Mohawk warriors, compared to the French force of 200 professional troops, 600 French Canadians, and 700 Abenaki and Caughnawaga allies.
>
> Casualty estimates vary greatly, with approximately 250 New Englanders killed or wounded, and an equal number of French Canadians and soldiers.
>
> French commander Major General Dieskau was wounded severely and captured in the battle. Dieskau would be kept prisoner until the war's conclusion in 1763.
>
> An important Mohawk ally to the British and Americans, Chief Hendrick Theyanoguin, commonly known as King Hendrick, was killed in the battle.
>
> Ephraim Williams, considered the founder of Williams College in western Massachusetts and for whom Williamstown was named, was killed in the battle.
>
> Native American battle casualties were seldom reported.
>
> William Johnson of New York had been appointed as a British major general to lead the assault against the French due to his influence with the Iroquois Six Nations. Though Johnson did not press on to capture Fort Saint-Frédéric, he had defeated the French troops and captured Major General Dieskau. For his success, Johnson would be knighted and soon named British Superintendent of Indian Affairs north of the Ohio River.

Late Sept. 1755 **In frontier New York, the building of *Fort William Henry* begins.**

Taking advantage of his victory over the French, Major General William Johnson orders the construction of Fort William Henry at the southern end of Lake George. Built by colonial militia forces, the fort is to serve as a base for launching military offensives against New France, and as a protective deterrent to French incursions southward into New York and New England.

> Note: William Johnson would bestow a new name on the French-claimed lake, Lac Du Saint Sacrement, renaming it *Lake George* in honor of King George II.

Oct. 1755 **The French begin building *Fort Carillon* at the southern edge of Lake Champlain.**

Located a mere forty miles north of Fort William Henry, the French construct Fort Carillon as a check to the British advance toward New France along the Lake Champlain corridor.

> Note: Fort Carillon would be captured by the British troops in 1759 and renamed *Fort Ticonderoga*. The remote New York fort would be destined to play a major role in the future American War for Independence due to its strategic location connecting Lake George and Lake Champlain.

Oct. 16, 1755 **Delaware warriors attack the Penn's Creek area of Pennsylvania.**

> Note: The defeat of General Braddock's troops, combined with French military and material support, had given the Indians a confidence that placed the Pennsylvania frontier settlers in peril.

Delaware raiding parties attack Penn's Creek, located on the Susquehanna River near present-day Selinsgrove. Launching their forest offensive from the Delaware town of *Kittanning,* the marauders attack the isolated homes of mostly German immigrants, killing and scalping thirteen inhabitants and capturing eleven others. Following the attack, the Indians divide into smaller groups and go their separate ways, killing twenty-five frontier settlers in total.

News of the vicious attacks sends an *Indian chill* throughout the region, and the settlers insist on revenge.

Note:	Most of the captives would be taken to the Delaware towns of the Muskingum River region in Ohio.
	In retaliation, a Pennsylvania militia would soon launch a counterstrike against Kittanning Town.

Nov. 24, 1755   **Shawnee and Delaware attack the Moravian mission of *Gnadenhutten* in Pennsylvania.**

Note:	The Indian mission town of Gnadenhutten, located near modern Lehighton, Pennsylvania, ministered to approximately 500 Christianized Delaware and Shawnee, many of whom resided with the missionaries in the settlement.

Eleven Moravian missionaries are killed outright or burn to death in an attic set aflame by the attackers. As a result, the Gnadenhutten mission is abandoned, and the nearby Moravian settlement of Bethlehem is ordered to be fortified.

Note:	Curiously, at the time of the onslaught, the Christian Indians had made themselves absent, causing many Whites to believe that they were either a part of the attack or had been warned of it by their kinsmen. Christian or not—most White settlers believed all Indians were savages, never to be trusted.
	Gnadenhutten, Pennsylvania, is often confused with another Moravian mission with the same name later built in eastern Ohio.

Dec. 17, 1755   **Pennsylvania authorizes three new forts for frontier protection.**

Benjamin Franklin directs George Croghan to begin constructing three forts of a size "large enough to house fifty men" to provide the isolated settlers shelter from Indian attacks.

1756   **Sam Adams is elected a tax collector in Boston.**

Note:	Many consider it ironic that Adams—a colonial tax collector—would become a protester of taxes paid to Britain and a firebrand for American independence.

Virginia dedicates half of its military budget to controlling the colony's African slaves.

Nova Scotia offers bounties for the scalps of Mi'kmaq and other hostile tribes.

Royal Governor Charles Lawrence declares, "And, we do hereby promise, by and with the consent of his Majesty's Council, a reward of 30 pounds for every live male Indian prisoner, above the age of sixteen years, brought in alive; or for a scalp of such male Indian twenty-five pounds, and twenty-five pounds for every Indian woman or child brought in alive."

Feb. 17, 1756   **William Johnson is commissioned as the northern superintendent for Great Britain's newly created *Department of Indian Affairs* and will report directly to London.**

Living in upstate New York, the British Superintendent of Iroquois Affairs, William Johnson, is appointed as the primary agent for Britain's Indian matters north of the Ohio River and granted broad powers to deal with the tribes—particularly the Iroquois League and its tribal allies. Paramount among Johnson's many goals is to keep the Iroquois from allying with the French. As Britain's Indian superintendent, William Johnson is instructed to allow no unauthorized transactions with the Northern Tribes but through him.

> Note: The Iroquois-speaking Johnson held much influence with the Six Nations. Up to this time, Johnson had been serving as the British superintendent of the Iroquois and had conducted the annual summer Indian conferences in Albany. Well-respected by all the tribes, William Johnson would prove to be a perfect fit for such an appointment.
>
> William Johnson's common-law Indian wife, Molly Brant, was the older sister of the future-famed Mohawk leader Joseph Brant. This connection would give Johnson additional influence with the Mohawk, the most powerful tribe of the Iroquois League.
>
> Johnson would continue to enrich himself with vast tracts of land acquired from the Iroquois, making him one of the largest landholders in colonial America.

Pennsylvania Indian trader and land speculator George Croghan is appointed Deputy Superintendent of Northern Indian Affairs.

Croghan is to be second-in-command to Superintendent William Johnson. Having much experience with the Ohio tribes, Croghan will concern himself primarily with the tribes of the Ohio Region, while Johnson holds sway over the Iroquois and other tribes of New York, eastern Pennsylvania, and New England.

> Note: George Croghan, like Superintendent William Johnson, was fluent in several Indian languages and would use his position and influence to further acquire vast personal acreages of frontier land.

Edmond Atkin is appointed Superintendent of Indian Affairs for Britain's Southern Department.

While visiting England, Atkin, a Charles Town merchant long engaged in the Indian trade and a member of the Governor's Council, is appointed Southern Superintendent of Indian Affairs due to his experience, connections, and two reports Atkin had submitted to the Board of Trade concerning trade relations and management of the Indians in North America. Edmond Adkin is to supervise the tribes south of the Ohio River.

Feb. 18, 1756   **The *Sandy River Campaign*: Virginians and Cherokee warriors begin a military expedition against Shawnee settlements near the Ohio River.**

As retribution for the previous summer's attacks on Virginia's frontier, including at Draper's Meadow, Major Andrew Lewis leads 200–300 Virginia militiamen and 80–100 Cherokee warriors in search of the Shawnee settlements, located near present-day Portsmouth, Ohio.

March 13, 1756   **The Sandy River Campaign against the Shawnee is called off.**

After only a month—rough terrain, winter cold, low supplies, a lack of game, and the loss of horses combined with other problems have led to general discontent and many of Lewis's men wish to return home. A vote is taken, but with only thirty men agreeing to proceed, the campaign is canceled, leaving the Shawnee unpunished.

<table>
<tr><td></td><td>Note:</td><td>The Cherokee warriors accompanying the expedition, quite content to continue, were disgusted by the decision to turn around.

The failed Sandy River Campaign would be an embarrassment for Virginia and embolden the warring Shawnee.</td></tr>
</table>

Spring 1756　　**In Virginia, Colonel George Washington leads a militia regiment guarding and fortifying frontier settlements against possible French or Indian attack.**

April 6, 1756　　**George Washington describes Indian fighting skills in a letter to Governor Dinwiddie.**

"[F]ive hundred Indians have it more in their power to annoy the inhabitants than ten times their number of regulars. For besides the advantageous way they have of fighting in the woods, their cunning and craft are not to be equaled, neither their activity and indefatigable sufferings. They prowl about like wolves, and like them, do their mischief by stealth. They depend upon their dexterity in hunting and upon the cattle of the inhabitants for provisions."

April 14, 1756　　**South Carolina Royal Governor James Glen protests the arrival of 900 French Acadians.**

After suffering frontier atrocities, Pennsylvania's governor declares war on the Delaware.

The Delaware and Shawnee have been attacking the frontier settlers, including the October attack upon Penn's Creek, and a pressured Pennsylvania Assembly—disregarding protests from the Quakers—offers bounties for Indian scalps.

<table>
<tr><td>Note:</td><td>There had always been tension in Pennsylvania between the Quakers and the western region's frontier settlers over how to best deal with the *Indian problem*.

Pennsylvania would offer "130 Pieces of Eight, for the Scalp of Every Male Indian Enemy, above the Age of Twelve Years" and "50 Pieces of Eight for the Scalp of Every Indian Woman" produced as evidence that the Indians had been killed.</td></tr>
</table>

May 1756　　**General Louis-Joseph de Montcalm arrives at Montreal to command the French military forces in North America.**

<table>
<tr><td>Note:</td><td>General Montcalm would become somewhat immortal in North American military history for leading French troops in the defense of Quebec against British General James Wolfe on September 13, 1759. The battle would prove fatal for both commanders.</td></tr>
</table>

May 8–9, 1756　　**Great Britain declares war against France, officially beginning the Seven Years' War.**

After two years of conflict in North America, Britain finally declares war against France.

<table>
<tr><td>Note:</td><td>France had complained that Britain was conducting a war without issuing a formal declaration. Britain had counterclaimed that a declaration of war was unnecessary, for it was fighting only to protect its territories from French invasions.

The Seven Years' War, commonly called the French and Indian War, had begun in 1754 in North America, and was therefore a nine-year conflict to the American colonials.</td></tr>
</table>

June 1756　　**France reciprocates and declares war against Great Britain.**

The next two years will fare well for the French and their Indian allies in the North American *forest war* against the British Army and American colonial forces.

> Note: By now, Britain's colonial subjects in North America, while proud to be British citizens, had become more distinctly—*Americans.*

King George II uses Hessians from his German homeland to help defend Great Britain.

At war with France and fearing a French invasion, George II imports German troops to protect the realm.

> Note: The large contingent of German troops arrived in Southampton, England, aboard 54 British transports on May 15, 1756. After being shuffled around England for a year, the Hessians would return to Germany in April 1757.

British Indian Superintendent William Johnson travels to *Onondaga* to persuade the Six Nations to support the king in his war with the French.

Superintendent Johnson also urges the Iroquois to set aside their historical animosities against the Cherokee. Johnson finds the Iroquois reluctant.

> Note: Onondaga Town, located near modern Syracuse, New York, was the capital or central town of the Iroquois Six Nations. It was here that the League's council fire was kept, and important conferences were held among tribal members.
>
> The Cherokee would tentatively support the English, but it would be rather short-lived, collapsing into the Anglo-Cherokee War of 1758.

1756

Wappinger lands in New York's Hudson Valley are confiscated by the Philipse family.

While most of the Wappinger warriors are off fighting alongside the British troops and American colonials, the wealthy Philipse family of New York takes advantage of the situation, appropriating 86,000 acres of Wappinger lands based on a dubious 1692 deed.

> Note: At this time, most of New York's Wappinger were living at Stockbridge, Massachusetts, with other Christian Indians while renting their Hudson Valley lands to White farmers—those same lands claimed by the Philipse family.
>
> At this time, much of the New York lands were claimed by wealthy Dutch landowners known as patroons—many of whom lived in the Netherlands. These vast tracts were often managed in a medieval-style patroon system whereby peasant farmers were forced to pay homage and rent in portions of cattle, crops, and labor to the owners, who in turn would permit them to work small acreages for themselves. Unable to purchase the lands they worked; the farmers held no security of tenure. Therefore, upon a farmer's death—the land would revert to the landlord.

July 1756

General John Campbell, aka Lord Loudoun, arrives as the new commander in chief of British forces in North America—and as Virginia's royal governor.

Lord Loudoun is to replace Massachusetts Governor William Shirley, who assumed command of the British troops following the death of Major General Edward Braddock.

> Note: Though appointed as Virginia's royal governor, the unpopular Lord Loudoun would focus on fighting a war with the French while Lieutenant Governor Robert Dinwiddie, who had until this point been serving as the colony's acting governor, would continue to administer Virginia's domestic affairs.
>
> Many royal governors in the American colonies were also British military officers.

| Summer 1756 | **British troops are housed in private homes for the only time in American history.** |

In Albany, New York—headquarters for the campaign against New France—barracks for the arriving troops are not yet completed. As such, Lord Loudoun declares that the people must temporarily house the British officers and troops. Though many citizens resist, the troops are forced upon them, and adding insult to injury and against local wishes, Lord Loudoun stores his gunpowder in an Albany church.

> Note: In Great Britain, under the *Mutiny Act,* the military could force the owners of inns and public houses to accommodate troops, with the owners to be compensated by the government. No such law gave Lord Loudoun this authority in the American colonies, but he did so anyway. The quartering of troops would soon become a heated issue between Great Britain and the colonial assemblies, later resulting in the Third Amendment of the United States Constitution.
>
> The belief that private citizens were on occasion forced to quarter British troops in their colonial homes remains a common historical misconception. Except in this one case in Albany, New York—it never happened.

| Aug. 2, 1756 | **Delaware warriors and French troops successfully attack *Fort Granville*, Pennsylvania.** |

With most of the garrison on patrol, and only twenty-four men left behind to guard the stockade, nearly 100 Delaware and 50 French decide that now is the time to attack the isolated frontier post. Opposing their attackers, Fort Granville's defenders manage to hold out until a fire is set and the fort's commander—Pennsylvania militia officer Lieutenant Edward Armstrong—is shot and killed while helping extinguish the flames.

Following the death of Lieutenant Armstrong, second-in-command Sergeant John Turner surrenders the fort under a promise of safe quarter, but Turner is instead tied to a stake and mercilessly tortured before being killed in front of the fellow prisoners, including children. After the fort is burned, most of the terrified captives are taken to the Illinois Country and from there transported by the French to New Orleans. In time, they are repatriated to England and eventually return to their Pennsylvania homes, ending a long and unusual odyssey.

> Note: Fort Granville, located near present-day Lewistown, Pennsylvania, had been recently built as a protective stockade under orders by Benjamin Franklin.

| Aug. 10–14, 1756 | **New York's Fort Oswego surrenders to General Montcalm—a major loss to the British.** |

Montcalm leads his French troops and allied Indians in a successful siege against the British fort, taking 1,700 men, women, and children as prisoners and seizing 121 British cannons: thereby effectively removing the British and American presence on Lake Ontario.

> Note: Located on the southern shore of Lake Ontario along the main French transportation route connecting New France with the western regions, Fort Oswego represented a major threat to the French, and they wanted it removed.
>
> General Montcalm, in North America only since May, had conducted a successful siege against Oswego, demonstrating that European-style frontal attacks could be effectively used in the North American theater.
>
> Fort Oswego would be reoccupied by the British and Americans the following year.

| Sept. 8, 1756 | **In western Pennsylvania, the Delaware town of *Kittanning* is destroyed.** |

> Note: With a population of nearly 400 residents, Kittanning was the largest Delaware town west of the Allegheny Mountains. Using their forest stronghold as a base, Delaware

> warriors had been launching frontier attacks against the encroaching White settlers, who in turn demanded that the Delaware be punished and forced completely from the region.

A 300-strong Pennsylvania militia led by Lieutenant Colonel John Armstrong attacks Kittanning setting fire to the entire town and shooting the Indians as they flee. Armstrong's men kill and scalp twelve Delaware, including the leader *Tewa*, known to the Whites as *Captain Jacobs,* and retrieve eleven White captives.

> Note: Most of the Delaware had managed to escape before the onslaught and fled westward to the Ohio Country taking their captives with them.
>
> Colonel John Armstrong, now touted as the *Hero of Kittanning*, estimated thirty to forty Indians had been killed in the campaign. For his efforts, Armstrong and his men collected £600 for their Delaware scalps.
>
> Armstrong's brother, Edward, had been killed by Delaware warriors at Pennsylvania's Fort Granville on August 2.

Nov. 1756   **The French press the Iroquois to join them in war against the English.**

Meeting with the French at Montreal, five of the six Iroquois tribes agree to remain neutral in the conflict, but the absent Mohawk will choose to support their British allies.

> Note: In addition, the French had been making inroads with the Southern Cherokee, trying to persuade them to turn against the English.
>
> Though the Kingdom of Great Britain had existed since 1707, most colonials in North America continued to identify as English, Scottish, or Irish, as well as German rather than yield to the more general term, British. The Indians, having used *English* for so many years, continued to classify the Whites generally as either English or French.

1756–1757   **South Carolina constructs *Fort Loudoun* in eastern Tennessee, the heart of the Cherokee Nation.**

> Note: To the British, Fort Loudoun's main purpose was to exert control over the Cherokee and keep away the French, located in Louisiana and extending into the regions of Mississippi and Alabama.
>
> To the Cherokee, Fort Loudoun represented the opening of a coveted trade post among them, symbolizing the promised British protections against their tribal enemies and the neighboring French. In return, the Cherokee agreed to provide 600 warriors to assist the English.

1757   **Needing funds for defense, Pennsylvania's assembly attempts to tax the land holdings of the colony's wealthy proprietors, which have thus far been held tax-free.**

In response, the Penn family will petition the King's Council arguing against it.

> Note: The council would agree with the Penns, calling it an affront to the Crown; nevertheless, in 1760, at the urging of Benjamin Franklin, the Penns would be taxed at the rate of the inhabitants.

Benjamin Franklin travels to England as an agent to represent Pennsylvania.

Franklin, an elected member of the Pennsylvania Assembly, arrives in London to represent the colony's interests and lobby on its behalf.

Jan. 1757 **British troops continue to arrive in New York City.**

The Seven Years' War is now an all-out war with France for control of North America and Great Britain intends to win it. Yet the arrival of so many troops in North America is bittersweet for the American colonials. On one hand, most are glad to see the troops and the protections they represent; on the other, they also represent the long arm of British authority which until now has been relatively absent. In addition, these thousands of new arrivals must be quartered and supplied, which causes burdens on those who are to provide it. For most of the war, that burden will fall mainly, but not exclusively, on the New York Assembly.

Jan. 3, 1757 **All outward-bound ships are prohibited from leaving North American ports.**

In New York, Lord Loudoun issues a temporary general embargo on American colonial trade as he secretly prepares for an upcoming military campaign against Louisbourg. By blocking outward-bound ships, Loudoun hopes to:

- Prevent intelligence from reaching the French.

- Keep vessels and seamen available for the upcoming campaign.

- Halt the illicit trade between the New England and the French sugar islands.

| Note: | Lasting six months, Lord Loudoun's embargo would result in economic pain for most of Britain's American colonies, raising prices on commodities including flour, cod, tobacco, corn, and lumber. In addition, the embargo would create a corn shortage in Great Britain, which imported great quantities from North America. |

Jan. 21, 1757 **The *Battle of the Snowshoes* is fought in upstate New York.**

While reconnoitering Fort Carillon on Lake Champlain, Rogers' Rangers are engaged by French troops and Ottawa warriors and battle to a draw.

| Note: | Fighting on snowshoes, Rogers's men were able to walk upon the snow, whereas the French and Ottawa floundered. The French would note this advantage when they wrote of the battle. |

June 1757 **A British fleet sails from New York to begin the campaign against Louisbourg.**

General John Campbell, aka Lord Loudoun, sails with a large British fleet bound for Halifax, Nova Scotia. Once at Halifax, Loudoun expects to rendezvous with another fleet under the command of British Admiral Francis Holbourne, as well as militia forces from New York and New England.

| Note: | The British believed that the capture of Louisbourg would render Quebec vulnerable, thus forcing France to withdraw troops from the frontier regions to protect Canada. |

June 27, 1757 **Lord Loudoun's embargo on seafaring trade is lifted.**

As the military campaign against Louisbourg gets underway, Lord Loudoun ends the embargo and permits the many harbored vessels to resume their business.

William Pitt becomes Great Britain's secretary of state.

Aug. 3–9, 1757   **French troops and Indian warriors capture Fort William Henry in northern New York.**

Located along the Lake Champlain corridor considered the *gateway to Canada*, the New Englanders have been using Fort William Henry as a staging point for raids against the French, and General Montcalm wants to drive them out. Leading a mixed force of 4,000 French troops, Canadian militiamen, and nearly 2,000 unruly Indians, the French commander successfully lays siege to the British fort.

Note: As part of the surrender terms, General Montcalm promised the fort's occupants—soldiers, women, children, servants, African slaves, and Indian allies—safe passage to the nearby British fort, *Fort Edward*. After taking oaths promising not to resume fighting for eighteen months, the prisoners would begin a sixteen-mile march accompanied by French guards to protect them from possible Indian atrocities.

This was General Montcalm's second successful military siege since his arrival in North America, the first having been against Fort Oswego one year before.

Aug. 10, 1757   **The occupants of Fort William Henry are massacred by Indians.**

Leaving Fort William Henry under a guarantee of safe passage, nearly 2,000 prisoners protected by 200 French troops begin the march southward to Fort Edward. But immediately upon their exit, the Indians quickly rush into the fort's hospital and begin killing the seventeen men left behind. As the slaughter continues, the Indians become increasingly *worked up*, growing ever more menacing and difficult for the French to control.

After killing those in the hospital, the Indians turn their attention to the marching captives. Writing of the slaughter, a private with Colonel Frye's regiment posted at Fort Edward wrote in his diary, "this Day when they Came to march the Savage Indiens Came upon them and Stript them of their Packs and Cloths and the most their Arms   then they Pickt out the negrows Melatows and Indiens and Dragd them Away and we Know not what is Become of them then   they fell to killing our men At A most DRedfull manner   they Ravesht the women and then Put them to the Slaugher young Children of the Regular forces had their Brains Dasht our Against the Stones and trees." For three hours the butchery continues to grow with little protest from the French guards who are rightfully concerned for their own safety. Unarmed and unprotected, many prisoners flee into the woods in search of refuge."

By the time the captives arrive at British Fort Edward, more than 200 have been killed outright and another 300 have been carried away by the Indians to meet their individual fates.

Note: Of the Indians' captives: some would be marched to Montreal to be exchanged for ransom, whereas others would not be as fortunate.

The British and Americans believed the massacre was an intentional treachery committed against unarmed prisoners by the French.

General Montcalm's forces would burn Fort William Henry to the ground before retreating northward.

As some in the fort's hospital had smallpox, the disease would soon spread among the Indians.

Aug. 1757   **The British military campaign against Louisbourg is canceled—for now.**

From Halifax, Admiral Francis Holbourne transports British troops and New England militia forces under the command of Lord Loudoun to begin the assault, but arriving near Louisbourg, the British find the French well prepared with 4,000 troops at the ready and several naval squadrons in the harbor. With Louisbourg so strongly reinforced, the indecisive Lord Loudoun abandons the campaign for now, but orders Admiral Holbourne's naval fleet to continue to patrol the Nova Scotia coast.

Nov. 3, 1757   **Georgia signs a peace treaty with the Creek.**

At war with the French, the southernmost British colony does not wish to also fight the Creek.

Dec. 1757   **British General John Forbes is promoted to brigadier general and given the task of capturing French Fort Duquesne.**

Where Braddock had failed, Brigadier General Forbes plans to succeed. Forbes's mission will be well-planned, well-manned, and well-protected as he slowly makes his way westward building the first road across Pennsylvania.

> Note: Political wrangling would continue between Virginia and Pennsylvania, for both colonies claimed the strategic Ohio Forks and the lands around it. The Virginians believed they would lose their claim to the region if the road was constructed across Pennsylvania. To mollify the Virginians, General Forbes stated that he would also improve *Braddock's Road* leading from Virginia to the Ohio headwaters.

Dec. 24, 1757   **"The rights and laws of an Englishman are carried with him wherever he may go."**

An English court issues the *Pratt–Yorke* opinion in a case involving the East India Tea Company's land acquisitions in India, ruling the following:

- English people carry English law with them wherever they may be. "Let an Englishman go where he will, he carries as much of law and liberty with him, as the nature of things will bear."

- Land is legally owned if it is obtained by the East India Company through negotiations with the inhabitants and not acquired by military force.

> Note: British and American land speculators in North America would view this court decision as also pertaining to the acquisition of Native American lands and interpret the decision to suit their particular legal needs.

1758   **General James Abercrombie replaces Lord Loudon as commander in chief of Britain's military forces in North America.**

Britain's war in North America has not fared well; the loss of Fort Oswego, Fort William Henry, and a canceled campaign against Louisbourg have led to the replacement of the unpopular Lord Loudon.

A second exodus: Additional French Acadians are removed from Nova Scotia.

In midst of another war with France, Britain mistrusts these French Canadians; as such, 4,000 Acadians will be transported to Britain or France.

> Note: During the expulsion of 1755–1756, large numbers of Acadians had been relocated to Britain's other North American colonies. But as the Americans had so vigorously protested their arrival, this time the French Catholics would be sent to Europe.

The first school in North America for Black children is opened in Philadelphia.

Sponsored by the Bray Associates, an Anglican philanthropic society, the school is opened despite opposition by White Philadelphians.

March 13, 1758 **In New York, Rogers' Rangers are decimated in the *Second Battle of the Snowshoes*.**

Leading 180 men from Fort Edward on a reconnaissance mission against Fort Carillon, Rogers engages in heated battle with French troops and their Nipissing allies, narrowly escaping with his life as nearly 140 of his men are killed or wounded.

May 29, 1758 **The long-anticipated campaign against Louisbourg gets underway as the British fleet sails from Halifax.**

Led by General Jeffery Amherst, the British forces at Halifax have been intensively training for the assault. But unlike the previous summer, this time the British are determined to succeed.

June–Nov. 1758 **The construction of *Forbes Road* begins a second campaign to capture Fort Duquesne.**

In Carlisle, Pennsylvania, with a force of 6,000 men accompanied by Indian allies, British General John Forbes begins constructing a road through Pennsylvania's wilderness to the Ohio Forks with the goal of capturing Fort Duquesne and driving the French from the region.

Still feeling the sting of General Braddock's 1755 defeat, General Forbes is determined not to repeat it. Therfore, Forbes orders that fortifications be built a day's journey apart as the expedition moves methodically westward. In addition, the sheer size of this military force helps ensure that the troops and roadbuilders will be unmolested.

Note:	Forbes's forces consisted of 4,000 Americans from Pennsylvania, Virginia, and North Carolina; 2,000 British regulars composed mainly of Scottish Highlanders; plus Indian allies—mostly Cherokee and Catawba warriors.
	The Forbes Road, nearly 200 miles in length, would make travel to the Ohio River much easier and help connect the isolated region to eastern Pennsylvania and the colonial capital, Philadelphia.

June 8, 1758 **The British siege against Louisbourg begins.**

An overwhelming force of 14,000 British troops and 200 New England rangers begins a land and sea assault against the mighty French fortress. Slow to begin, the bombardment dramatically increases in intensity once the British are able to establish effective positions.

July 8, 1758 **In New York's frontier, the British suffer a disastrous defeat at the *Battle of Carillon*.**

Led by General James Abercrombie, 15,000 British troops assisted by colonial militiamen from New England, New York, and New Jersey attempt to capture French Fort Carillon defended by General Louis-Joseph Montcalm. With superior numbers, Abercrombie battles a well-entrenched French force of 3,500 outside the fortress walls in a poorly planned assault. Without the support of cannons, Abercrombie launches several frontal attacks against the French line, but the British troops are "cut down like grass" under a barrage of withering fire.

During the intense lopsided battle, 2,000 British regulars are killed or wounded; the New York and New England troops lose 300; and the French but 350. In addition, General George Howe—considered by some to be the best general in the British Army—is killed in the assault.

Note:	General George Howe was the older brother of General William Howe and Admiral Richard Howe—both destined to play major roles leading British troops in the American War for Independence.

July 26, 1758   **Fort Louisbourg—the guardian of New France—surrenders.**

Under siege for seven weeks, the British naval guns have had their effect, reducing the fort's stone walls and interior buildings. Now, after mounting stout resistance, the outnumbered French surrender to General Jeffery Amherst.

Note:	This was the second conquest of Louisbourg. The French fortress had been first captured by New England troops in 1745 during King George's War but was returned to France three years later by the Treaty of Aix-la-Chapelle.
	The fall of Louisbourg would open the St. Lawrence River to British forces intent on securing Quebec.
	Casualty numbers vary, but losses were approximately 500 British dead or wounded and 172 French.

The term *Yankee* is used to describe the New Englanders.

British officers, when interacting with the Americans, often consider themselves superior and more refined than their *country cousins*. As such, many treat the colonial officials, militia troops, and citizens with a certain amount of haughty contempt and would begin referring to them as *Yankees*, generally meaning a simpleton or fool.

Note:	In a turnabout, the derisive moniker would be proudly embraced by the Americans.
	Though thoroughly researched, the exact origin of the term *Yankee* is unclear. The first known use of the word is attributed to British General James Wolfe during the 1758 Louisbourg campaign.

Summer 1758   **The Forbes expedition continues its slow progress across Pennsylvania's frontier.**

Note:	Due to being severely ill, General Forbes would lag behind during most of the expedition, leaving much of the command to the Swiss mercenary Colonel Henry Bouquet.
	The Western Tribes were extremely alarmed by news of a road being constructed into the heart of their country, west of the Allegheny Mountains.

Aug. 28, 1758   **Fort Frontenac surrenders to an army of American militiamen.**

British Colonel John Bradstreet leads 135 British regulars and 3,000 New York and New England militiamen against the important French fort and trade post located on Lake Ontario's northeastern shore. Beginning the bombardment on August 26, Bradstreet's forces easily overwhelm the 100 French soldiers defending the fort.

Note:	Constructed in 1673, Fort Frontenac commanded a vital position connecting the St. Lawrence River with Lake Ontario and thus served as an important link between New France and the French lands to the west and south.
	In 1764, Colonel Bradstreet would lead a rather inglorious expedition to Detroit during the Indian war known today as *Pontiac's Rebellion*.

Aug. 29, 1758   **The *Brotherton Reservation* is established—the first Indian reservation in North America.**

After buying the remaining Delaware (Lenape) lands in New Jersey, approximately 200 Christian Delaware, known locally as the *Brotherton Community*, are permitted to remain in the colony and are allotted a 3,000-acre reservation near modern Shamong Township. Overseen by Reverend John

116

Brainerd, the reservation operates a saw and grist mill but never becomes financially successful. In addition, White incursions onto reservation lands will bring disunity to the tribe.

> Note: On January 6, 1780, the Brotherton would issue a proclamation declaring that all White incursions upon their land must stop and that any past agreements permitting their use were void. The Delaware would state their goal as "living in better friendship with the whites," for "there is some which does not like white people for their Neighbours, for fear of their not agreeing as they ought to do."
>
> The Brotherton Reservation would be sold by the state of New Jersey in 1801, with the profits dispersed among the tribal members. The following year, most of the remaining Christian Delaware would either join with the Oneida in New Stockbridge, New York, or integrate among New Jersey's White communities.

Aug.–Sept. 1758   **General Forbes sends advance troops to construct *Fort Loyalhanna* within fifty miles of Fort Duquesne.**

Nearing his objective, Forbes sends Major James Grant ahead to prepare fortifications to be used as a base for the British Army. It is from here that General Forbes plans to ready his troops for the assault against the French fort.

Early Sept. 1758   **Virginia Colonel George Washington joins the Forbes expedition.**

Washington, leading the First Virginia Regiment, joins the expedition near modern Raystown Lake, Pennsylvania.

> Note: As a Virginian and a member of the Ohio Land Company, Washington was not in favor of the road being built across Pennsylvania, believing it would hurt Virginia by cementing Pennsylvania's claims to the Ohio Forks.

Sept. 1758   **Britain's North American commander in chief, General James Abercrombie, is replaced by General Jeffery Amherst.**

London has learned of Abercrombie's disastrous defeat attempting to capture French Fort Carillon, and of the death of his second-in-command, General George Howe. Consequently, General Abercrombie is recalled to England and replaced by General Amherst.

> Note: Amherst was now the fifth commander in chief of Britain's North American war against the French, after: General Edward Braddock in 1755, killed by Indians; Massachusetts Governor William Shirley, who temporarily replaced Braddock from 1755 to 1756; General John Campbell, commonly known as Lord Loudoun, commander in chief from 1756 to 1757; and General James Abercrombie, from 1757 to 1758.

Sept. 14, 1758   **British and Virginia troops are slaughtered in the *Battle of Fort Duquesne*.**

Acting without orders, British Major James Grant leads 800 troops, including the 1st Highland Regiment, from the newly constructed Fort Loyalhanna to reconnoiter Fort Duquesne. Falsely believing Fort Duquesne contains few defenders, Grant decides to attack. Hoping their presence remains undetected, Major Grant prepares a ruse to ambush the unsuspecting French as they rush from the fort.

The attack begins by the Scottish Highlanders announcing themselves with beating drums and blaring bagpipes to the surprised French. Unfortunately for the British, the tables are quickly turned as Major Grant is captured and his troops—both British and Virginian—suffer nearly 350 casualties, including many taken as captives, whereas the French and Indians lose but eight.

Note:	Though Major Grant's forces had suffered defeat—the main British Army was still approaching and the French wondered what could be done to halt its advance; Fort Duquesne contained only 600 French regulars, some Indian allies, and the fort's walls were too thin to ward off cannon fire.
	Accompanying Major Grant were Virginia troops under the command of Virginia Colonel Andrew Lewis. Though assigned to guard the rear baggage, Lewis and his men had rushed forward during the battle to assist the British troops resulting in Lewis's capture. Taken to Quebec, Colonel Lewis would be released in late 1759.

Oct. 12, 1758

The British camp—Fort Loyalhanna—is attacked by French and Indian forces from Fort Duquesne.

Attempting to thwart the British advance, French troops and several hundred Indian warriors launch a pre-emptive strike against Fort Loyalhanna before General Braddock and the main body of British troops can arrive. After four hours of battle, the French and Indians fail to take the fort and retreat to Fort Duquesne.

Oct. 26, 1758

The *Treaty of Easton* brings an uneasy Indian peace in Pennsylvania.

The royal governors of New Jersey and Pennsylvania gather with more than 500 Indians representing thirteen tribal nations in Easton, Pennsylvania, near Philadelphia. Meeting for a week, colonial representatives work to bring an end to their conflict with the Shawnee and Delaware, and to keep the tribes from allying with the French—particularly in the defense of Fort Duquesne.

The following form part of the agreement:

- Most of the attending tribes agree to neutrality in the war between the French and English.

- The Iroquois relinquish their claims to New Jersey lands after Governor Bernard agrees to pay the tribe 800 Spanish Dollars.

- The Delaware (Lenape) agree to relinquish claims to their remaining lands in New Jersey in exchange for large blocks of lands west of the Susquehanna River.

- The Allegheny Mountains are designated as the western boundary for White settlement and the lands of the Ohio Valley westward are reserved for the Indians.

Note:	The Delaware were still aching over being cheated in the Walking Purchase of 1737.
	In 1754, the Iroquois had sold the Wyoming Valley to Connecticut's Susquehanna Company for £2,000 angering the Delaware who claimed the land as their own. In the future, the Pennsylvania governor would agree to treat directly with the Delaware instead of going through the Six Nations.
	The tribes were very concerned about the construction of the Forbes Road across their lands and the presence of the British troops. To allay this concern, the Indians were assured that the soldiers would leave once the French were defeated and their lands would be returned. For these and other reasons, the tribes agreed to stay neutral.
	The Treaty of Easton would serve as a forerunner to Britain's Proclamation of 1763 barring White intrusions into the Indian lands west of the Appalachian Mountains.

Nov. 3, 1758

Nearly 4,000 troops—British regulars, Virginians, and allied Indian warriors—are assembled at Fort Loyalhanna.

Unsure whether to attack or make winter quarters, a vote is taken: the troops shall prepare winter quarters and attack Fort Duquesne in the spring.

> Note: Beginning the expedition in June with approximately 6,000 men, Forbes's numbers had been reduced along the way due to: desertions; captures (General Grant and his men); manning the new fortifications built along the way; and other sundry acts leading to the attrition.

Nov. 12, 1758   **George Washington's troops engage in a deadly firefight with fellow Virginians outside Fort Loyalhanna.**

Responding to reports of a French and Indian raiding party approaching from Fort Duquesne, General Forbes dispatches Virginia Colonel George Mercer and his 2nd Virginia Regiment to find and engage the enemy.

In the late afternoon, hearing distant gunshots, General Forbes sends Colonel George Washington and his 1st Virginia Regiment to assist Mercer. Not arriving until nightfall, the two groups nearly collide in the dark woods and Mercer's men—believing Washington's regiment to be French troops—begin a firefight with their fellow Virginians. By the time the mistake is realized, of the 500 troops involved, fourteen are dead, and another twenty-six are wounded.

> Note: The Virginia firefight would be the last military engagement by the Forbes expedition.
>
> The only account of the fight, written by a participant, placed the fault on Colonel Washington. Yet in later years, Washington would blame it all on his friend Colonel George Mercer and paint himself as the hero.
>
> Fighting in uniform for the French, Richard Johnson of Lancaster, Pennsylvania, was taken prisoner by Colonel Mercer. Claiming he had been captured and forced into service, Johnson informed General Forbes: the French were short on supplies; Fort Duquesne was weakly defended; and many of the Indians were deserting. As such, Forbes changed his plan and decided to attack the French fort immediately.

Nov. 14, 1758   **The Forbes expedition begins an advance against Fort Duquesne—only fifty miles away.**

Forced to follow the roadbuilders, General Forbes's army slowly ebbs its way westward, fully expecting to engage the French within a week to ten days.

Nov. 25, 1758   **The French retreat after destroying Fort Duquesne.**

Unable to successfully oppose the approaching British Army, French commander François-Marie Le Marchand de Lignery orders the fort destroyed as the French troops begin an eighty-five-mile retreat northward to Fort Machault during the dark of night.

> Note: Fort Duquesne was destroyed by igniting eighty barrels of gunpowder, causing an explosion that could be heard for miles.

The British and Virginia troops arrive at Fort Duquesne and find it deserted.

Buoyed by his success, the jubilant General Forbes names the site *Pittsburgh* in honor of William Pitt, leader of Parliament's House of Commons, and renames Fort Loyalhanna as *Fort Ligonier* in honor of Britain's Commander in Chief of the Forces, Sir John Ligonier.

> Note: The British were greeted with the appalling sight of Major Grant's mutilated Highlanders. Surrounding the fort, the Indians had placed the Scotsmen's heads and kilts atop pike poles to serve as a warning to the approaching troops.

General Forbes—ill for nearly the entire expedition—would become worse, suffering severe dysentery. Placing Colonel Henry Bouquet in command of the expedition, Forbes would depart Fort Ligonier on Dec. 3. Transported by litter to Philadelphia, General Forbes would die four months later, probably of stomach cancer.

Late 1758

The *Anglo-Cherokee War* begins and soon spreads throughout the frontier regions of Tennessee, Virginia, and the Carolinas.

A three-year war begins when a group of Cherokee warriors returning to their homes after assisting the Forbes expedition, steal horses while passing through Virginia. In retaliation, Virginians attack and kill twenty Cherokee and claim the scalps are Shawnee in order to collect the bounty. In revenge for the murders, the Cherokee launch attacks on White settlements in North Carolina and the conflict quickly escalates. As the war spreads in scope, the entire southern frontier will be at war with the Indians at their western doors.

> Note: The Cherokee accompanying General Forbes had been promised goods and presents that were not forthcoming. These and other issues had caused them to abandon the expedition in disgust and return to their homes.
>
> Operating out of *Fort Toulouse* near the confluence of the Coosa and Alabama Rivers, the French were busily lobbying the Cherokee to abandon their British allies and to instead "drive them from their lands."
>
> Due to the outbreak of hostilities, trading powder and lead to the Cherokee would be forbidden, but the French—at war with the British—were quite happy to provide it.
>
> The 1758–1761 Anglo-Cherokee War would also be known as the *War with those in Red Coats*, or the *War with the English*.

1759

Britain's naval forces defeat the Spanish and French fleets in the West Indies, capturing many of their island colonies.

> Note: Some islands would be returned following the conclusion of the Seven Years' War, but others, including Grenada and Tobago, would be retained by Great Britain.

Spring 1759

The construction of *Fort Pitt* begins at the Ohio Forks.

Under the command of Colonel Henry Bouquet, construction of the Britain's Fort Pitt begins at the confluence of the Allegheny and Monongahela Rivers. The frontier fortress is to be a large and elaborate structure meant to project an image of power to the Indians and the French.

> Note: Pittsburgh, located at the head of the Ohio River, would become a *gateway to the interior* for the future United States as thousands of settlers would use the site as a launch point for traveling west.

July 6, 1759

French Fort Niagara comes under attack by British troops and American colonial forces.

British General John Prideaux leads 2,000 British regulars, 1,000 New York and Rhode Island militiamen, and 1,000 Iroquois warriors in a siege against Fort Niagara—defended by a mere 200 French regulars and 300 French-Canadians.

> Note: On July 19, General Prideaux would be killed by a shell fragment. Prideaux's command would be filled by British Indian Superintendent William Johnson, who had accompanied the army and was responsible for the support of the Iroquois warriors.

Early July 1759

The French cancel a counterattack against Fort Pitt.

At Fort Machault, additional troops and supplies have arrived as the French prepare to retake control of the Ohio Forks before the British fort can be completed. But as more than 2,000 French regulars, French Canadians, and Indians ready themselves, the attack is called off. Having received news that Fort Niagara is currently under siege, the French troops instead hurry northward in hopes of relieving the strategic post.

July 23–26, 1759 **The *Battle of Ticonderoga*: The French abandon Fort Carillon under a British onslaught.**

Led by General Jeffery Amherst, a 12,000-strong army of British troops, supported by New York and New England militiamen, lays siege to the French fortress in upstate New York. After sustaining three days of cannon bombardment, Fort Carillon's 400 French defenders evacuate during the night, but before leaving, they try to render the fort useless by igniting the powder magazine. The explosion fails to destroy the fort's walls and the British take occupation the following day.

> Note: One year earlier, British General James Abercrombie had disastrously failed to capture Fort Carillon. Now, under the leadership of General Jeffery Amherst, the tide of war seemed to be turning against the French.
>
> The British would rename Fort Carillon as *Fort Ticonderoga*. Ticonderoga was an Iroquois word meaning "between two waters."

July 26, 1759 **Fort Niagara is captured by British, American, and Iroquois forces.**

After sustaining a three-week siege, the fort's commander Captain Pierre Pouchot surrenders.

> Note: Located between Lake Erie and Lake Ontario, Fort Niagara was an essential link connecting New France with its western lands in North America. The fort's capitulation represented a major prize for the British.
>
> The French had lost Louisbourg, Fort Frontenac, Fort Duquesne, Fort Carillon, and now Fort Niagara as the British noose seemed to be tightening.

Aug. 1759 **The French destroy their remaining Pennsylvania forts and abandon the region.**

The French decide to consolidate their military forces to save their higher priority—New France itself. As such, the untenable Fort Machault, Fort Le Boeuf, and Fort Presque Isle are ordered destroyed as the French troops retreat to Canada in hopes of saving Montreal and Quebec.

Sept. 13, 1759 **The *Battle for Quebec*: A climactic battle of the Seven Years' War in North America.**

British General James Wolfe leads an attack force of 4,400 against the French fortress of Quebec. During the night, Wolfe's troops secretly scramble up a cliff and assemble on the plain outside the fort surprising French General Montcalm, who had expected their approach from another direction. In command of a 4,500-strong French army, Montcalm chooses to engage the British directly in a frontal assault rather than staying inside the secure fortress and awaiting reinforcements.

Both commanders suffer fatal wounds during the hour-long battle. British General James Wolfe dies soon after being struck three times, whereas French General Louis-Joseph Montcalm—wounded twice during the French retreat—dies the following day.

Sept. 18, 1759 **A great British victory—the French surrender Quebec.**

> Note: The death of General Montcalm and fall of Quebec were severe blows to France.
>
> In April 1760, France would unsuccessfully attempt to recapture Quebec.

> Previously, Quebec had been captured only once—in 1629 by forces led by Englishmen David Kirke during the 1627–1629 Anglo-French War.

Oct. 4, 1759 **French-allied Abenaki are massacred at the Jesuit mission *Saint Francis*.**

Having traveled 185 miles north from Crown Point to destroy the Abenaki town, Rogers' Rangers surprise the Indian residents and mercilessly slaughter nearly 200 old men, women, and children.

After freeing the English captives and collecting Indian scalps for bounty, Rogers and his men flee southward but are soon pursued by Abenaki warriors. During their forest flight, the group is forced to endure starvation and depravations, with reports of cannibalism to stay alive.

> Note: Saint Francis, located near modern Pierreville, Quebec, was regularly used as a base for launching Abenaki raids against the English settlements to the south. Therefore, reports of the massacre would generate little sympathy in New England and New York.
>
> Due to his atrocities against them, the Abenaki would name Robert Rogers—the *White Devil*.

Oct. 17, 1759 **A Cherokee peace delegation arrives at Charles Town, South Carolina, hoping to parley with the royal governor.**

The Cherokee, numbering eighty in total, return homeward after Governor Lyttelton refuses to meet.

Mid-Oct. 1759 **South Carolina Governor William Lyttelton declares all-out war against the Cherokee.**

Dec. 9, 1759 **Cherokee leaders are made prisoners at *Fort Prince George*, South Carolina.**

Arriving at the frontier fort on their return from Charles Town, twenty-two Cherokee headmen are taken prisoner at the orders of Governor Lyttleton, but the rest are free to go. Placed in chains, the Cherokee hostages are to be released only in exchange for those warriors responsible for the recent frontier attacks.

> Note: Fort Prince George was located near present-day Six-Mile, South Carolina.

Mid-1700s **American colonials—particularly New Englanders—are much involved in maritime trade; transporting goods between Great Britain, North America, the West Indies, and Africa.**

This lucrative trade system has created wealth and social standing for many North American transporters and colonial merchants.

> Note: In future years, many of these powerful and influential merchants and shippers would wield oppositional powers to Britain's royal colonial governors in America.

The majority of Africans arriving in North America pass through Sullivan's Island, South Carolina.

Unloaded as human chattel, the Africans are sorted and inspected to confirm that they are disease-free before being sold at the slave market in Charles Town.

> Note: Arriving directly from Africa, these slaves—derogatorily referred to as *Saltwaters*—were less valued than those born in North America due to being generally more troublesome, independent, and *resistant to the yoke*.

Jan. 1760   **Smallpox is raging in South Carolina, affecting Whites, Africans, and Indians.**

Jan. 26, 1760   **With Fort Loudoun under Cherokee threats, a slave volunteers to carry an emergency message to the South Carolina governor.**

Fort Loudoun's commander, British Captain Paul Demere, offers a slave, Abraham, his freedom if he is willing to travel through the hostile Cherokee territory and deliver an urgent request for assistance to Governor Lyttleton at Charles Town.

> Note: Two previous messengers, a British soldier and an unnamed courier, had been killed attempting to get past the Cherokee warriors surrounding the fort.
>
> The attack against Fort Loudoun was partially in response to the Cherokee leaders taken captive at Fort Prince George.
>
> Located 400 miles west of Charles Town at present-day Vonore, Tennessee, Fort Loudoun was the most remote British fort in the Carolinas.

Abraham agrees and walks the first leg of his journey to Fort Prince George, then onward to *Fort Ninety-Six*. There, given a horse to finish his journey, Abraham arrives at Charles Town on February 13—nineteen days after leaving Fort Loudoun.

> Note: Abraham's story would be printed in the *South Carolina Gazette* three days after his arrival and Charles Town residents would learn of his heroic actions. As promised, Abraham received his freedom.

Feb. 1760   **In New York, the Mohawk complain to British Indian Superintendent William Johnson of the continued encroachment of their lands.**

Feb. 1, 1760   **In South Carolina, Cherokee warriors attack a wagon train carrying 150 fleeing refugees.**

Abandoning the settlement of Long Cane for the safety of *Fort Moore,* the slow-moving caravan becomes bogged down and is attacked by 100 Cherokee warriors. Twenty-three settlers are killed, fourteen are captured, and nine children are scalped but manage to survive.

> Note: Known in history as the *Long Cane Massacre*, the dead were later buried in a mass grave near present-day Troy, North Carolina.
>
> Future South Carolina Senator John C. Calhoun's grandmother, Catherine, was among those killed.

Feb. 3, 1760   **Cherokee warriors attack Fort Ninety-Six, South Carolina.**

The Cherokee attack the remote frontier garrison, whose defenders, according to the *South Carolina Gazette*, consist of "33 resolute White Men and 12 Stout Negroes, all armed." After attempting to take the fort and shooting from the woods for hours, the Indians quit the attack and burn the settlement's abandoned houses to the ground.

Feb. 16, 1760   **The Cherokee hostages at Fort Prince George, South Carolina, are massacred.**

In a botched attempt to free their chiefs, Cherokee warriors lure the commander, British Lieutenant Richard Cotymore, from the fort and kill him. During the ensuing melee, the Indian prisoners manage to stab two of their White guards before all Cherokee hostages are shot down by the fort's panicked occupants.

> Note: Of the original twenty-two Cherokee leaders taken captive on December 9, three had earlier escaped and five had died, leaving fourteen prisoners. Now, all fourteen headmen were dead, and the Cherokee would respond with fury.

Feb. 27, 1760   **Cherokee warriors attack *Fort Dobbs*, North Carolina.**

The only fort in North Carolina's frontier area, Fort Dobbs, is besieged by sixty Cherokee, who are eventually driven off by the superior firepower of the fort's garrison.

March 3, 1760   **In South Carolina, Fort Ninety-Six is attacked a second time.**

Though the fort has been reinforced since the February attack, the garrison is currently suffering a smallpox outbreak. For two days, 250 Cherokee warriors attack Fort Ninety-Six before finally retreating as a South Carolina relief force approaches.

> Note: As an isolated post and settlement located along the well-traveled *Cherokee Path*— Fort Ninety-Six was an easy target.
>
> The post had received its name due to being ninety-six miles from the nearest Cherokee village, *Keowe.*

South Carolina requests British military assistance to quell the Cherokee hostilities.

Royal Governor William Lyttelton writes to the British commander in chief, General Jeffery Amherst, in New York, requesting that he send troops to Charles Town to campaign against the overwhelming Cherokee.

March 20, 1760   **Cherokee warriors begin a near five-month siege of the isolated Fort Loudoun.**

Boston is devastated by the *Great Fire* of 1760—the largest fire in the city's history.

Three hundred and fifty buildings are destroyed as the fire races on, leaving 1,000 residents without habitation.

> Note: Boston had burned previously in October 1711. Hence, the 1760 fire is often referred to as Boston's *Second Great Fire.*

April–May 1760   **British troops arrive at Charles Town to campaign against the Cherokee.**

General Jeffery Amherst has redeployed 1,500 British regulars from New York under the command of Colonel Archibald Montgomerie to assist South Carolina.

> Note: Great Britain's war to conquer New France had been going well, with only Montreal yet to be taken. As such, Amherst had enough manpower to send troops to South Carolina.

May 1760   **British regulars set out to punish the Cherokee and relieve the beleaguered frontier forts.**

Colonel Montgomerie leads a combined force of British regulars, Carolina militiamen, and Catawba warriors into the Cherokee country of western North Carolina. Using the well-established practice for reducing the Indians to submission, Montgomerie's army attacks the Cherokee with superior firepower; burns their towns; and destroys their food stocks, whether stored or in the fields.

May–July 1760   *Tacky's Rebellion*: **Britain is shocked by a vast slave uprising in Jamaica.**

The revolt involves hundreds of enslaved Africans who join with *Tacky,* a former African chief, in an attempt to kill the Whites and take over the entire island. Launching their attack, the Africans enjoy initial success, but Tacky is eventually killed and his followers are hunted down by Jamaica's Maroon militias. By the rebellion's end, nearly 400 Africans are killed, 600 will be sent to Honduras, and the Jamaican slave codes become more restrictive.

> Note: With the White population of Jamaica greatly outnumbered by the African slaves, all rebellions would be crushed with utmost severity to deter others. In addition, news of any such revolts, large or small, would always to be suppressed to keep such ideas from spreading.

The British build *Fort Venango* in western Pennsylvania.

The French abandoned Pennsylvania the previous summer to focus their military strength on protecting New France. Now, without a French presence in the region, the British finish Fort Pitt and begin construction of Fort Venango—a small post located near former French Fort Machault at the strategic confluence of the Allegheny River and French Creek.

> Note: With the French troops vacating the western regions, it was important that Britain quickly fill the void to prevent French reoccupation and to assert themselves over the French-allied tribes.

June 27, 1760   **In North Carolina, the Cherokee repulse British forces at the *Battle of Echoee Pass*.**

Colonel Archibald Montgomerie leads 1,200 British regulars and Carolina militiamen to attack the Cherokee Middle Town of *Echoe,* but the Cherokee strike first.

Near modern Otto, North Carolina, warriors led by *Oconostota* attack the advancing army in a preemptive strike killing twenty men and wounding seventy, forcing Colonel Montgomerie to turn his troops around. After leaving most of his supplies and the wounded at Fort Prince George, Colonel Montgomerie and his men continue their retreat to Charles Town.

> Note: Part of Montgomerie's mission had been to relieve Fort Loudoun, under siege by Cherokee warriors since March 20. Instead, the isolated frontier fort would be left to its fate.
>
> Colonel Montgomerie would return to New York in August, after placing his second-in-command, British Major James Grant, in charge of the Cherokee campaign.

July 4, 1760   **Frederick Calvert accepts the 1732 border agreement between Pennsylvania and Maryland.**

The border survey around northern Delaware had begun earlier but was halted after Frederick Calvert, the 6th Lord Baltimore, protested that Maryland was not bound by the 1732 agreement. Now, under pressure from the king, Calvert relents, paving the way for an official survey to be made between the two quarreling colonies.

Summer 1760   **The British build *Fort Schlosser* near Niagara Falls to control the strategic portage between Lake Erie and Lake Ontario.**

The British are attempting to establish control over the transportation routes between New France and the western regions as the Seven Years' War continues to wind down. Already having built and manned forts along the important Venango Path, the British now fortify the *Niagara Portage.*

> Note: The Seneca considered Fort Schlosser an intrusion into their lands and a threat to the tribe's control of the portage trail around Niagara Falls.

Though the tribes of the Iroquois League were usually in agreement, this was not always the case. The British relationship with the Western Seneca was the least secure of the Six Nations.

| 1760 | **In New York, American colonials aboard the *Sampson* fire upon an approaching barge from the HBS *Winchester* to avoid impressment.** |

Killing several British sailors by their action, the seamen flee their ship and disappear into the city, concealed from the sheriff and the militia sent to apprehend them.

| Aug. 7, 1760 | **In desperation, Fort Loudoun surrenders to the Cherokee under promise of safety.** |

Under siege since March, the isolated frontier settlers—180 men and 60 women and children—have been starved to submission and surrender after being promised safe passage to South Carolina's Fort Prince George, 160 miles to the east.

Note: As part of the surrender terms, the fort's occupants agreed to leave behind all gunpowder. Instead, the group buried it hoping to deceive the *savages*. After the settlers began their trek to Fort Prince George, the Indians would discover the gunpowder. The deception only added to their fury.

| Aug. 8, 1760 | **The survivors of Fort Loudoun are attacked in an act of Cherokee retribution.** |

Having camped for the night, the famished survivors are attacked at daybreak by 700 Cherokee warriors. Able to offer little resistance, the large group is taken captive, and the Indians kill twenty-four White captives in revenge for the Cherokee headmen killed at Fort Prince George in February.

Note: Included among those killed was the fort's commander, British Captain Paul Demere. Having been particularly rude and haughty to the Cherokee, the Indians singled out Demere for punishment. After scalping Captain Demere, the Cherokee forced him to entertain them by dancing, then horrendously killed him in front of the other captives.

The French in Louisiana would rejoice at the news of Fort Loudoun's destruction, considered a trespass on French-claimed lands.

| Sept. 8, 1760 | **Montreal, the last French bastion in Canada, surrenders, ending most of the fighting in the North American theater of the Seven Years' War.** |

With Quebec under British control and little hope for victory, the last French governor of New France, Pierre de Rigaud, surrenders Montreal to British General Jeffery Amherst.

Note: French Louisiana—as well as France's westernmost forts, including Fort Detroit—had remained relatively unscathed, as most of the war had been fought in the northeast regions of New France.

Fighting between France and Great Britain would continue in Europe, finally ending with the Treaty of Paris 1763.

Though the French would surrender to the British—their Indian allies would not. Stung by the events, the French-allied tribes would war alone against the English.

| Sept. 1760 | **Sir Jeffery Amherst is appointed governor general of British North America.** |

General Amherst becomes the first governor of the new *British Quebec*, serving until 1763.

Oct. 25, 1760   **King George II dies, and George William Frederick becomes Britain's King George III.**

George II, the last foreign-born British monarch and currently the oldest, dies at age seventy-seven while sitting on the toilet. The king's grandson, Prince George William Frederick is heir to the throne due to his father, Prince Friedrich, having died nine years earlier.

> Note: George III's coronation would not take place until September 22, 1761.
>
> Only twenty-two years old, George William Frederick would be often called the *Boy King* during his early reign.
>
> King George III, being the first Hanoverian monarch to have been born in England, would use this fact to reassure those Britons yet harboring anti-German sentiments by declaring in his accession speech, "Born and educated in this country, I glory in the name of Britain."

George III inherits Britain's Seven Years' War—and the necessity of securing revenues to wage it.

As such, the young king and his administration will authorize better enforcement of Britain's Navigation Acts, which have been largely ignored and are difficult to enforce.

> Note: The American colonials had been permitted to: govern themselves; elect their own officials; enact their own laws; and tax themselves for the purpose of their own internal needs. This policy, referred to today as *salutary neglect,* had created a false sense of autonomy, or independence, from Britain's authority—particularly among the independent-minded New Englanders.

Nov. 29, 1760   **Fort Detroit is transferred to the British as the French continue to vacate the western regions.**

> Note: After the fall of Montreal, the governor-general of New France had surrendered Canada, including Fort Detroit, to the British.
>
> The French-allied tribes would be alarmed at the change of events, for the *English* had long been their hated foes.

1761   **In need of revenue, Britain decides to better enforce the 1733 Molasses Act.**

To assist the royal government in its crackdown on colonial smuggling and the ongoing evasion of duties, Massachusetts Governor Francis Bernard approves the use of *writs of assistance* authorizing custom house officials to inspect for suspected goods that have ducked the tax.

> Note: Writs of assistance were court-ordered general search warrants granting customs officers authority to search any building, ship, or private home when seeking contraband. In addition, the writs granted the customs officers authority to call on American colonial officials (e.g., sheriffs, justices of the peace, and constables) to assist them in the execution of their duties.

George Washington inherits his brother's Virginia estate, Mount Vernon.

Lawrence Washington had died in 1752 at his Mount Vernon home and now, upon the death of his widowed wife Anne Fairfax, Mount Vernon is inherited by Lawrence's younger brother, George.

> Note: Lawrence Washington's brother Augustine, also older than George, had been given first-inheritance rights but he instead chose other properties, enabling George to receive the Mount Vernon estate.

To assert themselves over the French-allied tribes of the Great Lakes, the British build *Fort Sandusky* at the western end of Lake Erie.

Fort Sandusky is to be but one of several forts linking Fort Pitt with Fort Detroit.

> Note: As the British began to take control of the former French lands, they would need to assert their authority by establishing a presence amongst the Western Tribes. As such, British troops would reoccupy many of the former French forts and begin the construction of additional others.

South Carolina's *Bounty Act* of 1761 encourages immigration to the colony.

With the Seven Years War and the Cherokee War nearly concluded, and the anticipation of Cherokee lands being opened for settlement, South Carolina passes the 1761 Bounty Act to encourage White immigration to the colony. The Act offers shippers £4 sterling cash for each Protestant passenger brought from Europe willing to settle in the *upcountry* of South Carolina.

> Note: South Carolina also encouraged and assisted Ireland's poor to migrate—if they were Protestants.
>
> As in Britain's other North American colonies, the recent arrivals to South Carolina—nearly always taking the contested western lands at the edge of *Indian Country*—would serve as a safety buffer for the more-established citizens of the eastern regions.

Feb. 24, 1761   **In Massachusetts, opposition arises to Great Britain's authority over the American colonies.**

Thirty-six-year-old James Otis, advocate general of the Admiralty Court in Boston, is requested to provide military escorts for royal customs officers and to promote support for writs of assistance. Instead, Otis takes the side of Boston's merchants and in an infuriated four-hour speech denounces the writs, declaring them to be "unconstitutional instruments of tyranny."

> John Adams would describe the scene sixty years later, recalling, "Otis was a flame of fire! … He burned everything before him. American independence was then and there born…"
>
> James Otis would resign his position as a British senior law officer and instead chose to represent the Boston merchants and maritime transporters.

Feb. 1761   **With the French threat in North America nearly eliminated, British General Jeffery Amherst reduces gift distributions to the Indians.**

> Note: A trade vacuum soon developed as the French bid *adieu* to their Indian allies and vacated the Great Lakes and western regions. With the French gone, the tribes had nowhere to turn for trade goods other than the despised English traders.

The Indians, accustomed to gift-giving and distributions by the Whites, have become dependent on them, and now General Amherst, having little respect for the Indian people, orders cuts to reduce costs and thus further alienates the tribes. British Superintendent of Northern Indian Affairs William Johnson warns Amherst against reducing the Indian trade gifts, but his advice is ignored. Johnson then writes, "Our people in general are ill calculated to maintain friendship with the Indians. They despise those in peace whom they fear to meet in war."

> Note: Like most people, the Indians preferred the efficiency, ease, and comforts that the European trade goods provided. Guns eased hunting and made a tribe more powerful, giving them an advantage over enemies. Copper pots and pans, mirrors, fire starters, knives, axes, hatchets, shovels, alcohol, beads, woven wool products, rope, fabrics and clothing, tea, sugar, wheat flour, candy, hats, rings, bells, playing cards—all and more were regularly traded to the tribes.

John Stuart is appointed as British Indian Superintendent for the Southern Department.

Former Superintendent Edmond Atkin has died, and Stuart, a Charles Town merchant, is appointed to replace him. Now, with John Stuart located in Charles Town and William Johnson in New York, the two Indian superintendents will wield much power and influence over Britain's policies with the tribes of Eastern North America.

> Note: John Stuart (once a Cherokee captive) and William Johnson had earned the Indians' trust by learning their languages and cultural ways and treating them respectfully.
>
> Both Stuart and Johnson would use their positions to ally the Indians against the American rebels in the future American War for Independence.

May–June 1761 **In South Carolina, the war against the Cherokee continues.**

Major James Grant, accompanied by Mohawk and Stockbridge scouts, leads 2,600 British troops and South Carolina militiamen against the Cherokee in the ongoing campaign to punish the Indians and break their ability to wage war. Cherokee towns and fields are burned as Grant's forces destroy at least fifteen towns and 15,000 acres of crops, including *Kituwah*—the heart of the Cherokee Nation. Soon depleted of *powder and shot*, the hungry Cherokee begin laying down their arms for peace.

> Note: Three years earlier, most of Major Grant's former Highland Regiment had been slaughtered at the Battle of Fort Duquesne and Grant himself had been temporarily held captive.

June 1761 **The British learn of war plans by the Western Seneca of Pennsylvania and New York.**

The Seneca are fomenting an uprising among the Western Tribes against the English, whom they see as arriving from across the mountains in ever-increasing numbers.

July 20, 1761 **Virginia makes peace with the Cherokee as the Anglo-Cherokee War winds down.**

The *Treaty of Long-Island-on-the-Holston* ends the three-year war between Virginia and the Cherokee Nation.

Aug. 1761 **Seven-year-old Phillis Wheatley arrives in Boston from Africa.**

Arriving frail and poorly dressed, the young girl is sold for a "trifle" to the financially secure Wheatley family of Boston. Named after the ship that brought her, Phillis—to be a house servant for the sickly Susannah Wheatley—will be treated somewhat like a family member and educated in the Wheatley household.

> Note: Unbeknownst at the time, Phillis Wheatly was destined to become the most well-known African in North America, receiving international acclaim through her literary talents.

Sept. 22, 1761 **In London, George William Frederick is coronated as King George III.**

George William Frederick and his wife Charlotte are carried in sedan chairs to Westminster and officially crowned king and queen of Great Britain in joyous celebration.

> Note: Though now officially coronated, George III had been on the throne for nearly a year.

Sept. 1761 — **At Fort Detroit, British Indian Superintendent William Johnson meets in council with the tribes of the lower Great Lakes, hoping to stem a possible Indian war.**

This is Johnson's first visit west to the former French fort. With regional Indian unrest due to the loss of their French allies and trade partners, Johnson begins the hard task of winning over the Western Tribes—long enemies of the English.

Dec. 18, 1761 — **The *Charles Town Treaty* ends the Anglo-Cherokee War.**

South Carolina signs a peace treaty with Cherokee representatives in Charles Town.

The following are among the terms:

- Both sides agree to return all captives.
- The Cherokee agree to expel all French from their lands.
- A pro-British Cherokee leader, *Attakullakulla*, commonly called *Little Carpenter*, is set up as the Cherokee *emperor*.
- The Lower Cherokee yield lands to South Carolina.

Dec. 1761 — **Spain places an embargo on Great Britain.**

Concerned about French losses in the ongoing war against Britain, Spain's King Charles III attempts to aid France by placing an embargo on British trade.

Jan. 4, 1762 — **Great Britain declares war on Spain, beginning the *Anglo-Spanish War*, to last until 1763.**

Learning of Spain's agreement to aid France, Britain declares war against Spain.

> Note: The year-long war would end with the Treaty of Paris of 1763.
>
> Spain's decision to assist France would result in the loss of La Florida.

1762 — ***Neolin*, a visionary Delaware prophet, influences many tribes of the Ohio region.**

Neolin preaches a doctrine of *separate paths* between the Whites and Indians. The Lenape mystic believes that the Indian people must purify themselves by driving the Whites and their corrupting influences from amongst them and return to the old ways of their people.

> Note: Neolin's teachings would be adopted by the Ottawa war chief Pontiac, among others, as many of the formerly French-allied tribes would soon set out to drive the English back across the mountains.

June 16, 1762 — **Three Cherokee leaders arrive in England to meet with King George III and become a public sensation.**

The Cherokee—*Ostenaco*, *Standing Turkey*, and *Wood Pigeon*—are escorted by Virginia Colonel Henry Timberlake but, unfortunately, the interpreter dies en route, and Timberlake speaks only a limited amount of Cherokee.

The Indians suffer seasickness throughout the voyage and immediately upon setting ashore at Plymouth, England, the painted Cherokee loudly begin a frightful-sounding song of deliverance that quickly draws a crowd so large it becomes difficult for the Indians and Timberlake to get to their inn.

The three Cherokee travel onward to London and while waiting for an audience with the king, visit the city's sights, including the Tower of London, and have their portraits painted by the famed Joshua Reynolds. The Cherokee are impressed by a large seventy-four-gun Man-of-War naval vessel and a play at the Sadler's Wells Theater but are less impressed by the cathedrals. In addition, they do not like a statue of Hercules with his club raised overhead and do not want to be around it. Though Timberlake protests that the Cherokee do not drink to excess at home, some of the Londoners enjoy inducing them to intoxication and watching the wild antics it produces.

Soon tiring of the gawking crowds that seem to always follow them, the Cherokee wish to withdraw from the public. With growing impatience, they ask Timberlake, "Why have we not yet met the King when we have traveled so far a distance to do so?"

When finally granted an audience, the three chiefs, having been convinced that Britain's king is second only to the almighty Creator, are quite surprised with King George III's youthfulness as well as his person and grandeur. Upon meeting the king, Ostenaco begins to prepare his pipe, as is the Cherokee custom to declare friendship, but Colonel Timberlake stops him, telling Ostenaco that even the greatest of men are blessed only by being allowed to kiss the king's hand.

The Cherokee offer King George III professions of friendship and faithful alliance, but with their interpreter dead, Timberlake simply translates the best he can. A new treaty with terms too detailed for Timberlake to interpret is presented to the Cherokee to take to Charles Town, where it is to be translated into their language. Before leaving, the Indians give the king gifts of pipes, wampum belts, and sacred objects representing Cherokee friendship.

> Note: A snafu would develop when the Cherokee expressed a desire to return to Virginia instead of South Carolina and refused to leave. To finally end the issue, the Indians were deceived, and their ship would sail for Charles Town on August 25.
>
> The favorable welcome the Cherokee had received in London caused resentment in the Carolina colonies, who had just fought a bloody three-year war against them.

June 1762

The dispute over the 1737 Walking Purchase between Pennsylvania and the Delaware is declared resolved by the Iroquois Council of Six Nations.

In Easton, Pennsylvania, Delaware Chief *Teedyuscung*, with the help of Quaker allies, continues to press charges that their lands had been fraudulently lost in the Walking Purchase of 1737 and that the issue has never been properly resolved. But without the support of the Iroquois, the Delaware are forced to accept their fate as large numbers of gifts are presented to settle the issue.

June 17, 1762

French forces capture St. John's, Newfoundland.

Great Britain has pulled troops from Newfoundland for greater military priorities—an attack against Cuba, which, if successful, will be followed by an attack against France's Louisiana. With Newfoundland now vulnerable and French war fortunes failing quickly, France hopes that the capture of Britain's valuable fishing colony will result in a better bargaining position during eventual peace negotiations.

Aug. 13, 1762

At war with Spain, British forces capture Havana, Cuba.

Under siege since June, Havana's *Moro Castle,* surrenders to British troops accompanied by American colonials.

Sept. 8, 1762

Boston lawyer James Otis publishes *A Vindication of the Conduct of the House of Representatives of the Province of Massachusetts Bay*.

In his publication, Otis argues in defense of Massachusetts's refusal to pay for the British ships protecting New England fisheries from French privateers.

Note:	Governor Bernard had made the request, but assembly had voted against it.

Sept. 15, 1762

The *Battle of Signal Hill*: The last major battle of the Seven Years' War in North America.

Led by General Jeffery Amherst, British regulars accompanied by New England militiamen attack a French detachment on St. John's Signal Hill, forcing the French to retreat to nearby Fort William to consolidate their troops. With the British now in charge of the tall hill, they can easily fire upon the French below, forcing their surrender three days later, leaving Newfoundland once again in possession of the British.

Nov. 1, 1762

After five years in London representing Pennsylvania's interests, Benjamin Franklin returns to Philadelphia.

Franklin, as one of only two North American postmaster generals, has reluctantly returned to the American colonies to inspect the post offices. Quite happy to be British, Benjamin Franklin harbors thoughts of perhaps returning to live permanently in England.

Note:	Franklin left his thirty-two-year-old son William in London. William Franklin would return to North America in February 1765 as the newly appointed royal governor of New Jersey.

Nov. 13, 1762

France secretly transfers Louisiana to Spain by the *Treaty of Fontainebleau*.

King Louis XV cedes all French territory west of the Mississippi, including the Isle of Orleans (New Orleans), to King Charles III of Spain. For the next eighteen months, the transfer will be kept secret from Great Britain, and even the French governor of Louisiana.

Note:	Spain would control Louisiana for the next thirty-eight years before returning the colony to France on October 1, 1800, by the *Third Treaty of San Ildefonso*.
	In 1803, France's Napoleon Bonaparte would sell Louisiana to the young United States, leading to the Corps of Discovery's (Lewis and Clark) expedition of 1804–1806 to the Pacific Ocean and back.

Parliament passes the *Revenue Act* of 1762, aka the *Customs Revenue Act*.

The Act's purpose is to halt the illegal but highly lucrative molasses trade between North America and the French West Indies. By tightening duty and navigational enforcements, the British Ministry hopes to suppress the regular circumventions of the 1733 Molasses Act.

The following are among the provisions of the Customs Revenue Act:

- There is to be strict enforcement of Britain's various Acts of trade.

- The British Ministry and Parliament will begin using the British Navy to enforce trade regulations by patrolling the North American coast and apprehending smugglers.

- The practice of customs officials living in England who rely on deputies in the colonies is to be ended.

- Writs of assistance are to be used by customs officers seeking illegal contraband.

- Immunity is to be given to British officers for mistaken seizures.

> Note: By granting customs officers and the British Navy authority to go after whomever they wished, the Revenue Act of 1762 would cause resentment among American merchants and transporters.

1762

The *Indian Trade Act* of 1762 enacts certain trade prohibitions.

Fearing hostilities by the French-allied tribes, any trade goods that can be used to rearm the Indians are prohibited—including guns, lead, gunpowder, knives, razors, flints, and hatchets. Enacted by Britain's Board of Trade, the ban results in extreme Indian frustrations as they have become very dependent on these goods which they consider essential for sustaining their livelihoods. Now, without the French traders to counterbalance the British, the trade prohibitions place the tribes in a bind, with scarcity and deprivation being the result.

> Note: Having defeated the French, the British incorrectly considered the French-allied tribes as having also been conquered, and now set about neutralizing them.
>
> Hoping to thwart British inroads with the Indians, many of the French had convinced the tribes that the English planned to kill them once they were disarmed.

Feb. 10, 1763

The *Treaty of Paris* ends the Seven Years' War, aka the French and Indian War.

The following are among the terms:

- France cedes to Britain all North American lands located east of the Mississippi River, except two small islands in the Gulf of St. Lawrence: St. Pierre and Miquelon.

> Note: Still French possessions today, the two islands were important for processing the French fish catch from the Grand Banks before it could be taken to Europe.
>
> Three months earlier, France had secretly ceded New Orleans and the Louisiana region west of the Mississippi to Spain. Both countries hoped to thwart eventual westward advances by Britain across the Mississippi River.

- Spain cedes to Britain all Spanish land claims east of the Mississippi, including Florida.

> Note: Britain would possess Florida until being returned to Spain in 1783 at the conclusion of the American War for Independence. The United States would acquire Florida from Spain in 1821 by the *Adams–Onís Treaty*.

- Britain returns Cuba to Spain.

- Britain returns to France the West Indies sugar islands of Martinique, St. Lucia, and Guadeloupe, but keeps Dominica, Tobago, and St. Vincent.

> Note: Britain had considered returning Canada to France and instead keeping the French sugar islands of the West Indies, but the British sugar industry had lobbied against it.

- French citizens living in the ceded French territories who do not wish to live under British rule have eighteen months to freely relocate to other French colonies.

The Seven Years' War has some additional results, including:

- Many in England and the colonies, heavily invested in North American real estate, are concerned that the values of their land holdings will drop due to the addition of New France to Britain's North American empire. Yet others eagerly await an expected granting of the former French lands to British and American investors.

- British and colonial trading companies foresee huge profits to be made in the lucrative Indian trade as they move to replace the former French traders.

- War expenditures have brought an increased wealth to Britain's North American colonies, but with the war's conclusion, the colonial economies will contract, ushering in a post-war recession.

- Immigration to North America, having ebbed during the war, will begin to increase.

- Britain now has undisputed control over much of North America, as well as the seas and shipping trade.

- As war has removed both the French and Spanish threat in North America, the American colonies are now less dependent on Britain for protection.

- The French-allied Indians feel abandoned to their English enemies. With the removal of the French as a counterweight, the Indians can no longer play one against the other.

Note:	This represented a great loss of tribal powers. With the French and Spanish removed from Eastern North America, Great Britain and the American colonies no longer needed the Indians as military allies.

- Britain leaves 10,000 troops in North America and firmly establishes its military headquarters in New York.

Note:	Approximately 6,000 British troops were stationed across the western frontier in isolated forts to assume control of the former French lands; establish British authority over the remaining French and their allied tribes; monitor the Indian trade; and maintain general frontier order. In time, many Americans would view their scarlet-coated protectors as a standing army and demand they be removed.

1763

Following the Seven Years' War, severe debt forces Great Britain to change its relationship with the North American colonies.

Britain is more than £122 million in debt, with £4.4 million interest per year. In addition to paying its war debt, Britain's costs now include establishing administrative control over the former French lands of North America, and the tougher task of securing the allegiance of the remaining French inhabitants and the French-allied tribes.

The western regions, in particular, require British expenditures associated with:

- Construction of new forts and the repair of the former French forts.

- Stationing of troops in the remote frontier.

- Huge increase in the quantity of presents and trade goods for distribution to the tribes.

- Need for military campaigns to suppress any Indian uprisings that shall arise.

In addition to the expense of governing the former French lands of North America, Britain has many costs associated with the regulation and administration of the massive British–colonial trade system, adding weight to the burden of an indebted Britain. Therefore, the royal government—King George III, his ministers, and the Parliament—all believe it is now time to reform the British imperial system by tightening the screws of trade enforcement in search of additional revenues.

"It is time for the Americans to pay their share."

Many in Great Britain believe the American colonials have been getting a free ride and the time for them to begin paying their fair share is long overdue. In their view, the North Americans receive the benefits and protections of the British Empire without paying the costs. Therefore, the British Ministry will begin to implement measures to enforce the kingdom's trade laws and revenue measures already in effect but are being ignored or loosely enforced. The enforcement of these measures and the passage of additional regulations will cause American resentment, as most of Britain's North American colonies will soon begin a drift from their *mother country*.

Note:	At the conclusion of the Seven Years' War, American sentiments toward Great Britain and King George III were at a peak—as nearly all were proud to be members of the British Empire.

March 1763   **The Western Tribes begin to learn of the cessation of French lands to the English.**

For most of the tribes, the French transfer of North American lands, known as *pays d'en haut*, represents a world turned upside-down as the French have been in Canada for more than 200 years. Rumors of the French departure leave the Indians alarmed as they ponder the consequences of the loss of such an important ally. With whom will they now trade? How can they check British claims on Indian lands without French assistance and firearms?

Note:	Many of the tribes were encouraged by the departing French to continue warring against the *English* and given false promise that their French friends would return.
	In the far-western forts of the Illinois and Mississippi regions, the French had not yet evacuated. As such, they would try to keep this new development from the Indians for as long as possible.

March 27, 1763   **In need of revenue, Parliament passes the *Excise bill* of 1763, aka the *Cider Act* or *Cider Tax*.**

The excise tax on cider and perry upsets the producers in West England and Wales and many refuse to pay by simply ignoring the tax, but the Act allows customs agents to search for illicit products which causes protests and civil unrest.

Opposition to the Act is led by William Pitt, who sees it as an intrusion on the people's liberties, declaring, "The poorest man may in his cottage bid defiance to all the forces of the crown. It may be frail—its roof may shake—the wind may blow through it—the storm may enter—the rain may enter—but the King of England cannot enter." The tax will be repealed in 1766.

Note:	The Cider Tax protests in Britain would be somewhat mirrored in North America by the future Stamp Act protests.
	Many historians believe the intrusions allowed to Britain's governmental authorities by the Cider Act would influence the Fourth Amendment of the United States Constitution.

April 4, 1763   **The first Georgia newspaper is published in Savannah, the *Georgia Gazette*.**

April 16, 1763   **George Grenville becomes prime minister of Great Britain and attempts to bring changes to Britain's financial situation.**

Faced with severe debt following the Seven Years' War, Grenville will try to restore Britain's finances by tightening the reins on government expenditures while seeking new revenue sources. As such, the prime minister sets his sights on the North American colonies. To Grenville, the

British are subsidizing the Americans, and it is time they pay their share. As such, Prime Minister Grenville will introduce certain tax measures on the North American colonists and unwittingly move many Americans toward independence.

> Note: Among Grenville's initiatives that would affect the North American colonies: the Proclamation of 1763; the 1764 (American) Revenue Act, aka the Sugar Act; the Currency Act of 1764; the Stamp Act of 1765; and the Quartering Act of 1765.
>
> Grenville would support the decision of his predecessor, former Prime Minster Lord Bute, to keep 10,000 troops stationed in North America.

April 27, 1763   **Near Detroit, the Indians attend a large intertribal conference and listen to the Ottawa *Pontiac* call for war against the English.**

Representatives of twenty-four tribes gather along the Ecorse River and agree to drive the English from their lands by destroying their frontier forts and forcing them to return across the mountains.

A great orator, Pontiac tells the massive crowd listening with rapt attention:

- To put aside their differences and to unite as one people in war against the English.

- To go home, prepare for war, and then attack the English in a coordinated strike that will be signaled to begin by an attack on Fort Detroit.

- That French soldiers will be crossing the ocean to help them in their struggle.

- That the French settlers are not to be harmed as they are friends and supporters of the Indians.

> Note: Following his visit with the Delaware prophet Neolin several months earlier, Pontiac had sought a personal vision quest. Like Neolin, the Great Spirit told Pontiac that the tribes had become too dependent on the White men's goods and should instead return to the traditional Indian ways and wipe the English invaders from their lands by striking while they were still few in number.
>
> Although the exact number of Native Americans attending Pontiac's council meeting is unknown, it is generally agreed that it was the largest intertribal war council yet to meet in the Western territories.

April 30, 1763   **In London, John Wilkes is arrested for publicly criticizing King George III.**

John Wilkes—a publisher and Member of Parliament—has written and published an article in issue No. 45 of his newspaper *The North Briton* criticizing the king's recent speech seeking Parliament's approval of the Treaty of Paris. Believing Britain's terms to be too generous to France, Wilkes published his caustic criticism on April 23. Arrested for sedition, Wilkes is placed in the Tower of London for a week before being released on the grounds of parliamentary privilege. Wilkes now sets to work—suing the government for damages.

> Note: Long a thorn in King George's side with his sharp wit and criticisms, Wilkes had also been particularly critical of the king's former prime minister and current advisor, the Scotsman John Stuart, 3rd Earl of Bute. By publishing his criticism of the king in issue No. 45 of his newspaper, Wilkes's allusion to the 1745 Jacobite Rising's near overthrow of King George III's grandfather could not be missed.

May 7, 1763   ***Pontiac's War* begins at Fort Detroit and quickly spreads throughout the Great Lakes region.**

Accompanied by 300 warriors, Pontiac attempts to capture Fort Detroit under pretense of council. Permitted to enter with sixty of his warriors, all secretly armed, his plot fails due to the fort's commander, Major Henry Gladwin, having been forewarned by a *Chippewa* woman. Facing an armed garrison ready to fight, Pontiac and his warriors peacefully remove themselves only to begin a furious attack two days later. Soon surrounded by nearly 1,000 warring Indians, the 120 British soldiers and twenty civilians inside Fort Detroit will be under siege for the next six months.

> Note: Pontiac's plan was to personally kill Major Gladwin as a signal to begin the attack.
>
> Pontiac's goal was to cut Detroit's communication and supply lines with the East. If the Indians could prevent reinforcements and supplies from reaching the isolated western fort, Pontiac hoped to force Fort Detroit's eventual surrender.
>
> The Indians would specifically kill all the English they could locate in the Detroit area. Though there were 2,000 French settlers living near Fort Detroit at the time, they were to be left unmolested, as they were considered friends.
>
> Many hundreds of soldiers and civilians would be killed during what would quickly become a pan-Indian uprising. In addition, thousands more would flee to the eastern cities, depopulating the frontier regions.
>
> The Western Indian War would not be known as Pontiac's War until the mid-1800s.

May 10, 1763 **Fort Detroit's second-in-command, British Captain Donald Campbell, is taken hostage.**

Captain Campbell, accompanied by an interpreter, voluntarily leaves the safety of Fort Detroit to negotiate with Pontiac, but in an act of duplicity—Campbell is held hostage by order of the Ottawa war chief.

May 16, 1763 *Fort Sandusky,* **in modern Ohio, is destroyed by Wyandot and Ottawa warriors, becoming the first western fort to fall.**

Indians appear and ask for council to gain access to the small British fort located near the western end of Lake Erie. Once inside, the warriors overcome the soldiers and traders, killing and scalping twenty-seven before burning the fort. The only survivor, commander Ensign Christopher Pauli, is taken captive but manages to escape a torturous death by being adopted by an Ottawa woman to replace her dead husband. Ensign Pauli later escapes and makes his way to Fort Detroit.

May 25, 1763 *Fort St. Joseph,* **in modern Michigan, falls to the Potawatomi.**

Eleven of the fort's fifteen defenders are killed outright as three others are taken captive, including the fort's commander, Ensign Francis Schlosser.

> Note: Schlosser would be released shortly in exchange for *Winama*—a Potawatomi chief held hostage by the British at Fort Detroit.

May 27, 1763 *Fort Miami,* **in modern Indiana, is captured by Miami warriors accompanied by Frenchmen.**

Unaware of the outbreak of the Indian war, British commander Ensign Robert Holmes is lured from the fort to treat a sick Indian and is immediately shot and killed. Unable to effectively resist, the fort's small garrison are offered their lives if they lay down their arms.

After a brief council, the fort's defenders surrender, but before being led off as captives, they watch as the French flag is hoisted over Fort Miami.

May 29, 1763 **The Western Indian War engulfs Pennsylvania as the countryside around Fort Pitt is attacked.**

Delaware warriors, led by *Wolf* and *Kickyuscung*, attack isolated frontier farms and settlements, causing panic among the region's settlers as they begin to stream into the already overcrowded fort.

> Note: Captain Simeon Ecuyer, with 230 troops under his command, would begin readying Fort Pitt's defensive works for an expected attack.

June 1, 1763   ***Fort Ouiatenon*, in modern Indiana, is taken by *Wea*, Kickapoo, and Mascouten warriors.**

Frenchmen accompanying the Indians save the lives of the British troops by giving the captors wampum for their exchange.

June 2, 1763   **In upper Michigan, *Fort Michilimackinac* is taken by the Chippewa, Ojibwe, and Sauk.**

Indian warriors gain access to the fort by pretending to play a game of *baggataway*, a forerunner to lacrosse, outside the fort's walls. The unsuspecting British soldiers come out to watch the play, and in a ruse, the Indians intentionally hit the ball through the fort's open gate and chase it inside to begin their attack. When they are finished, fifteen of the thirty-five men garrisoning the fort have been killed outright, while another five are led off to be tortured to death.

> Note: Located on the Mackinac Strait, the isolated Fort Michilimackinac had enjoyed a good relationship with the local tribes while conducting trade and small interactions. At the time of the attack, the troops were unaware that an Indian war had begun.

June 3, 1763   **The *Mississippi Land Company* is created to secure large grants of the newly acquired French lands of the Mississippi River region and its waterways.**

Hoping to take advantage of Great Britain's acquisition of the former French lands in North America, fifty prominent and influential shareholders in Virginia, Maryland, and London create the Mississippi Land Company. The investors include George Washington and his brother Augustine, as well as the wealthy Lee family—Arthur Lee, Richard Henry Lee, and Francis Lightfoot Lee.

> Note: The company, a closed group, was limited to fifty *inside* investors, with nine of the fifty shares being reserved for certain investors in London to help ensure the grant.
>
> Though the Proclamation of 1763 would prohibit settlement west of the Appalachian Mountains, the company's investors would believe the prohibition to be but a temporary measure, issued only to quell the current Indian unrest.
>
> The Mississippi Land Company should not be confused with the former French Mississippi Company, in operation from 1684 to 1721.
>
> Both Richard Henry Lee and Francis Lightfoot Lee would be future signers of the U.S. Declaration of Independence.

Summer 1763   **British General Jeffery Amherst, stationed in New York, issues orders for all Indians engaged in fighting to be put to death.**

June 15, 1763   **In Wisconsin, *Fort Edward Augustus*, aka *Fort La Bay*, is abandoned to the Indians.**

The westernmost British outpost, located at modern Green Bay, is deemed indefensible and ordered abandoned.

June 16, 1763   **Fort Venango, in western Pennsylvania, is overwhelmed by Seneca and Shawnee warriors.**

Approximately fifty warriors approach the fort feigning friendship and request permission to council, which is granted. Once inside, the Indians launch a surprise attack killing the fort's fifteen soldiers and capturing alive the commander, Lieutenant Francis Gordon. Wasting little time, the Seneca leader, *Kyashuta,* brings pen and paper to Gordon and dictates the Indians' grievances for fighting the English as Gordon writes them down.

Kyashuta states that the two major reasons for the fighting are the lack of powder and lead supplied them for their needs, and the continued construction and occupation of frontier forts after promises not to do so. After finishing his assigned task, the Indians kill Lieutenant Gordon by slow torture and burn Fort Venango to the ground.

| June 17, 1763 | **Fort Presque Isle, located on Pennsylvania's Lake Erie shore, is destroyed by hundreds of Indian warriors.** |

Two days earlier, nearly 250 Chippewa, Ottawa, and Huron arrived from the Detroit region in war canoes to join Seneca warriors in an attack against Fort Presque Isle ordered by Pontiac. Now under assault a second day and hunkered in the blockhouse, thirty-three British troops under the command of Ensign John Christie surrender rather than be roasted alive as the Indians prepare to burn the building. Promised safe passage to either Fort Pitt or Fort Niagara, Ensign Christie and his men are instead made prisoners and divided among the Indians. After the fort is burned, the frightened soldiers are marched away in various directions to their individual fates.

> Note: Two men had escaped unseen during the surrender.
>
> The Seneca, members of the Six Nations, had acted without the League's sanction.
>
> With some war canoes reaching nearly 20 feet in length—these large canoes were capable of quickly transporting many Indian warriors.

| June 18, 1763 | **In western Pennsylvania, Fort Le Boeuf is burned to the ground.** |

Five armed Seneca warriors arrive outside Fort Le Boeuf and feign friendship and good intentions, asking to be allowed to sleep within the fort's parade grounds. Denied permission, the fort's commander, Ensign George Price, orders the gates locked against them.

The attack begins that night with the Seneca shooting fire arrows against Fort Le Boeuf's roof and walls, setting the fort aflame. Rather than perish, the fourteen British soldiers narrowly escape out a back window and into the dark woods in an attempt to reach Fort Venango.

> Note: Unknown to the escapees, Fort Venango had also been destroyed.
>
> After wandering in the forest for eight days, Ensign Price and seven of his men would arrive at Fort Pitt on June 26. The other seven soldiers were lost.

The Indian war in Pennsylvania continues to spread as Fort Ligonier comes under attack.

After a day-long gun battle with plenty of *hot fire*, the Indians withdraw as night falls.

| June 21, 1763 | **Fort Ligonier, packed with panicked refugees, is attacked a second time.** |

In a ruse, fifteen British soldiers chase four Indians only to be ambushed by nearly 100 warriors lying in wait along a creek bank. The Indians pursue the fleeing soldiers but are slowed by marshy ground allowing the troops to safely return to the fort.

| June 1763 | **In Pennsylvania, *Fort Lyttleton* is abandoned.** |

The smallest post along the Forbes Road is ordered vacated, and the fort's three sole defenders join their British comrades at nearby Fort Bedford.

June 22, 1763   **Pennsylvania's Fort Bedford comes under attack by Delaware and Shawnee warriors.**

The Indians begin a six-week siege against Fort Pitt.

Delaware, Shawnee, Mingo, and Huron warriors begin the siege by attacking the fort's cattle and driving off the horses. In response, Captain Simeon Ecuyer orders his soldiers to the ramparts, but the men are greeted by withering fire from hundreds of secluded warriors who kill two of the fort's defenders.

> Note: Panic abounded among the region's settlers as more than 500 would eventually crowd themselves into Fort Pitt, bringing horrific tales of Indian atrocities.
>
> At his New York headquarters, British Commander in Chief General Jeffery Amherst would authorize a military expedition led by Colonel Henry Bouquet to relieve the beleaguered fort.
>
> Fort Pitt and Fort Detroit were both major military bastions not easily taken. As in medieval siege warfare, the Indians had surrounded each fort and begun a protracted containment while cutting off supplies and hoping to pick off stragglers and any arriving reinforcements.

June 24, 1763   **At Fort Pitt, smallpox-infested blankets are given to the Delaware.**

Two Delaware, *Turtleheart* and *Mamaltee,* approach the fort to parley. When the talks are finished, the Indians are given hospital blankets to hopefully spread smallpox among their people. Captain Simeon Ecuyer writes of the deed, "We gave them two blankets and a handkerchief out of the smallpox hospital." The Indian trader and owner of vast frontier lands William Trent writes in his journal, "I hope it will have the desired effect."

June 29, 1763   **British General Amherst suggests using smallpox against the warring tribes.**

Colonel Henry Bouquet, in Philadelphia hastily readying a relief force bound for Fort Pitt, receives communications from General Amherst suggesting smallpox be induced among the Indians there to *reduce them*. Colonel Bouquet responds that he will try to spread the disease among them by blankets and adds that he wishes they could use the Spanish method against the Indians, "hunting them down with English dogs followed by Rangers and Light Horse to extirpate or remove that vermin."

June 30, 1763   **British troop reinforcements arrive at the besieged Fort Detroit.**

The sloop *Michigan* arrives from Fort Niagara with fifty soldiers under the command of Lieutenant Abraham Cuyler. Upon spying the *Michigan*'s approach, the fort's beleaguered garrison cheer till their throats are raw, while others weep tears of joy.

July 3, 1763   **Pontiac learns that the war between France and Britain has officially ended.**

The news of the European peace has arrived aboard the *Michigan* and is disseminated to the Indians in hope that they might give up the attack. Shocked, incensed, and in disbelief upon hearing the news—Pontiac vows to continue the war against the English.

140

July 4, 1763   **At Detroit, British Captain Donald Campbell is tortured and killed within sight of his troops.**

Captain Campbell, held hostage for eight weeks by Pontiac, is killed by Chippewa Chief *Wasson* in revenge for his favorite nephew having been killed by the English. Despite Pontiac's promises of safety to Campbell, Wasson simply ties the British officer to a picket fence within sight of the fort's defenders and proceeds to slowly and methodically kill him. Wasson then cuts out the captain's heart and eats a part before tossing it to other warriors who do the same. Campbell's body is then hacked to pieces and thrown into the Detroit River.

July 9, 1763   **Hoping to completely isolate Detroit, Pontiac attempts to burn the *Michigan*—the fort's only lifeline to the outside world.**

Under siege for two months, the remote frontier fort is dependent on the sloop for supplies and reinforcements from Fort Niagara. Therefore, Pontiac attempts to set the *Michigan* ablaze by floating a burning barge downstream to collide with the anchored vessel. Though nearly succeeding, the plan fails.

Note:	Pontiac had fought alongside French General Montcalm at Quebec and had seen this ploy used against British ships on the St. Lawrence River.

Late July 1763   **Colonel Henry Bouquet's relief forces reach Fort Bedford, only 100 miles from Fort Pitt.**

Having arduously marched from Philadelphia along the Forbes Road, Colonel Bouquet pauses his 500-man army to rest and regroup before continuing. From this point forward, Bouquet's men, mostly Scottish Highlanders and Pennsylvania volunteers, are to remain on high alert as they travel the remaining miles to the besieged fort.

In New York, the British seek Iroquois assistance in the war with the Western Tribes.

Though the Iroquois reluctantly agree, they will do little in the conflict.

Note:	The Seneca, westernmost tribe of the Six Nations, were known as the League's "Keepers of the Western Door." Located near the Western Tribes and the scene of conflict, the Seneca—sensing an Indian victory—had joined the war to drive away the English. This act of independence sowed new divisions among the Six Nations, for the Iroquois were historical allies of Great Britain.

July 29, 1763   **Fort Detroit receives additional troop reinforcements and supplies.**

The number of soldiers at Detroit nearly doubles when 280 British regulars under the command of Captain John Dalyell arrive aboard twenty-three batteaux from Fort Niagara carrying bales and barrels of critical provisions. Upon sight of the seemingly endless parade of arriving vessels, the Detroit garrison shout out three cheers, rejoicing at their good fortune.

July 31, 1763   **Near Detroit, the British suffer a disastrous defeat in the *Battle of Bloody Run*.**

In a daring night attack, Captain Dalyell leads 250 troops in an attempt to *turn the tables* on the Indians by launching an assault against Pontiac's camp, but Dalyell and his men are discovered and ambushed by Chippewa, Wyandot, and Ottawa warriors. Forced to retreat, the British suffer thirty-eight wounded and twenty-three killed, including the recently arrived Captain John Dalyell—at Detroit for only two days.

Note:	Captain Dalyell's head would be placed atop a pole in front of Pontiac's lodge.

Aug. 1763   **British General Jeffery Amherst—held responsible for the Western Indian War—is recalled to London to report to the Board of Trade.**

General Amherst sails to England, leaving Major General Thomas Gage as the acting commander of Britain's troops in North America.

Note:	General Gage would gain future fame as commander of British forces in North America during the outbreak of Massachusetts hostilities in 1774.
	George Washington and Thomas Gage had made acquaintance during the failed 1755 Braddock campaign (Gage was then a British lieutenant colonel). At that time, neither man could have imagined that within twenty years they would become commanding foes.

Aug. 1, 1763   **The siege against Fort Pitt is abandoned as the Indians rush to ambuscade the approaching British relief force.**

Having learned that Colonel Bouquet's army has departed Fort Bedford, the Indian warriors set out to intercept them in battle.

Aug. 5–6, 1763   **The *Battle of Bushy Run*: The Indians engage in fierce fighting with Bouquet's troops but fail to stop their advance.**

Mingo, Delaware, Shawnee, and Huron warriors ambush Colonel Bouquet's army twenty-five miles east of Fort Pitt at today's Jeannette, Pennsylvania. After two days of bloody battle, the Indians give way and disperse, allowing the expedition to continue onward.

Note:	Bouquet's forces suffered sixty killed, with Indian losses estimated to be nearly the same.

Aug. 20, 1763   **Arriving to the joy of its occupants, Colonel Henry Bouquet reaches Fort Pitt.**

Note:	With the arrival of Colonel Bouquet, the siege against Fort Pitt would end, and the fortunes of war—initially favoring the Indians—would begin to turn against them.
	Hundreds of White prisoners remained captives of the Western Tribes, but as military operations required both men and funding—it would be a year before a rescue expedition into the Ohio Country could be mustered.
	Fort Pitt would stand successfully for the remainder of Pontiac's War.
	Both Colonel Henry Bouquet and Fort Pitt's commander Captain Simeon Ecuyer were Swiss mercenaries serving in the British Army.

Sept. 9, 1763   **In London, William Franklin is commissioned as the new royal governor of New Jersey.**

Having finished his law studies at Middle Temple and been admitted to the bar, William Franklin is appointed governor of New Jersey due to his father's influence.

The Mississippi Land Company petitions the king for 2.5 million acres of western lands.

The company requests a grant of 2.5 million acres of Britain's newly acquired lands along the Mississippi River and its tributaries. If so granted:

- Each of the company's fifty shareholders is to receive 50,000 acres for individual ownership.

- The lands are to lie on the upper Mississippi River and the lower Ohio River.

The company requests:

- "That the settlement be protected from the insults of Savages by his Majesty's Forces."

- "That the Lands be obtained if possible clear of all composition money, expenses, and quit rents for the space of twelve years or longer upon condition that we settle the same in that time if not interrupted by the Savages."

In addition, the company will suggest that Britain build two fortified settlements within the region.

> Note: The company's requests would be promptly denied before the year was out. Undeterred, the investors would unsuccessfully reapply in 1765, and a final time in 1768.
>
> Most of the disappointed Virginia investors, notably among them George Washington and members of the Lee family, would soon fight to sever ties from Great Britain.

Sept. 14, 1763   **Seneca warriors annihilate British troops in the *Battle of Devil's Hole*.**

Nearly 300 Seneca warriors attack a thirty-wagon convoy portaging around Niagara Falls. The surprised waggoneers are sprung upon and completely routed while passing along the edge of a steep ravine, losing twenty-one of the twenty-three men in the lopsided battle.

British forces in the area learn of the attack and rush to relieve the waggoneers, but they too are overwhelmed as the Indians kill eighty-one soldiers and wound eight.

> Note: In total, the Seneca killed 127 men while claiming to have lost only one warrior in the battle—the worst British disaster of Pontiac's War.
>
> The wagon train had been carrying supplies bound for the relief of Fort Detroit. Now, those supplies were secured by the Indians.

Oct. 7, 1763   **King George III issues the *Royal Proclamation* of 1763.**

With the end of the Seven Years' War, Great Britain seeks to establish authority and governance over the former lands of New France. But though Britain's war with the French is over—the war with the Western Indians is not. Therefore, hoping to appease the warring tribes and bring a permanent peace to the frontier, Great Britain creates an *Indian reserve* beyond the Appalachian Mountains.

The Royal Proclamation of 1763 states the following:

- A western boundary is established beyond which no settlers will be permitted to cross. Henceforth, settlement is to be allowed only on lands draining into the Atlantic that have been properly purchased from the Indians. The restrictive border is to be the *Eastern Continental Divide,* running roughly north to south through the

Appalachian Mountains. All Crown lands draining westward are to be held in reserve for the Indians, and any White settlers living west of the divide are to voluntarily remove themselves.

> **Note:** The boundary barring White migration west of the Appalachian Mountains would quickly become known as the *Proclamation Line of 1763*, or simply, the *Proclamation Line*.

- The private purchase of Indian lands is prohibited.

- Every person wishing to conduct trade with the Indians may do so only with a proper license issued by the governor or commander in chief of the colony in which the trader resides and is required to follow trade regulations.

- The British military is to be responsible for apprehending fugitives from justice that flee to the reserved Indian lands and delivering them to the colony in which the crime was committed to stand trial.

- Three new colonial boundaries are defined on the North American mainland: East Florida, West Florida, and Quebec. In the West Indies, the island colony of Granada is created.

- Land grants will be given free of charge in the newly formed colonies and any other British colony of North America to discharged British soldiers who have served in America and are currently residing there or are yet serving soon to be discharged. The land allocations also apply to veterans of the British Navy who have served in North America. The free allotments shall be:

  - 50 acres for a private.

  - 200 acres for a noncommissioned officer.

  - 2,000 acres for a staff officer.

  - 3,000 acres for a captain.

  - 5,000 acres for a rank above field officer.

The Proclamation of 1763 is designed to:

- Help populate Britain's newly acquired territories by redirecting the western migration northward into Canada and southward into Florida.

> **Note:** Many of the remaining Spanish and French citizens felt abandoned to their historical enemy and were hostile to British authority. By infusing large numbers of *British citizens* among them, Britain hoped to more easily gain control over its new North American lands and the people already living there.

- Create a peace with the Western Tribes by recognizing the Indians as owners of the land and thus reduce the expenditures required to fight them.

- Help retain the values of the eastern colonial land holdings.

> **Note:** Land prices, then as now, are subject to supply and demand. Therefore, by keeping the newly acquired French lands from entering the market, the value of lands already under ownership would remain higher.

Britain is to station 6,000 soldiers in various western forts to:

- Protect its new territories from re-encroachment by France.

- Exert control over the Western Tribes, most of whom are former French allies.

- Guard against unlawful intrusions.

- Monitor the Indian trade.

> Note: This stationing of regular troops in the western frontier regions would represent the first *standing army* in British America.

The Proclamation of 1763 represents a big change in accustomed practices, upsetting many. Land speculators in England and the colonies resent the restrictions. To be barred from the western lands means that the situation is just as it was under French control. The Americans have helped defeat the French; why should they not reap the territorial spoils of war?

Many correctly believe the Royal Proclamation is designed to curb western development and immigration. Several royal governors, also deeply invested in land speculations, will refuse to enforce the Proclamation's prohibitive boundary and encourage settlers to ignore it.

> Note: No matter the law, the British government was reluctant to use force to remove encroachers. White settlers, including Daniel Boone, would ignore the ban and continue to move west; by 1782, more than 30,000 would live illegally in Kentucky.
>
> The Proclamation of 1763 is alluded to in grievance seven of the U.S. Declaration of Independence.

Oct. 30, 1763   **Philadelphia is rattled by a rare earthquake.**

The *Pennsylvania Gazette* described the event thus: "On Sunday last, about a quarter after four in the afternoon, we had a smart schock of an earthquake here, which so alarmed the congregations of most of the places of worship in town, that the service was immediately broke up; but happily no damage was done."

Nov. 3, 1763   **The *Dismal Swamp Land Company* is formed by George Washington.**

> Note: The Great Dismal Swamp, with an original size estimated at 1 million acres, was located on Virginia's border with North Carolina. At that time, the dense swamp was so inhospitable that runaway slaves sought its cover as sanctuary and set up communities within its midst.

Washington and nine other Virginia investors form the Dismal Swamp Land Company and apply to the Virginia Council for a 40,000-acre grant of lands. The company investors believe portions of the swamp can be used for agriculture if they can be drained and surveyed. Their request is granted, and each of the ten members receives 4,000 acres, or one tenth of the shares.

> Note: George Washington agreed to help survey the project.
>
> The work was to be conducted by African slaves. As it was estimated that the project would require "Fifty able male labouring Slaves," each of the ten investors was to furnish five such slaves for his share by the next July to be delivered to the project managers.
>
> One investor, Thomas Nelson, would become a signer of the U.S. Declaration of Independence.
>
> Interest in the project would wane over time. In 1795, Washington would sell his 4,000-acre share to General Henry Lee, Jr., aka Light-Horse Harry (father of Civil War Confederate General Robert E. Lee). The land would revert to Washington's estate in 1809 after Lee could no longer make payments.

Nov. 10, 1763   **In Great Britain, the gadfly John Wilkes becomes a champion of liberty to the public.**

Wilkes wins his lawsuit seeking damages for his arrest and confinement in the Tower of London the previous May and is awarded a settlement of £4,000.

The *Treaty of Augusta* is signed with the Southern Tribes, aka the *Treaty of Perfect and Perpetual Peace and Friendship*.

Britain's Southern Indian Superintendent John Stuart, along with the governors of South Carolina, Georgia, North Carolina, and the lieutenant governor of Virginia meet in Augusta, Georgia, with nearly 1,000 Native Americans representing the Cherokee, Creek, Catawba, Chickasaw, and Choctaw nations.

The following points are discussed at the conference:

- The tribes are informed of the new boundary and told its purpose is to keep the peace, with Whites to live on the eastern side of the Appalachians and Indian people to the west.

- South Carolina recognizes the eastern boundary of the Cherokee.

- The Catawba are granted a 225-square-mile reservation in present-day York County, South Carolina.

Note:	The reservation still exists, and the Catawba are the only federally recognized Native American tribe in South Carolina today.

- The Creek, aka Muscogee, cede their Atlantic coastal lands to Georgia, running from the Altamaha River southward to St. Mary's River.

Note:	By this time, the Whites controlled nearly all former Indian lands on the Atlantic Coast of North America.

Nov. 12, 1763   **London publisher and Member of Parliament John Wilkes *tweaks the king's nose* yet again.**

Flushed with his victorious lawsuit, John Wilkes sets to work and pushes liberty of the press to an extreme by renewing his attacks and republishing issue No. 45 of *The North Briton*. This time, Wilkes also publishes thirteen copies of a pornographic poem entitled "Essay on Woman" as a parody of Alexander Pope's "Essay on Man." In the poem Wilkes defames John Montagu, 4th Earl of Sandwich, with innuendos of sexual impropriety, who reads the poem to the House of Lords causing a commotion leading to Wilkes being charged with printing impious libel. At the same time, the House of Commons declares the poem blasphemous and obscene and calls on Wilkes to answer charges. Luckily or unluckily for Wilkes, the next day he receives a serious abdominal wound in a duel, rendering him unable to appear.

Note:	John Wilkes would flee to France by the end of the year and be expelled from Britain's Parliament on January 11, 1764. Refusing to appear before Parliament for judgment, Wilkes would be declared an outlaw on November 1, 1764.

Nov. 15, 1763   **Charles Mason and Jeremiah Dixon arrive in Philadelphia to survey an official boundary between Pennsylvania and Maryland.**

The exact location of the border between the two colonies has long been a source of dispute and violence. Therefore, each colony's proprietors—the Penn family and the Calvert family—have agreed to fund the project.

Mason, an English astronomer, and Dixon, an English surveyor, soon begin their survey through the western forest marking a dividing line between the two colonies.

Note:	Frontier warfare with the Indians would create constant apprehension for the two surveyors, who would begin surveying in the spring of 1764 as a team of axmen set to work clearing a nine-yard-wide lane westward for 233 miles through the forest.

Nov. 1763   **The Pennsylvania frontier is in frenzied panic, and Indian hatred is at a high.**

Due to the ongoing Indian war, frontier settlers have formed armed *Indian patrols* to guard against the feared attacks which strike suddenly and without warning, leaving mutilated corpses in their wake. When patrolling for hostile Indians, all Indians become suspect—including the Christian Indians living near the Moravian mission of *Bethlehem*—and grave threats are made against them.

Note:	Throughout early American history, the formation of Indian patrols was quite common during times of frontier conflict. With Pennsylvania seemingly under endless Indian attacks, many frontier settlers believed the pacifist Quaker government in Philadelphia was abetting the tribes by failing to act against them. As such, near Paxton, Pennsylvania, a vigilante group composed mostly of Scotch-Irish settlers would be formed, calling itself the *Paxton Boys*. With emotions running out of control, most of the group and their supporters believed that all Indians should simply be killed.

Christian Indians are moved to Philadelphia for protection from hostile Whites.

The Indians have been living together peacefully in the villages of *Nain* and *Wechquetank,* but with frontier passions at a dangerous level, the peace-loving *Moravian* are relocated to the safety of Philadelphia's Province Island—with the Delaware River providing a protective moat.

Note:	Located south of the city, Province Island had been serving as Philadelphia's infirmary and the arriving Indians were to be housed there only temporarily. However, as neither New York nor New Jersey would accept them, these Christian converts and others would be forced to remain in the island's barracks until 1765.
	Stemming from the region of Moravia in today's Czech Republic, the Protestant missionaries traveled the world to introduce Christianity to non-Christian native people. The Indian converts in Pennsylvania were called Moravian or the *Moravian Tribe* and lived collectively in isolated settlements to practice their faith unmolested. As Christians, the Moravian were untrusted by their fellow Indians—but as Indians—they were untrusted by the Whites.

Dec. 2, 1763   **The oldest surviving Jewish synagogue in the United States is built in Rhode Island.**

The *Touro Synagogue* is dedicated in Newport, Rhode Island.

Note:	Today, the Touro Synagogue is the only surviving synagogue from the American colonial period and is listed as a national historic site.

Dec. 1763   **At Fort Pitt, Indians complain about the lack of the cheap trade goods promised to them after the defeat of the French.**

With the French gone, the tribes have no choice for trade and can only complain.

Dec. 14, 1763   **The Paxton Boys murder peaceful Indians near Harrisburg, Pennsylvania.**

Fifty-seven men from Paxton attack the small Indian village of *Conestoga Town* at dawn, killing and scalping six Susquehannock—more commonly known as Conestoga—and proceed to burn the Indians' cabins to the ground.

Note:	Fourteen Conestoga were away selling their woven wares at a nearby town at the time of the attack. Arriving home the following day, the Indians would be horrified to discover the ghastly scene. With their lives in danger, the Conestoga would be placed in Lancaster jail's workhouse under the protective care of the sheriff.
	The Conestoga were well-known to the wider community of regional settlers. Remnants of the once powerful Susquehannock, this small group had adopted many

of the Whites' customs—including Christianity—and earned money by making and selling brooms and other products.

To justify their actions, the Paxton Boys would claim that both the Conestoga and the Moravian were secretly in league with the warring Indians and were providing them with intelligence and aid.

The massacre site is located in today's Paxtang Borough of Harrisburg, Pennsylvania.

Dec. 22, 1763   **Pennsylvania Governor John Penn offers a reward for the apprehension of the Paxton culprits.**

> Note: Penn's proclamation concerning the Paxton Boys would not be published in the Philadelphia paper until December 29. In the meantime, it was Governor Penn's intention to protect the small group of surviving Conestoga by moving them hastily to Philadelphia to join with the Moravian on Province Island.

Dec. 27, 1763   **The *Conestoga Massacre*: Conestoga held at the Lancaster jail workhouse are brutally murdered.**

Approximately fifty Paxton Boys brush aside the jailkeeper and begin slaughtering the Conestoga with knives and tomahawks killing six adults and ten children. Learning of the murders, the Pennsylvania government is aghast and ups the reward for the apprehension of those involved.

> Note: Though many locals were ashamed of the murderous atrocity, others—consumed with Indian hatred—were supportive and simply wanted the Indians exterminated. Therefore, the rewards offered by the *Indian lovers* of Philadelphia would be ignored.
>
> Three of today's few reminders of the Conestoga existence are the village of Conestoga, Pennsylvania; the Conestoga River; and the historical Conestoga wagon.

Dec. 1763   **The Paxton Boys turn their wrath toward the colonial officials in Philadelphia.**

Learning of Governor Penn's call for their arrest and that the Moravian are being sheltered in Philadelphia, the Paxton Boys and their growing number of supporters turn their outrage toward the colony's Quaker officials. In general, the frontier Whites are angry that the Pennsylvania Assembly is willing to spend money to protect Indians but will not spend the necessary funds to protect them.

Jan. 1, 1764   **New York's *Provisional Act,* supporting the quartering of British troops, expires.**

During the Seven Years' War, the New York Assembly was happy to host the King's troops and enjoyed the security they provided by being based in New York. But now that the French threat has passed, the New Yorkers are reluctant to continue their support.

> Note: During the recent war, General Thomas Gage had experienced firsthand the difficulties of securing proper accommodations and logistical support for British troops in the American colonies. Now, with the New York Assembly reluctant to provide the necessary funds, a major problem existed for General Gage.

Jan. 2, 1764   **Pennsylvania Governor John Penn issues a second proclamation calling for the arrest of the Paxton Boys' ringleaders.**

Published in the newspapers on January 5 and again on January 12, a £200 reward is offered for taking into custody any one of the three Paxton leaders. In addition, a pardon is offered to the Paxton Boys not directly involved in the killings if they apprehend and secure the wanted men.

Jan. 1764

Panic ensues in Philadelphia as the Paxton Boys march on the city to present their grievances to the colonial government.

Two hundred fifty Paxton Boys—augmented by a growing number of frontier supporters—descend into mobbish vigilantes, intent on terrorizing Pennsylvania's officials and murdering the Moravian held on Province Island.

Note: Many in Philadelphia feared that the approaching mob numbered in the thousands and set about to oppose them.

Feb. 6, 1764

The Paxton mob is stopped at Germantown by a large force of citizens armed with small cannons to greet them.

Governor John Penn sends a delegation led by Benjamin Franklin to negotiate with the vigilantes, but they demand to present their grievances directly to the colonial officials. Franklin negotiates with the angry mob and agrees to permit one of the protestors, Matthew Smith, to present their grievances, but demands that the others turn around and disperse in the knowledge that their complaints will be addressed by the assembly.

Note: The grievances were contained in a pamphlet addressed to officials entitled, *The Declaration and Remonstrance of the distressed and bleeding Frontier Inhabitants.*

The Paxton crisis would further divide Pennsylvania politics between those supporting the Penn proprietorship and those against the family's continued oversight.

None of the Paxton Boys would ever be brought to justice.

What will happen to the Moravian?

The Christian Indians, mostly Delaware and Mahican, are given permission by the Iroquois to move westward to Pennsylvania's Wyalusing Valley, away from the hostile Whites. There, they found the settlement of *Friedenshuetten,* but in 1771, they are again forced to move after the land is sold to Pennsylvania by the Iroquois. At the invitation of the Western Delaware, the Moravian relocate near the Tuscarawas River in Ohio creating mission settlements with schools and churches under the direction of the Moravian missionary David Zeisberger.

In September 1781, during the American War for Independence, British authorities force the Moravian to move closer to Fort Detroit due to the frontier conflicts; however, before the end of that winter, the Indians' food supplies become desperately low. Hoping to avoid starvation, some of the Moravian are permitted to return to their abandoned towns to retrieve supplies left behind and to harvest any corn yet standing in the winter fields.

Arriving at their former settlement of Gnadenhutten, the Moravian are taken prisoner while gathering corn by 160 militiamen from Fort Pitt led by Colonel David Williamson. Seeking the hostile Indians responsible for recent attacks in western Pennsylvania, Williamson accuses the Moravian of having committed the frontier atrocities. Ignoring their pleas of innocence, the Indians are separated into two groups, with the men placed in one cabin and the women and children in another. After being bound, the Indians are told they are to be killed the next day.

Hearing their fate, the Moravian spend the night singing and praying, and as promised, on March 8, 1782, the entire group is executed. Forced to stand facing the cabin walls, the Christian Moravian—twenty-eight men, twenty-nine women, and thirty-nine children—are killed one at a time by mallet blows to the head. At the conclusion of the grisly deed, all are scalped before the Pennsylvania men set fire to the buildings. One boy, feigning death, escapes through a small window to serve witness to the infamous deed.

Note:	No charges would ever be filed against the murderers.
	Following the American War for Independence, many Moravian would relocate to Michigan, and others to the Ontario region of Canada.

Feb. 1764   **William Franklin arrives from London as New Jersey's royal governor.**

The new governor arrives with his wife, Elizabeth, to a welcoming crowd.

Note:	In stark contrast to his initial welcome, William Franklin would leave the royal governor's office in chains; arrested January 5, 1776, at the order of the Second Continental Congress for remaining loyal to Britain.

Great Britain has become the most powerful country in Europe, but maintaining the Empire's military might is expensive.

Note:	With few European allies, most in Britain believed a large military was necessary.

March 17, 1764   **Parliament's House of Commons debates imposing a stamp tax on Britain's colonies.**

Note:	Word of the stamp tax debate would soon cross the Atlantic and create alarm. In response, influential leaders in the American colonies would immediately set to work to thwart the idea.
	Nearly all the American colonies had agents employed in Britain to lobby for their interests and to keep the colonial assemblies and merchants abreast of the latest political news from London.

April 5, 1764   **Britain's *American Revenue Act* of 1764, aka the *Sugar Act*, is passed.**

At Lord Grenville's urging, Parliament passes the 1764 American Revenue Act as an amended extension of the 1733 Molasses Act—which has been little enforced and mostly ignored. The American Revenue Act, officially entitled *An act for granting certain duties in the British colonies and plantations in America*, is designed to better enforce the collection of duties as allowed under the 1733 Molasses Act and is to be considered perpetual, with enforcement to begin on September 29, 1764. The revenues generated by the collection of duties are to:

- Pay the necessary expenses for defending, protecting, and securing British colonies and plantations in America.

- Pay the costs for enforcement of the Act.

The American Revenue Act imposes new or higher duties on foreign imports to the colonies, including sugar, indigo, coffee, wine (excluding French wine), silk, goods of Persia, China, or East India, calicos, and linen cloth imported or brought into any British colony or plantation in America.

Note:	Importers of such enumerated articles were to post bonds of £2,000 for each ship.

Regarding duties to be paid on foreign sugars: the duty on molasses is reduced from 6 pence to 3 per gallon; the duty for raw sugar is kept the same; and the duty is increased on refined sugar. However, unlike the past, the duties are to be rigorously enforced and collected.

Note:	Though the tax on molasses was a 50 percent reduction, in reality it represented a 3-pence increase as most shippers and importers had been paying no duty at all due to smuggling and lax enforcement of the 1733 Molasses Act.
	Sugar was by far the most lucrative of the colonial trades. Therefore, Great Britain hoped to press the American colonial merchants to buy British sugar and molasses

from the planters in Barbados and Jamaica, while attempting to eliminate the cheaper Spanish and French sugar from the North American market.

The American Revenue Act of 1764, or Sugar Act, disallows the importation of foreign rum or spirits into any of his Majesty's dominions. The Act includes that:

- Importers of rum must carry a legal certificate issued by a British justice of the peace describing their ship's contents and origin.

- Upon arrival at a legal port of entry, the shippers are to present such certificates to the proper customs officer and take an oath swearing the contents are the same.

- If a shipper has no certificate but can show that the products are of British origin and that no fraud is intended, the regular duties shall apply.

The cargo of wine importers in violation of the law is to be seized and publicly sold by the proper customs official within twenty days to the highest bidder. The proceeds are to pay the proper duty owed, and any remainder is be returned to the importer. If the price bid for the wine is not sufficient to pay the duty, then the wine shall instead be destroyed, and the casks returned to the importer.

The American Revenue Act prohibits the shipping of colonial lumber and iron directly to Ireland or any port in Europe; all must be shipped directly to Great Britain beginning September 26, 1764.

The following points relate to the enforcement of the 1764 Revenue Act:

- Any British ship within two leagues (seven miles) of shore with such goods aboard without proper certification showing that bond has been paid; or any such ship arriving in Great Britain or Britain's colonies without presenting such certificate to a customs official at the time of arrival—such ship's cargo shall be forfeited, and the ship seized and prosecuted according to law.

- No goods liable to the payment of duties may be shipped from the colonies without proper papers showing the duties have been paid.

Note: This did not apply to ships without certificates hauling salt from Europe to the fisheries in New England, Newfoundland, Pennsylvania, New York, and Nova Scotia, or wherever else allowed by law.

The term *British ship* included the American ships—as all were at the time British.

- The falsifying or forging of papers shall result in a £500 fine.

- Any foreign ship anchored or hovering within two leagues of shore has forty-eight hours to depart to its destination after being requested to do so by the British customs officer. Apart from cases in which compliance is not possible, any ship in noncompliance shall be seized and prosecuted.

Note: This did not apply to French fishing ships in specific coastal waters of Newfoundland.

- Any British ship entering, leaving, hovering, or at anchor within two leagues of the French islands of St. Pierre and Miquelon found to have taken any goods aboard or dropped them off shall be seized, and such goods shall be forfeited and lost.

Note: These islands, located south of Newfoundland in the Gulf of St. Lawrence, were remnants of France's former North American empire. Though small, they were important islands used for processing fish caught by French fisherman. As such, they were a natural point for staging illegal smuggling operations between the French and American colonials.

- All goods unlisted on the certificate, which shall be found after the shipper has made his report to the customs officer, are to be forfeited and lost.

- If goods or merchandise liable to payment of duties are loaded for export or unloaded on import before proper duties are paid, or if prohibited goods are imported or exported contrary to the meaning of any Act of Parliament, every person assisting or otherwise concerned in the loading or unloading, or to the receiver of such illegal goods, shall forfeit treble the value of such goods, "and all the boats, horses, cattle, and other carriages whatsoever made use of in the loading, landing, removing, carriage, or conveyance of any of the aforesaid goods, shall also be forfeited and lost, and shall and may be seized and prosecuted by any officer of his Majesty's Customs, as herein after mentioned."

- Any customs officer causing the import or export of such goods, or helping the evasion of duties through fraudulence or falsification, shall be fined £50 for every offense.

- Every governor or commander in chief of any of his Majesty's colonies or plantations is required to take a solemn oath to do his utmost to observe and enforce the law.

- Those smugglers caught in Great Britain are to be prosecuted at Westminster, England, or in the Court of Exchequer in Scotland.

- Those smugglers caught in the colonies must pay all fines in British pounds sterling. Penalties and forfeitures are to be dealt with in the Admiralty or Vice Admiralty Courts, not in colonial civil courts.

After deducting the costs of prosecution, penalties and forfeitures recovered in the Americas are to be divided as follows:

- A third is to be paid into the hands of the customs officer at the port where the penalties and forfeitures are recovered for the use of the king.

- A third is to be paid to the governor or commander in chief of the colony.

- A third is to be paid to the person who should seize, inform, and sue for the same, except for seizures made at sea by commanders or officers of the British Navy.

Excepting such seizures as shall be made at sea by the commanders or officers of his Majesty's ships or vessels of war duly authorized to make such seizures, after deducting the costs of prosecution, penalties and forfeitures are to be divided as follows:

- One moiety is to be collected by the customs officer for the king's use.

- The other moiety to him or them who shall seize, inform, and sue for the same.

In addition, the following provisions apply:

- If a ship is seized, the owner is responsible to show that its contents are legal; it is not the customs officer's responsibility to prove them illegal.

- If the accused shall be found innocent but the judge rules there was probable cause, the ship and its contents (or the value thereof) shall be returned, but not more than 2 pence in damages shall be awarded.

- That any persons being sued in Great Britain or America for anything done in pursuance of the Revenue Act, or any other Customs Act, if the defendant can show that they acted in good faith in their pursuance of the law, the jury must find for the defendant.

The British Ministry views the new legislation as just and necessary, stating:

- The Revenue Act "is just and necessary and it is to be used towards defraying the expenses of defending, protecting, and securing the said colonies and plantations whose commerce has been happily enlarged as by the recent peace" (referring to the end of the Seven Years' War, aka the French and Indian War). In addition, Britain assures the colonists that the money will stay in America, to be used for the war and the administrative costs of the colonies.

The American reaction to the 1764 Revenue Act (Sugar Act) is mild due to:

- Unlike the upcoming 1765 Stamp Act, which will affect everyone, colonial protests against the Revenue Act are rare outside of Massachusetts and Rhode Island, where the Act's effects are mostly limited to the New England's rum producers, shipping industry, and in particular—the smugglers of molasses and sugar.

- The Revenue Act's duties are to be directly paid by the transporters and not by the general public. Though this causes a slight increase in the price of rum, sugar, and sugar products, it is an indirect tax—buried in the price and unnoticed by most.

- Though the Revenue Act also includes increased taxes on other imported goods, most are luxury items affecting the wealthy more than the average colonial.

- At a time of economic downturn following the recent war, many colonial merchants believe that Britain is trying to destroy American trade with foreign colonies.

Note:	Though the protected price of British sugar benefited New England rum distillers, it would not be appreciated. More objectionable to the colonial merchants were the stricter bonding regulations for shipmasters, whose cargoes would be subject to seizure and confiscation by British customs commissioners.
	Many believed the Revenue Act would have disastrous effects on Massachusetts and New England shipping, yet the Act would never really be enforced as smuggling had become a way of life for merchants and transporters alike. The North Americans were *far from home* and a long culture of salutary neglect by Great Britain made sure the laws would be mostly ignored, resulting in little money collected. Therefore, the British Ministry under Lord Grenville would continue to tighten control over the colonies, threatening to send warships to patrol the American coastline in search of smugglers and to crack down on the rampant bribery of customs officials.
	Boston's Sam Adams would be opposed to the 1764 Revenue Act, decrying that only the American colonists had the right to tax themselves. America enriched England by spending millions on British imports; therefore, taxes would only hurt the profitable trade between them. In the end, the greatest objection of the Americans was the precedent it would set.

The 1764 Revenue Act establishes a *Super-Vice Admiralty Court* in Halifax, Nova Scotia, with jurisdiction from Florida to Newfoundland.

Though this new super-court does not replace the authority of the existing courts, the Vice Admiralty Court in Halifax may be used when British naval officials believe that local bias will free a guilty man. The presiding judge at Halifax is to be from Great Britain and not the colonies, and failure to appear in court as commanded will result in a guilty verdict.

Note:	This would create a no-win situation for those Americans accused of certain maritime violations, including smuggling. Failing to appear at remote and distant Halifax, Nova Scotia, would render a guilty verdict as all accused were presumed guilty unless proven otherwise.

> In 1768, due to a constant overload of cases at the Halifax Court, additional Vice Admiralty Courts would be established in Boston, Philadelphia, and Charles Town to assist the judicial enforcement of British navigation and trade law in the American colonies.

April 19, 1764 **The *1764 Currency Act* is passed by Parliament, to be effective from September 1, 1764.**

Great Britain attempts to establish economic uniformity and control over the hodgepodge of printed monies and bills of credit used by the American colonies in conducting business. As the valuations fluctuate greatly, quarrels frequently arise over debt repayment, causing merchants in Britain to complain about losing money to the Americans. The 1764 Currency Act is an attempt to bring order to the chaotic economic system.

The following are among the provisions of the Act:

- No colonial legislation may order the printing of paper bills or bills of credit of any kind or denomination whatsoever to be used as bills of payment.

- The great quantities of bills already in circulation are to be called in and no colonial assembly may pass Acts prolonging their legal tender. Any such Act will be considered void.

- Any colonial governor, after September 1, 1776, giving his assent to such Acts contrary to the 1764 Currency Act shall be fined £1,000 for each offense and be removed from office.

Some effects of the Currency Act are as follows:

- British merchants are protected from being forced to accept colonial *paper* as payment, causing hard currency (silver and gold coins known as *specie*) to flow from the American colonies to England. As specie is scarce in the colonies, this will cause other commodities to be used as mediums of trade and barter in North America.

- The colonial economies are hurt as the Act comes into force during a post-war economic depression.

- Many Americans now want more economic self-determination, believing that Parliament and the British Ministry have little idea of their situation. The Currency Act is a reminder that they are under the *British thumb*.

1764 **Tasked with enforcing Great Britain's trade laws, the British fleet becomes an adversary to those involved in illicit trade.**

The Seven Years' War is over and the British Navy—no longer fighting the French and Spanish—turns its attention to apprehending colonial smugglers in what will become a game of cat-and-mouse during the years leading to the American War for Independence.

Brown University is established in Providence, Rhode Island.

> Note: Originally called the College of Rhode Island, the school would be renamed in 1804 after a wealthy donor, Nicolas Brown.

April 21, 1764 **The French residents of Louisiana learn that they are under Spain's authority.**

France informs the Louisiana governor that the colony was secretly transferred to Spain by the *Treaty of Fontainebleau* eighteen months earlier.

	Note: Upon hearing the news, many French vow to leave Louisiana rather than remain as France continues the process of vacating its former lands in North America.

Spring 1764	**Smallpox breaks out in Boston.**
	Note: Inoculations were dangerous. The method involved making a shallow incision into the skin and therein placing a thread laced with live pustular matter. The recipient then prepared to get sick but would later emerge immune to the dreaded disease—if they didn't die in the process.

Pennsylvania's political tensions continue over the Penn family's proprietorship.

Benjamin Franklin helps lead an unsuccessful effort to curtail the power of the Penns by having Pennsylvania placed under royal control.

	Note: The Penn family—proprietors of Pennsylvania since 1681—held the power to override the assembly's legislation; and until 1760, had been exempt from paying taxes on their vast landholdings. In addition, many Pennsylvanians were unhappy with the Quaker family's reluctance to *go after the Indians* who were upsetting the peace.

May 24, 1764	**Massachusetts learns Parliament has passed the American Revenue Act, aka the Sugar Act.**

At a Boston town meeting, the participants are upset to learn of the Revenue Act's passage. In response, Sam Adams and others denounce the tax and propose that the colonies unite in opposition to it.

	Note: The first calls for a nonimportation (boycott) of British goods would be raised at this meeting in order to provide Massachusetts a legal means to protest the Act.

June 1764	**Massachusetts organizes a *Committee of Correspondence* to begin communications with the other North American colonies.**

The Massachusetts General Court (Assembly) hopes to create a unified opposition to the Currency Act and the enforcement of Britain's trade and navigation laws as called for by the 1764 American Revenue Act.

	Note: Long considered an independent thorn, Massachusetts would only add to its trouble-making reputation as it began a campaign to unify colonial opposition to the Revenue Act. In response, Britain would focus its efforts to quell the American unrest on Boston—the epicenter of the resistance.

July 9, 1764	**Provincial gunners fire on the British schooner HBS *St. John* in Newport, Rhode Island.**

British naval patrols are already cruising the Rhode Island Coast and the Rhode Islanders—heavily involved in smuggling and rum production—resent their presence. The HBS *St. John* has raised the Rhode Islanders' ire by seizing a New York molasses ship and impressing a local sailor against his will. Now leaving Newport without paying for the ship's supplies, including pigs and chickens, Governor Stephen Hopkins orders gunners at Fort George on Goat Island to fire on the *St. John* as the British ship sails away.

	Note: The impressed sailor, Thomas Moss, had been rescued by a crowd who pelted stones at his British captors while Moss waited to be transported away.
	Many historians consider the firing on the HBS *St. John* the earliest act of open hostility in the coming American rebellion.

The Rhode Island governor, Stephen Hopkins, would be a signer of the U.S. Declaration of Independence.

July 1764   **Boston lawyer James Otis publishes *The Rights of the British Colonies Asserted and Proved*.**

In his essay, Otis argues for American representation in Parliament and questions Great Britain's right to tax the colonies without it. Otis writes, "No parts of His Majesty's dominions can be taxed without their consent; that every part has a right to be represented in the supreme or some subordinated legislature; that the refusal of this would seem to be a contradiction in practice to the theory of the constitution."

The essay continues, stating, "Every British subject born on the continent of America, or in any other of the British dominions, is by the law of God and nature, by the common law, and by act of parliament, (exclusive of all charters from the Crown) entitled to all the natural, essential, inherent and inseparable rights of our fellow subjects in Great Britain."

Note: Otis's declarations concerning taxes would soon render to its essence: "*Taxation without representation is tyranny.*" These words would make Otis a colonial celebrity.

This was the first published questioning of Britain's authority to levy taxes against the American colonists.

July 26, 1764   **With the Indian war raging, atrocities continue in Pennsylvania's frontier.**

Near Mercersburg, a raiding party of four Delaware warriors from the Muskingum region of the Ohio Country horrendously mutilate and scalp a pregnant woman. The next day, the same Indians attack a school, killing and scalping teacher Enoch Brown and nine of the students before escaping into the forest with four captives. Two additional children—scalped and left for dead—survive to provide witness.

Note: These horrific events created fascinating press in colonial newspapers and helped feed a hatred against the Indians.

Summer 1764   **Pennsylvania reintroduces scalp bounties against the warring Shawnee and Delaware.**

Lieutenant Governor John Penn offers bounties for the scalps of Shawnee, Delaware, and others in confederacy with them for having "butchered great Numbers of the Inhabitants, burnt and destroyed their Habitations, and laid waste the Country." The bounties to be paid: "For every Male Indian Enemy, above Ten Years old, who shall be taken prisoner, and delivered at any Forts garrisoned by the Troops in the Pay of this Province, or at any of the County Towns, to the Keeper of the common Goals there, the Sum of ONE HUNDRED AND FIFTY SPANISH DOLLARS, OR PIECES OF EIGHT. For every Female Indian Enemy, taken Prisoner and brought in as aforesaid; and for every Male Indian Enemy, of Ten Years old or under, taken Prisoner and delivered as aforesaid, the Sum of ONE HUNDRED AND THIRTY PIECES OF EIGHT. For the Scalp of every MALE INDIAN ENEMY, above the Age of Ten Years, produced as Evidence of their being killed, the Sum of ONE HUNDRED AND THIRTY-FOUR PIECES OF EIGHT. And for the SCALP of every FEMALE INDIAN ENEMY, above the Age of Ten Years, produced as Evidence of their being killed, the Sum of FIFTY PIECES OF EIGHT. AND that there shall be paid to every Officer or Officers, Soldier or Soldiers, as are or shall be in the Pay of this Province, who shall take, bring in, and produce any INDIAN ENEMY PRISONER or Scalp, as aforesaid, ONE HALF of the said several and respective PREMIUMS and BOUNTIES.

Note: Spanish silver dollars were commonly cut into eighths for smaller denomination purposes; thus, they were called *Pieces of Eight*.

The British military prepares an offensive against the warring Western Tribes.

From his military headquarters in New York, Acting Commander in Chief General Thomas Gage issues a two-pronged plan to end the Indian hostilities:

- A northern campaign—led by Colonel John Bradstreet—is to begin at Fort Schlosser at Niagara, New York, and sail westward along Lake Erie's southern shore to Fort Detroit.

- A southern prong—led by Colonel Henry Bouquet—is to march from Fort Pitt directly into the heart of the Delaware Country at the headwaters of the Muskingum River in eastern Ohio.

If possible, both military regiments are to eventually rendezvous.

Note:	The overall mission was to subdue and pacify the warring tribes, secure the return of White prisoners, and assert Britain's authority. As many of the Indians disbelieved the French were permanently gone, it was important to convince them that their former allies would not be returning.

July–Aug. 1764   **The *Fort Niagara Treaty*: The British seek Iroquois assistance in the Western Indian War.**

Meeting in Niagara, British Indian Superintendent William Johnson attempts to brighten the Covenant Chain; return the warring Senecas to the British fold; and enlist the Six Nations to *take up the hatchet* against the Western Tribes—but they resist.

Note:	As punishment for the Devil's Hole attack the previous September, the Seneca were forced to relinquish a mile-wide strip on both sides of the Niagara River called the *Mile Reserve*, blocking them from the river and the Niagara Falls. This was a particularly harsh punishment as the portage connecting Lake Ontario and Lake Erie had long been controlled by the Seneca, who profited by hiring themselves as porters for both the French and English.

Summer 1764   **In Boston, Samuel Adams campaigns against the American Revenue Act, arguing that if the taxes are not opposed, others will surely follow.**

Early Aug. 1764   **From western New York, the Bradstreet expedition sets out for Fort Detroit.**

Westward-bound with a force of 1,800—800 British regulars, 73 sailors, 766 colonial troops, and 150 Iroquois allies—Colonel John Bradstreet departs Fort Schlosser in longboats and begins a voyage along Lake Erie's southern shore to relieve the besieged Fort Detroit. Then, after pacifying Pontiac and the hostile tribes of the Great Lakes, Bradstreet is to march south into the Ohio country in conjunction with Colonel Henry Bouquet to target the warring Shawnee and Delaware.

Note:	Though the plan called for the two military offensives—Bradstreet's and Bouquet's—to take place simultaneously, Colonel Bouquet had been delayed at Carlisle, Pennsylvania, due to insufficient numbers. In need of colonial troops and additional supplies, Bouquet would continue to ready his army as best he could while the Pennsylvania Assembly dragged its feet in providing the necessary funds (Virginia and Maryland had both refused).
	Longboats, aka shallops were open boats with oars and sails, quite susceptible to the elements.

Aug. 1764   **In the western Carolinas, groups know as *regulators* patrol the frontier regions keeping watch.**

People in the frontier regions often arrived ahead of the security provided by an established government. As such, it was common for the isolated settlers to form citizen patrols to fill the void. In the Carolinas, civilian patrol groups are formed under the general name of regulators in response to the dangers posed by the French, hostile Indians, highwaymen, fugitives, and runaway slaves.

Seeds of revolt: Regional divisions have developed in North Carolina.

As people continue to move westward into the remote interior regions, provincial differences have emerged between the established coastal elites and the poor hill farmers of the western Piedmont region. The eastern tidewater planters, merchants, and lawyers—enjoying both wealth and control of the North Carolina Assembly—are little inclined to hearken to the remonstrances of the frontier farmers who view the established government officials as "unjust and dishonest," engaging in extortion, embezzlement, and other schemes to benefit themselves at the expense of the poor. The following are among the main issues:

- The western North Carolina region is generally poor, with a newer population. Hence, the hardscrabble farmers have little political influence with the colonial government at New Bern.

- The frontier settlers believe their property taxes are unfairly high. Many feel they should be charged less than the easterners as their lands are much less valuable than the fertile coastal lands.

- Land prices remain high due to speculators and wealthy newcomers moving into the region and taking economic and political power from locals.

- Western Carolina has suffered recent droughts and reduced crop yields, leaving many farmers poorer than before.

- High fees, confiscated lands, and unaccounted taxes paid to dishonest sheriffs have caused the frontier people to suffer.

- Many of North Carolina's poor view both the courts and the sheriffs as corrupt and caring little for their needs.

Nonimportation is used for the first time as Massachusetts calls for a boycott of certain luxury goods from Great Britain.

Urging a repeal of the looming Revenue Act and the Currency Act, Massachusetts flexes its economic muscle by calling for nonimportation of certain nonessential goods manufactured in Great Britain and sold in Massachusetts. In response, shop owners pledge to no longer import lace, ruffles, mourning clothes and gloves (usually handed out at funerals), as well as other items. In addition, Boston's silversmiths and blacksmiths agree to boycott leather workwear.

Note:	Though limited in scope, Massachusetts's economic boycott was designed to be a wake-up call to British merchants.
	The term *boycott* did not yet exist. The term would be first used in Ireland during the 1880s by tenants collectively resisting high taxes and evictions by an absentee landlord, Charles Cunningham Boycott.

Nonimportation will become an economic weapon of choice for the Americans.

Great Britain imports huge quantities of natural resources from North America and exports massive amounts of goods regularly used and consumed by the American colonials. This ever-increasing multiplicity of goods and manufactures shipped to North America generates vast wealth for Britain, and thus the Americans employ a strategy allowing them to stay within the law while hopefully bringing enough pressure to bear on Britain's economy to secure their demands.

Aug. 12, 1764   **En route to Fort Detroit, Colonel Bradstreet meets with Indian leaders at Pennsylvania's Presque Isle.**

Having learned of the military campaigns launched against them, ten Delaware and Shawnee leaders arrive to meet with the British commander stating that they have been sent to negotiate a peace. Though Colonel Bradstreet has authority only to create a temporary truce with the warring tribes, he oversteps his bounds and negotiates an agreement.

The following are among the terms:

- The Indians agree to recognize British authority; cease hostilities; and deliver their prisoners to Colonel Bradstreet during his return from Fort Detroit.

- Colonel Bradstreet agrees not to attack the Shawnee and Delaware towns, and to halt the Bouquet expedition expected to be sent against them from Fort Pitt.

Aug. 26, 1764   **The Bradstreet expedition reaches the beleaguered Fort Detroit.**

While meeting with tribal leaders, Colonel Bradstreet once again exceeds his authority by making unauthorized agreements.

Note: Colonel Bradstreet was mistakenly convinced that the Western Tribes would forsake their French allies and accept British authority.

As part of his agreement, Bradstreet chose not to destroy the Indian villages near Sandusky as General Gage had ordered him. As such, Gage would later condemn Bradstreet for making treaties and failing parts of his objective.

Though Pontiac refused to meet with Bradstreet, the famed Ottawa war leader would send a peace belt to the British colonel before leaving for the Illinois Country—still occupied by remaining French troops.

Sept. 1, 1764   **The 1764 Currency Act goes into effect.**

The printing of paper money or bills of credit is now prohibited in all of Britain's North American colonies.

Note: The previous Currency Act of 1751 had applied only to New England. Now, by applying to all the American colonies, the 1764 Currency Act would help foster a growing cohesiveness among them.

Many Americans believed the Currency Act would cripple the colonial economies.

Sept. 14, 1764   **British Colonel John Bradstreet's forces leave Fort Detroit and begin their return to Niagara's Fort Schlosser.**

Sept. 17, 1764   **Colonel Henry Bouquet arrives at Fort Pitt to launch a military campaign against the warring Delaware and Shawnee in Ohio.**

After long delays, Bouquet has finally arrived with a contingent of British regulars and 700 Pennsylvanians.

Note: During the 200-mile march from Carlisle, Bouquet had lost 300 of his Pennsylvania troops to desertion.

Sept. 29, 1764   **The American Revenue Act of 1764 (Sugar Act) goes into effect.**

Autumn 1764   **Four Cherokee chiefs travel to London to meet with King George III.**

For a second time, Virginia's Colonel Henry Timberlake accompanies Cherokee leaders to London. The Cherokee wish to meet with the king and request he enforce the Proclamation of 1763 banning White encroachments onto their tribal lands. As the Cherokee have previously complained to the royal governors to no avail, they now attempt to take their message directly to the king. This trip, unlike Colonel Timberlake's visit in 1762, is not considered a success and leaves the Indians disappointed. The following are among the many misfortunes:

- One of five original Cherokee dies just before departing Charles Town.

- A second Cherokee dies soon after arriving in England.

- The remaining three Cherokee are denied an audience with the king, for their visit has not been officially sponsored.

- While visiting the Strand Theatre, three New York Mohawk also arrive, causing confusion and quite a sensation for the theater patrons.

> Note: The Mohawk were completing a tour of Ireland and England.

In addition, Colonel Timberlake is accused of using *his Indians* to make money and told to take them home at his own expense. However, Timberlake refuses, warning that *these people* could start a war over the ill treatment they have received during their stay.

> Note: The British Ministry would eventually relent and pay for the Cherokee to return to South Carolina.

The Massachusetts nonimportation movement remains generally moribund.

Despite it having little actual economic effect—as a major consumer of British goods—Massachusetts has fired an economic warning shot *across the British bow*.

> Note: Although Massachusetts's nonimportation campaign against the 1764 American Revenue Act neither greatly materialized nor spread to other colonies, it helped set the stage for future protests that would erupt over the 1765 Stamp Act—including a second boycott of British goods.
>
> Neither the American Revenue Act nor the Currency Act would be repealed by Parliament due to nonimportation.

Oct. 1, 1764   **A mobbish election takes place in Philadelphia between supporters and non-supporters of the Penn family.**

The election is to decide whether Pennsylvania shall remain under the continued proprietorship of the Penn family or become a royal province by transferring control of Pennsylvania to the Crown. Benjamin Franklin, running for re-election to the colonial assembly, leads the efforts to oust the Penns which results in Franklin's double disappointment—the Pennsylvanians keep the Penn family as proprietors, and Benjamin Franklin fails to be re-elected.

> Note: The threat to civil rule represented by the Paxton Boys had frightened the Philadelphians. As such, the fear had been successfully used as a campaign issue by the Penns and their supporters to retain control of the colony.
>
> Sailing to London within a month, Franklin would continue to lobby against the Penn family's proprietorship of Pennsylvania.

Oct. 3, 1764   **Colonel Henry Bouquet leads an army from Fort Pitt to subdue the Delaware and Shawnee.**

With a goal to pacify the warring tribes and secure a return of English captives, Colonel Bouquet sets out with 1,500 men to the Delaware towns of the Tuscarawas region in eastern Ohio. Though commanding a formidable force, Bouquet proceeds cautiously during the two-week journey hoping to intimidate the Indians along the way.

> Note: The Bouquet expedition—the second prong of Britain's military offensive against the warring tribes—had been delayed due to the reluctance of Pennsylvania's assembly to provide funding to raise troops. By the time Bouquet's army finally departed Fort Pitt, Colonel Bradstreet's forces were returning from their mission to Fort Detroit.

Oct. 17, 1764   **The Indians are alarmed that Bouquet's army has reached the Tuscarawas River.**

Colonel Bouquet is met by Delaware chiefs who bring eighteen White captives to be given up as a show of good faith. The Indians are rightfully worried over this seemingly unstoppable English army approaching their villages and fear the probable destruction of their towns and fields. To further intimidate the Delaware chiefs, Colonel Bouquet refuses to halt and continues directly to the Indian towns.

> Note: The Muskingum River area hosted several important central towns of the Delaware and Shawnee. Among these Indians also lived a number of Mingo—offshoots of the Western Seneca.
>
> The Shawnee and Delaware tribes shared a close historical relationship. As a sign of respect, the Shawnee referred to the Delaware as *uncles*.

Oct. 18, 1764   **"We carry all to her hive." The New York Assembly petitions Parliament's House of Commons in objection to the Revenue and Currency Acts, and foremost—for being taxed without representation.**

The New York petition:

- Objects to taxes imposed "upon Subjects here, by Laws to be passed there," asserting the right that only the people may tax themselves. The assembly "conceive that this Innovation, will greatly affect the Interest of the Crown and Nation, and reduce the Colony to absolute ruin."

- Asserts that New York has both suffered and sacrificed for the Crown: "It has been their particular Misfortune, to be exposed to the Incursions of the Canadians, and the more barbarous Irruptions of the Savages of the Desert, as may appear by all the Maps of this Country; and in many Wars, we have suffered an immense Loss of Blood and Treasure, to repel the Foe, and maintain a valuable Dependency upon the British Crown."

- Asserts that New York has always paid "equal to our Abilities," and that in the past conquest of Canada, "our contributions surpassed our Strength ... to which we had loyally and voluntarily submitted."

- Asserts that free states must be granted exemption from involuntary taxes, "Without such a Right vested in themselves, exclusive of all others there can be no Liberty, no Happiness, and no Security; it is inseparable from the very Idea of Property, for who can call that his own, which may be taken away at the Pleasure of another?"

The petition also includes the following:

- "His Majesty has nowhere in the British dominion, more faithful subjects nor Britain more submissive and affectionate Sons than those of New York."

- "And if our Contributions to the Support of the Government upon this Continent, or for the Maintenance of an army, to awe and subdue the Savages should be thought necessary, why shall it be presumed with a Trial, that we more than others, will refuse to hearken to a just Requisition from the Crown?"

- "Nor will the Candor of the Commons of Great Britain, contrueour Earnestness to maintain this Plea, to arise from a Desire of Independency upon the supreme Power of the Parliament. Of so extravagant a Disregard to our own Interests we cannot be guilty. From what other Quarter can we hope for Protection? We reject the thought with utmost Abhorrence."

- "What can be more apparent, than that the State which exercises a Sovereignty in Commerce can draw all the Wealth its Colonies into its own Stock? And has not the whole Trade of North-America, that growing Magazine of wealth, been from the Beginning, directed, restrained, and prohibited at the sole pleasure of Parliament?"

- "A Freedom to drive all Kinds of Traffick in a Subordination to, and not inconsistent with, the British Trade; and an Exemption from all Duties in such a Course of Commerce, is humbly claimed by the Colonies, as the most essential of all the Rights to which they are intitled, as Colonists from, and connected, in the common Bond of Liberty, with the uninslaved Sons of Great-Britain."

- "... the whole Wealth of a Country may be effectively drawn off, by the Exaction of Duties, and by any other Tax upon their Estates."

The conclusions are as follows:

- "And therefore, the General Assembly of New York, in Fidelity to their Constituents, cannot but express the most earnest Supplication, that the Parliament will charge our Commerce with no other Duties, than a necessary Regard to the Particular Trade of Great-Britain, evidently demands; but leave it to the legislative Power of the Colony, to impose all other Burthens upon its own People, which the publick Exigencies may require."

- "Permit us, also, in Defence of our Attachment to the Mother Country, to add, what your Merchants (to whom we boldly make the Appeal) know to be an undoubted Truth; that this Continent contains some of the most useful of her Subjects. Such is the Nature of our Produce, that all we acquire is less than sufficient to purchase what we want of your Manufactures; all our riches must flow into Great Britain. As such, we contribute immensely to the National Stock. ... The more extensive our Traffick, the Greater her Gains; we carry all to her Hive, and consume our Returns."

The petition continues, stating that New York is:

- Opposed to the Revenue Act (Sugar Act), banning trade with the foreign sugar colonies.

- Opposed to the ban on the exportation of lumber to Ireland.

- Opposed to the laws of trade that "change the Current of Justice from the common Law, and subject Controversies of the utmost Importance to the Decisions of the Vice Admiralty Courts, who proceed not according to the old wholesome Laws of the Land, nor are always filled with Judges of approved Knowledge and Integrity."

- Opposed to the Currency Act rendering the colonial paper money nonlegal tender. The petition states that paper currency is often used in emergencies during war due to costs exceeding the colony's ability to pay, thus rendering paper currency an expedient answer only to be used as long as necessary for want of money.

The petition concludes: "The General Assembly of this Colony have no desire to derogate from the Power of the Parliament of Great-Britain; but they cannot avoid deprecating the Loss of such Rights as they have hitherto enjoyed, Rights established in the first Dawn of our Constitution, founded upon the most substantial Reasons, confirmed by invariable Usage, conducive to the best Ends; never abused to bad Purposes, and with the Loss, of which Liberty, Property and all the Benefits of Life, tumble into Insecurity and Ruin: Rights, the Deprivation of which, will dispirit the People, abate their Industry, discourage Trade, introduce Discord, Poverty and Slavery; or by depopulating the Colonies, turn a vast, fertile, prosperous Region, into a dreary Wilderness; impoverish Great-Britain, and shake the Power and Independency of the most opulent and flourishing Empire in the World."

In Ohio, the Bouquet expedition arrives at the headwaters of the Muskingum—the heart of the Delaware.

Aghast that an English army is in their very midst, the Delaware leaders sue for peace, but Colonel Bouquet initially rejects their overtures, telling them they are to be punished for warring against the English. However, during negotiations, Colonel Bouquet agrees to spare their villages from destruction if:

- The Indians return all English captives within twelve days.

- They provide each captive with enough supplies for the return trip to Fort Pitt.

- They provide six Indians hostages—two Shawnee, two Seneca (Mingo), and two Delaware—to show good intent and to assure that additional captives will be returned.

- The Delaware and Shawnee agree to travel to New York the following summer to meet with British Indian Superintendent William Johnson to work out a peace.

The Indians agree to the terms and Bouquet's army establishes a nearby camp to await the arrival of the captives.

Note:	Colonel Bouquet was able to subdue the Indians without firing a shot.
	The site of the Delaware towns was at present-day Coshocton, Ohio.

Oct. 19, 1764   **En route from Fort Detroit, the Bradstreet expedition suffers terrible losses in a great lakeside storm.**

While camped on the Lake Erie shore near present-day Cleveland, a fierce storm damages half of the fifty-six-boat flotilla. With the loss of so many vessels, Bradstreet's army is forced to bury its heavy cannons, and many of the troops must return overland to Fort Schlosser.

Note:	The two British campaigns against the warring tribes would have very different results in achieving their military objectives. When completed, Colonel Bradstreet would be blamed for his failures, whereas Colonel Bouquet would be lauded for his success.

Nov. 1, 1764   **Benjamin Franklin returns to Great Britain as a colonial agent for Pennsylvania.**

Franklin, as a member of the Pennsylvania Assembly, had previously lived in London representing the colony's interests. Now, having lost his re-election bid, the influential *Doctor Franklin* is employed by the assembly and returns to London to lobby on Pennsylvania's behalf.

Note:	This was Franklin's third trip to England, and it would be his longest stay—eleven years. Combined, Benjamin Franklin would live in London for nearly 18 years of his adult life.
	Once again, Franklin left his common-law wife Deborah in Philadelphia. Though she would suffer a series of strokes in 1768, her husband would choose not to return, and Deborah Franklin would die alone on December 19, 1774.
	The influential Benjamin Franklin would be later employed to also represent the interests of New Jersey, Massachusetts, and Georgia.
	Benjamin Franklin was not a doctor. He had received honorary degrees from the University of St. Andrews in 1759 and from Oxford in 1762 due to his significant contributions to science. To Franklin, it was an honor of which he was quite proud.

Nov. 3, 1764   **Massachusetts petitions the king in protest of the American Revenue Act.**

The following are among the petition's assertions:

- The Act represents a hardship on Massachusetts.

- The Act shuts off an established outlet for the inferior portions of the fish catch normally traded with the French islands in return for French molasses. Without this market, the price of fish will rise in Europe, and the French will undersell and destroy the nursery of English seamen.

Note:	The *inferior* catch was used to feed the African slaves of the French sugar islands.

- The trade restraints imposed on exporting timber and lumber to Great Britain only hinder the development and clearing of the uncultivated lands.

- The powers given to distant Admiralty Courts make it likely that accused but innocent men will lose disputed property.

- The extended powers of the Admiralty Courts deprive the colonists of trial by jury.

- Every Act of Parliament distinguishing the colonists from their fellow subjects living in Britain creates concern and grief.

- Britain is warned against imposing a stamp tax upon the colonists, as recently debated in the House of Commons, and against further consideration until the next session of Parliament.

- It is the colonists' hope that the liberties they have enjoyed continue.

- The depressed economy makes it impossible for the people to pay tax.

- The scarcity of money has had a detrimental effect on the American economy.

- Due to the unbalanced trade with Britain, wealth is drained away to Britain. This will result in a loss of trade by British merchants, for Americans will be unable to pay for goods.

- Britain benefits by the colonials, as they are taxed to support internal government and forced to consume British goods and manufactures.

- "Therefore, all things considered, we are here as fully burdened as our fellow subjects in Britain."

- "Therefore, the government receives a greater benefit from us living here rather than if we were returned to England and paid the additional taxes there."

- "We pray to be relieved of the burdens placed upon us by the late Acts of Parliament, and that the colonists be able to keep their own internal taxing power as in the past until more full representation of the state and condition of the colonies and the state of Great Britain in regard to them."

Nov. 5, 1764 **Boston's Pope's Day violence is particularly savage.**

The anti-Catholic event is celebrated yearly in Boston with a great brawl taking place between the town's two major gangs—the South End and the North End. These rivals annually engage in a competition to capture the other's pope effigy and this year's event is especially violent, with Boston authorities attempting to stop the brutal melee as one person is killed and others are severely injured.

Nov. 16, 1764 **General Thomas Gage is appointed commander in chief of Britain's troops in North America.**

General Gage has been the *acting* commander in chief since General Jeffery Amherst was recalled to London one year ago. With General Amherst having no interest in returning to North America, Gage's position now becomes official.

Nov. 18, 1764 **A huge military success: The Bouquet expedition begins its return to Fort Pitt with 200 recovered captives.**

Many of the captives have lived so long among the Indians that they do not wish to return and must be forced to do so. A number of the women, having been adopted into the tribes, now have Indian husbands and mixed-race children. Most of the younger captives do not speak English, have no memory of their previous lives, and do not wish to leave with these White strangers. As such, some of the captives escape during the march to Fort Pitt and return to their Indian families and friends. As agreed, in return for ending the hostilities and returning their captives, Colonel Bouquet spares destruction of the Delaware towns and promises to return in six months with presents.

Note	The Bouquet and Bradstreet expeditions basically ended the Western Indian War against the English, known today as Pontiac's Rebellion.

Nov. 1764 **Now officially in charge, General Gage writes to Parliament requesting additional powers for Britain's military forces in North America.**

From his headquarters in New York, Gage requests that Great Britain's *Mutiny, Desertions and Payment of Army Act*—more commonly referred to as the *Mutiny Act*—be amended to apply to the American colonies.

Note:	Most legal interpretations had determined that Britain's Mutiny Act (requiring that quarters be provided for troops on the march) did not apply to the American colonies, but Gage wanted the Act changed. Needing quarters and supplies should he have to march the British troops, General Gage sought the power to order that both be provided and paid for by the colonial assemblies, if deemed necessary.

Dec. 18, 1764 **Virginia's House of Burgesses petitions Parliament against introducing a stamp tax.**

Having learned the House of Commons had on the "17th day of March last," declined a measure calling for a stamp tax to be placed on the American colonies to be used "towards defending, protecting, and securing the British colonies and plantations in America,"—the Virginia Assembly is alarmed. Though the measure had been defeated, Parliament agreed to revisit the idea during its next session; thus, the assembly generates a petition in opposition stating, "the Council and Burgesses of Virginia, met in General Assembly, judge it their indispensable duty, in a respectful manner but with decent firmness, to remonstrate against such a measure, that at least a cession of those rights, which in their opinion must be infringed by that procedure, may not be inferred from their silence, at so important a crisis."

Included among the petition's assertions:

- That we should be taxed only by representatives chosen by us.

- That we retain all rights and immunities of British subjects.

- That Parliament does not have the power to tax the colonists shown formerly as the people cannot be represented.

- That even if it were proper for Parliament to impose the tax, it would prove ruinous to Virginia, now in a weakened state after recently contributing so much to the last war.

- This duty, added to the cost born by Virginia in fighting the restless Indians of her frontier, combined with the scarcity of cash in circulation and the low value of Virginia staples in the market would prove intolerable.

- That such an additional load placed on the colonies would not outweigh the negative effects on Great Britain—which depends on the colonies for her prosperity and represent a continued treasure if not discouraged. The colonies provide agricultural products and in return buy British manufactured goods with consumption increasing daily. This happy intercourse must be interrupted if we are forced to manufacture due to extreme poverty of articles normally purchased from Britain.

The Virginia the petition concludes:

- "From these considerations it is hoped that the Honourable House of Commons will not prosecute a measure, which those who may suffer it cannot but look upon as fitter for exiles driven from their native country after ignominiously forfeiting her favours and protection, than for the prosperity of *Britons*, who have at all times been forward to demonstrate all due reverence to the mother-kingdom, and are so instrumental in promoting her glory and felicity; and that *British* patriots will never consent to the exercise of anticonstitutional power; which even in this remote corner may be dangerous in its example to the interior parts of the *British* Empire, and will certainly be detrimental to its commerce."

1765   **More than 7,000 Africans arrive at Charles Town, South Carolina.**

Enslaved Africans, now 60 percent of the South Carolina population, are a very real concern for the Whites.

Note: At this time, approximately one in every five people in Britain's North American colonies was an African slave.

The steam engine is greatly improved and helps usher in Britain's Industrial Revolution.

Long dependent on water wheels, windmills, and animals for driving machinery, Scottish inventor James Watt's steam engine exponentially increases the world's mechanical powers.

Note: Coal would quickly become the primary fuel for creating steam to drive the many large machines that would be created. With ample coal deposits in Great Britain, another industry would be born—coal mining. In short time, London would be well known for its smoke-filled skies and soot-covered buildings.

The first medical school in the present-day United States begins at the University of Pennsylvania.

French Acadians begin a twenty-year migration to Louisiana.

Spain offers passage and land grants to Acadians who are willing to move to Louisiana.

> Note: Spain was only nominally in control of France's former Louisiana Colony and needed to increase the colony's population to hold back the encroaching British. Therefore, with so many French Acadians wanting to leave Canada rather than live under British authority, Spain created a destination for them. These French Catholics, as well as others already dispersed, would begin a migration to Louisiana and form the basis of the modern Cajun community located there yet today.
>
> *Cajun* comes from the word Acadian.

Jan. 1765

Britain continues forward with economic measures designed to defray the cost of defending its North American colonies.

Under the leadership of Prime Minister Lord George Grenville, Parliament continues to push for the American colonists—now costing Britain £200,000 a year—to pay their fair share.

> Note: With the French threat finally removed, many Americans saw no need to pay for unnecessary protections and preferred that Great Britain recall its troops.

Feb. 2, 1765

In London, Benjamin Franklin and other colonial agents dismiss American protests against the 1764 Revenue Act and give tentative consent for introducing a stamp tax in the colonies.

> Note: Misjudging the public's sentiments, several colonial leaders, including Franklin and Richard Henry Lee of Virginia, initially hoped to secure positions as stamp commissioners, which would later sully their reputations with their American brethren. Franklin was also responsible for Pennsylvania's stamp agent John Hughes being appointed to his position. As a result, Franklin's house in Philadelphia would come under attack while he was living in London.

Feb. 27, 1765

The *Stamp Act* is approved by Parliament's House of Commons for the purpose of raising a revenue from "his Majesty's dominions in America."

The Stamp Act still needs be approved by the House of Lords and King George III.

The term *sons of liberty* is used for the first time.

During Parliamentary debate over the stamp tax, Isaac Barre refers to the Americans opposed to the tax as "these sons of liberty."

> Note: Upon learning of Barre's words, many Americans resisting the Stamp Act would warmly embrace his description and a new moniker was born.

March 1765

Three disappointed Cherokee leave London and sail home to North America.

Returning with them to Charles Town, South Carolina, is Colonel Timberlake, who is now monetarily broke. In gratitude for his efforts to help them, the Cherokee offer Timberlake asylum in their country but he politely declines the invitation. Disappointed with their experience, and with two of the original Indian delegates dead, Timberlake is concerned that these retuning Cherokee leaders will stir up trouble among their brethren once they return to their towns and people.

In western Pennsylvania, a vigilante militia known as the *Black Boys* is formed to stop illegal trade goods from reaching the Western Tribes.

Large profits await the many unscrupulous Indian traders and East Coast merchants who, in the name of money, disregard the laws, ignore the consequences, and continue to trade prohibited goods—guns, lead, powder, knives, tomahawks, and rum. In addition, certain British military officers and colonial officials are themselves actively involved in the illicit trade, while others are paid to simply *look the other way*.

With Forbes's Road leading directly west to Fort Pitt and the Ohio River, it is a natural route for the flow of legal and illegal trade goods to the formidable tribes of the interior regions. Living along Forbes's Road near Fort Loudoun, James Smith and his Black Boys patrol will attempt to interrupt the flow of contraband—particularly weapons—through their region of Pennsylvania.

Note:	To hide their identities, the Black Boys would blacken their faces with soot before going on patrol, giving them their name.
	Indian hatred in Pennsylvania's frontier regions was in full swing as the people felt little supported by the British Ministry or the Penn government. This perception had given rise to Pennsylvania's Paxton Boys in 1764, and now to James Smith's Black Boys, as the frontier people *went it alone* to protect themselves against the warring Indians.

March 5, 1765   **A large pack train is stopped by Pennsylvania's Black Boys near Fort Loudoun.**

Suspected of carrying illegal trade goods, James Smith's vigilantes demand to inspect the train's cargo, but the pack drivers refuse. After sharp words and threats are exchanged, the eighty-one-horse pack train continues slowly westward toward Fort Pitt.

March 6, 1765   **The *Black Boys Rebellion* begins in Pennsylvania.**

During a snowstorm near modern McConnellsburg, eleven members of Smith's Black Boys, dressed as Indians, overtake the pack train and force it to halt by firing shots. Claiming to be acting in self-defense by prohibiting illegal goods from reaching the Ohio tribes, the disguised vigilantes shoot several pack horses and destroy many of the trade goods before fleeing. Immediately following the attack, the drivers return to Fort Loudoun and the fort's commander, British Lieutenant Charles Grant, sends a patrol of Royal Highlanders to arrest the culprits.

Note:	To assist with Indian negotiations at Fort Pitt, Deputy Superintendent of Indian Affairs George Croghan had been issued a military pass to trade with the tribes. Croghan—unopposed to making money—often used his official pass as a cover to transport prohibited trade goods from Philadelphia along Forbes's Road.

In New York, the Wappinger declare themselves to be the rightful owners of the Hudson Valley lands—but a court disagrees.

Confiscated from the Wappinger in 1756 by the wealthy and influential Philipse family, Wappinger sachem Daniel Ninham attempts to regain the tribe's lost lands by hiring a lawyer. However, in court the defendant Beverly Robinson produces a questionable 1692 treaty supposedly signing away the Wappinger lands to Adolph Philipse—his wife's deceased great-uncle. Therefore, the civil authorities rule against the Indians in favor of Robinson.

March 8, 1765   **In London, the Stamp Act is approved by Parliament's House of Lords.**

In frontier Pennsylvania, a British patrol arrests eight Black Boy militiamen.

Charged with attacking the pack train two days earlier, the men are arrested and taken to Fort Loudoun under guard.

March 9, 1765   **The first armed assault against British military troops by Americans?**

James Smith, leading 300 armed men, surrounds small Fort Loudoun, Pennsylvania, and demands the release of the eight Black Boys and the return of their confiscated firearms. Under siege and with little recourse, Lieutenant Charles Grant sends out runners to solicit aid but all are captured.

Though Grant had initially refused Smith's demands, now, with Fort Loudoun completely encircled and several of his troops held captive, the British commander has little choice and agrees to exchange prisoners and return the confiscated arms. However, the following day after the prisoners are exchanged, Lieutenant Grant refuses to return the weapons.

Note: Not a shot was fired during the entire siege.

James Smith would consider Lieutenant Grant's refusal to return the firearms a serious offence, and he was determined to retrieve them.

The actions of Smith's Black Boys would be published in British newspapers beginning on May 23 in the *London Chronicle*.

March 1765   **King George III approves the Stamp Act—the first direct tax on Britain's colonies.**

Scheduled to begin on November 1, 1765, the tax is designed to raise revenue throughout the British Empire. In the American colonies, the revenues shall be specifically used to pay one third of the cost of maintaining 10,000 troops in North America. The British troops are to: serve as a defense force for the Americans; keep the peace with the Indians; and monitor the former French lands west of the Appalachian Mountains—including the enforcement of the Proclamation of 1763 prohibiting unauthorized White intrusions.

The Stamp Act:

- Taxes all sorts of printed matter—deeds, marriage licenses, pamphlets, advertisements, broadsides, ships' papers, insurance documents, handbills, newspapers, diplomas, wills, customs documents, playing cards, etc.

- Introduces penalty provisions, including eliminating jury trials for violators.

Note: Unlike the 1764 American Revenue Act (Sugar Act), which primarily affected merchants and shippers, the stamp tax was to be a direct tax.

The amount paid for a stamped paper would vary depending on its purpose. As examples: a stamped paper granting license to practice law required a £10 fee; a license to sell wine or retail liquor required a duty of £3; a full sheet of paper for printing pamphlets had a 1-penny fee; an almanac required a 4-pence tax; a fee for playing dice was 10 shillings; and a pack of playing cards was a mere shilling.

Many American colonial leaders were already at work organizing resistance to the tax, hoping to bring about its repeal before it would go into effect, November 1. As a result of their efforts and the efforts of others, the summer of 1765 would be a summer of protests and open rebellion in Britain's North American colonies.

The British had been paying a stamp tax in England for years as a way of generating revenue. In addition, the Stamp Act would apply to all of Britain's colonies—not just the Americans. These included Jamacia, Barbados, East and West Florida, Quebec, Nova Scotia, etc. Therefore, the American complaints would garner little sympathy across the Atlantic.

Unlike today's postage stamps, a revenue stamp was an embossed stamp—a stamp imprinted on paper. The stamping would take place in England before the required papers were sent to Britain's colonies. Unable to be stamped on vellum (calfskin), the stamp would be instead embossed on paper and cut out to be stapled onto the vellum in order to show that the tax had been paid.

March 24, 1765 **Parliament passes the *Quartering Act* of 1765 to better meet the needs of the movement of his Majesty's troops in the American colonies.**

"There may be occasions for marching and quartering of regiments and companies of his Majesty's forces in several parts of his Majesty's dominions in America: and whereas the publick houses and barracks, in his Majesty's dominions in America, may not be sufficient to supply quarters for such forces: and whereas it is expedient and necessary that carriages and other conveniences, upon the march of troops in his Majesty's dominions in America, should be supplied for that purpose."

The following provisions concern the quartering of soldiers on the march:

- Local town officers or justices of the peace are required to quarter and billet troops in barracks provided by the colonies.

- Where room is insufficient, troops shall be billeted in "barracks, inns, livery stables, ale-house, victualling-houses, and houses of sellers of wine by retail to be drank in their own houses or places thereunto belonging, and all houses of persons selling of rum, brandy, water, cyder or metheglin, by retail, to be drank in houses."

- If there is still insufficient room, the governor and council for each province are to appoint a person to appropriate and prepare uninhabited houses, outhouses, barns, or other buildings to quarter remaining troops.

Note: Only space deemed necessary to accommodate the number of troops present was to be made ready.

- The commanding officer is to provide written notice as early as possible to the governor of the affected colony of troop numbers and movements so that the appointed person may prepare the necessary lodgings.

- Military officers violating this Act or forcing others to violate it, under witness of two, are to be cashiered from the military.

- If any person providing quarters shall find himself aggrieved by bearing a greater load in proportion to his neighbors and shall complain to the justice of the peace, such justice shall have the power to relieve such person by removing so many soldiers and quartering them upon such other person or persons to receive such soldiers accordingly.

- The officers and soldiers so quartered and billeted as aforesaid (except such as shall be quartered in the barracks, and hired uninhabited houses or other building aforesaid) shall be received and furnished with diet, and small beer, cyder, or rum mixed with water by the owners of the inns livery stables, alehouses, victualling-houses, and other houses in which they are permitted to be quartered by this Act, paying and allowing the same the several rates herein after mentioned to be payable out of the subsistence-money for diet and small beer, cyder, or rum mixed with water.

Note:	Rum mixed with water was called *grog*. The traditional mix was 4:1 water to rum.

- That all such officers and soldiers so put and placed in such barracks or hired uninhabited houses, out-houses, barns, or other buildings, shall from time to time be furnished and supplied by the person authorized or appointed for such purpose, with fire, candles, vinegar, and salt, bedding, utensil for dressing victuals, small beer, or cyder, not exceeding five pints, or half a pint of rum mixed with a quart of water, to each man, without paying anything for the same.

Note:	Anyone who provided these goods and services to the troops was to be reimbursed by the respective colonial administration.

- If any constable, magistrate, or other chief officer so charged with quartering officers and soldiers shall neglect or refuse for a space of two hours to quarter or billet such officers and soldiers after having been given sufficient notice before the arrival of such forces, or shall receive demand, contract, or agree for, any sum or sums of money, or any reward whatsoever, for or on account of excusing any person or persons whatsoever from quartering or receiving into his, her, or their house or houses, any officer or soldiers liable by this Act to be quartered or billeted upon him or her, shall refuse to receive or victual and such officer or soldier, or shall refuse to furnish or allow the several things herein before directed to be furnished at the rate herein mentioned, if convicted before a magistrate of the common law court, of the colony where the offense shall be committed, every such constable, magistrate, or other chief officer or person so offending shall forfeit for every such offence, the sum of five pound sterling, or any sum of money not exceeding five pounds nor less than forty shillings for every offense. The sum to be paid to the treasury of the province or colony.

The following provisions concern carriages to be used for the King's troops:

- All justices of the peace, if requested by the king, or the general of his forces, or of the commanding officer, shall issue warrants to the constables, magistrates, or civil officers of the districts or municipalities through which they are ordered to march, make ready carriages with able men to drive them allowing them reasonable time to do so.

- If sufficient carriages are not to be found, warrants for the same are to be delivered to the next town, village, or township, officers for the same to make up the deficiency.

- That the pay or hire for a New York wagon, carrying 1,200 pounds gross weight, shall be seven pence sterling for each mile, and for every other carriage in that and every other colony in his Majesty's dominions in America, in the same proportion.

- Pay shall be paid daily into the hands of the drivers until such carriages are discharged from service for the use of their owners.

- No such wagon is required to carry more than 1,200 pounds weight.

- No such carriage is obliged to travel more than a day's march, if, within that time they shall arrive at another place where other carriages may be procured. If they do not, they shall be obliged to continue until they shall arrive at such a place where sufficient carriages for the service of the forces may be procured.

- Penalty for a public officer who shall neglect or refuse to execute such warrants of the justices of the peace for providing carriages and man, shall be fined for every offense any sum not exceeding forty shillings sterling, nor less than twenty shilling to be paid into the treasury of the province where the crime shall be committed.

- If the procured wagons or other carriages are to be taken for long marches beyond the settlements, an appraisal shall be made by two different persons (one chosen by the commanding officer and the other by the owner) of the value of such horses and carriages at the time of taking them up and a certificate issued for the value. If lost or destroyed, the owner shall produce the certificate to the paymaster of his Majesty's guards and garrisons and be paid for the loss.

The following provisions concern the many British military desertions:

- That it shall be lawful for any civil official to apprehend any person who may be reasonably suspected of being a deserter and to be brought before a justice of the peace or chief magistrate.

- If found to be a deserter by examination or the testimony of two witnesses, he is to be conveyed to the jail, house of correction, or prison and to notify the commander in chief of his Majesty's forces in order that the prisoner may be proceeded against according to law.

- The jailers are to be reimbursed for the deserter's time of stay but shall not be entitled to any fee or reward.

- Any person helping a deserter by harboring, concealing, or by offering assistance is to be fined the sum of £5 for each offense.

- Any person who buys arms, clothes, caps, or other furniture belonging to the king from any soldier or deserter or cause to color such clothes to be changed is to be fined £5.

| Note: | If the offender could not pay within four days, they were to be jailed without bail for three months or publicly whipped at the discretion of the justice. |

- A £5 reward is to be paid to the informers of deserters if convicted.

| Note: | The reward was to be paid using the money collected by the fines. |

- No commission officer shall break open any house, within his Majesty's dominions in America, to search for deserters, without a warrant from the justice of the peace, and in the daytime.

- Every commissioned officer who shall, in the night, or without warrant, forcibly enter a dwelling-house, or outhouses of any person whatsoever, under pretense of searching for deserters, shall, upon due proof, forfeit the sum of £20.

The following provisions concern civilian crimes at military installations and others committed outside the bounds of civil jurisdictions:

- Whereas many crimes committed have been and may be committed by several person, not being soldiers, at several forts and garrisons and other places which are not within the limits of jurisdiction of any civil government, and not subject to court martial, whereof several great crimes and offences may go unpunished, to the great scandal of government, that from the twenty-fourth day of March, one thousand seven hundred and sixty five, if any person or persons, not being a soldier or soldiers, do or shall commit any crime or crimes, or offence or offences, in any of the said forts, garrisons, or places, within his Majesty's dominions in America, which are not within the limits or jurisdiction of any civil government hitherto established, it shall and may be lawful for any person or persons to apprehend such offender or offenders, and to carry, him, her or them, before the commanding officer for the time being of his Majesty's forces there.

- The accused offender charged under oath and in writing, is to be taken into custody by the commanding officer and safely held to convey and deliver, or cause to be conveyed and delivered, with all convenient speed to the civil magistrate in the next adjoining province to be administered and be dealt with according by the civil magistrate according to law as if the crime had been committed within the jurisdiction of the court.

Note:	Some frontier posts were beyond the reach and authority of civil law and civilians committing crimes there were not subject to the usual military courts martial, which created a legal quandary. The Quartering Act attempted to remedy those situations.

The following provisions concern the military's right to commandeer ferries for its use:

- That the commanding officer has lawful right to use any ferry in their march, either to share with other passengers, or to bar other passengers and hire the entire ferry for the needs of the troops and shall pay the rate of one half the regular rate.

- If no regular ferry exists, and the officer has need to hire boats for the troops crossing, officers are to pay the regular rates that people normally pay.

Note:	Overshadowed by the Stamp Act, resistance to the 1765 Quartering Act would be minimal as the complaints from the colonial assemblies were more concerned with providing the funds to pay for it rather than any loss of liberty. Most of the colonies, excepting Massachusetts, at least partially complied. Pennsylvania, currently fighting a war against the Shawnee and Delaware, was the only colony to fully comply, though the greatest financial burden fell on New York—headquarters for Great Britain's military forces in North America.
	Many of the 10,000 British soldiers in North America would be stationed in American port cities causing resentment. Feeling watched and controlled by the troops, most Americans would oppose being forced to support them. As Benjamin Franklin wrote of the Quartering Act, "That it would put it in the Power of the Captain General to oppress the Province at pleasure."
	Passed as an amendment to Britain's 1765 Mutiny Act, the Quartering Act of 1765 was scheduled to expire on March 24, 1767, but would be amended and renewed for two additional years, finally expiring in 1770. On June 2, 1774, Parliament would pass the Quartering Act of 1774.

May 7, 1765   **In western Pennsylvania, the Black Boy engage in a firefight with British troops.**

A second pack train containing Indian trade goods destined for Fort Pitt is stopped by James Smith's men. As before, several of the horses are killed, but this time the pack drivers are tied up and flogged. One driver manages to escape and returns to Fort Loudoun for assistance. A British military patrol immediately sets out, and the attackers are soon found.

With no intention of being arrested, the Black Boys challenge the patrol's authority, and a firefight breaks out during which one of Smith's men is wounded and taken prisoner. As the fight continues, a large number of Black Boys arrive and the dozen British soldiers quickly find themselves overwhelmed. With their retreat cut off, the troops are forced to release their wounded captive in order to make haste to nearby Fort Bedford.

May 10, 1765   **Fort Loudoun is surrounded by James Smith and 150 Black Boys.**

James Smith, accompanied and supported by the county justice, William Smith, demands the right to inspect the pack train's goods to search for contraband destined for the Indians, but British Lieutenant Charles Grant refuses.

Note: Justice William Smith was James Smith's brother-in-law, and both Smiths suspected Lieutenant Grant to be involved in the illicit Indian trade.

May 28, 1765   **British Lieutenant Charles Grant is taken prisoner by the Black Boy vigilantes.**

Apprehended while riding with a small patrol, Lieutenant Grant is held overnight in the woods and threatened with personal harm if he does not return the long rifles taken on March 9. Although Grant states that he possesses no such authority, he eventually relents, and Smith agrees to release him, but only after Grant posts a £40 bond to be forfeited if the arms are not returned within five days.

Note: Lieutenant Grant would be released in Mercerville, Pennsylvania, after the bond was paid—but the firearms were not returned

In New York, British General Gage would learn of the frontier attacks and demand Pennsylvania Governor John Penn put a stop to the rebellion.

May 29, 1765   **In reaction to the Stamp Act's passage, Patrick Henry introduces seven resolutions to Virginia's House of Burgesses.**

The bold resolutions are tabled until the following day for debate and vote.

May 30, 1765   **Patrick Henry gives his maiden speech to the Virginia Assembly and begins a rise to fame.**

In a defense of his resolutions concerning the Stamp Act, the young and fiery Patrick Henry denounces Parliament and warns King George III to profit from the example of Julius Caesar's assassination by Brutus. The brash twenty-nine-year-old Henry is interrupted by cries of "Treason!" to which he supposedly replies, "If this be treason—make the most of it!"

Note: Patrick Henry would gain fame as one of early America's most powerful orators, gaining support by speaking a language that the everyman could understand.

In opposition to the tax, Virginia's House of Burgesses passes its *Stamp Act Resolves*.

1. "*Resolved*, that the first Adventurers and Settlers of his Majestie's Colony and Dominion brought with them and transmitted to their Posterity and all other his Majestie's Subjects since inhabiting in this his Majestie's said Colony all the Priviledges, Franchises & Immunities that have at any Time been held, enjoyed, & possessed by the People of Great Britain.

2. "*Resolved*, that by the two royal Charters granted by King James the first the Colonists aforesaid are declared intituled to all the Priviledges, Liberties &

Immunities of Denizens and natural born Subjects, to all Intents and Purposes as if they had been abiding and born within the Realm of England.

3. *"Resolved*, that the Taxation of the People by themselves or by Persons chosen by themselves to represent them who can only know what Taxes the People are able to bear and the easiest Mode of raising them and are equally affected by such Taxes themselves is the distinguishing Characteristic of British Freedom and without which the ancient Constitution cannot subsist.

4. *"Resolved*, that his Majestie's liege People of this most ancient Colony have uninteruptedly enjoyed the Right of being thus governed by their own assembly in the Article of their Taxes and internal Police and that the same hath never been forfeited or yielded up, but hath been constantly recognized by the Kings and People of Great Britain.

5. *"Resolved*, therefore that the General Assembly of this Colony have the only and sole exclusive Right & Power to lay Taxes and Impositions upon the Inhabitants of this Colony and that every Attempt to vest such Power in any Person or Persons whatsoever, other than the General Assembly aforesaid has a manifest Tendency to destroy British as well as American Freedom."

Note:	Henry's fifth resolve, after having been initially accepted by only one vote, would be rescinded the next day and erased from the official journal due to pressure from the elder assemblymen.

Patrick Henry introduces two additional resolves that fail to pass.

6. *"Resolved*, that his Majestie's liege People, the Inhabitants of this Colony, are not bound to yield obedience to any law or ordinance whatever, designed to impose any Taxation whatsoever upon them other than the laws or ordinances of the General Assembly aforesaid.

7. *"Resolved*, that any Person who shall, by speaking or writing assert or maintain that any Person or Persons other than the General Assembly of this Colony, have any right or power to impose or lay any Taxation on the People here shall be deemed an Enemy to his Majestie's Colony."

Note:	Though Henry's fifth resolve was rescinded and the sixth and seventh were not approved, all seven resolves were published in the American colonial newspapers, helping to spread his radical thoughts.
	By the end of the year, eight other colonial assemblies would issue similar resolves regarding the Stamp Act.
	Virginia's Stamp Act Resolves are commonly referred to as the *Virginia Resolves*.

June 1765 **Massachusetts proposes a *Stamp Act Congress* to meet in New York City in October.**

At the urging of Boston's Samuel Adams during a meeting of the Massachusetts General Court, James Otis calls for the formation of an intercolonial Stamp Act Congress. In response, Massachusetts issues *circulars* (letters) to the legislatures of "the several Colonies on this Continent" calling for a congress of colonial representatives in order to form a unified response to the stamp tax.

Note:	When learning of the General Court's call for a Stamp Act Congress, Governor Bernard would shut down the assembly and request the British Ministry increase its number of civil offices to tighten control over Massachusetts.

June 4, 1765 **The *Maidstone Affair*: Troubles break out in Newport, Rhode Island, over a British naval impressment.**

The HBS *Maidstone* intercepts a Newport ship returning from Africa and impresses the entire crew, which includes several local inhabitants. That evening, a boat from the *Maidstone* docks at the wharf and an angry crowd of 500, mostly sailors and boys, drags and carries the boat to Newport's common and burn it in celebration.

Note:	When called upon by royal authorities to produce the rioters for justice, Governor Stephen Hopkins would answer that they could not be found. Hopkins went on to state, "that, by the best information I can get, no person of the least note was concerned in the riot; the persons who committed the crime consisting altogether of the dregs of the people, and a number of boys and negroes."

Late Spring 1765 **The *Regulator Movement*: Organized resistance to the North Carolina government begins.**

By mid-1765, the western frontier farmers of North Carolina are fed up and begin speaking out and organizing more extreme resistance to the civil authorities. Bound together by common grievances, the Regulators begin petitioning the assembly in New Bern, but their petitions are ignored. Choosing to run some of their members for political office, the Regulators manage to get representatives elected to the colonial assembly, but their numbers are too few to be significant as the government and its courts continue to favor the civil officials and the influential wealthy. As a result, the North Carolina Regulators will begin to harass officials, withhold taxes, shut down civil courts, and issue demands for corrupt officials to resign.

June 6, 1765 **An Address to the People of Granville County, aka the Nutbush Address, is made in North Carolina.**

Demanding reforms, local schoolteacher George Sims delivers an address in graphic language to his neighbors and the community of Granville County denouncing the abuse of power that the people of the Piedmont are forced to endure, including:

- Excessive taxes.

- Excessive legal fees.

- Excessive rents.

- The abuse of power by a local official and political kingpin, Samuel Benton, and Benton's improper use of public funds.

Sims continues his speech, arguing against arbitrary tyranny and encouraging the farmers to refuse to pay the many varied, and often onerous, legal fees charged them.

Note:	Though Sims did not encourage violence, he would be jailed and sued by Samuel Benton.
	At the encouragement of others, three years later, Sims's Nutbush Address would be resurrected and printed, adding fuel to the fire of the growing Regulator Movement.

Pennsylvania resumes the Indian trade and opens it to non-licensed traders.

Now that the Western Indian War has nearly ended, Governor John Penn reopens Pennsylvania's Indian trade, but now permits non-licensed traders to participate.

Note:	The profitable Indian trade had come to a standstill during the recent war, and with the French now gone, a great trade vacuum had been created that the Pennsylvanians wished to help fill.

July 13, 1765 **Lord Rockingham becomes Great Britain's prime minister, replacing George Grenville.**

King George III dismisses Grenville as prime minister and names Charles Wadsworth-Wentworth, aka Lord Rockingham, as his replacement.

> Note: Though in his post for only one year, Prime Minister Lord Rockingham would be somewhat supportive of the American colonists, managing to repeal the Stamp Act.

July 1765 **Warring tribes from the Ohio region meet in New York for a peace conference.**

Among those arriving are the Delaware and Shawnee, as part of the agreement with Colonel Henry Bouquet eight months earlier in return for Bouquet having spared their Muskingum towns from destruction.

> Note: The meeting site, Johnson Hall, was the new estate of British Indian Superintendent William Johnson and his Mohawk wife, Molly Brant. Johnson Hall was located near today's Johnstown, New York.

July 30, 1765 **Under political pressure, Pennsylvania Governor John Penn calls Justice William Smith before him to account for the attacks against the Indian traders and the British troops.**

Having been charged with encouraging and protecting the Black Boys vigilantes, William Smith faces Governor Penn and gives a stirring defense: "The right of self-defense in the absence of government protection." The county justice emotionally defends the actions of his brother-in-law James Smith, citing John Locke's premise that self-defense is justified if the government fails in its duty to protect the citizens' rights to life, liberty, and property. Therefore, the actions of James Smith and his followers represented civil law, and Lieutenant Grant had been the one to act improperly.

As a result of Justice William Smith's stirring defense, he is acquitted of the charges and a warrant will be later issued for British Lieutenant Grant's arrest in connection to the illegal trade.

> Note: The political movement to oust the Penn family as proprietors of Pennsylvania would continue. As the colony's wealthiest family and its largest landholders, the assembly and many citizens wished to rid the colony of the Penns and the Quaker influences. Now, the unpopular Governor Penn was in a political pinch as he inquired into the behaviors of James Smith and his Black Boys, who were popularly supported by the frontier people.
>
> Governor John Penn was politically destined to be the last of the Penns to preside over Pennsylvania, as his family's long proprietorship would be finally swept aside by the American War for Independence.

Aug. 2, 1765 **South Carolina becomes the first colony to declare it will attend the Stamp Act Congress.**

Answering the call from Massachusetts for an intercolonial congress to be held in New York, South Carolina selects three delegates to represent the colony: John Rutledge, Christopher Gadsden, and Thomas Lynch—all strong supporters of American colonial rights.

Summer 1765 **Hoping to conclude the Western Indian War, the British send an expedition to find the Ottawa war leader Pontiac.**

Assistant Superintendent of Indian Affairs George Croghan travels to the distant Illinois region to meet with Pontiac and invite him to conference with Superintendent William Johnson in a peace council at Fort Ontario the following summer.

> Note: Fort Ontario was located at present-day Oswego, New York.

American opposition to the Stamp Act continues to grow.

The following are among the reasons for the growing opposition:

- Unlike the taxes paid to regulate colonial trade and commerce, the stamp tax is to generate funds directly from the colonists for the purpose of supporting British troops in America—troops that most colonists did not want. Previously, the Americans had only been directly taxed by their colonial legislatures.

- The tax is to be represented by a visual symbol on every paper a person is likely to read or need, and will therefore be literally *in one's face*, serving as a daily reminder and a source of constant irritation.

- The tax has been issued without consultation or approval by the colonial assemblies. As a direct tax on the people, it interferes with the internal affairs of the colonies and ignores the American colonial tradition of self-government.

- The tax is to be overseen by stamp agents, with enforcement and infractions to be dealt with by the Vice Admiralty Courts—without juries—rather than by civilian courts.

- The tax will affect all classes of people, as everybody is to pay it. The poor are unused to paying taxes, for most colonial taxation consists of property taxes or duties paid by merchants.

Note:	In London, Benjamin Franklin suggested that the Americans would need to be represented in Parliament if such taxes were to be imposed.
	Since the Stamp Act would not take effect until November 1, 1765, this gap would allow time for colonial opposition leaders to mount vigorous campaigns against it.

In Boston, the *Loyal Nine* meet to organize opposition to the Stamp Act.

Nine members of Boston's influential *Caucus Club* meet in secret to decide what actions are necessary to bring about the Stamp Act's repeal. This small but determined group of political leaders—to be known as the Loyal Nine—will print and distribute anti-Stamp Act pamphlets and broadsides, organize protests, and create general unrest in Boston against the looming tax.

Note:	The Loyal Nine would quickly enlist the support of a Boston shoemaker and gang leader, Ebenezer Mackintosh. As such, the Loyal Nine (and later, the Sons of Liberty) would use Mackintosh to quickly summon large numbers of people, and—after whipping them into a frenzy—provide the crowd with a target for its wrath. This ability represented a powerful tool for the political group.
	The tactic of hiring mobs to protest and riot had long been used in England.
	The Loyal Nine would dissolve by the year's end as the members merged with Boston's Sons of Liberty.
	Founded in 1720, Boston's Caucus Club was a cabal of influential men that dominated Boston's politics. The members met at the Green Dragon Tavern, often called the "Headquarters of the Revolution."

The Stamp Act gives rise to the formation of *Sons of Liberty* groups throughout the colonies.

Adopting their collective label from Isaac Barre's speech to Parliament on February 27, 1765, numerous colonial groups and individuals actively resisting the Stamp Act begin calling themselves Sons of Liberty.

Note:	The general strategy of resistance to the tax would be to prevent the unloading of the arriving stamps and force the colonial stamp tax agents to resign their posts. To accomplish these ends—threats, intimidation, and destruction of personal property would all be used.

Formed to oppose the stamp tax, many of the various Sons of Liberty groups would continue to operate after the Stamp Act's repeal, but with a much greater goal—complete independence from Britain.

When the American colonists spoke and wrote about resistance to the *stamps,* they meant resistance to the *papers* that had been embossed (stamped) in England before being sent to the colonies. There would be no arriving stamps, only stamped papers.

Boston's Sons of Liberty are organized under the leadership of Sam Adams.

Consisting mostly of wharfingers, artisans, and shipyard workers, the Sons of Liberty are fronted by Boston's leaders and influential merchants. As such, the diverse members can easily summon people to action and help link the town's lower sorts with the upper class.

Aug. 14, 1765   **The first violence of the *Stamp Act Rebellion* begins.**

In South Boston, two large effigies representing a stamp agent and a British jackboot are suspended by hangman's nooses from the branches of a large elm tree that has traditionally served as a community meeting site. Lieutenant Governor Thomas Hutchinson sends the sheriff to cut the effigies down, but the sheriff reports that more than 1,000 people are there and the situation is thus too dangerous.

After listening to speakers, the mobbish crowd takes down the effigies and proceeds to parade them through the Boston streets as the large group continues to grow and soon numbers between 2,000 and 3,000. Emboldened by its increasing size, the mob becomes riotous and proceeds to destroy the nearly completed office structure of the stamp commissioner, Andrew Oliver. Following the destruction of Oliver's office, the rioters behead one effigy and then burn both to a cheering crowd. Still unsatisfied, some of the rioters proceed to Oliver's house and the stamp commissioner quickly goes into hiding. The arriving mob smashes his windows, breaks through the barricaded doors, splinters his furniture, and proceeds to destroy his entire house leaving only the walls and a part of the roof. Adding insult to injury, the crowd then burns Oliver's prized riding coach before finally departing.

Note: Fearing the rioters, Massachusetts Governor Francis Bernard had retired to the safety of Boston's Fort Castle William.

Andrew Oliver—Thomas Hutchinson's brother-in-law—was also the attorney general for Massachusetts.

Aug. 15, 1765   **Andrew Oliver resigns his position as Massachusetts's stamp tax commissioner.**

The horror of a mob destroying his personal residence while in pursuit of his person has had its intended effect.

Aug. 26, 1765   **Boston mobs rampage against three British officials' houses, including that of Massachusetts Lieutenant Governor Thomas Hutchinson.**

William Story and Benjamin Hallowell both suffer damages, but the largest attack is conducted against Hutchinson's magnificent home. Though the lieutenant governor manages to safely flee—his house is destroyed.

Note: Having destroyed the home of Attorney General Andrew Oliver, and now having also demolished the house of Lieutenant Governor Thomas Hutchinson, much of the *moral high ground* of Boston's Stamp Act protestors had been lost. The colonial leaders' strategy to keep Britain on the moral defensive was now shattered as the royal authorities would use the Boston riots to further tarnish the American image.

In Annapolis, Maryland, citizens create an effigy of the colony's stamp agent and burn it at the gallows.

Information has been published in the paper that the Maryland native Zachariah Hood is due to arrive from London as the colony's stamp distributor, but the crowd is determined to keep him away.

Aug. 27, 1765   **Many of Boston's *better citizens* meet in Faneuil Hall objecting to the recent violence.**

> Note: As the Stamp Act protests became increasingly destructive, many citizens would decry the actions of the rioters and wished not to be associated with them.
>
> In Britain's view, the American colonials seemed to be lawless rabble; unappreciative of the many benefits received by being members of the Empire, including the British Constitution.

Rhode Islanders protest the Stamp Act.

Crowds haul effigies of Rhode Island stamp agent Augustus Johnston and two prominent merchant supporters of the stamp tax through the Newport streets before finally suspending them fifteen feet in the air and burning both to grand cheers.

Aug. 28, 1765   **The Stamp Act protests in Rhode Island degenerate.**

Out for a second day of protests, the Newport crowd turns ugly as the protesters—consisting of the *lower sort*—careens out of control with lots of criminal mischief.

Aug. 29, 1765   **Rhode Island's stamp agent resigns.**

On the third continuous day of protests, Augustus Johnston resigns as stamp agent after being threatened and hanged once again in effigy by the Newport mob.

> Note: Augustus Johnston was also the colony's attorney general. Well-liked by the people, Johnston believed he would be safe; but as the mob sought him out, Johnson would quickly change his mind and take refuge aboard the HBS *Cygnet*.

Maryland's stamp agent arrives from England, but the crowds refuse to permit him to disembark.

Arriving at Annapolis, stamp agent Zachariah Hood is greeted by an angry crowd demanding he resign his position, which he refuses to do. Yet within days—after additional threats are made against him—Hood will secretly flee on horseback to New York.

Aug. 30, 1765   **New York's stamp agent resigns.**

Fearing for his personal safety, stamp agent James McEvers also worries his house will be targeted and pulled down by the crowds.

Sept. 1765   **Massachusetts Governor Francis Bernard asserts Parliament's authority to tax the colonists.**

Bernard urges the Massachusetts General Court to comply with the stamp tax, which only makes him more unpopular with the people.

Sept. 1765 **George Grenville and Virginia's stamp agent are hanged in effigy in Leedstown.**

> Note: Virginia's stamp agent, George Mercer, was still in England at the time.

Sept. 2, 1765 **In Annapolis, Maryland, a crowd pulls down the warehouse of stamp agent Zachariah Hood.**

Upon learning that Hood had escaped two days earlier, an angry crowd of 300 to 400 people proceed to destroy his warehouse.

> Note: Hunted down by the Sons of Liberty, Zachariah Hood would formally resign as Maryland's stamp agent on November 28, 1765, at Flushing, New York.

New Jersey's stamp agent resigns.

Having arrived from England with his commission papers, William Coxe is unable to find lodging as the landlord is afraid the people will pull down the house if he permits Coxe to stay.

Sept. 5, 1765 **Royal Governor Bernard acknowledges the Stamp Act is unenforceable in Massachusetts.**

Sept. 9, 1765 **In Boston, the dreaded *stamps* finally arrive.**

Readying for the looming November deadline, the stamped papers are unloaded and placed under armed guard in Fort Castle William.

> Note: November 1, 1765—the date on which the stamp's usage was required to begin—was only fifty-two days away.

New Hampshire's stamp agent resigns.

Arriving in Boston from London, George Meserve is met by a crowd demanding his resignation. To placate the people, Meserve complies and the crowd issues three cheers in jubilation.

> Note: George Meserve believed his appeasement was only temporary, for he fully expected the people's opposition to subside after the colony's business would come to an abrupt halt without the stamps necessary to conduct it.

There is growing pressure in Britain's North American colonies to carry on business—with or without the required stamps.

Sept. 11, 1765 **Boston's *Liberty Tree* receives its official designation.**

A large copper plate is nailed on the tree's trunk declaring it the "Tree of Liberty." The Boston Sons of Liberty will hold political meetings under the tree, placing a flagstaff in its branches with a red ensign to signify when they are to gather.

> Note: The large elm was often decorated with banners and lanterns. The shaded area under its branches would be called *Liberty Hall*.
>
> Word of Boston's Liberty Tree would spread, inspiring other communities throughout the American colonies to adopt their own *liberty trees* as symbols of dissent.
>
> Though uncertain, many historians credit members of Boston's Loyal Nine with emplacing the copper plate and bestowing the tree with the moniker, Liberty Tree.

Sept. 12, 1765	**New Hampshire's stamp agent resigns—for the second time.**

Having been forced to resign in Boston three days earlier, George Meserve arrives in Portsmouth and is forced to resign once more, this time witnessed by the New Hampshire citizens.

Sept. 15, 1765	**News arrives in North America that Britain's Grenville administration has been replaced.**

A new British prime minister—Charles Watson-Wentworth, aka Lord Rockingham—has come into office. As former Prime Minister George Grenville had been most responsible for the Stamp Act, this news gives the Americans hope that the tax may yet be annulled as many believe Lord Rockingham will be more sympathetic to their protests.

Sept. 16, 1765	**Benjamin Franklin's house in Philadelphia is threatened by Stamp Act protestors.**

To protect the house from the mob, Deborah Franklin and friends arm themselves and barricade the doors. Mrs. Franklin then stands guard from an upstairs window while her friends guard from below.

> Note: Many protesters in Philadelphia had threatened to pull down the houses of those responsible for the stamp tax and its distribution, and they suspected Benjamin Franklin—living in London—to be a secret author of the tax and an agent for it. Many in the crowd accused Franklin of trying to fatten his purse by supporting the tax. Thus, the threats against his Philadelphia home were very real.

Sept. 19, 1765	**Connecticut's stamp tax agent is forced to resign.**

Having already been subjected to harassment and burned in effigy, stamp agent Jared Ingersoll is now intercepted on his way to an assembly meeting at Hartford by a crowd of 500 people demanding his resignation. The mobbish crowd refuses to let him proceed until he reads a resignation letter prepared for him. Faced with little choice, Ingersoll resigns his commission.

Sept. 21, 1765	**In Woodridge, New Jersey, the *Constitutional Courant* is published and distributed in response to the Stamp Act.**

Published secretly by William Goddard, the so-called newspaper is more of a broadside manifesto opposing the Stamp Act. Containing only one page, the newspaper's header is a drawing of Benjamin Franklin's segmented snake with the caption "Join or Die" followed by three anti-Stamp Act essays signed by pseudonyms. With the Stamp Act Congress preparing to meet in New York, this one-edition paper is designed to influence public opinion by calling for the American colonies to unite in opposition to the dreaded tax. In addition, though the paper argues against violence, it attempts to put the recent riots in a positive light by suggesting there was little alternative.

Dated September 21, 1765, the *Constitutional Courant* is distributed widely in New York City and reprinted in Philadelphia and Boston.

> Note: The newspaper's printing would cause a fruitless inquiry into its origin by the royal officials.
>
> Benjamin Franklin, a moderate, would not support the use of his cartoon for the Stamp Act cause.

Oct. 5, 1765	**In Philadelphia, a muffled statehouse bell is rung to announce the arrival of the stamps as a crowd of thousands gathers.**

A ship has arrived from London carrying the despised stamps and commission papers naming John Hughes to be Pennsylvania's stamp agent. As a result, an unruly crowd gathers at the Pennsylvania

State House and demands Hughes resign his post. The protestors send a seven-member committee to meet with the agent, and though Hughes refuses to resign, he agrees not to distribute the stamps.

Note:	John Hughes had been recommended to his commission by Benjamin Franklin.
	The muffled bell that tolled protesting the arrival of the stamps in Philadelphia is today's Liberty Bell of Independence Hall.

Oct. 7–25, 1765   **The Stamp Act Congress meets for nearly three weeks in New York City to create a unified plan for colonial resistance.**

Meeting in New York's City Hall, nine of Britain's North American colonies are represented:

- South Carolina, Maryland, Pennsylvania, Delaware, New Jersey, New York, Connecticut, Massachusetts, and Rhode Island. Georgia sends representatives but only to transcribe the proceedings.

Not attending are:

- Nova Scotia—due to the assembly's strong financial ties to England.

- East Florida, West Florida, and Quebec. As newly formed British colonies— they have not yet established assemblies and have not been invited.

Note:	Most of the delegates were meeting each other for the first time as acquaintances were made and political views were shared. As expected, agreements and disagreements existed among them.
	The British Board of Trade was alarmed that the colonies were acting in union without the express authority of the Crown.
	Though New York hosted the Stamp Act Congress, New York's royal lieutenant governor, Cadwallader Colden, considered the intercolonial meeting to be illegal.
	By forcing the Stamp Act's repeal, some of the delegates believed that they were helping Britain maintain a strong union with the American colonies. They argued that enforcement of the tax would surely lead to political disunion—something they did not wish to see.
	To most historians, the Stamp Act Congress represented the second major intercolonial meeting of the North American colonies; the first being the Albany Conference in 1754.
	The meeting site—New York's City Hall—would serve as the first seat of government for the new United States, causing it to be renamed *Federal Hall*. On April 30, 1789, George Washington would be sworn in as the first United States president on the building's balcony.

Oct. 1765   **The North American colonies begin to unify in common cause.**

Opposition to the Stamp Act creates a collective identity for the American colonists for the tax affects all—rich and poor, young and old, urban and rural, north and south.

Oct. 10, 1765   **British troops take control of *Fort de Chartres*—the last French fort remaining east of the Mississippi River.**

In an official ceremony, Captain Thomas Stirling and the 42nd Highland Regiment hoist Britain's Union Flag, much to the disappointment of the forty French soldiers readying to depart.

> Note: Located in today's southwestern Illinois, the transfer of Fort de Chartres represented the final dissolution of New France—France's former forest empire in North America.
>
> British troops had previously attempted to reach the remote western fort, but Ottawa resistance had prevented them.

Oct. 19, 1765   **In Charles Town, South Carolina, violence breaks out as people protest the Stamp Act.**

Though the identity of South Carolina's stamp agent has not been publicly announced, most believe it to be George Saxby, currently returning from England. With both Saxby and the despised stamps expected to soon arrive, 2,000 protestors drag his effigy through the streets and burn it on the town common accompanied by cheers. With the crowd now roused to a frenzy, the demonstration degenerates as the protestors attack a house owned by Saxby. While proceeding to stone and ransack the building, several issue threats that they shall kill Saxby upon his return.

> Note: The stamps would arrive at Charles Town the following day, further agitating the people. Hoping to quiet the whole affair, the officials would announce that no stamps were to be landed in town, but that they would instead be stored at Fort Johnston until it was necessary to remove them.

In Wilmington, North Carolina, a raucous crowd protests the Stamp Act with a giant bonfire.

A crowd of 500 sets alight a massive pile of timber fueled by barrels of tar and burns in effigy the king's adviser, former British Prime Minister, John Stuart, aka the Earl of Bute.

> Note: Two weeks later, the same Wilmington crowd would hold a funeral for *Lady Liberty* after symbolically strangling her.

In New York, the Stamp Act Congress creates a *Declaration of Rights and Grievances*.

"The members of this Congress, sincerely devoted, with the warmest sentiments of affection and duty to his Majesty's Person and Government, inviolably attached to the present happy establishment of the Protestant succession, and with minds deeply impressed by a sense of the present and impending misfortunes of the British colonies on this continent; having considered as maturely as time will permit the circumstances of the said colonies, esteem it our indispensable duty to make the following declarations, of our humble opinion, respecting the most essential rights and liberties of the colonists, and of the grievances under which they labour, by reason of several late Acts of Parliament.

     I.   That his Majesty's subjects in these colonies, owe the same allegiance to the Crown of Great Britain, that is owing from his subjects born within the realm, and all due subordination to that august body, the Parliament of Great Britain.

     II.   That his Majesty's liege subjects in these colonies, are entitled to all the inherent rights and liberties of his natural born subjects within the kingdom of Great Britain.

     III.   That it is inseparably essential to the freedom of a people, and the undoubted right of Englishmen, that no taxes be imposed on them, but with their own consent, given personally, or by their representatives.

     IV.   That the people of these colonies are not, and from their local circumstances cannot be, represented in the House of Commons in Great Britain.

     V.   That the only representatives of the people of these colonies, are persons chosen therein by themselves, and that no taxes ever have been, or can be constitutionally imposed on them, but by their respective legislatures.

VI.   That all supplies to the Crown, being free gifts of the people, it is unreasonable and inconsistent with the principles and spirit of the British Constitution, for the people of Great Britain to grant to his Majesty the property of the colonists.

VII.   That trial by jury is the inherent and invaluable right of every British subject in these colonies.

VIII.   That the late Act of Parliament, entitled, An Act for granting and applying certain Stamp Duties, and other Duties, in the British colonies and plantations in America, etc., by imposing taxes on the inhabitants of these colonies, and the said Act, and several other Acts, by extending the jurisdiction of the courts of Admiralty beyond its ancient limits, have a manifest tendency to subvert the rights and liberties of the colonists.

IX.   That the duties imposed by several late Acts of Parliament, from the peculiar circumstances of these colonies, will be extremely burthensome and grievous; and from the scarcity of specie, the payment of them absolutely impracticable.

X.   That as the profits of the trade of these colonies ultimately center in Great Britain, to pay for the manufactures which they are obliged to take from thence, they eventually contribute very largely to all supplies granted there to the Crown.

XI.   That the restrictions imposed by several late Acts of Parliament, on the trade of these colonies, will render them unable to purchase the manufactures of Great Britain.

XII.   That the increase, prosperity, and happiness of these colonies, depend on the full and free enjoyment of their rights and liberties, and an intercourse with Great Britain mutually affectionate and advantageous.

XIII.   That it is the right of the British subjects in these colonies, to petition the King, or either House of Parliament.

Lastly, That it is the indispensable duty of these colonies, to the best of sovereigns, to the mother country, and to themselves, to endeavour by a loyal and dutiful address to his Majesty, and humble applications to both Houses of Parliament, to procure the repeal of the Act for granting and applying certain stamp duties, of all clauses of any other Acts of Parliament, whereby the jurisdiction of the Admiralty is extended as aforesaid, and of the other late Acts for the restriction of American commerce."

> Note: The sentiments expressed by the Stamp Act Congress echoed John Locke's 1689 *Two Treatises of Government*: "Government is founded on a social contract to protect the individual's right to life, liberty, and estate." This belief would be postulated in the U.S. Declaration of Independence as "Life, Liberty, and the Pursuit of Happiness."

The Stamp Act Congress agrees to the nonimportation of tax stamps.

If the import of the stamps is not permitted, they cannot be used.

> Note: Though the Stamp Act Congress called for all colonies to boycott the stamps, it did not call for a boycott of British goods. At this time, that issue would be left to others.

Oct. 22, 1765   **Stamps arrive in New York, aboard the HBS *Edward.***

Anchoring safely offshore, the ship's captain is greeted by 2,000 protestors clamoring for him to return to England.

Oct. 22–23, 1765 **The Stamp Act Congress labors to create petitions to be presented to the king, the House of Lords, and the House of Commons.**

Oct. 24, 1765 **In New York, the stamps are secretly unloaded and stored at Fort George.**

The news causes unrest and warnings against their usage by New York's Sons of Liberty.

Tensions are high as the Stamp Act Congress finalizes the petitions to the king and Parliament.

Debates and arguments take place amongst the men, leading to a particularly heated exchange between chairman Timothy Ruggles of Massachusetts and Thomas McKean from Delaware. Feeling insulted, an aggrieved Ruggles challenges McKean to a duel which does not take place.

Note: Of the delegations attending the Stamp Act Congress, three colonies refused to sign the petitions—New York, Connecticut, and South Carolina. Massachusetts, Pennsylvania, Delaware, Maryland, New Jersey, and Rhode Island did sign. Georgia had attended only to observe.

The Stamp Act petitions were the first petitions presented to the king and Parliament in the name of multiple American colonies acting in cooperation as a group. Previously, each colony had acted mainly in its own interest, but the looming stamp tax had created a new cooperation among them and a feeling of common cause.

All three petitions would be rejected on the grounds that the Stamp Act Congress was an extralegal and unconstitutional assemblage with no authority to meet or petition.

Timothy Ruggles would move to Nova Scotia during the War for Independence. As a result of his steadfast support for Great Britain, Ruggles would be banished from Massachusetts and suffer his house and properties confiscated under authority of the 1778 *Massachusetts Banishment Act*.

Oct. 25, 1765 **The Stamp Act Congress adjourns.**

After meeting for three weeks in New York, the Stamp Act Congress adjourns and the delegates ready themselves for their journeys home.

Note: The congress had not been about colonial independence, for nearly all the delegates were loyal to the king and proud members of the British Empire. Rather, the Stamp Act Congress had been called to help bring together these rather disparate colonies in unity of mutual opposition to the stamp tax by creating: a joint statement concerning colonial rights; petitions for the king and Parliament; and a common resistance strategy for ensuring the Stamp Act's eventual repeal.

Seven of the Stamp Act delegates would become future signatories to the U.S. Declaration of Independence.

Georgia's stamp agent is burned in effigy.

With Georgia's stamp agent yet to arrive from England, Savannah's Sons of Liberty meet and decide that he must be forced to resign.

Oct. 26, 1765 **In Charles Town, the South Carolina stamp agents resign.**

Fearing for their safety, stamp inspector George Saxby and distributer Caleb Lloyd are lodging at Charles Town's Fort Johnston. The previous week's violence has had its effect; with additional threats being made against them, both men now resign their commission.

Oct. 31, 1765   **To oppose the Stamp Act, New York merchants agree to a nonimportation of British goods.**

The New York merchants are soon joined by others in Boston and Philadelphia as an economic war is launched against Great Britain. In all, more than 1,000 colonial merchants will participate in the nonimportation movement as the Americans hope British merchants will lobby their government for the Stamp Act's repeal.

Virginia's stamp agent resigns his position due to threats against him.

Arriving in Williamsburg from London, stamp agent George Mercer is accosted by crowds and jeered as he makes his way to meet with the House of Burgesses. Finding no support, Mercer resigns his position after being insulted by the people and burned in effigy.

New York's Sons of Liberty form a committee to correspond with supporters in other colonies.

Hoping to create a unified and coordinated resistance to the Stamp Act, these various committees of correspondence will steadily evolve into an organized intercolonial network of communications carried by secret couriers.

Protestors in Newport, Rhode Island, hold a public funeral for liberty.

By October's end, nearly all colonial stamp agents have resigned due to intimidation.

The American colonists have successfully pressured most stamp agents to relinquish their commissions. Only the North Carolina, Pennsylvania and Georgia commissioners have not yet resigned. Without a stamp agent to distribute the stamps—they cannot be used.

> Note: This refers only to the stamp agents assigned to the thirteen colonies that would collectively make up the *original* United States. When thinking of Britain's colonies in North America, we tend not to include East and West Florida, nor the British colonies in Canada, nor the colonies of the West Indies. Yet the Stamp Act also applied to them.
>
> North Carolina's stamp agent, Dr. William Huston, would resign November 16; Georgia's stamp agent, George Angus, would not arrive from London until early January; and Pennsylvania's stamp agent John Hughes agreed not to distribute the stamps.

Nov. 1765   **Philadelphia merchants agree to nonimportation until the Stamp Act is repealed.**

A farmers' revolt begins in New York, to become known as the *Hudson Valley Land Riots*.

The wealthy Philipse family owns nearly half of the lands in Dutchess County and thereby controls much of the lives of the estate's tenant farmers. Upset with new lease terms being forced upon them, the farmers learn that the wealthy Lord Van Rensselaer pays but a gratuitous £4 and 12 shillings in rent for 200,000 acres.

With little control over their lives, the farmers' resentments continue to grow as they must either agree to new leases or be ousted from their farms. Facing evictions and threats of jail for those delinquent in rents, the farmers' frustrations have thus far led only to impasse. But now, with the Stamp Act resistance in full swing, the aggrieved farmers are swept by the tide of protest in the

American colonies and choose to rebel. The maverick Hudson Valley farmers choose William Prendergast—a neighbor and fellow farmer—to lead them as they form their own militia bands vowing to stop what they see as injustices by the wealthy and to free any farmers that may be jailed.

Note:	The revolting New York farmers would be labeled *levellers*, a disparaging term borrowed from England where the term was regularly used to denigrate those striving for human rights and a more equitable distribution of wealth.
	In the Hudson River Valley, Rensselaerswyck Manor totaled 1,000,000 acres; Philipse Manor had 200,000 acres; and Beekman Manor a mere 100,000. Nearly every acre of Dutchess County's 825 square miles had been patented to a handful of absentee Dutch landlords known as patroons.

Nov. 1, 1765   **The Stamp Act begins, and protests erupt throughout Britain's North American colonies.**

Bells toll. Ships' flags are flying at half-mast. Shops are shuttered. Newspapers are published with drawings of skulls and bones occupying the spot on which the stamps were to have been prominently displayed.

Note:	Colonial newspaper editors would play a big part in keeping the issue stirred up.

Funeral protests are conducted in the streets of American cities. In Portsmouth, New Hampshire, a funeral for liberty is held after the crowd first stones a stamp agent effigy tied to a pole. In Middletown, Connecticut, effigies are burned to a cheering crowd. In Boston, angry citizens gather at the Liberty Tree and hang effigies of British officials from its limbs and—after listening to stirring speeches—the crowd cuts them down and proceeds to Boston's gallows where they are hanged to rousing cheers.

In New York, after two days of street protests, a part of the crowd breaks away and destroys Lieutenant Governor Colden's prized coach and sleigh. Other rioters continue to the home of British Major Thomas James, who once said that the stamp tax would be "forced down the Americans' throats." Now, in symbolic retribution, the crowd destroys the British major's house.

Note:	Though New York's stamp agent had resigned, many people felt that Lieutenant Governor Colden might use the King's troops to force the stamps upon them. Serving as Britain's military headquarters and seat of power in North America, it was highly likely that Colden would attempt to make New York an example to the other colonies.

Though the Stamp Act is officially in effect, the stamps cannot be distributed for use.

Nearly all stamp commissioners have resigned or fled, and an impasse now exists between the American colonists and Great Britain.

All colonial vessels are now required to conduct business using stamped papers.

Note:	Most merchants had sent their ships to sea before the November 1 deadline to avoid the tax.

With no stamps available, the American colonial courts cannot function.

Most courts are forced to close as they are obligated to conduct business and legal transactions using stamped papers.

Former Prime Minister Lord Grenville calls for sending troops to the American colonies to enforce the Stamp Act.

Benjamin Franklin—living in London as a colonial agent—opposes the idea and speaks against it, stating that it will only lead to trouble.

Nov. 2, 1765   **Virginia advises customs collectors to ignore the ban on shipping without stamped papers.**

> Note: Philadelphia, Newport, Portsmouth, and New Haven would soon follow.

In most colonial ports, customs officers have little power to enforce the Stamp Act.

Lacking sufficient protections, many customs officials are outright intimidated by the many threats made against them. A Philadelphia customs officer writes perceptively concerning the stamps, "We must now submit to necessity, and do without them, or else in a little time, people will learn to do without either them or us."

> Note: Though we often speak of *British* customs officials, most of the customs workers in North America were born in the American colonies.

Nov. 5, 1765   **Afraid of violence erupting during the annual Pope's Day festivities, Boston authorities help broker a truce between the town's two major gangs.**

Last year's celebration left one person dead and others severely injured and authorities do not want it repeated. Now, with the people of Boston agitated by the recent Stamp Act protests, town officials are so concerned about the possibility of major violence that a truce is brokered between Boston's two major gangs—the North End and the South End. To keep the peace, the South End's leader, Captain Ebenezer Mackintosh, has been selected as grand marshal of the annual parade. Beginning at noon and dressed in a martial uniform, Mackintosh leads thousands of cheering Bostonians through the town streets, ending with a large bonfire on Copp's Hill.

> Note: In 1765, the annual Pope's Day celebration would be described in Boston as "the Anniversary of the Commemoration of the happy Deliverance of the English Nation from the Popish Plot."

Nov. 16, 1765   **In frontier Pennsylvania, the Black Boys lays siege to Fort Loudoun.**

Ongoing confrontations with Lieutenant Charles Grant have brought James Smith and his followers to attack Fort Loudoun to retrieve the group's arms held since March. In addition, the group wishes to force away the despised British lieutenant—long suspected of involvement in the illegal trade with the Indians. Beginning around 7 p.m., 100 Black Boy militiamen fire hundreds of shots into the small fort until Lieutenant Grant finally agrees to turn over the arms—not to Smith, but to local magistrate William McDowell. As such, James Smith agrees to end the siege and Lieutenant Grant is escorted by Smith's men to Fort Bedford, forty miles to the west.

> Note: With the Western Indian War ebbing to a close, so too would Pennsylvania's frontier conflict known today as *Smith's Rebellion,* as James Smith soon headed west to explore Kentucky. Returning to Pennsylvania, Smith would be arrested for murder in 1769 but would be found innocent. In the 1780s, Smith would move to Kentucky with his family and there became a successful Presbyterian missionary among the tribes aided by his knowledge of Native American culture. Before his death, James

Smith would write a treatise on Indian fighting tactics and warfare that would become a manual for the United States Army.

Under threats, North Carolina's stamp agent, Dr. William Houston, resigns his commission.

While visiting Governor Tryon, Dr. Houston is met by 500 men who demand he resign his office. In his defense, Houston claims to be unaware that he has been named the colony's stamp agent.

Note: The stamps would not arrive in North Carolina until November 20, 1765.

Nov. 18, 1765   **North Carolina Governor William Tryon fails to calm the people's anger over the Stamp Act.**

The royal governor attempts to placate the people by inviting the community to a feast of reconciliation and ordering the Brunswick militia to muster. Hoping to conciliate the militiamen by roasting an ox and providing free beer—they instead throw the roast into the river and pour the beer onto the ground.

Nov. 30, 1765   **A public funeral for liberty is held in Fredericktown, New Jersey.**

Dec. 1765   **Usage of the term, Sons of Liberty, continues to spread in the American colonies— particularly in New England and New York—signifying support for the Stamp Act's repeal.**

Connecticut and New York form a military alliance, agreeing to march to the other's assistance if necessary.

Dec. 5, 1765   **In Savannah, Georgia, the expected stamps arrive from London, long overdue.**

Arriving at the mouth of the Savannah River aboard the HBS *Speedwell*, the stamps are unloaded and stored in a warehouse without incident.

Note: The colony's stamp agent had not yet arrived from England, so there was no one in Georgia to issue the stamps. Placed in a bind, Governor Wright ignored the petitions from local merchants to conduct business without them. Instead, the royal governor would continue to keep the port closed until the authorized agent arrived to dispense the stamps.

Dec. 7, 1765   **British General Thomas Gage orders updated maps to be made of New York City and its surrounding countryside due to the growing unrest of the people.**

Should military force be necessary, Gage knows that he and his troops cannot match the colonists' intimate knowledge of the region; therefore, General Gage requests maps to be made for his use.

Dec. 13, 1765   **General Gage asks Governor Henry Moore to request funds from the New York Assembly to properly accommodate the additional troops scheduled to soon arrive.**

Note: As Britain's North American military headquarters, New York was the main port for troops arriving from and departing to England; and served as a stage point for launching the various military campaigns conducted in North America. As such, New York felt overwhelmed and unduly burdened, and the assembly had begun to balk.

New York had originally wanted the British Army headquartered in the city to ensure protection during the recent Seven Years' War with the French. Therefore, the assembly had agreed to fund the troops stationed there, as authorized by New York's Provisional Act, but the Act had expired two years before. Many citizens now considered the British military presence in New York to be a standing army and questioned its necessity and purpose.

In the past, the American colonial authorities had exercised near total control over the formation, the funding, and the eventual disbandment of their armies. These militia-provincial forces were always temporary in nature and manned by citizens of the locale under the direct control of the colonial assemblies. Now, with seemingly ever-increasing numbers of British troops amongst them, the New Yorkers had begun to feel they were not only losing control of the military—but were operating increasingly *under its control*. With General Gage requesting more funds, many wondered, "Is the sky the limit?" For the next four years, General Gage and the New York Assembly would engage in a tug-of-war over funds and the provisioning of quarters for the British troops—one exercise of control left to the colonial assemblies.

Dec. 17, 1765   **The New York Sons of Liberty are posting "libellous and rebellious" advertisements around the city, accompanied by other acts of defiance.**

As reported by General Gage's mapmaker John Montresor, "That night, the Effigies of Lord Colville, Mr. Grenville, and General Murray were paraded several times through the streets amidst a large concourse of people who halted first where the Governor was in company and gave three Huzzas, [after which] they were carried to the Common and burnt."

Boston Harbor opens for business without the required stamps.

Though ships are not legally permitted to sail without proper papers, no stamps are available and Boston Harbor is bottled up. Therefore, under pressure from the influential merchants and the shadowy Sons of Liberty, Boston's customs officials agree to provide ship clearances without them.

Note: Customs officers were under great pressure to clear ships for sea. With personal threats being made against them and mobs threatening to storm Boston's customs house, the officials agreed to let the ships sail, rationalizing that no stamps were available for their use.

The reopening of the colonial harbors represented a partial victory for the Americans as the debate and lobbying over the Stamp Act continued to rage in London.

Jan. 1766   **Defiance to the stamp tax is having its desired effect.**

The American colonials won't allow the stamps to be used and yet the law says they must—thus creating an economic and political crisis. Though concerned about the rule of law, British merchants do not wish to alienate the colonists, nor jeopardize their corresponding profits, as many businesses come to an economic standstill. This loss of market, combined with the debts owed them by the Americans, has British merchants demanding the Stamp Act's repeal.

Ignoring the Stamp Act—all northern ports in the American colonies are now open for shipping.

Note: By the end of February, the southern colonial ports would also be open.

British troops arrive in New York with no quarters to receive them.

Mostly veterans of the Seven Years' War in Europe, 1,500 arriving troops are required to remain on board their transports until accommodations can be worked out due to New York's refusal to provide for them.

The New York Assembly refuses full compliance of the requisite funds for General Gage's troops.

The assembly argues that its share, in relation to the other colonies, is an undue burden due to the British military being headquartered in New York.

Note:	Britain's Rockingham administration would see the refusal as an act of defiance, and as such, would pass the New York Restraining Act in June 1767.

Maryland relents and permits ships to sail without papers stamped for clearance.

Jan. 2, 1766   **A near riot occurs in Savannah, Georgia.**

With the stamp agent due to arrive from London, nearly 200 protesters march on the Savannah warehouse and demand the stamps be removed. Royal Governor Wright meets with them and manages to placate the group, who eventually return to their homes.

Jan. 7, 1766   **The Port of Savannah is opened as Georgia begins using the despised stamps.**

Georgia's stamp agent, George Angus, has arrived and begins distributing the stamps to various merchants. Bowing to economic pressures, the merchants reluctantly use them to conduct business.

Note:	During January, sixty ships using properly stamped papers would be cleared to sail from Savannah.
	Of the thirteen colonies to become the future United States, Georgia was the only colony to use the stamps.

Several of Britain's North American colonies comply with the Stamp Act.

In addition to Georgia—Nova Scotia, Newfoundland, Quebec, East Florida, West Florida, and Britain's island colonies in the West Indies—choose to use the stamps; however, though compliant, most turn a blind eye to the defiant colonies and permit business between them to continue despite the law.

Jan. 9, 1766   **Portsmouth, New Hampshire, erects the first *liberty pole* in the North American colonies.**

According to legend, Portsmouth's Sons of Liberty erect a liberty pole beside the town's bridge to show opposition to the Stamp Act. The large pole is hoisted with a banner proclaiming "Liberty, Property and No Stamp."

Note:	Whether truth or legend we do not know; but the Portsmouth citizens would rename the bridge, *Liberty Bridge*.
	The first documented raising of a liberty pole would take place in New York City on June 4, 1766.
	Many coastal towns would have their own liberty poles or liberty trees to rally supporters.

The liberty pole, long used in Europe as a symbol to represent freedom, had been introduced to English political culture by King William III and quickly became associated with England's hallowed 1689 Declaration of Rights. Later adopted by the American colonists to show opposition to British tyranny, these poles of various sizes were often festooned with ribbons and other colorful adornments and nearly always topped with a *Phrygian cap* (a red stocking cap) before being planted in the ground. Seen correctly as acts of defiance, most royal authorities simply tolerated their presence, but, to the British troops stationed in the colonies, their erection often became a game of cat-and-mouse as the soldiers would often destroy a pole, only for the colonists to plant another in its place.

Jan. 14, 1766   **William Pitt—known as the *great commoner*—delivers a powerful speech to Parliament, protesting the assembly's declared right to tax the American colonies.**

A supporter of the colonies, Pitt reminds Parliament that the Americans are *sons* of England and not its *bastards*. In his speech, Pitt puts forth:

- That he rejoices at America's rebellion to the stamp tax.

- That if the Americans voluntarily fall to becoming slaves, the rest of Britain will be next.

- That it is unfair to tax a people without representatives to speak for them.

- That Britain uses America's bounties to benefit itself.

- That Parliament has a sovereign and supreme power to legislate over America and to bind and restrain it, if it wishes.

- That there is a plain distinction between taxes levied for raising a revenue, and duties imposed for the regulation of trade.

- That Great Britain profits £2 million annually from the colonial trade and need not seek to gain yet more.

- That the colonies have been previously mismanaged by England.

- That in spite of talk of America's growing power and strength, the force of Great Britain "could crush America to atoms."

- That if America falls to Britain, like a drunk man, she will embrace the pillars of the state and pull down the constitution along with her.

- That though America has wronged, it has been due to madness driven by injustice: "Will you punish her for madness that you have occasioned? Are you to sheathe your swords into the bowels of your countrymen?"

- That toward America, Britain should take the view as a man to his wife: "Be to her faults a little blind. Be to her virtues very kind."

Pitt concludes his speech by stating: "Upon the whole, I will beg leave to tell the House what is really my opinion. It is, that the Stamp Act be repealed absolutely, totally, and immediately; that the reason for the repeal should be assigned, because it was founded on an erroneous principle. At the same time, let the sovereign authority of this country over the colonies be asserted in as strong terms as can be devised, and be made to extend every point of legislation whatsoever: that we may bind their trade, confine their manufactures, and exercise every power whatsoever—*except that of taking money out of their pockets without their consent.*"

On both sides of the Atlantic the stamp tax continues to be debated: In Parliament and the colonial assemblies; in the newspapers; and in North America—often violently in the streets.

Jan. 27, 1766   **Under threat, Georgia Governor James Wright orders the stamps moved to Fort George.**

Governor Wright has learned that 600 rural people are planning to march on Savannah to oppose the stamps. Concerned that the stamps are to be destroyed, Governor Wright orders them moved from a Savannah warehouse to Fort George on Cockspur Island.

Feb. 1766   **Leedstown, Virginia issues the *Leedstown Resolves*, repudiating the Stamp Act.**

Led by Richard Henry Lee, more than 100 influential citizens sign the resolves, aka the *Westmoreland Resolves*, pledging to prevent the tax from going into effect "at every hazard, and, paying no regard to danger or to death" and to make sure that anyone who attempts to enforce it will face "immediate danger and disgrace."

General Gage begins transferring troops from the western forts to the eastern regions to help quell civil unrest.

With the recent Indian war quieting down, British frontier troops are available for other uses.

Note:	The soldiers were stationed in *Indian Country* to keep the peace and to monitor trade and the overall situation. Their absence would leave the frontier more vulnerable.

Feb. 4, 1766   **Georgia ends its use of the stamps.**

Facing 300 armed and angry citizens demanding he prohibit further distribution of the stamps; Governor James Wright orders the stamps removed from Fort George and placed on board the HBS *Speedwell*. Now, ensconced aboard the ship, the stamps cannot be issued; thus, Georgia is forced to operate without them.

Feb. 13, 1766   **Benjamin Franklin testifies before Parliament regarding the Stamp Act.**

Note:	Franklin had become the unofficial spokesman for the colonies in London and many Britons now turned to him to assess the situation *across the waters*.

For four hours, the influential Doctor Franklin answers questions submitted by Members of the House of Commons concerning a variety of issues, including: colonial taxation, representation, economics, and—most importantly—the present unrest over the stamp tax.

During his appearance, Franklin tells the British MPs that there is not enough currency in the colonies for the people to pay the tax and that they will not do so except by force of arms. The sixty-year-old Franklin warns that if soldiers are sent to America to enforce the Stamp Act, they will not *find* a rebellion but will instead *create* one. Throughout his testimony Franklin attempts to put the Americans in a positive light, describing them as devoted children opposed only to internal taxes, and not to taxes on trade.

Note:	With Britain's relationship with the American colonies steadily deteriorating, many believed Franklin was correct and that it was time to repeal the Stamp Act, yet Parliament needed to save face. The question thus became, "How to do both?"
	Franklin's remarks would be published both in London and the American colonies and many attribute his testimony as having *sealed the deal* for the Stamp Act's repeal.

Residents of Elizabeth Town, New Jersey threaten to hang any stamp distributor.

Mid-Feb. 1766   **Charles Town permits ships to sail without properly stamped papers.**

South Carolina stamp agent Caleb Lloyd reaffirms his resignation, and with no one to distribute the stamps, Governor William Bull now permits ships to sail without them.

Feb. 18, 1766   **A customs officer is seized in Brunswick, North Carolina.**

Nearly 1,000 men march on Brunswick and seize the customs collector, William Dry, forcing him to open the port and release three confiscated ships that are to be sent to the Vice Admiralty Court in Halifax. In addition, the intimidated Dry takes an oath before the unruly crowd promising to no longer support the Stamp Act. The next day the large group marches to confront Governor Tryon.

Feb. 22, 1766   **The Stamp Act is repealed by Parliament.**

Under intense internal and external pressures, Parliament reluctantly repeals the measure. Now the repeal must be approved by the king.

> Note: The Stamp Act's repeal was mainly due to the lobbying of British merchants rather than to the howling protests from across the Atlantic.

Feb. 28, 1766   **London merchants warn their Boston trade partners of the importance of repudiating violent protests.**

They sign the letter, "Your affectionate friends, and humble servants."

March 1766   **The first recorded *tar and feathering* in North America takes place in Norfolk, Virginia.**

Believed to be an informer of smugglers, William Smith is tarred and feathered and paraded through the streets to the beat of a drum. Followed by a jeering crowd while pelted with stones and rotten eggs, Smith is taken to the town wharf and tossed into the water.

> Note: The threat of being tarred and feathered would be mostly limited to local informers, defiers of nonimportation, and lower-level customs workers in an effort to intimidate them from doing their jobs.
>
> The punishment—usually delivered as a form of mob violence—dated back to the Crusades and King Richard I.

March 17, 1766   **British merchants draft a petition urging the king to rescind the Stamp Act.**

March 18, 1766   **King George III gives his royal assent to the Stamp Act's repeal.**

The repeal is to go into effect beginning May 1, 1766.

> Note: Two months would pass before word of the Stamp Act's repeal reached the Americans.

Parliament passes the *Declaratory Act* to assert its authority over the Americans.

Though Parliament repeals the Stamp Act, it also wishes to reassert its authority over Britain's colonies and thus passes the Declaratory Act, declaring Parliament's right to make laws binding on the colonies "in all cases whatsoever"—meaning that the American colonists are subordinate to British parliamentary powers.

Note:	Parliament wished to specifically state its authority to tax the Americans, but William Pitt had successfully argued against it. Though Pitt's actions furthered his positive reputation in the colonies, this did not settle a basic question: Does Parliament have the power to directly tax British citizens living in Britain's colonies?
	Some colonial leaders would consider the Declaratory Act to be a form of political slavery and a clipping of American power assertions.
	Despite those in opposition, many Americans—proud to be part of the Kingdom of Great Britain—would agree with the Declaratory Act.
	Great Britain would attempt to strengthen the enforcement powers of the various royal agents and civil officers in the American colonies by additional troops. Many in London felt that had there previously been more troops, they might have prevented the Stamp Act riots.
	Though Britain could not admit it, much less accept it, the problem was simply that its American colonies, like children, had matured. After years of permitting the colonists a liberal hand over their own affairs, Britain's attempts to reassert control were a case of too little, too late, and too far away.

March 19, 1766　　**In Falmouth, Maine, destructive riots are led by the Sons of Liberty.**

In the dead of night, thirty rioters dressed loosely as Indians launch a surprise attack with guns and axes against the home of Richard King. The unpopular King, a successful businessman and supporter of the stamp tax, is targeted by his disguised neighbors, many of whom are indebted to him due to extended credits. The rioters break out King's windows, wreck his furniture, and then burn, destroy, and carry off his papers and business records while his family and servants cower in fear.

Two days later, a sign appears attached to King's gate warning that if anyone is arrested for the crime, those responsible for the arrests shall have their houses burned and be killed, cut into pieces, and tossed into the flames. It is signed, "The Sons of Liberty."

Note:	One year later, the rioters would return to King's restored residence and destroy it beyond repair. For the rest of his life, a determined Richard King would seek redress for the injustices against him.
	Boston attorney John Adams would represent King in his unsuccessful lawsuit.

Spring 1766　　**Wappinger sachem Daniel Ninham sails to London to appeal his case to King George III.**

Funded by sympathetic New York tenants, seven Wappinger sail to England to address the king but are refused, for they have neither an official invitation nor a letter of introduction from New York authorities. Instead, Chief Ninham meets with Britain's secretary of state and the Board of Trade. After listening to the plight of the Wappinger, Lord Shelburne will instruct New York Governor Moore to "take under your most serious consideration the case of these distressed people and turn your thoughts to every possible measure that may obtain for them a just and lasting satisfaction and that you take on yourself as far as justice and the reason of the thing shall demand the office of their advocate and protector."

Early April 1766　　**In New York, rumors abound that Britain's Royal fleet is to arrive and force the stamp tax upon the people.**

Unaware that the Stamp Act has been ordered repealed, many Sons of Liberty leaders prepare to resist—by force if necessary.

Late April 1766   **Armed New York farmers march on New York City, as the Hudson Valley Land Riots continue to grow.**

Three farmers have been arrested and taken to New York City for *safe keeping*, far from their revolting brethren. With plans of securing their release, William Prendergast and 500 armed followers march south causing panic as the disgruntled farmers reach King's Bridge leading to Manhattan. When warned of his actions, Prendergast replies, "Mobs have overcome kings before and why should they not overcome now?"

> Note: Referring to themselves as Sons of Liberty, the rebelling farmers hoped the city's laborers would join them and that the New York Sons of Liberty would support their cause—but they would not.
>
> Afraid the anti-rent rebellion would spread; the patroons and New York authorities called for their suppression.
>
> As a precaution, British General Thomas Gage would order men to the protection of Fort George at the southern tip of Manhattan Island.

May 1, 1766   **The Stamp Act is officially terminated, ending one and a half years of British-American political turmoil.**

Though the Stamp Act had been in effect for only six months, the issue was debated and protested for a year beforehand.

Prendergast's army of rebel farmers negotiates with New York Governor Henry Moore.

At the outskirts of New York City, Prendergast sends six representatives to Fort George to meet with Governor Moore and present their grievances. Hoping to quell the situation, Moore tells the rebel delegates he will not intervene on behalf of the patroons which gives them satisfaction and most of the farmers begin a homeward retreat.

> Note: Buoyed by success, Prendergast's support would continue to grow as his followers soon numbered between 1,700 and 2,000 men, causing concern among New York's government officials and the wealthy landlords. Unhappy with Governor Moore's tepid response, New York's city council would place a £100 reward on Prendergast's head and demands that Governor Moore enlist the British Army to subdue the rebels.

May 16, 1766   **Boston learns of the Stamp Act's repeal and the people rejoice.**

The news quickly travels throughout the town as people gather in the streets to celebrate accompanied by cheers and the ringing of church bells. As day turns into night, the raucous festivities continue with the normally dark streets illuminated by bonfires and fire pyramids.

> Note: In Boston, the merchant John Hancock would provide wine for the celebrants on Boston Common—which helped increase his popularity—while John Adams would write that he had witnessed "such a grand exhibition and fireworks as were never before seen in America."

In North America, William Pitt is celebrated as a champion of American liberties.

The influential Member of Parliament is celebrated in the colonies for his efforts to repeal the stamp tax and his general support for the Americans.

June 4, 1766	**New York raises it first liberty pole in celebration of the Stamp Act's repeal and the king's birthday.**

> Note: The liberty pole erected at City Hall Park would become an important symbol to the New York radicals, providing a rallying site to assemble and stir up trouble.
>
> The British soldiers stationed in New York City were upset that the assembly had not provided the funds required for their support and viewed the raising of the liberty pole as another act of American defiance.

June 13, 1766	**Once again, Governor Moore requests funds from the New York Assembly for the quartering of British troops.**

Additional troops are expected from England and the quartering issues have not been resolved.

June 19, 1766	**The New York Assembly denies Governor Moore's request for military funding; declaring the colony has insufficient resources.**

June 1766	**British troops are ordered to march against Prendergast's army.**

Having proclaimed the rebel leaders guilty of high treason, the New York Provincial Council requests that General Gage send troops to kill or capture William Prendergast and defeat the rebel army, now nearly 2,000-strong. Gage agrees and sends the 28th Grenadiers from Albany led by Major Richard Browne to help restore order to Dutchess County.

> Note: General Thomas Gage sent the 28th Grenadiers to Poughkeepsie, and the 46th Regiment to Claverack to aid Sheriff Harmanus Schuyler.
>
> Some historians consider this to be the first ordering of British troops directly against Americans.

June 23, 1766	**The New York Assembly commissions statues of William Pitt and King George III.**

Wishing to erect a statue honoring William Pitt but not wanting to offend the king, the assembly also orders a statue of George III astride his horse, which will be placed on Bowling Green in New York City.

> Note: The statue of George III—the first equestrian statue in North America—would be pulled down on July 9, 1776, by a raucous crowd celebrating the passage of the American Declaration of Independence.

Like New York, the South Carolina Assembly commissions a statue of William Pitt.

The assembly allows £7,000 for defraying the expense for a marble statue to be made in England of William Pitt.

> Note: Four years later, William Pitt would become the first public official to be honored with a statue in North America when South Carolina would erect the finished work in Charles Town on July 5, 1770.

Late June 1766	**In New York, Prendergast's army begins to disperse after learning it is being hunted by British regulars.**

Approximately 100 of the remaining rebels split into two groups; one led by William Prendergast and the other by Robert Noble.

June 26, 1766	**Prendergast's army battles the sheriff's militia.**

Landowner Stephen Van Rensselaer II, accompanied by Sheriff Harmanus Schuyler and 105 New York militiamen, are met by 50 of the revolting farmers armed mostly with clubs and sticks under the command of Robert Nichols. The two groups face off with a mere fence separating them before the sheriff orders, "Fire!" The one-way volley kills a farmer, wounds others, and one militiaman is killed by friendly fire. Most of the rebels flee into the woods, but others retreat to a nearby house and a firefight ensues resulting in one farmer killed and seven of the sheriff's men wounded. The farmers continue to battle causing Sheriff Schuyler to seek the assistance of Major Richard Browne and his British regulars. But Major Browne—busily in pursuit of William Prendergast—declines to aid Sheriff Schuyler.

> Note: At the fence, a farmer with a broken leg complained in misery to the Sheriff's men upon being lifted that he "would rather die than be carried off" so they shot him and left him to die.
>
> The wealthy patroon Stephen Van Rensselaer II was married to Catherine Livingston, the daughter of Philip Livingston, a future signer of the American Declaration of Independence.

July 2, 1766	**British troops are killed pursuing Prendergast's army; but they defeat the rebels.**

With the singular goal of capturing William Prendergast, Major Browne and his Grenadiers continue their pursuit but are ambushed by rebels hidden in a cornfield. Leaving two British soldiers dead, the farmers flee to a hilltop house as the troops advance against them. With little hope remaining, the farmers soon wave a white flag and are taken prisoner, but Major Browne has missed his quarry—rebel leader William Prendergast has escaped.

July 24, 1766	**Pontiac signs an agreement ending the Western Indian War against the English.**

Meeting at Fort Ontario, Canada, the Ottawa war leader Pontiac signs a peace treaty with British Indian Superintendent William Johnson, ending one of the most successful Indian wars in American history. As part of the agreement, Pontiac is granted a full pardon for his role in the war.

July 28, 1766	**Rebel leader William Prendergast surrenders to New York authorities on his own accord.**

Accompanied by his wife Mehitable Wing, Prendergast turns himself in and is promptly shipped to New York City to stand trial.

> Note: Prendergast would be transported by boat as the authorities considered the situation too dangerous to send him overland; fearing his rebel supporters would free him.

July 30, 1766	**William Pitt becomes Britain's prime minister, replacing Lord Rockingham.**

News of Pitt's selection will be well received in the American colonies.

> Note: With the French gone from North America; the repeal of the Stamp Act; and a new administration governing Great Britain; most in Britain and the colonies believed better relations were ahead.

Aug. 1766	**Boston's Sons of Liberty organize a commemoration of the Stamp Act riots—one year past.**

The Sons of Liberty believe their cause to be noble and their resistance to British authority to be lawful. As such, most feel it is important to keep the public somewhat *whipped up* or agitated to provide a ready reserve of pressure to exert if necessary.

Meeting at Kaskaskia, Illinois, Western Tribes agree that all French lands purchased by past treaty will be transferred to Great Britain.

All other lands are to be retained by the Indians.

Aug. 6, 1766   **In New York, William Prendergast goes on trial for high treason.**

Prendergast, described as a "sober, honest, and industrious Farmer much beloved by his neighbors," conducts his own defense with the aid of his wife, Mehitable. Found guilty, the jury recommends mercy, but the court orders him to be hanged, drawn and quartered. Therefore, Prendergast is scheduled for execution on September 28.

> Note: Shocked at the judgment, Prendergast's tearful wife would ride seventy miles to meet with Governor Henry Moore, and after much pleading, Moore would issue a stay of execution pending an appeal to King George III. In addition, the court could not find anyone willing to execute Prendergast in such a manner—even with a disguised identity.
>
> The court—controlled by the wealthy patroons—wanted to use the grisly execution of Prendergast as a deterrent to others who might wish to rebel against them.

Aug. 10, 1766   **New York City's first liberty pole is destroyed.**

Tensions come to blows between citizens and British troops as the soldiers manage to chop down the liberty pole, defiantly raised at City Hall Park two months earlier.

> Note: Though a second liberty pole would be quickly raised, within a few days it too would be destroyed. This back-and-forth battle would continue for more than ten years.

Aug. 11, 1766   **John Wentworth the Younger becomes New Hampshire's last royal governor.**

> Note: Serving for nine years, Wentworth would be forced from office by armed mobs in the summer of 1775.

Sept. 23, 1766   **A third liberty pole is erected in New York City.**

Royal Governor Moore orders the British troops to disregard the offending pole.

Dec. 1766   **Having suffered greatly in the recent Indian wars, New York's assembly calls for an intercolonial meeting.**

New York wishes to treat with the tribes as a unified colonial group rather than individually, but the idea is nixed by the British Ministry, suspecting *ulterior designs*.

Dec. 5, 1766   **The Massachusetts Assembly passes the *Indemnity Act* in an attempt to put the Stamp Act riots behind it.**

Officially titled "An act for Granting Compensation to the Sufferers, and of Free and General Pardon, Indemnity and Oblivion to the Offenders in the Late Times," the Act is Massachusetts's attempt to put an end to all suits, controversies, and prosecutions related to the riots, hopefully drawing a veil over the *late unhappy excesses* and pleasing the Crown.

Dec. 15, 1766   **The New York Assembly petitions Governor Moore against the 1765 Quartering Act.**

The petition states:

- "That compliance would please us, but we cannot."

- "An unfair burden is placed on New York compared to its neighbors."

- "The 1765 Quartering Act only applies to soldiers *on the march*."

- "We are told to prepare to quarter any soldier who enters the Province for an entire year—this would ruin us financially and is unsupportable."

Dec. 19, 1766   **Royal Governor Moore prorogues the New York Assembly for noncompliance with the 1765 Quartering Act.**

Jan. 1767   **"Americans ought to pay for the troops protecting them."**

Former Prime Minister George Grenville, now serving as Britain's Chancellor of the Exchequer, states that the Americans should pay the expenses of maintaining British troops in North America, since the troops are stationed there for the benefit and defense of the Americans.

Note: The Chancellor of the Exchequer served as Great Britain's chief financial officer, administering the state's revenues and expenditures.

New York farmer and rebel leader William Prendergast receives a pardon.

Pardoned by King George III, the act makes William Prendergast a lifelong supporter of the king and Great Britain.

Note: The Prendergast Rebellion would be but one of several anti-rent revolts against the wealthy patroons and the feudal property leases in New York.

March 1767   **Wappinger sachem Daniel Ninham fruitlessly refiles his lawsuit to reclaim the tribe's lands in New York's Hudson Valley.**

Chief Ninham states that the Wappinger would never prevail to sell their New York lands and all claims to the contrary are false. Witnesses on Ninham's behalf—relatives of the Philipse family—claim they heard Adolph Philipse once say that he had never bought the land from the Indians but should have. In addition, no lawful deed of conveyance has ever been recorded or recognized. Despite the evidence, the council rules that the Wappinger tribe have no right to title.

Following the trial, the defense lawyer sums up the court's ruling against the Wappinger: "Observing upon the Dangerous Consequences of admitting such Kind of Complaints. This will be Dangerous Tendencey; Twill open a Door to the greatest Mischiefs, inasmuch as a great part of the Lands in the Province are supposed to lie under much the Same Situation; and upon the whole intimated, that it would therefore, by no means do, to give Heed to the present Complaint."

What will become of the Wappinger?

In the future years:

- Approximately 250 Wappinger are forced to move to the Stockbridge Indian Town in western Massachusetts and join with the Mohican community.

- Wappinger warriors volunteer and fight during the American War for Independence as the *Stockbridge Militia Company*, pledging, "Wherever your armies go, there we will go; you shall always find us by your side; and if providence calls us to sacrifice our Lives in the field of battle, we will fall where you fall. And lay our bones by yours. Nor shall peace ever be made between our nation and the Red Coats until our brothers—the white people—lead the way." Comprised of Munsee, Mohican, and Wappinger, the Indian warriors assist in many American military campaigns, including the 1775 capture of Fort Ticonderoga; the 1775-1776 siege of Boston; and the 1777 battles of Saratoga and Monmouth.

- On August 31, 1778, the Indians suffer tragedy during the Battle of Kingsbridge after being ambushed by British troops. Though they fight gallantly, many Wappinger are massacred by *shot and saber*, including Chief Daniel Ninham and his son Abraham.

- In the mid-1780s, the surviving Wappinger at Stockbridge, Massachusetts—predominately grieving widows and children—move north to join the Oneida near Oneida Lake, New York, and form the community of New Stockbridge.

- In 1818, due to pressures from New York land speculators, the Wappinger relocate to Michigan, and later to Wisconsin.

- In 1839, as part of the United States' *Indian Removal Act of 1832*, the Wappinger relocate to Kansas and Oklahoma; however, in the 1840s, some tribal members return to Wisconsin, where their descendants remain.

Note: Today, the Stockbridge-Munsee-Mohican Indian Nation operates a casino, golf course, and resort in Shawano County, Wisconsin.

         Like all Native American tribes—the history, contribution, sacrifices, and influences of the Wappinger on the formation of the United States are today largely forgotten.

March 18, 1767   **For a third time—British troops destroy New York's liberty pole.**

Many citizens gather at the pole to celebrate the one-year anniversary of the king's repeal of the Stamp Act. The haughty celebratory defiance disturbs the soldiers and they cut down the pole.

March 19, 1767   **A fourth liberty pole is raised in New York in an ongoing battle of wills.**

Determined to prevail against the British troops, resolute New Yorkers secure the festooned pole with iron bars and hoops so it cannot be chopped down. The Sons of Liberty and others try to guard what has become to all—a symbol of anti-British defiance.

March 24, 1767   **The 1765 Mutiny Act, aka the Quartering Act, is renewed by Parliament.**

In London, Benjamin Franklin stresses that Americans are opposed to paying internal taxes levied against them by Parliament, rather than external taxes.

Britain's Chancellor of the Exchequer Charles Townshend listens carefully to Franklin's words.

May 13, 1767   **Parliament rejects the Massachusetts Indemnity Act.**

Passed by the Massachusetts General Court on December 5, 1766, to hopefully settle the political and legal issues surrounding the 1765 Boston Riots, the Act is rejected by Parliament, as advised by the Privy Council.

> Note: First presented to the Board of Trade on March 12, 1767, the Massachusetts Indemnity Act had been forwarded to the law officers of the Crown. On April 10, the officers reported that, "the Governor, Council, and Assembly of the Massachusetts Bay have not by the Constitution of that Province, any original Power to enact a Law of General Pardon, Indemnity and Oblivion … without previous Communication of the Grace and Pleasure of the Crown."
>
> Though the Massachusetts Indemnity Act was rejected, the colony would make compensatory payments to those royal officials who had suffered damages.

Chancellor of the Exchequer Charles Townshend proposes a new approach for raising revenue from the American colonials.

Townshend believes Great Britain can raise an additional £40,000 for the Treasury by imposing duties on certain exports to the colonies that they cannot do without, but to be successful, the new laws must be enforced. The taxes are not to be direct internal taxes like the troublesome stamp tax, but rather indirect external taxes.

> Note: These taxes, combined with the several Acts passed by Parliament to enforce American compliance, will become known collectively as Britain's *Townshend Acts*.
>
> The Townshend Acts would include the New York Restraining Act of 1767, passed on June 5, 1767; the Revenue Act of 1767, passed on June 26, 1767; the Commissioners of Customs Act of 1767, passed on June 29, 1767; the Indemnity Act of 1767, passed on June 29, 1767; and the Vice Admiralty Court Act of 1768, passed on July 6, 1768.
>
> The Revenue Act of 1767 would be often referred to as the *Townshend Revenue Act,* or more simply—the *Townshend duties*

June 5, 1767   **The *New York Restraining Act* is passed by Parliament.**

The Act calls for the suspension of the New York Assembly beginning on October 1, 1767, if it does not provide funding and support for the King's troops as required by the Quartering Act. British Chancellor of the Exchequer Charles Townshend orders Royal Governor Moore to "interrupt" the assembly's operations until it approves the requisite funds necessary for the support of the troops.

> Note: The New York Assembly considered itself an independent body following autonomous legislative traditions, and therefore resented being told what to do.
>
> The suspension of colonial assemblies would be alluded to in grievance number five of the U.S. Declaration of Independence.

June 8, 1767   **The *Pennsylvania Gazette* publishes observations concerning affairs from Benjamin Franklin in London.**

Having attended Parliament's debate over the Massachusetts Indemnity Act, Franklin warns not only will the Act be rejected, but Massachusetts can expect severe censure as well. In addition, Franklin expresses concern that America's friends in Parliament are outnumbered by those against them. Therefore, with Parliament's mood as it is, the colonies can expect violent resolutions against America.

> Note: Though Massachusetts did not know it at the time, the Indemnity Act had been rejected three weeks earlier. News and correspondences sent between Great Britain and the North American colonies normally required four to six weeks to arrive.

Late June 1767   **Faced with suspension, the New York Assembly agrees to partially fund the quartering of British troops.**

Aware that Parliament was passing legislation (New York Restraining Act) calling for the assembly's suspension beginning October 1 if it did not comply with the Quartering Act, the assembly begrudgingly votes to provide partial funding.

1767   **Tea drinking has become an established British custom; however, though consumption is immense—the East India Company is losing money.**

The East India Company has been Britain's sole *legal* importer of tea; however, the company has always been forced to compete against Dutch tea—easily smuggled into both Great Britain and the colonies. In 1721, Parliament had attempted to remedy the situation by requiring all tea brought into the kingdom be imported by the East India Company and pass through the London warehouses before distribution. Yet over the subsequent years, actual enforcement has been but a sieve as smugglers and merchants alike ignore the law, and the illegal trade continues to flourish. As such, the East India Company is losing money, and by it, Great Britain is also losing tax revenue—nearly £400,000 annually in uncollected duties. To stem the losses, Britain's Board of Trade wishes to drive Dutch tea from the British market by undercutting Dutch prices and through better enforcement of the trade restrictions.

> Note: Among the stockholders in the East India Company were royalty, nobles, and wealthy British merchants who were rightfully concerned about company profits. Therefore, by saving the East India Company—these influential investors were also saving themselves.
>
> More than 1 million pounds of tea were consumed annually in the American colonies alone.

June 26, 1767   **The *Revenue Act* of 1767 is passed by Parliament.**

Though the Stamp Act has been revoked, the British Ministry and Parliament still need additional revenues to pay for customs enforcements in North America and the British troops stationed there. Therefore, Parliament passes the Revenue Act of 1767—an external (indirect) tax placed mainly on paper, paint, glass, and tea imported into the North American colonies—believing that by taxing these necessary items not produced in the colonies, the tax will be hard to avoid. Parliament expects to raise £40,000 annually by the Act.

The Revenue Act's stated purpose is as follows: "Revenues shall be used for defraying the charge of the administration of justice, and the support of civil government, in such provinces as it shall be found necessary; and towards defraying the expenses of defending, protecting and securing the said dominions."

Beginning November 20, 1767: "there shall be raised, levied, collected, and paid, unto his Majesty, his heirs, and successors, for and upon the respective Goods herein after mentioned, which shall be imported from Great Britain into any colony or plantation in America which now is or hereafter may be, under the dominion of his Majesty, his heirs, or successors, the several Rates and Duties."

The 1767 Revenue Act's provisions include:

- A duty on glass (crown, plate, flint, white, and green) at a tax per hundred-weight of 4 shillings and 8 pence.

- A duty on red lead and white lead (used with paint) at a tax per hundred-weight of 2 shillings.

- A duty on colours (paints) at a tax per hundred-weight of 2 shillings.

- A duty on tea at a tax per pound of 3 pence.

- A duty on paper, to vary depending on the type of paper; all paper not made in Britain is to be taxed at a higher rate.

Note: Paper was very important in the American colonies; used extensively from print to packing and so much more. The 1767 Revenue Act listed nearly seventy different paper types and the specific tax on each. Though the Revenue Act mirrored the Stamp Act, the duties would be rolled into the overall price and did not have a stamp affixed; thus, avoiding a visual irritant that would remind the people that a tax had been paid.

- Duties placed on certain silks, calicoes, linens, and stuffs, printed, painted, or stained (silk handkerchiefs excepted) to the sum of 6 pence for every yard in length, reckoning half a yard for the breadth.

- Reduced export duties on cocoa (chocolate) and coffee grown in the British kingdom, in the hopes of encouraging production in the colonies.

- A discontinuation of the duties on log wood (raw logs) exported from the colonies beginning July 20, 1767.

- Duty-free exportation of rice to other parts of the kingdom until December 1, 1767.

"All rates and duties, charged by this act upon goods imported into any British American colony or plantation, shall be deemed, and are hereby declared to be, sterling money of Great Britain; and shall be collected, recovered, and paid to the amount of the value which such nominal sums bear in Great Britain."

To prevent fraud and regulate abuses, "it is lawful for any officer of his Majesty's customs, authorized by writ of assistance under the seal of his Majesty's Court or Exchequer, to take a constable, headborough, or other public officer inhabiting near unto the place, and in the day-time to enter and go into any house, shop, cellar, warehouse, or room or other place, and, in case of resistance, to break open doors, chests, trunks, and other package there, to seize, and from thence to bring, any kinds of goods or merchandize whatsoever prohibited or uncustomed, and to put and secure the same in his Majesty's store-house next to the place where such seizure shall be made."

"That from and after the said twentieth day of November, one thousand seven hundred and sixty-seven, such writs of assistance, to authorize and impower the officer of his Majesty's customs to enter and go into any house, warehouse, shop, cellar, or other place, in the British colonies of plantations of America, to search for and seize prohibited or uncustomed goods, in the manner directed by the said recited acts, shall and may be granted by the said superior or supreme courts of justice having jurisdiction within such colony or plantation respectively."

Note: Writs of assistance allowed by the 1767 Revenue Act would permit the customs officers to search for goods subject to duties.

"Customs officers sued in pursuance of their duties may plead the general issue and use this Act for their defense and are therefore protected if his actions were done in pursuance of and by authority of this Act. If the judgment is for the defendant, he shall receive treble costs from the plaintiff."

> Note: By granting itself authority to pay the salaries of certain royally appointed judges and officials, the British Ministry hoped to remove the financial leverage currently wielded over such Crown officers by the colonial assemblies. In addition, it was believed that by paying the judges' salaries directly from Britain's coffers, it would better retain the loyalty of the royal officers operating in America, thus ensuring better compliance with British trade regulations.
>
> By paying the import duties at the port of entry, they would be *hidden* from the consumer by being folded into the overall price.
>
> The 1767 Revenue Act allowed leeway in pursuance by customs officers, using *good faith in pursuit of the law* as a defense against suits. If a ship's owner brought a suit against a customs official, the onus of proof was on the owner. If the lawsuit was lost, the owner would be charged three times the court costs.
>
> The 1767 Revenue Act would be met with resistance in the colonies as many would question and resist any control from the mother country across the ocean. To many Americans—the purpose of the tax was worse than the tax itself.

June 29, 1767 **The *Indemnity Act* of 1767 lowers the price of British tea to save the East India Company— on the verge of financial collapse.**

"An Act for taking off the Inland Duty of One Shilling per Pound Weight upon all Black and Singlo Teas consumed in Great Britain; and for granting a Drawback upon the Exportation of Teas to Ireland, and the British Dominions in America, for limited Time, upon such Indemnification to be made in respect thereof by the East India Company, as is therein mentioned; for permitting the Exportation of Teas in smaller Quantities than One Lot to Ireland or the said Dominions in America; and for preventing Teas seized and condemned from being consumed in Great Britain."

The 1767 Indemnity Act's provisions include:

- A removal of the 1-shilling tax per pound of weight on all black and Singlo tea consumed in Great Britain.

- A drawback of the 25 percent duty normally charged for tea exported to Ireland and the American colonies, thus lowering the price, and hopefully ensuring more sales. For five years, tea importers shall receive a drawback of the whole duties payable upon the importation of such teas which shall be made to the exporter.

- "All the monies which shall be paid into the receipt of his Majesty's exchequer in pursuance of this Act shall be applied to such uses and purposes, and in such proportions, as the present duties on teas are now made applicable."

- "No tea shall be exported to the kingdom of Ireland, or to any of his Majesty's plantations in America, in any chest, cask, tub, or package whatsoever other than that in which it was originally imported into Great Britain; nor in any less quantities than in the entire lot or lots in which the same was sold at the sale."

- "All teas which shall be seized and condemned for being illegally imported, or for any other cause, shall not be sold for consumption within this kingdom, but shall be exported to Ireland, or to the British colonies in America; and that no such teas, after the sale thereof, shall be delivered out of any warehouse belonging to his Majesty, otherwise than for exportation as aforesaid, or be exported in any package containing a less quantity than fifty pounds weight."

- "Lawsuits brought in pursuance of the law found in favor of the defendant shall be paid treble cost."

Note:	At selected future dates, the East India Company was required to indemnify His Majesty's Exchequer for the Crown's lost revenue. The company, now in financial trouble, expected to repay the government from the profits to be produced by increased tea sales to Ireland and the American colonies. Though the 1767 Revenue Act had enacted a 3-pence tea tax, the Indemnity Act offset that tax by allowing a drawback on the duties previously paid on tea exports. Thus, tea prices would be lower than the Irish and Americans had been previously paying.
	The Indemnity Act was to begin on July 5, 1767; and would expire on July 5, 1772.
	Those involved in the smuggled Dutch tea trade were rightfully concerned that the lowered prices of East India tea would undercut their market prices both in Great Britain and in the American colonies—which was the Act's intent.

The *Commissioners of Customs Act* of 1767 is passed to supervise customs enforcement in North America.

The overall purpose of "An Act to Enable his Majesty to Put the Customs, and Other Duties, in the British Dominions in America, and the Execution of the Laws Relating to Trade There, under the Management of Commissioners to be Appointed for that Purpose, and to be Resident in the Said Dominions" is to transfer customs enforcement authority concerning American colonial trade from Britain to North America.

The Commissioners of Customs Act's provisions include:

- An *American Board of Customs and Commissioners* is to be established, with its headquarters in Boston, the seat of the American resistance.

- The new American Board of Customs and Commissioners is to consist of five commissioners, who will reside in Boston.

Note:	Parliament and the British Board of Trade planned to assert authority and enforce the 1767 Revenue Act and other trade regulations by putting customs agents *on the ground* and locating the new American Customs Board in Boston rather than trying to control affairs from London. By granting the Boston commissioners the same authority as the commissioners of customs in Great Britain, the Board of Trade hoped to eliminate the many appeals to London which greatly delayed and obstructed commerce and trade. Yet such authority granted to officials operating at great distances from Britain would make the situation ripe for illegal profiteering as bribes would be offered for officers to *look the other way.* Many officers would entrap merchants by being lax on technical violations and then suddenly becoming strict. In addition, customs officers would often bring false charges using paid witnesses as all persons charged were assumed guilty unless they could prove otherwise.

- An increased number of tax collectors and customs agents are to be stationed in the colonies.

Note:	Americans were employed by the British Customs to enforce the various trade regulations in North America, and many would suffer for it. Often harassed with verbal and physical intimidation, a certain few would be grievously injured simply for doing their job.

- Customs officials are to be paid directly by the Crown through revenues generated by trade enforcements, for the British government wishes to have the customs officers independent of American influence and control.

- Custom officers are empowered to seize vessels violating the law and sell both the ships and their cargo.

| July 1767 | **Hoping to force a repeal of the 1767 Revenue Act, calls begin in North America for nonimportation of certain British goods.** |

> Note: British merchants and American colonists were tightly bound by symbiotic economic interests. In debt to British manufacturers and financiers due to expanded credits and a large American market, the colonial business leaders would play their *economic cards* hoping to influence British policy through the pain of lost revenues.

The nonimportation movement will grow slowly over the next several years, first in Boston, followed by New York and Philadelphia, and eventually broadening to include the Southern merchants. As the calls for a boycott spread, the issue becomes a moral cause for the Americans as their views become more entrenched, and their resolves harden.

> Note: The nonimportation movement protesting the 1767 Navigation Act would vary somewhat among the different colonies as each had its own particular interests. Beginning seriously in 1769, most colonies would join the boycott by the end of that year—but each with its own plan and degree of enforcement.
>
> Many in Britain's government complained of the insubordinate wretches across the sea who dared question Parliament's authority and that of the British Ministry. Now, the American noncompliance would become a direct challenge to Britain as *two could play the game.*

| Mid-Aug. 1767 | **New York's Sons of Liberty demand that all "market people should not sell any provisions to any of the officers or soldiers" quartered within the city.** |

The British troops stationed in New York are still awaiting adequate funds to be provided by the colonial assembly and the Sons of Liberty want to keep it that way, depriving the soldiers of everything in order to drive them away.

> Note: In New York, the British soldiers often sought second jobs as laborers or dockworkers to supplement their low pay, but pressure was now put on employers not to hire them.

| Sept. 4, 1767 | **Charles Townshend dies: Britain's former Prime Minister and the current Chancellor of the Exchequer.** |

> Note: News of Townshend's death would reach North America in early October to little sympathy. But as Townshend had been the man most responsible for Britain's current fiscal policy toward the colonies, many American leaders would wonder, "Now what?"

| Oct. 1, 1767 | **Though scheduled to begin, the New York Restraining Act is not enforced.** |

Under pressure from the New York Assembly, Royal Governor Henry Moore decides against proroguing the assembly due to its June compliance for funds—though considered to be partial and inadequate—as the assembly continues to resist Parliament's demand that New York provide for the funding of the British troops stationed there.

| Oct. 9, 1767 | **In western Pennsylvania, the Iroquois force the Mason-Dixon survey to end short of its commission.** |

After having cleared a nine-yard-wide line through the forest for 233 miles, the survey team is halted by arriving Mohawk. Having reached the *Warriors Path* running north and south through the Appalachians, the Indians tell the men they have gone as far as the Iroquois have permitted and they must turn back. Though the assignment is to survey to a point five degrees west of the Delaware River, the team of surveyors, axmen, and supporters is forced to turn around—thirty-four miles short of its goal.

> Note: The Iroquois had grown increasingly resentful as the Whites cleared a path mile after mile into the western forest. The survey team had been stopped previously by the Mohawk at Mile 162, and only after Indian Superintendent William Johnson paid the Iroquois an additional £500 was the survey permitted to continue.
>
> Indian warfare was always a threat to the isolated survey team and took its toll on the surveyors' nerves. At Mile 216, twenty-six members of the team had quit due to Indian fears and had to be replaced.
>
> As markers, survey stones had been laid every mile, and *crown stones* made in England were placed every five miles.
>
> The survey had begun in the spring of 1764 and was halted nearly four years later.
>
> The uncompleted survey between Pennsylvania and Maryland would be finished by others in 1784.
>
> The survey boundary would not be known as the *Mason-Dixon line* for another fifty years.
>
> In the future, the Mason-Dixon line would be considered the unofficial border between the Northern and Southern region of the Eastern United States.

The British Ministry creates a new *American Department* to superintend the North American colonies.

With relations rapidly deteriorating between Great Britain and the American colonies, the ministry removes the responsibility for overseeing the colonies from Britain's *Southern Department* and instead creates an *American Department* to better deal with colonial affairs in North America.

> Note: Affairs concerning Britain's colonies had been mainly run by the Board of Trade and a committee of the Privy Council. Now, a new office—the *Secretary of State for the Colonies*—would be established as a cabinet-level position to help supervise Britain's colonies in North America.

Concerned about the increasing numbers of slaves, Virginia officials double the import tariff on newly arriving Africans.

Oct. 1767

In Boston, calls continue for a nonimportation of British goods.

A broadside appears containing the names of 650 Bostonians pledging nonimportation.

> Note: Though the Americans would oppose the collective Townshend Acts, it was the Revenue Act of 1767, or Townshend duties, that would become the target of their collective ire.

Autumn 1767

Frontiersman Daniel Boone, in violation of the Proclamation of 1763, enters the Kentucky region for the first time.

Living in North Carolina's Yadkin Valley, Boone and his brother Squire unsuccessfully attempt to find the famed Indian hunting grounds that lay to the west.

> Note: British law prohibited Whites from traveling west of the Appalachian Mountains without permission; yet to those settlers living in the western forest regions of North

America—London and the reach of British law seemed distant and would be therefore mostly ignored.

In 1784, Daniel Boone—an able frontiersman and Indian fighter—would gain instant fame and future legendary status in American history due to John Filson's publication, *The Adventures of Col. Daniel Boone.*

Nov. 1767

In Massachusetts, Governor Bernard's salary is made independent of the General Court.

The assembly's control over the royal governor's salary has always served as a check to the governor's power. This change causes the General Court great concern over what is seen as the further loss of Massachusetts self-government.

Note: If deemed necessary, royal governors' salaries could now to be paid directly by Great Britain from the funds expected to be collected by the Revenue Act of 1767.

Nov. 4, 1767

In Boston, British officers of the newly created American Board of Customs arrive to a cool reception.

Arriving from London, the customs commissioners feel unwelcome, unwanted, intimidated, and isolated as they set about exercising their official duties. As such, the new customs officials will request that British troops be sent to Boston for their safety.

Note: William Burch, Henry Hulton, and Charles Paxton arrived to join John Temple and John Robinson as customs commissioners. Samuel Venner arrived as secretary to the board, John Porter as comptroller general, and John Williams as inspector general, along with a number of clerks.

Many in Boston seethed over the creation of the American Customs Board and its arriving officers, who were to now live amongst them. These sentiments would be reciprocated by the British commissioners. Two years hence, John Robinson would pummel the famed Boston lawyer James Otis senseless after Otis picked a fight with the British customs commissioner.

The arrival of these custom officers to Boston is alluded to in the tenth grievance of the U.S. Declaration of Independence.

Nov. 20, 1767

The 1767 Revenue Act officially begins in Britain's North American colonies.

Dec. 1767

***Letters from a Farmer in Pennsylvania to the Inhabitants of the Colonies* is published.**

John Dickinson, a Pennsylvania legislator and lawyer, publishes the first of twelve essays critical of the 1767 Revenue Act and Parliament under the pseudonym "a Pennsylvania Farmer." Though Dickinson acknowledges Parliament's authority to raise colonial revenue for the purpose of regulating trade, he denies its authority to raise a general revenue from the colonies by imposing internal taxes upon the colonists. Therefore, the Townshend duties are unconstitutional. Dickinson also denounces the suspension of New York's assembly for noncompliance with the Quartering Act. Published in the *Pennsylvania Chronicle*, Dickinson's essays are written for the common man and widely reproduced, earning him fame throughout the American colonies.

Note: Dickinson's twelve essays were published from December 1767 to February 1768.

In 1776, as a member of the Second Continental Congress, John Dickinson would refuse to sign the Declaration of Independence, still hoping for reconciliation with Britain.

Dec. 30, 1767

The Massachusetts General Court is called into session, urging action against Great Britain.

The Massachusetts Assembly debates a resolution attacking the Townshend duties; a petition to the king; and a circular letter to be forwarded to Britain's colonies in North America.

> Note: Written by Sam Adams and James Otis, the explosive letter—later known as the *Massachusetts Circular Letter*—would be approved and sent in February 1768.

Jan. 12, 1768   **Massachusetts approves a petition to King George III and his ministers.**

The petition addresses issues of property rights, taxation, and the colony's subjugation by royal officials and requests the removal of Royal Governor Francis Bernard. Authored by Sam Adams, the petition also stresses Massachusetts's continued loyalty and unity with Great Britain.

> Note: Like Massachusetts, Pennsylvania and Virginia also petitioned the king protesting the Townshend duties, but none the petitions would be considered.

Jan. 20, 1768   **A petition from King George III is presented to the Massachusetts Assembly.**

The king requests that the Massachusetts General Court compensate the petitioners who suffered loss in the riots of March 19, 1766, in Cumberland County (present-day Portland, Maine).

Feb. 1768   **In New York, a new assembly is formed to secure proper funds for the British troops stationed there.**

The new assembly will also frustrate Governor Moore as it proves to be less compliant than the previous one.

"No Taxation without Representation" appears in print for the first time.

Reporting on Lord Camdon's recent speech to Parliament regarding Britain's 1766 Declaratory Act, *The London Magazine* prints the summary headline, "No Taxation without Representation" and the words quickly become a catchphrase for the American colonists.

Feb. 11, 1768   **The Massachusetts Circular Letter is approved and sent to the colonial legislatures.**

"The House of Representatives of this province have taken into their serious consideration the great difficulties that must accrue to themselves and their constituents by the operation of several Acts of Parliament, imposing duties and taxes on the American colonies.

As it is a subject in which every colony is deeply interested, they have no reason to doubt but your house is deeply impressed with its importance, and that such constitutional measures will be come into as are proper. It seems to be necessary that all possible care should be taken that the representatives of the several assemblies, upon so delicate a point, should harmonize with each other. The House, therefore, hope that this letter will be candidly considered in no other light than as expressing a disposition freely to communicate their mind to a sister colony, upon a common concern, in the same manner as they would be glad to receive the sentiments of your or any other house of assembly on the continent.

The House have humbly represented to the ministry their own sentiments, that his Majesty's high court of Parliament is the supreme legislative power over the whole empire; that in all free states the constitution is fixed, and as the supreme legislative derives its power and authority from the constitution, it cannot overleap the bounds of it without destroying its own foundation; that the constitution ascertains and limits both sovereignty and allegiance, and, therefore, his Majesty's American subjects, who acknowledge themselves bound by the ties of allegiance, have an equitable claim to the full enjoyment of the fundamental rules of the British constitution; that it is an essential, unalterable right in nature, engrafted into the British constitution, as a fundamental law, and ever held sacred and irrevocable by the subjects within the realm, that what a man has honestly acquired is absolutely his own, which he may freely give, but cannot be taken from him without his consent; that the American subjects may, therefore, exclusive of any consideration of charter rights, with a decent firmness, adapted to the character of free men and subjects, assert this natural and constitutional right.

It is, moreover, their humble opinion, which they express with the greatest deference to the wisdom of the Parliament, that the Acts made there, imposing duties on the people of this province, with the sole and express purpose of raising a revenue, are infringements of their natural and constitutional rights; because, as they are not represented in the British Parliament, his Majesty's commons in Britain, by those Acts, grant their property without their consent.

This House further are of opinion that their constituents, considering their local circumstances, cannot, by any possibility, be represented in the Parliament; and that it will forever be impracticable, that they should be equally represented there, and consequently, not at all; being separated by an ocean of a thousand leagues. That his Majesty's royal predecessors, for this reason, were graciously pleased to form a subordinate legislature here, that their subjects might enjoy the unalienable right of a representation; also, that considering the utter impracticability of their ever being fully and equally represented in Parliament, and the great expense that must unavoidably attend even a partial representation there, this House think that a taxation of their constituents, even without their consent, grievous as it is, would be preferable to any representation that could be admitted for them there.

Upon these principles, and also considering that were the right in Parliament ever so clear, yet, for obvious reasons, it would be beyond the rules of equity that their constituents should be taxed on the manufactures of Great Britain here, in addition to the duties they pay for them in England, and other advantages arising to Great Britain, from the Acts of trade, this House have preferred a humble, dutiful, and loyal petition, to our most gracious sovereign, and made such representations to his Majesty's ministers, as they apprehended would tend to obtain redress. They have also submitted to consideration, whether any people can be said to enjoy any degree of freedom if the Crown, in addition to its undoubted authority of constituting a governor, should appoint him such a stipend as it may judge proper, without the consent of the people, and at their expense; and whether, while the judges of the land, and other civil officers, hold not their commissions during good behaviour, their having salaries appointed for them by the Crown, independent of the people, hath not a tendency to subvert the principles of equity, and endanger the happiness and security of the subject.

In addition to these measures, the House have written a letter to their agent which he is directed to lay before the ministry; wherein they take notice of the hardships of the Act for preventing mutiny and desertion, which requires the governor and council to provide enumerated articles for the king's marching troops, and the people to pay the expenses; and also, the commission of the gentlemen appointed commissioners of the customs, to reside in America, which authorizes them to make as many appointments as they think fit, and to pay the appointees what sum they please, for whose malconduct they are not accountable; from whence it may happen that officers of the Crown may be multiplied to such a degree as to become dangerous to the liberty of the people, by virtue of a commission, which does not appear to this House to derive any such advantages to trade as many have supposed.

These are the sentiments and proceedings of this House; and as they have too much reason to believe that the enemies of the colonies have represented them to his Majesty's ministers, and to the Parliament, as factious, disloyal, and having a disposition to make themselves independent of the mother country, they have taken occasion, in the most humble terms, to assure his Majesty, and his ministers, that, with regard to the people of this province, and, as they doubt not, of all the colonies, the charge is unjust. The House is fully satisfied that your assembly is too generous and liberal in sentiment to believe that this letter proceeds from an ambition of taking the lead, or dictating to the other assemblies. They freely submit their opinions to the judgment of others; and shall take it kind in your house to point out to them anything further that may be thought necessary.

This House cannot conclude, without expressing their firm confidence in the king, our common head and father, that the united and dutiful supplications of his distressed American subjects will meet with his royal and favourable acceptance."

> Note: The Circular Letter had been drafted in December 1767 by James Otis and Sam Adams but was only now approved and sent.
>
> The Massachusetts Circular Letter's request for a response would ensure a debate of its contents and a corresponding reply by the colonial assemblies.
>
> The circular letter would be received enthusiastically by the other colonies as a new colonial union continued to grow—with Massachusetts leading the way.

Feb. 27, 1768   **The Earl of Hillsborough is appointed as the *American Secretary of State for the Colonies*.**

Wills Hill, aka Lord Hillsborough, is appointed as head of the newly created department for better managing American colonial affairs.

> Note: Lord Hillsborough would have a rough road ahead of him as American relations with Great Britain continued to deteriorate.

March 4, 1768   **Massachusetts Governor Francis Bernard dissolves the General Court.**

The royal governor labels the Circular Letter to be seditious, and as a result, suspends the assembly.

March 12, 1768   **Boston merchants agree to a nonimportation of goods from Great Britain.**

To protest the Townshend Acts—particularly the 1767 Revenue Act—no British goods are to be purchased for the next eighteen months, except for those goods necessary for the fishing industry.

> Note: Colonial nonimportation had been first used in 1764 with limited success against the 1764 Revenue Act (Sugar Act), and more successfully against the Stamp Act in 1765. Now, once again, the Americans would choose to leverage their economic might against Great Britain.
>
> The Boston boycott would be expanded and formalized on August 1, 1768. In addition, Massachusetts would appeal to the other colonies to join in nonimportation.

The *Treaty of Johnson Hall*: The Cherokee and the Iroquois make a peace.

Meeting in New York at Superintendent William Johnson's plantation home, *Johnson Hall*, the two Indian nations *bury the hatchet* between them after many years as enemies.

> Note: Despite the Proclamation Line of 1763 forbidding unauthorized intrusions west of the Appalachian Mountains, the speculators in frontier lands had plans for moving settlers into the regions of modern West Virginia and Kentucky. As both the Iroquois and Cherokee nations claimed sovereignty over those territories, it was important to first end hostilities between them before negotiations could begin, and to obtain the tribes' permission for new intrusions—if possible. Yet this looked unlikely, for the Iroquois complained to Johnson about the endless encroachment of White settlers, now nearing the Ohio River.
>
> Previous truces between the Iroquois and Cherokee had been brokered by British officials in 1742 and 1756, but both had been short-lived.

March 18, 1768   **Boston customs officials are prevented from doing their duty by armed men.**

Under cover of night, Daniel Malcom, a well-to-do Boston smuggler of tea and wine, unloads sixty casks of wine onto an island in Boston Bay to avoid paying the required duties. The operation is guarded from British customs inspectors by men armed with clubs. Prevented from inspecting Malcom's ship, the customs officials feel the need for additional help if they are ever to do their jobs effectively.

> Note: Daniel Malcom would be buried in Boston's Copp's Hill Cemetery. According to legend, Malcom asked to be buried ten feet down instead of six so that the British could not get him in death for what they hadn't in life. Malcom's gravestone yet today has visible damage caused by lead balls shot into it by British soldiers in an act of defacement.

April 1768   **A copy of the Massachusetts Circular Letter reaches London.**

Lord Hillsborough—the new British minister of American colonial affairs—considers the Circular Letter dangerous and factious, to be viewed with contempt. As such, Hillsborough orders the Massachusetts General Court to rescind it.

> Note: Great Britain was concerned about the possibility of Boston's rebellion spreading to other colonies and did not want the Americans networking independently of London or perhaps calling for an intercolonial congress.

At Fort Pitt, tribal leaders from the Ohio region complain about the steady encroachments and murder of their people by the Whites.

Illegal settlements continue to spring up and the Indians—Shawnee, Mingo, and Delaware—want them removed as the British authorities try to mollify the tribes with presents and promises.

April 8, 1768   **In Hillsborough, North Carolina, the Regulators intimidate a tax collector in open defiance of the civil authorities.**

Seventy well-armed Regulators ride to the home of tax collector Edward Fanning to retrieve a horse that has been confiscated from its owner for unpaid taxes. Before departing with the horse, the Regulators shoot rifle balls into Fanning's house as a warning. In response, Fanning calls out the local militia, orders two of the Regulator leaders arrested, and requests Governor Tryon send military assistance to suppress the growing anti-government rebellion in the western region.

In Boston, customs officials are thwarted from searching John Hancock's ship, the *Lydia*.

Attempting to search the vessel for illegal contraband, Hancock insists that the officers produce an authorized warrant. As they have none, Hancock demands they leave.

> Note: John Hancock, one of the richest men in Boston and long suspected of smuggling, would now become a specific target for the new American Board of Customs—determined to enforce the Crown rules. Conversely, Hancock, along with Sam Adams and others, would lead Boston's resistance to the Townshend duties.

April 14, 1768   **The Massachusetts Circular Letter is endorsed by Virginia's House of Burgesses.**

April 21, 1768   **Lord Hillsborough writes to the colonial governors concerning the Massachusetts Circular Letter.**

Hoping to stem any support for the Massachusetts Circular Letter by other American colonies, Lord Hillsborough writes a circular letter to Britain's royal governors. In his correspondence,

Hillsborough includes a copy of the Massachusetts letter and directs the governors to dissolve the assemblies if they give "countenance to the seditious paper." In addition, Hillsborough directs Massachusetts Governor Francis Bernard to order the colony's General Court to rescind the Circular Letter or be permanently suspended.

> Note: Before the royal governors received Lord Hillsborough's orders, three colonial assemblies had already approved the Massachusetts Circular Letter. After Hillsborough's letter arrived in mid-May, the assemblies would view his directives as a curtailment of their free right to correspond. Therefore, ignoring the American secretary's orders, eight more assemblies would endorse the Massachusetts Circular Letter as a more common unity between the colonies began to develop.
>
> To many historians, the political commotion caused by the Massachusetts Circular Letter—at that time—stood second only to the Stamp Act protests of 1765.

Late April 1768   **North Carolina Regulator leaders are arrested.**

Two men, Herman Husband and William Butler, are jailed by Crown official Edward Fanning for their part in the unrest of April 8.

April 27, 1768   **In London, John Wilkes is sent to prison and becomes a public hero on both sides of the Atlantic.**

After a four-and-a-half-year exile, Wilkes had returned from France on February 6, and in defiance of the charges against him—refused to submit a king's pardon. Levied a £1,000 fine and sentenced to prison for twenty-two months, the publisher and former Member of Parliament is rescued by a mob of supporters while being escorted to jail, but Wilkes chooses to serve his punishment as the large crowd outside the prison only continues to grow.

> Note: Though confined, Wilkes would continue to fight, using his newspaper and quoting England's cherished Magna Carta as his defense for liberty. Expelled from Parliament, Wilkes would campaign for office from jail and be re-elected, only to be re-expelled in 1769.
>
> Wilkes's seditious article had been published in issue 45 of the *North Briton* and hence the number forty-five became synonymous with *liberty* as the public in Great Britain and the American colonies followed his case with interest, viewing Wilkes as an underdog against a powerful government. Known as a champion for liberty, John Wilkes would become a popular figure to many Americans for supporting the colonists' struggle for independence.
>
> The future assassin of Abraham Lincoln, John Wilkes Booth, was a distant relative of Wilkes and was named in his honor.

May 2, 1768   **In North Carolina, the jailed Regulator leaders are released to avoid violence.**

A Regulator force numbering 700 rides toward Hillsborough, North Carolina, to free Herman Husband and William Butler, but the men are released by frightened authorities before the vigilantes' arrival.

May 3, 1768   **In Newport, a British officer kills a Rhode Island man.**

While taking a stroll, three naval officers from the HBS *Senegal* get into a war of words with a group of young men. The altercation rapidly deteriorates and ends with the British midshipman, Thomas Careless, killing local shoemaker Henry Sparker with his sword and wounding another. The Newport coroner labels Sparker's death as willful murder, and the three officers are ordered arrested. Lieutenant Careless is charged with murder and his two companions are charged as accessories to the crime.

> Note: In June, the three British officers would be acquitted on pleas of self-defense by the Rhode Island Superior Court of Judicature.

May 6, 1768 **The New Jersey Assembly endorses the Massachusetts Circular Letter.**

May 9, 1768 **A Boston customs officer is forcefully detained while smugglers unload a ship.**

Customs officer Thomas Kirke arrives to inspect John Hancock's *Liberty*, suspected of containing a load of contraband Madeira wine. Hoping to sway the officer's resolve, Captain John Marshall offers a bribe, but Kirke—intent on doing his job—refuses. Therefore, Captain Marshall orders the dutiful officer locked in the ship's hold rendering him unable to stop the unloading or to witness it happening. When finished, Hancock's men release Officer Kirke and threaten him to dare not report it.

> Note: Bribery had long been a successful tactic of smugglers. Now, with the American Customs Board located directly in Boston, the old rules seemed to no longer apply as British customs enforcement tightened its grip.

May 10, 1768 **The *Massacre of St. George's Fields*: In London, military troops are used against the supporters of John Wilkes.**

Up to 15,000 people gather at St. George's Fields near King's Bench Prison to show their support for the imprisoned Wilkes. Fearful of a riot erupting and the possible freeing of Wilkes, authorities send soldiers to keep back the crowd. Goaded by the people, the troops kill a man and the situation only worsens. The Riot Act is read giving the unruly crowd one hour to disperse but the order is ignored. Now, pelted with stones, the soldiers fire on the crowd resulting in eleven deaths. Though the people disperse, word of the massacre quickly spreads, causing riots to flare up throughout London.

May 17, 1768 **In a display of British power, the battleship HBS *Romney* arrives in Boston.**

The arrival of the huge ship-of-war is an attempt to bring order by serving as a warning to local smugglers and troublemakers. As expected, the lethal British vessel—with its fifty guns—is intimidating to the Bostonians and the ship's appearance in Boston's harbor *changes the game*.

Late May 1768 **In Boston, British press gang operations stir hostilities.**

Captain John Corner of the HBS *Romney* sends press gangs ashore to impress seamen into service. Resenting the *Romney*'s presence, a crowd rescues an impressed sailor by hurling insults and rocks at the naval gang. In response, Captain Corner trains the battleship's guns on the defiant crowd but holds his fire.

> Note: Captain Corner's orders not to inflame the populace had somewhat tied his hands.

Britain's Board of Trade rules against the New York Assembly.

The Board of Trade, upon review, disagrees with Royal Governor Henry Moore and rules that the assembly has satisfied neither the demands of the 1765 Quartering Act nor the Restraining Act of 1767. Therefore, the assembly should have been suspended on October 1; however, since it was not—all New York laws and Acts passed after that date are to be considered invalid.

	Note: Ruled to be in noncompliance, the assembly would be dissolved, and new elections held the following year.

1768

Philadelphia merchants begin trading in the remote Illinois region.

The merchants hope to earn great profits by filling the Indian trade void created by the French absence. In addition to selling goods to the tribes, the merchants wish to supply the British troops stationed in the western frontier forts.

> **Note:** In 1773, these same Philadelphia merchants would form the Illinois Company and purchase vast tracts of Indian lands, despite the prohibitions against it.

June 8, 1768

At his New York military headquarters, British General Thomas Gage receives instructions from London to send "such Force as You shall think necessary to Boston."

With the support of American Secretary of State Lord Hillsborough, General Gage is authorized to transfer troops to Boston to maintain civil order and to tamp down the growing insubordination.

June 9, 1768

In Boston, orders are issued to seize John Hancock's ship, the *Liberty*—long suspected of smuggling.

Due to the occurrence on May 9, the head customs collector in Boston orders the *Liberty* seized.

> **Note:** The customs officer, Thomas Kirke, had been too intimidated to report the incident due to the threats made against him by Hancock's men. But now, backed by the presence of the HBS *Romney*, Kirke had told the truth to the head customs officer, Joseph Harrison, who ordered the *Liberty* seized.

June 10, 1768

The *Liberty Riot*: Violence erupts against the British customs commissioners in Boston.

John Hancock's docked ship, the *Liberty*, is seized by British marines from the HBS *Romney* for suspected smuggling and the forced detention of customs agent Thomas Kirke. During the *Liberty's* seizure, customs comptroller Benjamin Hallowell and head customs commissioner Joseph Harrison scuffle with a protesting dockside crowd. After being roughed up, the two customs officials manage to make their escape as the *Liberty* is latched to the *Romney* by the marines and towed away.

As word of the incident spreads, people continue to arrive at the docks and the angry crowd soon numbers 3,000. Unable to save Hancock's ship, the protestors again turn their hostilities toward the now-absent British customs commissioners and seek them out. Failing to find the two officials, the unruly crowd satisfies itself by shattering the windows of each man's home, and in a further act of retribution, carries Commissioner Harrison's pleasure boat to the town common and burns it in a large bonfire in raucous celebration.

The British customs commissioners and Governor Bernard feel threatened by the situation in Boston and will request troops be sent for their protection.

> **Note:** The *Liberty Incident* is considered one of the first acts of direct and open violence against the newly established American Customs Board.

The Connecticut Assembly endorses the Massachusetts Circular Letter.

June 11, 1768

In Boston, the British customs commissioners repair to the safety of HBS *Romney*.

Harassed, intimidated, and offered little protection, the threatened royal officials feel compelled to move their customs operations to Fort Castle William.

Lord Hillsborough writes to the Massachusetts royal governor that British troops are to be sent to Boston.

In a letter to Governor Bernard, Lord Hillsborough writes, "It is but too evident … that the Authority of Civil Power is too weak to enforce Obedience to the Laws, and preserve that Peace and good Order, which is essential to the Happiness of every State and his Majesty has thought fit … to direct the Commander in Chief of his Majesty's Forces in America to station One Regiment at least in the Town of Boston, and to garrison, and if necessary to repair, the Fort or Castle of William and Mary …"

Note:	General Gage would send two regiments: the 14th and 29th Regiments of Foot from Nova Scotia. In addition, the British Navy would send five ships.

June 30, 1768

The Massachusetts General Court is suspended after refusing to rescind the Circular Letter.

In a direct rebuke to Governor Bernard and Lord Hillsborough, the Massachusetts General Court votes 92-17 against rescinding its letter. In consequence, the following day Governor Bernard prorogues the assembly until the next scheduled elections in May 1769—eleven months away.

July 6, 1768

The 1768 *Vice Admiralty Court Act* is passed to help enforce Britain's trade laws, and to more easily prosecute violators of those laws.

The purpose of "An Act for the more easy and effectual recovery of the Penalty's and Forfeitures inflicted by the Acts of Parliament relating to the Trade or Revenues of the British Colonies and plantations in America" is as follows:

- To better contribute to due collections of his Majesty's revenue.

- To prevent and punish fraud relating to the same.

- To provide a more speedy and effectual administration of justice within the colonies and plantations.

- To establish a sufficient number of Vice Admiralty Courts at "proper and convenient places" within the said colonies and plantations.

The Super-Vice Admiralty Court at Halifax overseeing colonial trade and nautical violations ranging from Florida to Newfoundland is to be replaced with four District Vice Admiralty Courts established in North America: Halifax, Nova Scotia; Boston, Massachusetts; Philadelphia, Pennsylvania; and Charles Town, South Carolina.

To keep the judges independent from colonial influences and to reduce graft, their salaries are to be paid by the Crown through revenues received by trade enforcements. If that is not sufficient, then the remainder is to be paid by funds from selling surplus naval stores.

Note:	The issue of judicial dependencies is listed in grievance nine of the U.S. Declaration of Independence.

The Vice Admiralty judges are expressly prohibited from accepting any fee or gratuity for any judgment given in their court or "business done in their respective Courts" under penalty of losing their position.

Note:	The Vice Admiralty Courts did not provide trial by jury, as required in civil courts.

The Vice Admiralty Court Act is to be effective from September 1, 1768.

Note:	Overall, the Vice Admiralty Court Act amended the 1764 Revenue Act (Sugar Act), which had created the Vice Admiralty Court at Halifax, Nova Scotia. The Halifax Court had been charged with handling and prosecuting nearly all North American

cases involving violations on the seas, particularly smuggling, and was thus overwhelmed by its caseloads. In addition, Halifax was geographically inconvenient, providing the Americans with a sound argument that it was too far from their home locales.

Britain also had a Vice Admiralty Court in Kingston, Jamaica, with jurisdiction in the West Indies.

American merchants, transporters, and ship owners would have but two reasons to appear before one of the District Vice Admiralty Courts—to be prosecuted, or to file suits of appeal for the recovery of confiscated or forfeited property.

Though Charles Townshend had died ten months earlier, the Vice Admiralty Court Act is usually considered to be one of the Townshend Acts.

July 1768   **London merchants are concerned by reports from North America that the Americans plan to use nonimportation to protest the 1767 Revenue Act, aka the Townshend duties.**

The British merchants do a great business with the Americans and do not wish for interruptions to the profitable flow of goods. In addition, as credit abounds between the two groups, the merchants are rightfully concerned about debt repayment by their American counterparts.

July 27, 1768   **Providence, Rhode Island, dedicates a large elm as its Liberty Tree.**

The tree is dedicated with a prayer by Rhode Islander Silas Downer: "We do, in the name and behalf of all the true sons of liberty in America, Great Britain, Ireland, Corsica, or wheresoever they may be dispersed throughout the world, dedicate and solemnly devote this tree to be a tree of liberty. May all our councils and deliberations under its venerable branches be guided by wisdom, and directed for the support and maintenance of that liberty which our renowned forefathers sought out and found under trees and in the wilderness. May it long flourish, and may the sons of liberty often repair hither to confirm and strengthen each other; when they look toward this sacred elm may they be penetrated with a sense of their duty to themselves and their posterity; and may they, like the house of David, grow stronger and stronger, while their enemies, like the house of Saul, shall grow weaker and weaker. Amen."

Note: As in Boston, the Providence citizens would gather under the tree's branches for news and meetings.

Summer 1768   **The second recorded tar and feathering in the American colonies takes place in Salem, Massachusetts.**

A man suspected of being an informant is tarred and feathered, placed in a cart, paraded through the streets, and then banished from Salem for six weeks.

In Boston, rumors are circulating that the King's troops are being sent to suppress the *rebelliousness of the people*.

The sobering news helps to enforce order as the people ponder its effects.

Note: Britain's customs officials were afraid to leave Fort Castle William until British troops could arrive to help guarantee their safety—allowing them to do their lawful jobs.

Alarmed by Boston's radicals and somewhat intimidated by the shadowy Sons of Liberty, Royal Governor Francis Bernard would begin looking for reasons to arrest the firebrand Sam Adams.

Aug. 1, 1768 **Massachusetts expands its economic war against Great Britain as Boston merchants issue a formal agreement concerning nonimportation.**

The *Boston Nonimportation Agreement* is as follows.

"The merchants and traders in the town of Boston having taken into consideration the deplorable situation of the trade, and the many difficulties it at present labours under on account of the scarcity of money, which is daily increasing for want of the other remittances to discharge our debts in Great Britain, and the large sums collected by the officers of the customs for duties on goods imported; the heavy taxes levied to discharge the debts contracted by the government in the late war; the embarrassments and restrictions laid on trade by several late Acts of Parliament; together with the bad success of our cod fishery this season, and by the discouraging prospect of the whale fishery, by which our principal sources of remittances are like to be greatly diminished, and we thereby rendered unable to pay the debts we owe the merchants in Great Britain, and to continue the importation of goods from thence:

We, the subscribers, in order to relieve the trade under those discouragements, to promote industry, frugality, and economy, and to discourage luxury and every kind of extravagance, do promise and engage to and with each other as follows:

- That we will not send for or import from Great Britain this fall, either on our own account, or on commission, any other goods than what are already ordered for the fall supply.

- That we will not send for or import any kind of goods or merchandise from Great Britain, either on our own account, or on commissions, or any otherwise, from January 1, 1769, to January 1, 1770, except salt, coals, fish hooks and lines, hemp, duck, bar lead and shot, wool-cards, and card-wire.

- That we will not, from and after January 1, 1769, import into this province any tea, paper, glass, or painters colours, until the Acts imposing duties on these articles have been repealed."

Note: The Boston Nonimportation Agreement was also created to serve as an example for other colonies.

More than sixty Boston merchants would join within a fortnight. Only sixteen would refuse.

Boston issues calls for the North American colonies to join the Massachusetts boycott.

With Massachusetts leading the way, supporters of nonimportation hope that an intercolonial boycott of British goods will bring enough economic pressure to force the British Ministry and Parliament to repeal the 1767 Revenue Act.

Note: The 1769 nonimportation movement would not be as unified as Boston radicals had wanted. Though others would join, most would choose to follow their own nonimportation policies.

Many British merchants would resent American nonimportation, for Parliament had already repealed the Stamp Act. Now, they would ask, "What do you Americans really want?"

Aug. 27, 1768 **New York merchants agree to nonimportation, hoping to repeal the Townshend duties.**

Sept. 8, 1768 **New York's nonimportation resolutions are published.**

Published in the *New York Journal*, the first two resolutions state that New York merchants:

1. "Will not send for from Great Britain, either upon our own account or on commission, any other goods than what we have already ordered.

2. "Will not import any kind of merchandise from Great Britain, either on our own account or on commission … that shall be shipped from Great Britain after the first day of November."

Sept. 13, 1768 **Boston demonstrates its strength by holding a gun show while passing resolutions concerning citizens' rights.**

Concerned about the expected arrival of British troops, the town's arms are put on display at Faneuil Hall during a town meeting *for cleaning* under pretext of a possible war with France.

> Note: Sam Adams wanted to distribute the arms to the attendees, but James Otis used his influence to dissuade Adams from urging armed resistance, which would have been treasonous.

The town meeting adopts several resolutions, including:

- An assertion of natural rights, and that these rights are carried by all citizens of the kingdom wherever they may be as if they had been born in England.

- That the citizens of Boston hold these rights and liberties, but at the same time acknowledge their firm and unshaken allegiance to the king.

- That the citizens of Boston will take all legal and constitutional measures to defend and maintain King George III and their liberties as granted by charter and as British subjects.

- That the Massachusetts Royal Charter permits only the General Court to levy taxes upon its citizens in defense of the king.

- That, as Parliament has said, to keep a standing army in the kingdom in times of peace is against the law, and that it is the indefeasible right of subjects to give their free consent to the raising and keeping of a standing army among them, and that without it would be a grievance.

> Note: Governor Bernard would send word of the militant meeting to General Gage in New York, which left both men concerned that the British troops would be met with armed resistance when they arrived.

Sept. 19, 1768 **Massachusetts Governor Bernard announces that British troops are being sent to Boston.**

Bernard confirms what has been long rumored—British regulars are on their way.

Sept. 1768 **North Carolina Governor Tryon arrives in Hillsborough accompanied by militia troops to ensure court proceedings are not disrupted by the Regulators.**

Expecting attempts to shut down the court, Tryon arrives with 1,400 well-armed militiamen as 3,700 Regulators retreat rather than challenge the governor's forces.

Sept. 22–29, '68 **The *Massachusetts Convention of Towns* meets in Boston.**

In response to Governor Bernard's announcement that British troops are expected to soon arrive, delegates from ninety-six Massachusetts towns and eight districts gather for an emergency meeting to discuss the people's options and to formulate a response.

During the week-long meeting, the delegates argue and debate among themselves with the conservatives urging for peaceful responses and the radicals calling for armed resistance. As the debate continues, Chairman Thomas Cushing uses his moderating influence to tamp the more violent designs, and the conservatives win out.

Though recognizing it has no legal authority to act, the convention decides to petition the governor to summon the General Court to session; and to petition the king requesting redress while also professing loyalty and its "love of peace and good order."

Note:	Though Governor Bernard had ordered the extralegal gathering to disband; the delegates chose to ignore his demands.
	Rumors had reached London that the Massachusetts militias would offer resistance to the landing of the King's troops.

Sept. 28, 1768   **British troops arrive in Boston Harbor aboard Royal ships.**

In an act of intimidation, Governor Bernard and the British officers decide to encamp the troops on Boston Common.

Note:	The citizens had expected the soldiers would be housed in Fort Castle William where barracks had been readied, but the island fortress was deemed too removed from the lawlessness to be effective. Therefore, the troops were to be placed in the town itself.
	The Bostonians had refused to provide alternative quarters, stating that the 1765 Quartering Act only applied if the barracks in Fort Castle William were filled.

Oct. 1, 1768   **Two regiments of British troops disembark in Boston as tensions increase.**

Beginning at noon in a display of military might, the troops are landed at Long Wharf "and marched into the Common, with muskets charged, bayonets fixed, colours flying, drums beating and fifes, &c. playing, making with the train of artillery upwards of 700 men."

Note:	Citizens watching the whole affair were shocked as the British regulars took quarters in various public places throughout the town, including the town hall. A large tent encampment was set up on Boston Common, permitting easy interactions between the soldiers and Boston's civilians.
	Most Bostonians resented this presence of armed troops in their midst, causing tensions and hostilities only to increase. Yet to Governor Bernard, customs personnel, and those citizens uncomfortable with civil disorder and Boston's increasing resistance to royal authority—the King's troops were a welcome sight.
	In London, Benjamin Franklin had warned of the dangers of young men with attitudes and likened the placement of troops in Boston to "setting up a magazine of gunpowder in a blacksmith's forge."

Oct. 14, 1768   **In South Carolina, the acquisition of Cherokee lands continues with the *Treaty of Hard Labor*.**

Encouraged by the frontier land speculators, settlers continue moving west in violation of the Proclamation of 1763. As such, Southern Indian Superintendent John Stuart meets with the Cherokee at Hard Labor, South Carolina, to secure additional lands. Using pressure accompanied by presents and promises, Stuart induces the Cherokee to cede their claims to the lands lying between the Allegheny Mountains and the Ohio River—basically most of modern West Virginia.

Note:	The Treaty of Hard Labor was an attempt to move the 1763 Proclamation Line westward as the land companies were *chomping at the bit* to settle the vast frontier

regions. Yet the Iroquois also had overlapping claims to the same lands. Therefore, approval by the Six Nations would still need to be acquired.

With the *English* pouring over the mountains, the Indians could see the *writing on the wall* as to the eventual outcome. Therefore, many tribes simply chose to sell those lands and receive something for them rather than nothing at all—especially lands with overlapping claims. As such, many inter-tribal wars erupted over tribes selling lands claimed by others.

Oct. 16, 1768   **British General Thomas Gage arrives in Boston.**

General Gage has traveled 200 miles overland from New York City to help oversee the stationing and garrisoning of the newly arrived troops.

Oct. 28, 1768   **Massachusetts refuses to comply with the 1765 Quartering Act.**

The British troops in Boston are considered armed occupiers, thus the Massachusetts General Court announces its refusal to provide for their support.

A Boston customs worker is tarred and feathered.

George Gailer, a former sailor aboard John Hancock's *Liberty* now working as a custom agent patrolling for violators, is stripped, tarred and feathered, and paraded through the streets while being struck with clubs and pelted with stones. In response, Gailer will sue several of his assailants that he recognizes among the crowd.

Nov. 2, 1768   **The richest man in Boston, John Hancock, is arrested.**

The charges are related to the *Liberty* incident of May 9, 1768. The wealthy Hancock tries to avoid arrest by offering huge sums of funds, but orders are orders, and Hancock is taken into custody.

> Note: John Hancock had until now managed to avoid arrest. But with troops occupying the town to back up the British custom officials; the authorities had ordered Hancock apprehended.

Nov. 5, 1768   **The Proclamation Line of 1763 is breached by the *Fort Stanwix Treaty* as the Ohio River becomes the new border—with Indians to the north and Whites to the south.**

> Note: Great fortunes were waiting to be made and land speculators, both in England and the American colonies, believed that if the Indian opposition could be removed, there would be no further need for the 1763 Proclamation Line barring western settlement. Working behind the scenes in London, Benjamin Franklin, with the help of influential investors, had already applied for permission to form the *Grand Ohio Company* in anticipation of the financial opportunities that would be afforded by the terms of the Fort Stanwix negotiations. Thus, Franklin advised his son, New Jersey Governor William Franklin, to attend the negotiations.

More than 3,000 Indians, mostly Iroquois, attend the meeting at Fort Stanwix, located in present-day Rome, New York. The negotiations, held with the approval of Britain's Board of Trade, are to quiet Indian affairs following the recent wars and to enable land speculators to sell their vast frontier holdings by moving the restrictive Proclamation Line farther west. Northern Indian Superintendent William Johnson—directed by the Board of Trade to negotiate a new boundary line running near Fort Stanwix south to the confluence of the Kanawha and Ohio Rivers—exceeds his directives and plies the Six Nations to relinquish their claims to lands south of the Ohio and westward to the mouth of the Tennessee River.

> Note: Like the Cherokee Treaty of Hard Labor, the Iroquois wished to relinquish only those lands forming today's West Virginia, but Johnson pushed them to give up rights to present-day Kentucky. Yet the purposefully uninvited Shawnee also had claims to Kentucky and would argue that the Iroquois had no right to sell. In addition, the Cherokee also claimed the Kentucky region, and as such, both tribes would resist the White settlers soon to arrive there.
>
> As Superintendent Johnson had greatly overstepped his directives, he would have to get the treaty approved by Britain's Board of Trade. Not wishing to begin another Indian war, the Board would request that Johnson renegotiate the massive land acquisition—but with such potential money to be made—Johnson refused and instead sent representatives to London to argue otherwise.
>
> A small group of wealthy Pennsylvania merchants—dubbed the *suffering traders* due to having lost merchandise during the recent Indian war—were granted lands east of the upper Ohio River in modern Pennsylvania as compensation by the Iroquois, known as the *Indiana Grant*. These men would form the *Indiana Land Company*, which would merge with the Grand Ohio Land Company the following year.
>
> The Indiana Land Company was the first use of the term *Indiana* and the source of the future state's name.

Nov. 8, 1768

King George III addresses the opening of Parliament, stating his intention to stamp out disobedience in the American colonies.

In his speech, the king states that although some of the misled colonists are returning to their sense of duty, other spirited factions are not yet extinguished, and troubles continue to break out afresh with violence and resistance to law. The capital (Boston) seems to be in a state of disobedience to all law and government, is subversive to the constitution, and might manifest a disposition to throw off its dependence on Great Britain. That he, with the help of Parliament, will defeat the mischievous designs of those turbulent and seditious people who have too successfully deluded numbers of his subjects in America, for, "if suffered to prevail, [it] cannot fail to produce the most fatal consequences to my colonies immediately; and, in the end, to all the dominions of my Crown." King George III then asks the House of Commons for support in suppressing the rebellion.

The British Parliament replies to King George III's speech.

After thanking the king for his constant attention pertaining to the great commercial interests of the country, Parliament expresses a common concern about the American colonists being misled by factious and designing men to commit acts of violence and resistance to execution of the law, "attended with circumstances that manifest a disposition to throw off their dependence on Great Britain." Parliament then states that though it is ready to contribute to the relief of any real grievance of his Majesty's American subjects, it also promises to give the king support of necessary measures to repress the spirit of disobedience and dissent in North America, to enforce submission to the laws, and to maintain the supremacy of Parliament over all dominions over every part of his Majesty's Crown: "That we, as a group, are ready to unite wherever the interests of our country and our attachment to Your Majesty is concerned, and will be happy, if by such an example, the deluded parts of Your Majesty's subjects may be induced to return to their sense of duty, and gratefully feel the blessings of the mildest Government and most perfect constitution."

> Note: Parliament had asked the king to take steps for "bringing to condign punishment the chief authors and instigators of the late disorder."
>
> In the words of Britain's Chancellor of the Exchequer Lord Frederick North, "America must fear you before she can love you."

Nov. 1768	**Parliament declares the actions in Massachusetts to be illegal, unconstitutional, and derogatory to the rights of the Crown and Parliament.**

Parliament also suggests Royal Governor Bernard investigate the persons most active in treasonous activities, to be perhaps sent to England for trial.

Nov. 24, 1768	**General Gage leaves Boston and returns to his headquarters in New York.**

Gage has spent a month in Boston supervising the deployment of British troops and conferring with Governor Francis Bernard about the state of current affairs.

Nov. 28, 1768	**In Boston, John Hancock's trial begins.**

Hancock faces charges regarding the *Liberty* incident of May 9, 1768. The trial will be delayed and drawn out, lasting four months.

> Note: Hancock was defended by John Adams, a future president of the United States.

Dec. 1768	**The Americans are alarmed to learn of King George III's address to Parliament.**

In his speech, the king promised to suppress colonial disobedience and asked the Parliament for its support, which the body has readily agreed to provide.

1769	**Great Britain permits Catholics to serve in the Granada Assembly.**

This goes against the long-established Test Acts barring Catholics from British public office. With so many French Catholics residing in Canada, this break from tradition causes alarm among Britain's Protestants colonies—particularly in New England.

St. John's Island becomes Britain's newest North American colony.

Formerly considered a part of Nova Scotia, St. John's Island becomes its own colony.

> Note: Due to confusion with Canada's St. John's, Newfoundland; and St. John, New Brunswick; St. John's Island would be renamed *Prince Edward Island* in 1798.

The American nonimportation movement begins in earnest.

Though Boston merchants have been boycotting most British goods since the previous summer, with British troops now occupying the town, things get serious as other colonies join the nonimportation movement.

> Note: The Townshend duties had been in effect for more than a year, and the Americans wanted them removed. By conducting an economic war with Great Britain, the colonial leaders hoped to bring Britain to its proper senses.
>
> Pressure would be brought to bear on all American colonial merchants to participate. For those who refused, particularly in the northern seaports, public humiliation and threats of violence would await.
>
> By the end of 1769, British exports to North America would fall by 38 percent.

A third New York Assembly is elected as Royal Governor Moore continues his attempts to secure adequate funding for the quartering of British troops in New York.

> Note: A more moderate assembly than the previous two, Governor Moore and General Gage hoped this new group of lawmakers would capitulate and grant the long-sought funds.

March 1769 **Philadelphia merchants agree to nonimportation.**

The merchants are under pressure by the artisans and craftsmen of the city to do so.

Maryland joins the nonimportation movement.

Nonimportation has become a battle of wills—as well as economics—between Great Britain and the American colonists.

Britain believes that the Americans cannot live without British-manufactured goods and the colonial coordination will soon fall apart, forcing the colonies one by one to return to the fold.

March 26, 1769 **The long-drawn-out trial of Boston's John Hancock abruptly ends.**

Without explanation, after extending the trial for four months—the prosecution drops the case.

> Note: Historians are not exactly sure why the charges were dropped. Some suggest the British authorities were concerned about the large amount of negative publicity a guilty verdict would have generated throughout the colonies. To others, it was simply due to Hancock's powerful influence and wealth.
>
> Though the charges did not bring a conviction, Hancock's ship would never be returned. The HBS *Liberty* was now used by the British Navy to patrol for customs violators. The ship would be burned by a mob in Newport, Rhode Island in July 1769.

April 4, 1769 **Boston prepares a petition to King George III.**

The Petition of the Boston Town Meeting:

- Stresses the Bostonians' devotion to the king.

- Minimizes the previous year's civil unrest against the British customs officials.

- Questions the need for the King's troops to be sent to Boston and seeks the reasons for their deployment. Believing Governor Bernard to be responsible for their presence, the petition requests access to Bernard's papers and the memorials of Boston's American commissioners of customs to ascertain what charges have been levied against them so that they might defend themselves.

> Note: The Boston petition would be presented to the king on June 2, 1769.
>
> While initially kept private, the petition would be made public and printed in the *Boston Gazette* on July 10 and July 24, 1769.

April 1769 **Copies of Governor Bernard's letters to London are received in Boston and published.**

Intercepted by Massachusetts agents in England, Bernard's letters have been forwarded to certain individuals in Boston and are promptly published in the *Boston Gazette*. In his correspondence, Governor Bernard had sought additional powers to his office, which—now known—only adds to the opposition against him as the Massachusetts Assembly formally requests that Bernard "might be forever removed from the Government of the Province."

April 20, 1769	**The great Ottawa war leader Pontiac is murdered near Cahokia, Illinois.**

Living in western Illinois and without his former influence, Pontiac is killed by a Peoria warrior to avenge the death of a family member three years earlier.

> Note: Some implied that Pontiac was clandestinely targeted by the British military, who wished him dead for his past deeds and his potential for causing future Indian unrest.
>
> Until 2010, the General Motors Company used Pontiac's name as a car brand, and his imagined likeness in various forms—both romanticized and abstract—as a hood ornament for its Pontiac cars until 1956.

April 22, 1769	**In Boston, a British naval officer is killed while trying to impress sailors.**

Lieutenant Henry Panton of the HBS *Rose* boards a merchant ship loaded with salt and attempts to apprehend several hiding Irish seamen for impressment, but the men refuse his orders to "Come out!" A midshipman accompanying Lieutenant Panton shoots one man in the arm, but the men still refuse to show themselves as seaman Michael Corbett warns that he will kill the British officer if he attempts to capture him. With that challenge, Lieutenant Panton grabs Corbett, who counters by thrusting a harpoon into the officer's neck and Panton soon bleeds to death. Corbett is promptly arrested and charged with murder.

> Note: Since the crime was committed *on the waters*, Corbett would be tried in Boston's Admiralty Court, but an important question remained legally vague and unresolved: "Does a sailor have a right to a jury trial in Admiralty Court?" Most agreed they did not.
>
> The slain Lieutenant Henry Panton would be given a large military funeral attended by 2,000 British soldiers and officers and was buried next to Boston's King's Chapel.

May 1769	**The Massachusetts General Court meets for the first time since being suspended nearly one year earlier by Governor Bernard.**

The assembly protests the presence of the British troops and refuses to appropriate money for their support.

In Providence, Rhode Island, a customs house tidewaiter is tarred and feathered.

Jesse Saville is seized while on duty and tarred and feathered. Though a £50 reward is offered for his assailants, they are never apprehended.

1769	**Britain's Indian policy continues:** *Keep the Indians divided.*

After traveling through Iroquois country, Indian Superintendent William Johnson has found the Six Nations and other tribes to be very unrestful over continued intrusions into the western lands. As such, Johnson urges formulating further divisions among them to keep each tribe against the others.

> Note: After the recent Western Indian War (to be later dubbed Pontiac's War), the British were determined to never again permit such an Indian alliance to be formed.

The first permanent White settlers move into Tennessee.

Having readied a cabin and planted fields of corn in order to stake a claim to the land, Virginia frontiersman William Bean moves his family and others to the confluence of Boone's Creek and the Watauga River.

> Note: Located at present-day Elizabethton, Tennessee, Bean soon would be followed by others from Virginia and North Carolina, all in violation of the Proclamation Line of 1763, and illegally settling in Cherokee lands.

May 7, 1769   **Virginia's House of Burgesses is suspended by the royal governor.**

Governor Botetourt shuts down the assembly for supporting the Massachusetts Circular Letter and preparing a set of resolves regarding the 1767 Revenue Act. In defiance, the burgesses move to the neighboring Raleigh Tavern and continue their work.

May 16, 1769   **The *Virginia Resolves* are adopted by the House of Burgesses.**

Written by George Mason and introduced by George Washington, the resolves condemn the "censuring" of the Massachusetts Circular Letter and state that:

- No colonist should be sent to England for trial.

- Only the assembly has the right to tax those living in Virginia.

- The colonies have a right to petition, either by themselves or in coordination with other colonies.

> Note: Massachusetts would be elated that Virginia, with its substantial influence, had decided to join its efforts.
>
> Other colonies would pass similar resolutions within the next several months.

May 18, 1769   **Virginia adopts a nonimportation agreement against Great Britain.**

Meeting at the Raleigh Tavern in defiance of Governor Botetourt, the Virginia trade agreement is signed by nearly all members of the House of Burgesses. Beginning September 1, 1769, the *Virginia Association* agrees to no longer import British goods upon which duties have been paid.

> Note: Though Virginia would be less militant in its nonimportation enforcements than its northern colonial neighbors, Virginia would be the last colony to end the boycott, in July 1771.
>
> The fifth resolution read, "That they will not import any slaves, or purchase any (hereafter) imported until the said Acts of Parliament are repealed."

1769   **In Great Britain, women still lose their legal identities upon marriage.**

A married couple is considered a single unit under the law, with the husband assuming all civic and legal duties for that unit. This legal view is reinforced by British jurist William Blackstone's commentaries on English law, upon which most North American colonial laws are based.

> Note: At this time, an unmarried woman had more legal rights than a married woman, who surrendered hers at the altar.

June 14, 1769   **A sensational murder trial begins in Boston over the killing of a British naval officer.**

A sailor, Michael Corbett, had killed Lieutenant Henry Panton of the HBS *Rose* two months earlier as Panton attempted to arrest him for impressment. Now, defended by lawyers John Adams and James Otis, Boston crowds gather to hear, and newspapers rush to report the trial.

The defense argues that Corbett's actions were justifiable homicide due to the facts that the British officer had neither notified nor sought permission from Governor Bernard or his agent before attempting to arrest the men for impressment. Therefore, since Lieutenant Panton had acted without legal authority, Corbett's actions to prevent his impressment were justified as self-defense. The commission agrees and the charges against Corbett are dropped.

> Note: Denied a jury, Michael Corbett was judged by a panel of five judges.
>
> Following the trial, British midshipman William Peacock would be arrested aboard the HBS *Rose* by the Boston sheriff for having shot the other seaman, John Ryan, in the arm during the skirmish of April 22.

July 20, 1769   **Hoping to tighten adherence to nonimportation, the New York Sons of Liberty publish the names of importers for public shaming and scrutiny.**

July 1769   **The town of New Haven, Connecticut, joins the nonimportation movement.**

> Note: The Connecticut Colony would not join the boycott until February 1770.

July 22, 1769   **South Carolina joins the boycott with the *Charles Town Nonimportation Agreement*.**

The South Carolina Resolutions are as follows:

I.   "That we will encourage and promote the use of North American manufactures in general, and those of this province in particular. And any of us, who are venders thereof, do encourage to sell and dispose of them, at the same rates as heretofore."

II.   "That we will, upon no pretense whatsoever, either upon our own account or on commission, import into this province any of the manufactures of Great Britain, or any other European or East India goods, either from Great Britain, Holland, or any other place, other than such as may have been shipped in consequence of former orders; excepting only Negro cloth, commonly called white and colored plains, not exceeding one shilling and six pence sterling per yard, canvas, bolting cloths, drugs and family medicines, plantation and workmen's tools, nails, firearms, bar steel, gunpowder, shot, lead, flints, wire cards and card wire, mill and grindstones, fish hooks, printed books and pamphlets, salt, coals, and saltpeter. And exclusive of these articles, we do solemnly promise and declare, that we will immediately countermand all orders to our correspondents in Great Britain, for shipping any such goods, wares, and merchandise. And we will sell and dispose of the goods we have on hand, or that may arrive in consequence of former orders at the same rates as heretofore."

III. "That we will use our utmost economy, in our persons, houses, and furniture; particularly, that we will give no mourning, or gloves, or scarves at funerals."

IV.   "That from and after the 1st day of January, 1770, we will not import, buy, or sell any Negroes that shall be brought into this province from Africa; nor, after the 1st day of October next, any Negroes that shall be imported from the West Indies, and any other place excepting from Africa as aforesaid. And that, if any goods or Negroes shall be sent to us, contrary to our agreement in this subscription, such goods shall be reshipped or stored, and such Negroes reshipped from this province, and not by any means offered for sale therein."

V.   "That we will not purchase from or sell for, any masters of vessels, transient persons, or non-subscribers, any kind of European or East India goods whatever, excepting coals and salt, after the 1st day of November next."

VI. "That as wines are subject to a heavy duty, we agree, not to import any on our account or commission, or purchase from any master of vessel, transient person, or non-subscriber, after the 1st day of January next."

VII. "Lastly, That we will not purchase any Negroes imported, or any goods or merchandise whatever, from any resident in this province, that refuses or neglects to sign this agreement, within one month from the date hereof; excepting it shall appear he has been unavoidably prevented from doing the same. And every subscriber who shall not, strictly and literally, adhere to this agreement, according to the true intent and meaning hereof, ought to be treated with the utmost contempt."

Aug. 1, 1769 · **Massachusetts Governor Francis Bernard is relieved of his duties and returns to England.**

Note:	Bernard had privately known of his impending recall since early May.
	Retaining personal and professional grievances against Massachusetts, the former governor, once safely in London, would advocate with zeal for structural changes to the colony's government.

Aug. 2, 1769 · **Massachusetts-born Thomas Hutchinson becomes acting governor over a colony in crisis.**

Having begun his political career in 1738 as a Boston selectman, Thomas Hutchinson is a veteran politician having served as Massachusetts's lieutenant governor since 1758. Well known to all, Hutchinson is not particularly liked by the people for he is supportive of many of Britain's colonial policies, thus guaranteeing him a most difficult role as he replaces the departing royal governor.

Note:	Four years earlier, Hutchinson's home had been destroyed by a mob during Boston's Stamp Act Riots.

Aug. 1769 · **Delaware joins the nonimportation movement.**

Many in Britain assert that the Americans want independence, but Benjamin Franklin assures them it is not so.

Parliament refuses the various colonial petitions opposing the 1767 Revenue Act, commonly called the Townshend duties.

Note:	Though Parliament refused to accept the petitions, the British legislative body was under great pressure to repeal the 1767 Revenue Act—not due to love for the Americans, but due to British economic losses and the lobbying of English merchants.

Aug. 13, 1769 · **The *Boston Chronicle* republishes the Massachusetts Nonimportation Agreement and lists those merchants refusing to participate.**

Sept. 5, 1769 · **In Boston, the famed Massachusetts lawyer James Otis is beaten senseless.**

Otis, having learned that Boston customs commissioner John Robinson has complained about him to authorities in London, replies by calling Robinson a blockhead and vows to "break Robinson's head." After issuing his threat, the hot-headed Otis seeks out the British commissioner at a nearby coffee house and begins the fight by demanding satisfaction from Robinson, but it ends with Otis beaten nearly to death by Robinson and his supporters.

Sept. 19, 1769   **Georgia joins the nonimportation movement.**

Sept. 29, 1769   *A Tradesman's Plea* **is published in Philadelphia, urging the continuation of nonimportation.**

In a letter addressed "To the Tradesmen, Farmers, and other Inhabitants of the City and County of Philadelphia," the anonymous author implores the readers not to abandon the nonimportation agreement: "Don't neglect the only Opportunity you will ever have of convincing the World that you are *real lovers* of Liberty … Remember the high Character our Province bears both at home and abroad. The eyes of the whole Continent are now fixed upon us, and will be much influenced by our Example. I conjure you, therefore, by the Ghosts of our Ancestors, who planted the once howling Wilderness we now inhabit—and who are now, perhaps, Spectators of our Conduct—I conjure you by the Love you bear to yourselves—to your Country—to your Posterity—and above all by the Homage you owe to Human Liberty, not to surrender upon such base Terms, but to assert your Freedom at the Expence of your Fortunes and your Blood … (Signed) A Tradesman."

Oct. 18, 1769   **New Jersey joins the nonimportation movement.**

Oct. 1769   **Newport, Rhode Island, joins the nonimportation movement.**

From this time forward, new orders shall not be placed from England until the Townshend duties are repealed. Those goods already ordered and scheduled to arrive are to be held in bond.

Note: Providence, Rhode Island, was still a holdout and extreme pressure would be exerted by the other colonies for the town to conform, including threats of boycotts against it. Providence would finally comply from January 1, 1770.

Nov. 1769   **North Carolina joins the nonimportation movement against British goods.**

The North Carolina Assembly votes to join other colonies in a *nonimportation association* and vows that after January 1770, "no slaves, wine, nor goods of British manufacture" will come into the colony.

A British captain in Boston advises his men to bayonet any civilian who troubles them.

The acquittal of Michael Corbett has had its effect. The British troops believe that Corbett had been plainly guilty of murdering Lieutenant Henry Panton and yet he had been set free. If murderers of the King's troops are to escape punishment by simply claiming self-defense, what should the troops to do to protect themselves?

Dec. 6, 1769   **Boston merchants urge more colonial uniformity in the nonimportation movement.**

Boston merchants meet and agree to send notice to the other colonial assemblies urging all to adopt a uniform plan of nonimportation, basing any and all orders from England upon the revocation of the Townshend duties and to confer with the other colonies' committees.

Dec. 15, 1769   **The New York Assembly attempts to comply with the 1765 Quartering Act by providing** *partial funds* **for the quartering of British troops.**

The assembly approves only £1,800 for the quartering of troops—inadequate funding—and anger rises within the British military as a result. Yet to those wishing to starve the British troops *out of the city*, this is seen as a capitulation to the very demands the two prior assemblies had refused. In particular, the New York Sons of Liberty are livid that they are now to fund at the people's expense, the very troops that many New Yorkers believe are stationed in the city only to serve as a long arm of control by Parliament and the British Ministry.

> Note: The New York Assembly would complain to Parliament that the difficulties produced by the 1764 Currency Act made it nearly impossible to pay for housing the troops. Therefore, Parliament would authorize New York to print £120,000 of paper money to be used only for the payment of public debts.
>
> The ongoing battle to secure adequate funding for the British troops stationed in New York had been going on for four years, and the assembly's decision to yield to pressure would further divide the people's sentiments. Many New York citizens were quite loyal to the king and Parliament and viewed the troops as a welcome and protective presence.

Dec. 16, 1769   **Seditious broadsides are distributed and posted in New York against the assembly.**

Due the assembly's funding of the British troops, Alexander McDougall, a leader of New York's Sons of Liberty, prints a broadside entitled *To the Betrayed Inhabitants of the City and Colony of New York*. Critical of the assembly, the broadsides are posted around the city causing turmoil.

> Note: Three weeks later—sparked by McDougall's broadside—the escalating tensions in New York would erupt into violence at the *Battle of Golden Hill*.

Dec. 22, 1769   **In London, the *Grand Ohio Company* is formed by investors from both sides of the Atlantic.**

The vast amount of land ceded by the Iroquois at the Treaty of Fort Stanwix is opposed by American Secretary of State Lord Hillsborough. Though Hillsborough considers the grant much too extensive, Benjamin Franklin, with the help of influential English investors, argues that the tribes have freely given the land as sovereign nations and that should suffice. With approval now reluctantly granted, Franklin and others form the Grand Ohio Company hoping to make vast profits from the sales of the newly acquired western frontier lands.

> Note: The Grand Ohio Company, aka the *Walpole Company* was named after a company investor, Thomas Walpole, nephew of former Prime Minister Robert Walpole.
>
> Both the Indiana Land Company and the Ohio Company would soon merge with the Grand Ohio Company as the investors joined forces.

Dec. 29, 1769   **A Boston mob attacks the printer of the *Boston Chronicle*.**

John Fleeming is severely beaten in a Boston street for refusing to publish essays critical of British trade policies written by local authors. Instead, the printer has chosen only to republish news from Europe, and essays supporting the royal government.

> Note: From an article of the incident published in the January 8, 1770, edition of the *Newport Mercury*: "From Boston we hear, that on the Evening of the 29th, Mr. — Fleeming, Printer of the Boston Chronicle, was attacked in one of the Streets of that Town, by a Number of Ruffians, who abused him very much; and, 'tis thought, he would have died of his Wounds on the Spot, had not a humane Negro, who knew him, taken him up and helped him to his Home."

Jan. 1770   **Tensions continue to rise in Boston between citizens and the British troops.**

Trying to diffuse the situation, Boston's leaders apply pressure on Massachusetts Lieutenant Governor Hutchinson to have the soldiers removed from the town and placed on Castle Island.

Jan. 13, 1770   **In New York City, British troops assault the liberty pole.**

A group of British soldiers attempt to bring down the fortified pole by sawing and packing it with gunpowder, but the fuse does not set off an explosion. As an angry crowd continues to grow, the outnumbered soldiers choose to abandon their task—for now.

Jan. 16, 1770   **Having stood for three years, New York's famed liberty pole is destroyed.**

British troops, using explosives, finally destroy the symbolic monument of the rebellious New Yorkers. To add insult to injury, the soldiers saw the pole into pieces and throw them before a tavern frequented by New York's Sons of Liberty.

> Note: The McDougall broadside, inadequate funding for the troops, and now the destruction of New York's liberty pole would bring the simmering tensions to a boil between the British *Redcoats* and the more radical element of the citizens.

Jan. 19, 1770   **The *Battle of Golden Hill*: Violence erupts in New York.**

British soldiers reply to the December 16 broadside by posting a handbill of their own warning New York's citizens that the Sons of Liberty are the real enemy of the people. The handbill also makes fun of the liberty pole's destruction and of those colonials believing that their freedoms depend on a "piece of wood." While distributing the handbill, two soldiers are apprehended to be dragged to the mayor's office, but the others escape and race to sound the alarm.

Twenty British troops soon arrive with cutlasses and fixed bayonets to demand the release of their comrades, but the soldiers—greatly outnumbered by jeering townspeople—instead begin a return to their barracks while followed and harassed by the crowd.

When the soldiers reach Golden Hill, additional reinforcements arrive and position themselves at the rear of the crowd trapping the citizens between them. With this change of events, the formerly retreating soldiers now turn and attack their attackers—cutting though the crowd with bayonets as a melee breaks out injuring several citizens seriously.

> Note: News of the *battle* would spread throughout the American colonies, adding to the existing tensions.
>
> Reports in London would incorrectly state that a citizen had been killed in the riot.
>
> The Battle of Golden Hill was the first significant conflict in New York between American colonials and British troops.
>
> The struggle over New York's liberty pole would be published in the papers, leading others to adopt the practice as a way of displaying their community's patriotic sentiments and defiance of British authority. Many colonial towns would engage in friendly competitions to outdo their neighbors by erecting taller poles.

Jan. 1770   **In Massachusetts, Acting Governor Thomas Hutchinson suffers a legal rebuke.**

Local justices deny Hutchinson's charge that Boston's *Association* meetings are illegal. If things remain peaceful, what laws are broken?

> Note: Governor Hutchinson had declared the meeting illegal to disrupt Massachusetts's participation in the boycott against Great Britain.

> The various colonial Associations were responsible for enacting and enforcing the nonimportation of British goods to the American colonies.

Jan. 22, 1770   **Boston newspapers continue to publish the names of those violating the nonimportation agreement.**

Attempting to publicly shame citizens and merchants into compliance, new names are added to the list, deemed "enemies to their country."

Jan. 28, 1770   **Lord Frederick North becomes the new prime minister of Great Britain.**

> Note: Replacing Augustus FitzRoy, Lord North would serve as Britain's prime minister throughout the American War for Independence.

Jan. 30, 1770   **The New York Sons of Liberty are denied permission to erect a new liberty pole on public property.**

Undeterred, they purchase private property near the former Golden Hill site.

Feb. 6, 1770   **New York's fifth and final liberty pole is raised.**

Hoping to prevent its destruction, the liberty pole is secured with iron bands and hoops for the first two-thirds of its height and sunk deeply into the ground.

> Note: On July 9, 1776, George Washington, accompanied by Alexander Hamilton, would read the Declaration of Independence to his troops at the liberty pole in New York's City Hall Park. Four months later—having stood for six and a half years—the famed pole would be destroyed by British troops in October 1776.

Feb. 7, 1770   **A Sons of Liberty leader is arrested by authorities in New York City.**

Alexander McDougall is charged with seditious libel for having written the broadside placed around town six weeks earlier, which ignited the problems leading to the Golden Hill Riot.

> Note: When released from jail, McDougall would be accompanied by a crowd of 600 cheering supporters.

Feb. 22, 1770   **The first death in the American War for Independence? An eleven-year-old boy is killed in Boston.**

Ebenezer Richardson, an unpopular employee of the Customs Department, happens upon some boys hanging a paper sign on a merchant's door listing the names of four Boston *importers* known to be violators of the nonimportation agreement. Richardson rips down their sign and the boys taunt him for being an *informer*. A gathering crowd begins pelting Richardson with stones and follows him to his home. After Richardson goes inside, the unruly crowd continues its assault by throwing rocks and breaking his house's windows and front door. The enraged Richardson moves to an upstairs window and fires a couple of random shots of buckshot into the crowd, killing eleven-year-old Christopher Seider and wounding another.

> Note: Ebenezer Richardson would be arrested and placed on trial on April 20, 1770.
>
> Boston physician Dr. Joseph Warren would perform Seider's autopsy. Dr. Warren would be a leader of the independence movement in Boston; the primary author of the *Suffolk Resolves*; and would die fighting in the battle of Bunker Hill.

Feb. 26, 1770   **Thousands join the funeral parade of Christopher Seider—Boston's young martyr for liberty.**

Attended by 2,000 citizens, Seider's funeral parade begins at Faneuil Hall and proceeds to the Liberty Tree for speeches, before finally moving onward to the cemetery.

Note:	Boston's radicals made the most of the occasion for propaganda purposes. Samuel Adams had planned Seider's funeral arrangements and had inscribed on Seider's casket, "Innocence itself is not safe." The Sons of Liberty would publish posters pushing its version of the event and calling to avenge the boy's death.
	Following the funeral of the young Seider, tensions in Boston were at an all-time high and would soon spill over into more violence between citizens and the hated British *Lobsterbacks* occupying and patrolling the town.

March 2–3, 1770 **The *Boston Ropewalk Brawl* erupts between British troops and rope makers.**

Note:	Many soldiers supplemented their meager pay by hiring themselves out for work, competing with civilian laborers.

A British soldier named Thomas Walker asks for work at John Gray's ropewalk and receives the reply, "You can go and clean my shit house!" More insults are traded, and a fight breaks out. Receiving the worst of it, Walker runs to his barracks and returns with comrades to exact revenge and a vicious fight begins. After receiving the worst of it, the outnumbered soldiers are driven away.

The next day, three soldiers return to renew the fight, but they too are beaten, which only inflames their ire.

Note:	One of the brawling soldiers, Matthew Kilroy, still seething from the fight, would shoot Boston citizens three days hence in what would become known as the *Boston Massacre*.

March 4, 1770   **A large number of British troops descend upon the ropewalk in an invasive search.**

The troops believe a missing comrade had been murdered during the previous day's brawl and search the premises.

Note:	Following the raid, a rumor would quickly spread that the soldiers planned to return the next day to attack the ropewalk and cut down Boston's sacred Liberty Tree.

March 5, 1770   **Prime Minister Lord North introduces a resolution to Parliament calling for the revocation of the 1767 Revenue Act.**

Most Members of Parliament wish to do so—but question how Parliament can relent to the Americans without yielding its authority.

Note:	Four years earlier, Great Britain had yielded to American protests against the Stamp Act, and Parliament did not wish to do so again.

The *Boston Massacre*: Eleven people are shot in a confrontation with British troops.

Note:	Only one week after the funeral of Christopher Seider and two days since the Ropewalk Brawl, the night of March 5 found tensions extremely high between many of Boston's citizens and the British troops. Rumors abounded that a local oysterman had been severely beaten by soldiers, the town's prized Liberty Tree was to be cut down, and that the British troops were posting notices stating they were to defend themselves against the Bostonians. In response, various groups roamed the streets

Serving guard near Boston's Custom House, Private Hugh White is harassed by two teenage boys, who abuse him with insults, going so far as to poke White in the chest. White responds by striking one teen in the head with the butt of his rifle and both boys cry out in alarm, causing the situation to quickly escalate. Hearing the commotion, people make their way to the Customs House as the young British private—fearing for his life—is surrounded by a menacing crowd.

Responding to the alarm, Captain Thomas Preston and seven British soldiers rush from the barracks with fixed bayonets and quickly form a protective semi-circle in front of the besieged Private White with their muskets lowered.

Church bells begin to ring and the angry crowd continues to grow, eventually numbering 300 to 400 people as many of Boston's more-ordinary citizens turn out to see what the fuss is about. Captain Preston orders the crowd to disperse, but they respond instead with taunts, flying oyster shells, coal, and chunks of ice daring Preston to fire while shouting that if he does—he will pay for his actions with his life.

Note: Many in the crowd did not believe that the soldiers would dare fire due to the restrictions of the Riot Act laws that required a sheriff to disperse a crowd by first *reading them the Riot Act* and then giving them one hour to comply.

The crowd continues to taunt and abuse the British soldiers who now fear for their lives. Captain Preston is hit with a club on the arm barely missing his head, while Private Hugh Montgomery is knocked to the ground by a thrown object during which his gun is knocked from his hands. Picking up both himself and his gun, Private Montgomery fires into the crowd and a several-second pause ensues—a momentary shock of consciousness—before the other soldiers also fire. Into the now surreal scene, Lieutenant Governor Thomas Hutchinson arrives and orders the soldiers to their barracks while trying to calm the crowd, promising that justice will be done.

Note: Three citizens were killed instantly; one would die the following day; and another would die nine days later. The six others shot in the attack would survive.

One of those killed, Crispus Attucks, was mixed race. Attucks had been born in Massachusetts to a Wampanoag mother and an enslaved African father.

Radicals in Boston, including Paul Revere, would use the killings to further agitate American hostilities toward Great Britain. Immediately dubbed the *Boston Massacre,* news of the event would rapidly spread throughout the North American colonies.

March 6, 1770 **British Captain Prescott is arrested and jailed by Boston's civil authorities.**

The seven relief soldiers, including the rescued Private White, are also arrested and jailed.

Boston lawyer John Adams agrees to represent the accused British soldiers.

Adams, along with lawyer Josiah Quincey, believes all men should receive a fair trial.

Boston citizens demand the British troops "out of our city."

An angry crowd of 4,000 Bostonians meets at Faneuil Hall, demanding the soldiers be removed immediately to the island fortress of Castle William in Boston Bay.

March 8, 1770 **Funeral services are held for those killed by the British troops.**

Shops in the town are closed and church bells ring in mourning as the four victims are laid to rest in Boston's Granary Burying Ground.

March 11, 1770   **Half of the British troops are relocated in an attempt to ease tensions in Boston.**

One of the two British regiments encamped in the town is removed to Castle Island at the demand of angry citizens.

> Note: People would find this half-measure unacceptable as Sam Adams and other leaders continued to pressure the acting governor, Thomas Hutchinson, warning him of armed citizens descending on Boston. As a result, Hutchinson would be convinced to remove both regiments to the island fortress.

Bostonian silversmith Paul Revere engraves a depiction of the Boston Massacre.

Revere's portrayal of the event is printed throughout the colonies, helping to spread anti-British sentiments.

March 13, 1770   **Captain Prescott and eight British soldiers are indicted for murder by a Boston grand jury.**

The nine military men will stand trial in a civilian court, but not until October, allowing time for passions to cool.

March 14, 1770   **The last Boston Massacre victim to die from his wounds, forgives the soldiers.**

Patrick Carr, shot through the abdomen and aware that his death is inevitable, chooses not to blame the soldiers for his fate. Carr believes that they had exercised undeserved patience before shooting into the crowd.

> Note: Patrick Carr, from Ireland, was the only Catholic among the victims. Carr's sentiments toward the British soldiers would cause him to be denounced by Sam Adams, who wished to promote the incident as a *massacre* for anti-British propaganda purposes.

March 16, 1770   **Massachusetts Lieutenant Governor Thomas Hutchinson sends his report to London concerning the killing of civilians by British troops.**

> Note: Though most Americans would label the March 5 shooting as the Boston Massacre, the British authorities would refer to it benignly as the *Incident on King Street*.

March 17, 1770   **A final funeral is held for those killed in the Boston Massacre.**

The fifth to die, Patrick Carr, like the others, is buried in Granary Burying Ground.

> Note: Boston would settle into a somewhat eerie state of calm after the shooting as the town awaited the eventual trial of the accused British soldiers. Both sides would spend the spring and summer locked in a fierce propaganda battle hoping to influence the outcome of the looming murder trials.

April 9, 1770   **Parliament repeals the Revenue Act of 1767, aka the Townshend duties.**

Succumbing to the effects of economic pressure due to nonimportation and the lobbying by British merchants; and not wishing to further alienate the Americans—Parliament votes to repeal the 1767 Revenue Act but retains the 3-pence per pound tax on tea.

> Note: Most Americans believed only they could tax themselves and that Great Britain had no legal authority to do so. Yet by retaining the tea tax—Parliament was demonstrating its right to tax the colonies.

April 12, 1770 **King George III gives his royal assent to the *Repeal Act*, ending the Revenue Act of 1767.**

The Repeal Act has the following results:

- Though some American colonials urge the continuation of nonimportation, the Revenue Act's repeal creates a general relaxing of the nonimportation movement and ushers in a two-year period of relative calm between Britain and its North American colonists.

- The tea issue settles down, and most American colonists either drink smuggled Dutch tea or the taxed East India tea, often determined by availability.

April 20, 1770 **The trial of Ebenezer Richardson takes place in Boston.**

Ebenezer Richardson and George Wilmot are placed on trial for the killing of young Christopher Seider on February 22. Though Richardson fired the lethal shot, Wilmot had gone into Richardson's house to assist him during the attack. After hearing testimony from multiple witnesses, the jury quickly exonerates Wilmot, but the trail for Richardson continues.

> Note: English law permitted a man to kill someone breaking into his house at night, but Richardson had shot Seider during the day.
>
> The people packing the courtroom, described by Judge Oliver as "a vast Concourse of Rabble," wanted Richardson declared guilty of murder.

After the evidence and arguments are finished, the jury—denied food, drink, or sleep until it reaches a verdict—begins its deliberations around 11 p.m. The following morning, Ebenezer Richardson is declared guilty of manslaughter but innocent of murder. Expecting a king's pardon due to being a civil servant, Richardson waits in jail without formal sentencing for two years until his pardon finally arrives.

> Note: Now a Boston pariah, Ebenezer Richardson would be pursued by crowds upon his release. Though Richardson would escape to Philadelphia, his identity would be found out, and—under threat of being tarred and feathered—Richardson would again flee and eventually moved to England for his safety.

In London, John Wilkes is released from prison to a hero's welcome.

After two years in prison, the champion of English liberty emerges more popular than ever among the people.

May 1770 **Colonial nonimportation begins to collapse after the 1767 Revenue Act is repealed—except for the 3-pence tax on tea.**

Many American merchants are hurting from nonimportation and wish to return to normal business. During May—Albany, Providence, and Newport merchants all agree to resume imports despite efforts by activists to keep the boycott alive.

In Boston, a customs worker is tarred and feathered by a raucous crowd.

Richard Owens, a tidewaiter for British customs, is tarred and feathered in retribution for ordering a ship in New London, Connecticut, to be seized for customs violations.

June 4, 1770	**In New York, the commissioned statues of King George III and William Pitt arrive from England.**
	Ordered four years earlier by the New York Assembly to commemorate the Stamp Act's repeal, the statues arrive on the king's birthday.
June 1770	**New York merchants—against the wishes of the Sons of Liberty—begin importing British goods.**
	In Boston, a merchant is paraded through the streets for defying nonimportation.
	Patrick McMaster, a wealthy Scottish merchant, is to be tarred and feathered but faints upon seeing the tarbrush. Spared this ignominious humiliation, McMaster is hauled through town on a cart to Roxbury and released.
July 5, 1770	**The first statue in North America dedicated to a public official is erected.**
	In Charles Town, South Carolina, a marble statue of William Pitt is erected to commemorate Pitt's help in repealing the Stamp Act.

> Note: Although Pitt's statue would be moved and damaged over the years, it stands today inside Charleston County Judicial Center. The statue's arms are both missing—one of which was shot off by a British cannonball on April 16, 1780.

Aug. 16, 1770	**A statue of King George III is erected in Bowling Green, New York.**
	The celebratory event is attended by most of the notable New York dignitaries, accompanied by drinks, festive music, and the firing of thirty-two brass cannons representing the king's thirty-two years of life.

> Note: The equestrian statue—depicting the king sitting boldly upon his horse—would be torn down on July 9, 1776, by American Continental soldiers and New York citizens after hearing the Declaration of Independence read aloud.

Sept. 7, 1770	**New York erects its second commissioned statue; this one of former British Prime Minister William Pitt.**
	Pitt is seen as the champion of American liberties, and his statue of white marble is placed at the intersection of Wall Street and William Street.

> Note: Pitt's statue would be decapitated and its arms broken off on September 15, 1780, by New York Loyalists.

Sept. 1770	**As the *Regulator Revolt* continues to grow in North Carolina, the rebels become more emboldened to violence.**
	The Hillsborough Superior Court is stormed by 150 Regulators, forcing a judge to flee as the group breaks up the court's proceeding before vandalizing it. Then, seeking out tax collector Edmund Fanning, the Regulators deliver him a severe beating while drinking his alcohol and burning his house and barn to the ground. The violence and corresponding threats cause the Hillsborough Courthouse to remain closed as the local officials now fear for their lives, and a much-shaken Edmund Fanning quickly leaves town.

Sept. 12, 1770 **Philadelphia ends its boycott of British goods as the American nonimportation movement continues to ebb.**

Oct.–Nov. 1770 **The Fort Stanwix Treaty has begun a western land rush as George Washington travels down the Ohio River claiming extensive land tracts.**

For nine weeks, Washington travels downriver accompanied by his friend William Crawford and a large party of surveyors, claiming lands recently opened to settlement by the Fort Stanwix Treaty. Hoping to obtain the best lands for themselves, the group travels as far as the Great Kanawha River in modern West Virginia. Washington and his party claim many thousands of acres, hoping to sell their lands to settlers already gathering at Fort Pitt readying to move westward.

Note: The Fort Stanwix Treaty would provide great economic opportunities for the various land companies and their investors.

Oct. 11, 1770 **Boston merchants agree to end their nonimportation of British goods.**

Oct. 18, 1770 **The *Treaty of Lochaber*: The Cherokee cede additional lands to the British Crown.**

During negotiations at Lochaber, South Carolina, Southern Indian Superintendent John Stuart secures Cherokee relinquishment of all remaining claims to the modern West Virginia region. In return, to satisfy the Cherokee, the treaty fixes *permanently* the western limits of new settlements by the Whites.

Oct. 24, 1770 **The first Boston Massacre trial gets under way.**

The trial begins for Captain Thomas Preston—accused of giving the orders to fire on the crowd.

Note: Captain Preston and his men had been in jail for eight months awaiting trial.

A second trial for the eight noncommissioned soldiers charged in the incident was scheduled to begin following the conclusion of Captain Preston's trial.

Oct. 30, 1770 **British Captain Thomas Preston is acquitted of manslaughter charges.**

After five days of testimony, Captain Preston is acquitted of all charges against him: *Not guilty*.

Note: To ensure a fair trial, the jurors were selected from outside the town of Boston.

Preston's trial was one of America's first trials to have lasted multiple days.

Nov. 27, 1770 **The second Boston Massacre trial begins.**

The guilt of the eight soldiers charged with manslaughter is to be considered individually during the joint trial.

Note: John Adams, having successfully served as a defense lawyer for Captain Preston, had also agreed to defend the noncommissioned soldiers.

Dec. 5, 1770 **A mixed verdict is reached in the second Boston Massacre trial.**

Six of the soldiers are acquitted, but two others are convicted of manslaughter with the possibility of hanging: Private Hugh Montgomery and Private Matthew Kilroy.

Note:	In the words of John Adams in his defense of the soldiers, "Facts are stubborn things; and whatever may be our wishes, our inclinations, or the dictates of our passion, they cannot alter the state of facts and evidence."

Dec. 12, 1770 **Charles Town, South Carolina ends its boycott of British goods.**

Dec. 14, 1770 **A sentencing hearing is held in Boston for the soldiers found guilty of manslaughter.**

The two British soldiers have prayed "benefit of clergy" which reduces their sentences to thumb-branding. Both men have the letter M for manslaughter branded at the base of their thumbs by the sheriff as defense attorney John Adams witnesses the punishment.

A period of relative calm settles upon Boston.

Following the trial of the British soldiers:

- British Captain Thomas Preston sails to England in late December never to return.

- Lieutenant Governor Hutchinson begins removing the remaining troops to Castle Island under pressure from Boston's town officials.

- The boycott of British goods basically ends now that the Townshend duties (except for the tax on tea) have been repealed.

Note:	After the Boston Massacre, many radicals, particularly in Massachusetts, would begin to work toward complete independence from Great Britain instead of simply righting grievances.

1771 **The American nonimportation of British goods has dissolved.**

Note:	Virginia, still a holdout, would end nonimportation by July 1771.

Jan. 15, 1771 **To suppress the Regulator Revolt in western North Carolina, the assembly passes the _Johnston Riot Act_.**

A rumor spreads stating that the Regulators are planning an assault on the colonial capital and the New Bern citizens are alarmed. In response, the North Carolina Assembly passes an Act based on England's Riot Act of 1714 in order to suppress the rebels with military force if necessary—after declaring them to be illegal rioters. The following are among the provisions of the Johnston Riot Act:

- Any unlawful assembly of ten or more must disperse within an hour after so being ordered by a judge or sheriff.

- Deputies cannot be charged for killing or maiming rioters.

- Emergency courts are to be established.

- The governor may raise a militia against the Regulators, paid by public expense.

- The Act is to be one year in duration.

Note:	The Regulators would ignore the Johnston Riot Act; dubbing it the _Bloody Act_ and simply added it to their list of grievances.

> Labeled rioters, the Regulators were to be suppressed by the colonial militia and could now be killed with impunity.

Governor Tryon orders the North Carolina Regulators to surrender.

The Regulators are ordered to surrender within sixty days or be declared outlaws and have their lands confiscated by the government for noncompliance.

Early 1771   **Benjamin Franklin, acting agent for Pennsylvania in London, is appointed to represent Massachusetts's interests.**

Franklin—also an agent for New Jersey and a former agent for Georgia—is regarded as the unofficial representative and spokesman for Britain's colonial America. Therefore, many in England regularly seek Doctor Franklin's advice regarding American political affairs.

> Note: Some Americans doubted Franklin's loyalty, particularly Boston's Sam Adams and Richard Henry Lee of Virginia.

1771   *Vandalia*: **A new British colony in North America?**

The Grand Ohio Company, aka the Walpole Company, wishes to spur sales of the recently acquired Indian lands by proposing a new British colony encompassing modern West Virginia and Kentucky. Hoping to buy land grants from the Crown, the company submits plans for a new governmental organization including the appointment of a royal governor, an assembly, and courts. The new colony will be named *Vandalia* in honor of Queen Charlotte, who descends from the Vandals of Europe.

> Note: Other names for the proposed colony would include *Pittsylvania* and *Westsylvania*.

March 1771   **In New York City, the HBS *Jersey* is converted to a British hospital ship.**

> Note: The large, aging vessel would serve as a floating hospital for British troops in New York until being converted into a prison ship in 1779.
>
> The HBS *Jersey* would house thousands of American prisoners of war in deplorable conditions until the British evacuated New York in 1783.
>
> Historians believe that up to 11,000 men died aboard British prison ships during the American War for Independence.

March 5, 1771   **The first commemoration of the Boston Massacre.**

A crowd numbering thousands attends a one-year anniversary of the Boston Massacre at the Old South Meeting House.

> Note: Boston's radical leaders would repeat this commemoration yearly causing an annual upwelling of irritation and troubles between the citizens and the British officials. Yet to other Bostonians, these solemn observances would be considered much ado about nothing. In their opinion, the "Massacre" had been just punishment for the rabble who had instigated the event.

March 14, 1771   **Lieutenant Governor Thomas Hutchinson is confirmed as governor of Massachusetts.**

The Massachusetts-born Hutchinson has been serving as acting governor since Governor Francis Bernard returned to England on August 1, 1769.

April 1771	**In Newport, Rhode Island, a customs official is accosted.**

During the night, collector of customs Charles Dudley goes alone aboard a vessel docked at Newport's wharf and is accosted by drunken sailors. Cruelly and scandalously abused, Dudley is threatened with his life if he reports the incident. Fearful of retribution and believing he will receive no justice in the civil courts, Dudley chooses not to file charges with the local authorities.

> Note: When learning of the event, American Secretary of State Lord Hillsborough would use the incident to highlight that the laws of the kingdom were being trampled with impunity in the colonies.

May 9, 1771	**Attempting to quash the Regulator insurrection, Governor Tryon leads a large army of militiamen to Hillsborough, North Carolina.**

With local judges afraid to open the courts due to threats from the Regulators, Governor William Tryon begins a 150-mile march from New Bern to protect them. In response, the Regulators ready themselves to resist Tryon's arriving forces.

May 16, 1771	**Frontier Regulators battle North Carolina militia forces in *the Battle of Alamance*.**

Twenty-eight miles west of Hillsborough, 2,000 Regulators (mostly farmers) face Governor Tryon's well-armed militia army of 1,600 in a standoff at Alamance Creek.

The Regulators wish to meet with Tryon for discussion, but he insists they first "lay down [their] arms and surrender up [their] leaders." The governor then reads the recently passed Johnston Riot Act giving the rebels one hour to disperse to avoid the effusion of blood, but they ignore the orders. By midday, having not received a response, Governor Tryon gives them one more warning, telling the rebels that if they should submit without resistance, he shall give them the best terms possible, but to resist would prove futile for they are no army and will be defeated.

With the two groups facing one another, some of the Regulators begin waving their hats defiantly, yelling, "Fire and be dammed." In response, Governor Tryon orders the rebels to be fired upon, and the militia cannons unload into the crowd causing the Regulators to scramble in retreat and return fire from behind trees and boulders. During a two-hour mismatched battle, many Regulators abandon the fight for they suffer from lack of arms, leadership, and organization.

> Note: The Regulators endured heavy casualties as a large unknown number were killed or wounded, and fifteen were taken prisoner.
>
> The North Carolina militia force suffered nine dead and sixty-one wounded.
>
> Governor Tryon was an experienced lieutenant colonel in the British Army who held few qualms regarding his ability to crush the Regulators and end the rebellion.

May 17, 1771	**Captured Regulator leader James Few is executed.**

Governor Tryon believes the Regulators are being led by a few individuals who control the masses; if the serpent's head is cut off, the movement will die.

> Note: James Few's wife and children were forced to watch his hanging.

Late May 1771	**Twelve more Regulators are sentenced for execution.**

At the Hillsborough Court House, twelve of the fourteen Regulators charged with treason are convicted and sentenced to be hanged.

June 19, 1771	**Six Regulators are hanged at Hillsborough, North Carolina, basically ending the revolt.**

Governor Tryon, hoping to end the rebellion by winning over the Regulators and regional people with benevolence and forgiveness, pardons six of the twelve convicted men. In addition, Tryon offers amnesty for those Regulators willing to take oaths of allegiance.

Note:	The six men saved from the noose were obliged to swear allegiance to the royal government. Within six weeks of the governor's amnesty offer, nearly 6,500 settlers in North Carolina's western region would also take oaths of allegiance.
	Outside the North Carolina frontier region, the Regulators were portrayed as outlaws, generating little sympathy except for some support in the Boston press.
	Governor Tryon would depart two days later to become royal governor of New York, replacing Governor John Murray, aka Lord Dunmore.
	On July 12, 1775, King George would pardon all former Regulators hoping to secure their support against the American rebels.

Summer 1771   **North Carolina Regulators move west to the Watauga frontier region.**

Hoping to escape their troubles, James Robertson leads sixteen Regulator families deep into Appalachia to begin life anew at the *Watauga* settlement. Located on Cherokee lands in present-day Tennessee, the arriving North Carolinians join the frontier settlement, which until now has been inhabited mostly by Virginians.

The Watauga settlers are ordered to remove themselves from Cherokee lands.

British Deputy Indian agent Alexander Cameron orders the people to vacate, because:

- They are west of the limits set by the Proclamation Line and thus beyond the jurisdictions of Virginia and North Carolina.

- They are on Cherokee land, and private purchase from the Indians is prohibited.

Note:	Most of the people living at Watauga would ignore Cameron's orders.
	These and other frontier settlers living west of the Proclamation Line were generally referred to as *overmountain people* by the colonial governors and others.

July 1771   **The American boycott of British goods ends completely as Virginia becomes the last colony to abandon nonimportation.**

Note:	In April 1770 Parliament had repealed the 1767 Revenue Act, thus the boycott begun three years earlier had lost its steam and purpose.

Secretary of State Lord Hillsborough denounces the ill-treatment customs officials receive in America.

Hillsborough complains of certain outrages committed on royal customs officers and "the neglect of the governors and civil magistrates in giving their assistance and protection." The secretary continues, "that some of the most violent of these outrages have been committed at Newport, in Rhode Island, particularly in April last, when the collector of his Majesty's customs at that port, was, in the execution of his duty, assaulted and grossly ill-treated, even to the danger of his life, by a number of the inhabitants, without any protection being given him; that, in general, the officers of the customs have received no support or countenance from that government, and have in vain applied to the superior court for writs of assistance in cases where such writs were adjudged necessary."

| 1771–1772 | **Iroquois delegates travel to the western regions to placate the hostile tribes and quell the threat of a new Indian alliance.** |

Though the Iroquois and Cherokee have negotiated agreements with the British, the tribes further west have not. The Shawnee, among others, consider the new boundaries barring White settlement as being too far west and threatening. Therefore, on behalf of British Indian Superintendent William Johnson, the Iroquois travel among the tribes to quiet matters.

> Note: By the terms of the 1768 Fort Stanwix Treaty, the Iroquois had granted away the lands of West Virginia and Kentucky—hunting grounds used and occupied by the Shawnee, Cherokee, and other regional tribes. Though the Cherokee had granted away the lands of West Virginia by the 1770 Lochaber Treaty—they had not granted away Kentucky.
>
> Pontiac's War had taught the British and Americans another hard lesson concerning the potency of the Indian tribes when allied in union. Never again did they wish to endure such a catastrophe.

| Sept. 25, 1771 | **John Murray, aka Lord Dunmore, becomes Virginia's new royal governor.** |

Lord Dunmore, like many of Virginia's gentry, seeks to secure a fortune by investing in frontier lands.

> Note: Appointed as governor of New York in 1770, Dunmore had been transferred to Virginia following the death of Governor Botetourt.
>
> Lord Dunmore would be Virginia's last royal governor; forced from office by American rebels in late 1775.

| 1772 | **Britain's 1772 *Credit Crisis* causes economic tensions to rise in the American colonies.** |

The British East India Company is in economic trouble due to fiscal mismanagement and the effects of India's *Great Bengal Famine*. As a result, the value of the East India Company's real estate holdings in the subcontinent drops precipitously, creating concerns about the company's ability to repay its loans. As bankruptcies increase, British merchants begin to demand payment on the debts owed them. The situation causes Britain's economic problems to spread to the American colonies, particularly in the Southern colonies, which rely on a system of credit to sufficiently operate. With less credit available and little gold or specie in North America for repayments, severe belt-tightening is the result.

> Note: The Great Bengal Famine of 1769–1773 would result in an estimated 10 million deaths in India.
>
> The East India Company was seen as a company too large to fail. The company's financial success was important to the overall British economy, and with so many influential investors, economic measures would soon be taken to save it.

| Jan. 1772 | **In Rhode Island, the HBS *Gaspee* arrives to assert British authority and enforce the kingdom's maritime trade laws.** |

The ship's commander, Lieutenant William Duddingston, is responsible for patrolling the coastal waters around Narragansett Bay, and many locals resent the *Gaspee*'s presence.

> Note: Lieutenant Duddingston, considered an overzealous enforcer of the laws, would detain ships, confiscate and impound cargos, and earn the general wrath of the Rhode Island merchants, who considered the *Gaspee*'s crew to be nothing but arrogant thieves.

Feb. 17, 1772 **While patrolling Narragansett Bay, the HBS *Gaspee* confiscates a load of smuggled molasses from the sloop *Fortune*.**

British Lieutenant Duddingston sends the impounded cargo to Boston for *safe keeping* as he does not trust it can be securely held from the sympathetic locals.

> Note: The Rhode Islanders would be infuriated that the *Fortune*'s confiscated goods, taken in Rhode Island waters, would be held in Boston. The colony's charter specifically required that crimes committed within Rhode Island must be tried within Rhode Island.

April 1772 **Parliament passes the *Dockyard Act* to prevent arson of the King's shipyards, vessels, and stores.**

The Dockyard Act stipulates a death sentence for anyone found guilty of setting fire to the King's ships or dockyards in Great Britain *or in the colonies*. In addition, the Act stipulates that those charged with arson under the Act are to be sent to England for trial.

> Note: The call for trials to be held in England for crimes committed in North America would cause American alarm and is alluded to in grievance nineteen in the U.S. Declaration of Independence.

Britain's Board of Trade and Plantations opposes creating the Vandalia Colony.

The British trade commissioners express opposition to the Vandalia project and refuse to recognize the Ohio River as the new *Indian boundary* as stipulated by the 1768 Fort Stanwix Treaty. Instead, the commissioners recommend that all settlements west of the Proclamation Line of 1763 be forbidden and demolished.

> Note: Many in Britain were against the creation of new colonies in the North American interior, viewing such designs as counterproductive to British interests. Lord Hillsborough's resistance to the Vandalia Colony and further western intrusions upon the Indians would help lead to his removal as Britain's American secretary of state as influential and disappointed investors in Britain and America considered both the Indians and Lord Hillsborough as impediments to their schemes.
>
> George Washington, hoping to cash in on the Vandalia project, directed his agents to survey and acquire 10,000 adjoining acres, but he would later back out.

April 14, 1772 **In Weare, New Hampshire, a sheriff and his deputy are beaten while trying to stop the illegal harvesting of white pines.**

The previous day, Sheriff Benjamin Whitling and Deputy John Quigley had arrested the owner of a sawmill, Ebenezer Mudgett, found to be in violation of the law. After Mudgett promised to provide bail the next morning, he was released and the two law officers overnighted in a nearby inn expecting Mudgett to deliver his bail as agreed. Instead, the sheriff and deputy are jostled from their sleep and severely beaten by twenty men with blackened faces and then driven from town to the sound of jeers.

> Note: Beginning in 1691, England had placed multiple restrictions on the harvesting of North America's large white pines, which were much valued as masts for the British Navy due to the lumber's superior qualities. The New England colonists resented the restrictions and regularly played cat-and-mouse with the authorities—or simply bribed them to ignore the illegal harvesting.
>
> As a symbol of New England and the region's defiance to the king, the white pine would be incorporated into the design of the historical *Pine Tree Flag*—first used by a naval squadron commissioned by George Washington in August 1775. The flag

shows a pine silhouetted against a white background with the words "An Appeal to Heaven."

| Spring 1772 | **In eastern Tennessee, the Watauga settlement negotiates a *lease* to remain on Cherokee lands.** |

Barred from buying land from the Indians and ordered to abandon their frontier homes, the Watauga settlers negotiate a ten-year lease with certain Cherokee leaders for $6,000, agreeing that no additional Whites to the area would be permitted.

> Note: The agreement was an uncertain legal maneuver. Though private purchases from the Indians were illegal—the law did not address *leasing*.
>
> Future hostilities would be inevitable; most Cherokee opposed the lease and White settlers would continue to intrude despite the agreement.

| May 8, 1772 | **The Watauga settlement creates a semi-autonomous government.** |

Having secured a lease from the Cherokee, the settlers form the *Watauga Association* and adopt the *Written Articles of Association*.

> Note: The Watauga Association was to be governed by a five-member board.
>
> The self-government of Watauga is often waxed romantically by some as the first freely adopted constitution in a region to become a part of the United States; the first government formed by native-born Americans; and the first British government west of the Appalachian Mountains.
>
> No copy of the Written Articles of Association survives, and all records of Watauga government have perished.
>
> As Watauga was outside the bounds of royal colonial government, the question would arise, "Under whose authority do the people operate and to whom do they legally answer and report?" As such, the governors of North Carolina and Virginia would declare the frontier settlement illegal.

| June 9, 1772 | **The HBS *Gaspee* runs aground while chasing smugglers off the Rhode Island coast.** |

News of the patrol ship's grounding quickly spreads as a group gathers at a Providence tavern to plan an attack against the despised British vessel, responsible for the *Fortune's* seizure four months earlier in Narragansett Bay.

| June 10, 1772 | **Near Providence, Rhode Islanders shoot a British naval officer and destroy the HBS *Gaspee*.** |

Under the dark of night, fifty-five men row eight longboats to the stranded British ship to surprise a sleeping and unsuspecting crew to arrest the *Gaspee's* commander under charges of illegally confiscating goods. Acting as the local sheriff, John Brown attempts to place Lieutenant William Duddingston under arrest, but the British lieutenant resists and in the resulting melee— Duddingston is felled by a musket ball to his arm. The wounded Lieutenant Duddingston and his crew are bound and rowed to shore as the predawn sky is lit by flames from the burning ship and its exploding munitions.

> Note: News of the *Gaspee Affair* would spread rapidly throughout the American colonies.
>
> Outraged by the Rhode Islanders' actions, the British Ministry would issue calls for an investigation and for the culprits to be arrested.
>
> With the recent passage of Britain's *Dockyard Act*, American colonists charged with arson of a King's ship are to be sent to England for trial under penalty of death.

However, charging the culprits with treason instead of arson would ensure that if arrested, their trials would take place in Rhode Island.

The investigation would conclude a year later with no arrests having been made due to sympathetic local courts; a lack of cooperation from witnesses; and the supportive sentiments of the public—alarming the British officials for the precedent it set.

June 22, 1772   **The *Somerset decision* deals a legal blow to slavery in England.**

The Somerset decision is issued by the English Court of King's Bench stating that a slave in England cannot be forcibly taken abroad by his master. James Somerset—enslaved in Africa; sold in Jamaica in 1749; and later resold in Virginia to Charles Stewart of Boston—had been brought to England by Stewart in 1768 to serve as a personal assistant. While living in England, James Somerset was influenced by British abolitionists who tried to help him avoid being returned to the American colonies. At their encouragement, James was baptized a Christian in February 1771 and then urged to *run away,* for the abolitionists wished to make a test case of his situation.

Note: Becoming a Christian would help arguments for James's freedom; many Britons believed that Christianized Africans could not, or at least should not, be enslaved.

To be baptized required James to receive *godparents.* Then, following baptism, his new godparents could legally initiate the necessary court proceedings on his behalf.

After disappearing, James was found aboard a ship bound for Jamaica. Somerset's godparents intervened and he was released by writ of *habeas corpus* beginning a legal wrangle over the issue of "whether James Somerset can be removed from England against his will."

Note: Abolitionists supported the defense for James Somerset, whereas British West Indian planters financed his owner, Charles Stewart, hoping the case would declare slavery to be legal in England once and for all.

The Somerset trial, published in newspapers, is incorrectly framed as a case to end slavery in England and its proceedings are followed both domestically and abroad—particularly in the colonial presses of North America and the West Indies.

Note: England had approximately 10,000 African *servants*—de facto slaves—though the practice stood on legs unsupported by common law.

Some colonial plantation owners, living either in England or the Americas, traveled between the continents with their household slaves used for domestic duties. If James Somerset prevailed, the slaveowners would be unable to continue this practice.

Somerset's defense argues that:

- Colonial laws concerning slavery have no effect on the laws in England.

- No English law supports or acknowledges slavery, and therefore it is illegal.

- No person can enslave himself by contract without his own consent.

The opposition argues that:

- Property is property, citing past legal cases in English history.

- It would be dangerous to free the Africans in England.

The verdict was: "The state of slavery is of such a nature that it is incapable of being introduced on any reasons, moral or political, but only by positive law, which preserves its force long after the reasons, occasions, and time itself from whence it was created, is erased from memory. It is so odious, that nothing can be suffered to support it, but positive law. Whatever inconveniences, therefore, may follow from the decision, I cannot say this case is allowed or approved by the law of England; and therefore the black must be discharged."

> Note: Contrary to popular belief, Judge Mansfield did not outlaw slavery in England, only ruling that a slave could not be removed from England against his will. Yet the British public and justices of the peace would view the decision as a blow to slavery, and many believed that it was only a matter of time until slavery would end.

The Somerset decision has the following effects:

- James Somerset is set free and will live the rest of his life in Britain.

- English abolitionists get a boost to their cause.

- The Somerset decision establishes a radical precedent and will help lead to an end of British participation in the Atlantic slave trade in 1807.

- No longer can slave owners travel to England with their slaves and compel them to return. Slavers in the colonies are rattled and unnerved, for it opens a legal window leading to the next obvious question: "Does this apply to the British colonies in North America and the West Indies as well?"

- Colonial and British slave holders see the court decision as a major economic and social threat.

> Note: Some today argue that the ruling helped the American colonies move toward independence from Great Britain, as those who profited from the slave system began wondering if a separation would provide the answer to this legal issue. As the end of British slavery seemed to be nearing—perhaps by becoming independent—the American colonists could protect slavery by their own laws.
>
> Some historians view the Somerset case as analogous to the future *Dred Scott* case in 1857.

July 1772   **At their annual summer conference, the Iroquois complain to Indian Superintendent William Johnson and the new governor of New York, William Tryon, concerning the continued loss of their lands.**

> Note: The Six Nations had long exaggerated their claims to the western lands at the expense of the other tribes. Having enriched themselves over the years by selling these dubious claims to the Whites, Iroquois power had begun to wane as the extent of their former domain had shrunk considerably.

July 1, 1772   **In London, the Privy Council preliminary approves the Grand Ohio Company's Vandalia Colony; but the colony will never materialize.**

The Vandalia Colony, aka *Westsylvania*—to be located along the shared border region of present-day West Virginia and Kentucky—will not receive the final Crown approval the investors seek due to the rapidly deteriorating events between Great Britain and the American colonies.

> Note: In the summer of 1776, settlers and land speculators supporting Vandalia statehood would petition the Second Continental Congress, but rivals would work against it, and the plan would be rejected. After the American War for Independence, the Vandalia Company would again apply for Vandalia statehood, but disputes over western lands between Pennsylvania and Virginia would prevent it.
>
> Whether called Vandalia, Westsylvania, or Pittsylvania, we are reminded of the proposed colony by the modern Westsylvania Jazz and Blues Festival held annually in the town of Indiana, Pennsylvania, and by today's Pittsylvania County in southern Virginia.

| July 5, 1772 | **Passed to benefit Britain's East India Company, the Indemnity Act of 1767 expires.** |

For five years the Indemnity Act has provided a rebate of 25 percent to the East India Company for the taxes paid on tea exported to the American colonies. Now, with the Act's expiration, the tea prices will have to go up, as the company—with massive surpluses of tea—is in financial straits.

| Aug. 27, 1772 | **Lord Hillsborough is replaced by Lord Dartmouth as secretary of state for the American colonies.** |

William Legge, aka Lord Dartmouth, will serve as Britain's American secretary of state until the outbreak of hostilities in 1775.

> Note: Though Lord Dartmouth would be viewed by many as being too soft on the Americans—like his predecessor, Lord Hillsborough—Dartmouth was opposed to their westward trespasses into Indian lands.

| Sept. 1772 | **The British garrison at Fort Pitt is reduced as soldiers are sent east to help quell the growing civil unrest.** |

Britain offers a £500 reward for the arrest of those responsible for burning the HBS *Gaspee*.

> Note: The reward would never be collected.

The British Crown declares its right to replace colonial judges and begins paying the salaries of certain judges directly.

The salaries of royal governors, judges, and other officials in America have traditionally been paid by the colonial assemblies. As such, many in Britain believe those assemblies wield an undue influence and control over the royal officials and support the change. Yet to the Americans, by losing the *power of the purse,* many consider this new situation a loss of control over their own affairs.

> Note: The British would view the American response as strange: "We're paying their salaries and you complain?"
>
> The direct payment of judges is alluded to in grievance nine of the U.S. Declaration of Independence.

| Nov. 2, 1772 | **Boston creates a *Committee of Correspondence* to communicate with other Massachusetts towns.** |

Sam Adams wishes to establish a reliable communications system connecting the Boston radicals with Massachusetts towns and others "friendly to the cause"—an underground network to be anchored by the trusted Committee of Correspondence. Adams hopes to use the communications network to:

- Explain the radicals' position on the people's rights and liberties.
- Show how Britain has violated and continues to violate those rights.
- Keep all informed about current events.

> Note: Within a year, committees of correspondence would be established in nearly all of the American colonies, helping to foster a growing cohesiveness among them.

| Nov. 1772 | **In London, Benjamin Franklin attempts to present a Massachusetts petition protesting the usurping of the colony's civil authority.** |

The petition to the British Ministry protests the loss of local control by having the royal governor's salary paid by the Crown instead of the Massachusetts General Court. Franklin is persuaded by Lord Dartmouth to keep the petition for now, and to present it at a better date and time.

| Nov. 20, 1772 | **Attempting to influence the other colonies, Boston's Committee of Correspondence issues a list of British violations of American liberties.** |

| Dec. 2, 1772 | **From London, Benjamin Franklin sends the Speaker of the Massachusetts Assembly, Thomas Cushing, a pilfered packet of incriminating papers written by Governor Hutchinson.** |

The letters, written a few years earlier, include private correspondences by Hutchinson and his brother-in-law, Massachusetts Attorney General Andrew Oliver, to British officials concerning the situation in Boston. In the letters, Hutchinson blames the unrest on a few intriguing individuals; urges that the remaining Townshend Acts be kept in place; and argues for British troops to be sent to Boston to restore order, suggesting, "There must be an abridgment of what are called English liberties."

> Note: The Hutchinson letters were among a collection of private papers written by certain officials and held in possession of Thomas Whately, once clerk to former Prime Minister Charles Townshend. But Whately had died six months earlier and the letters had been mysteriously given to Franklin.
>
> Though unethical, as an agent of Massachusetts, Franklin desired to secretly expose Hutchinson and Oliver's private correspondences, as both men greatly influenced Parliamentary policy toward Massachusetts.

| Jan. 6, 1773 | **Enslaved Africans petition the Massachusetts General Court for their freedom.** |

With the support of abolitionists, a slave named *Felix* has penned the petition on behalf of a group of Boston slaves. The petition states that the Africans overall are of good character and their freedom would contribute to the public good. The slaves describe their stark condition—"We have no Wives. No Children. We have no City. No Country. But we have a Father in Heaven, and we are determined, as far as his Grace shall enable us, and as far as our degraded contemptuous Life will admit, to keep his Commandments: Especially will we be obedient to our Masters, so long as God in his sovereign Providence shall suffer us to be holden in Bondage."

The petition concludes: "We humbly beg Leave to add but this one Thing more: We pray for such Relief only, which by no Possibility can ever be productive of the least Wrong or Injury to our Masters; but to us will be as Life from the dead."

| Feb. 6, 1773 | **New York's statue honoring William Pitt is vandalized.** |

Reacting to the vandalism, the New York Assembly imposes a penalty of £500 or one year in jail for defacing either of New York's two public statues—the other being the equine statue of King George III.

> Note: William Pitt's New York statue had stood unmolested since September 1770.

| March 1773 | **Virginia's House of Burgesses creates an eleven-member Committee of Correspondence.** |

Virginia's assembly issues a call for each of the North American colonies to do the same in order to enable the sharing of communications between them.

| April 20, 1773 | **Enslaved Africans repetition Governor Thomas Hutchinson and the Massachusetts General Court for freedom and relief.** |

The petition thanks the General Court for debating the issue in its previous session and hopes freedom shall be granted in the next. The petition states that the Africans, if freed, will not demand just pay for past servitude as it would be detrimental to their present masters, but ask only for ample relief, which, as men, they have a right to. "As free men, we are willing to submit to the law made in regard to us until we can remove ourselves to the coast of Africa to build a settlement there—which we intend to do."

| Note: | By stating that they planned to move to Africa, the slaves hoped to make their emancipation more likely, for many White Americans feared the idea of Africans living among them as free men. |
| | *Liberia* would be founded on Africa's western coast to receive freed slaves from the United States. Sponsored by the American Colonization Society, Liberia—meaning "free place"— would begin receiving ex-slaves from the United States in 1822, eventually totaling nearly 12,000 people. |

| May 10, 1773 | **The *Tea Act* of 1773 is passed by Britain's Parliament.** |

With the East India Company $600 million in debt, the Tea Act is designed to stave off financial ruin by allowing the company to dispose of its excess tea in the American market.

The Tea Act brings about the following changes:

- Eliminates the import duty on tea imported into Great Britain.

- Retains the 3-pence-per-pound duty on tea shipped to the American colonies.

- Permits the East India Company to ship its tea directly to the colonies rather than first routing it through London and the auction houses as formerly required

- Eliminates the American transporters from the market.

- Eliminates most of the colonial wholesale tea merchants. Now, the tea is to be received only by special company consignees located in New York, Charles Town, Philadelphia, and Boston.

| Note: | Though the 1767 Revenue Act, aka Townshend duties, had been repealed in April 1770—the Act's 3-pence tax on tea had been retained. The tea tax would continue to be collected in the colonial ports by customs officers—to be paid within twenty days of a ship's arrival. |
| | By eliminating the private shippers, retail middlemen, and the London import tax by shipping tea directly to the American colonies, it was hoped that the resulting cheaper-priced tea would help save the East India Company and drive out the Dutch competitors. |

Most Americans react to the Tea Act with resentment.

Among the main grievances:

- Many colonial leaders see this as a grab for money and power by the British Crown and the East India Company. Are the Americans simply being used to reward the company's mismanagement and save its financial backers from ruin?

- The American wholesale tea merchants and transporters resent being eliminated from the business. Unlike before, all tea imports are to be now funneled through a few select individuals serving as company consignees.

- Other colonial merchants also resent the Tea Act, perceiving it as furthering the British East India's monopoly over the tea trade and setting a bad precedent. Could not Britain thus grant other monopolies to the East India Company, or to other favored groups and individuals?

- By retaining the 3 pence tax on tea, Parliament was maintaining its right to tax the Americans—whether the Americans liked it or not.

Note:	The American colonial merchants were a rich, powerful, and influential group, and many had grown distrustful of the British and their intentions.
	Many American consumers preferred the cheaper smuggled Dutch tea. As such, both they and those involved in the lucrative business of providing it, would resent the British government's attempt to eliminate the Dutch tea from the market.

The Tea Act becomes a matter of principle and an easy target of defiance.

Former colonial protests had forced the repeal of the 1765 Stamp Act and 1767 Townshend Revenue Act—except for its 3-pence tax on tea. As such, the 1773 Tea Act becomes a reminder of this remaining tax, and many believe it is time to finish the job. Beginning in Philadelphia and New York, Sons of Liberty groups mobilize the people against it by reviving the sentiment of *No taxation without representation!*

Note:	For five and a half years, the colonists had been paying the 3-pence tea tax, but the issue had become somewhat like a *sleeping dog*. Now, the passage of the Tea Act would come to represent *the kick that woke the dog*.
	Boston's Sam Adams and other radicals of the various Committees of Correspondence objected to the Tea Act and would work to further the people's opposition to it.
	The Sons of Liberty would put pressure on the tea consignees to refuse to receive the tea and to resign their posts.
	Women, as the primary consumers of tea, would play an active role in the boycotts.

June 1, 1773   **The *Second Treaty of Augusta*: Georgia receives large tracts of Creek and Cherokee lands.**

The Cherokee are heavily in debt to the traders and request a meeting to deal with the issue. At the conference, the Indians agree to the following:

- The Cherokee relinquish more than 2 million acres of land to Georgia in exchange for debt forgiveness.

- The Creek (Muskogee) cede claim to 675,000 acres known as the *Oconee-Ogeechee Strip*. The area—jointly claimed by both the Cherokee and the Creek—was previously granted to Georgia by the Cherokee, upsetting the Creek who received nothing. Now, in exchange for debt forgiveness and promises of firearms, powder, and lead, the Creek resentfully relinquish the rights to their prized hunting area in what becomes known as the *New Purchase*.

Note:	When trading with the Indians, it was a common ploy to overextend credit to the tribes. Then, when the debts became too great to pay, their lands would become a last resource for exchange.

June 1773   **Governor Hutchinson's private papers are published in the *Boston Gazette*, causing a furor in Massachusetts.**

Against Franklin's wishes, John Adams, as leader of Massachusetts's Committee of Correspondence, has the letters published, creating an immediate outcry as citizens learn that

Hutchinson had earlier urged Britain to send additional troops to Boston and called for a curtailment of the people's liberties.

> Note: The publications would only increase the opposition to Governor Hutchinson and Lieutenant Governor Andrew Oliver.
>
> The surreptitious reading of correspondences between royal officials in North America and those in Great Britain was not unusual, but Governor Hutchinson's private papers had now become a public matter—on both sides of the Atlantic.
>
> The source of the letters, Benjamin Franklin, was kept confidential.
>
> Hutchinson's letters would also be published in the *Massachusetts Spy* and printed in various pamphlets to be read throughout the colonies.

The Massachusetts General Court petitions the king and the British Ministry to remove Governor Hutchinson and Lieutenant Governor Oliver from office.

The petition calls for both men's removal due to lack of public confidence. Employed as an agent for Massachusetts, the petition will be presented by Benjamin Franklin.

June 8, 1773   **Leaving his New York headquarters, General Thomas Gage sails to London.**

General Gage has been granted a year's leave to deal with family affairs—and to consult with British government officials concerning the situation in America.

Summer 1773   **Using the Ohio River, the first migration into western Virginia and Kentucky begins.**

Surveyors, traders, and those seeking the choicest lands by arriving before the others soon to follow, begin to trickle down the Ohio River as the Shawnee take notice of this new situation.

> Note: Though the Iroquois had relinquished claims to the Kentucky region by both the 1752 Logstown Treaty and the 1768 Fort Stanwix Treaty, other tribes had not. The western region had long served as prime hunting grounds for the Indians, and neither the Cherokee nor Shawnee wished to relinquish Kentucky to White intrusions.
>
> Many of the early settlers entering the region would establish claims to frontier lands by a method known as *tomahawk rights*: Simply girdle some trees at the head of a water spring or other prominent site and cut your initials into them. Though unsophisticated, this forest signage system effectively showed other newcomers that the land was already claimed. Invariably, these *tomahawk marks* would incense the Indians when discovered—for the marks meant the Whites were now upon them.

July 5, 1773   **The recently formed *Illinois Company* purchases Indian lands in frontier Illinois.**

Despite British prohibitions against the private purchase of Indian lands, the Illinois Company, composed of Philadelphia merchants, buys two large tracts of lands from the *Kaskaskia, Peoria,* and *Cahokia* tribes.

> Note: The company's investors knew of the *Pratt-Yorke* decision made on December 24, 1757, regarding lands acquired in India by the British East India Company and favorably interpreted it as authorization for their purchase.
>
> Britain's Board of Trade would not recognize the Illinois Company's dubious claims; therefore, the investors turned to Virginia Governor Lord Dunmore, who—in return for his influential assistance—joined with company investors hoping to enrich himself.

July 1773 **London learns of the stolen Hutchinson letters and of their publication in Boston.**

The news causes a furor in Great Britain; how dare Massachusetts publish private letters! As a result—accusations begin. Who in London pilfered the letters and forwarded them to Massachusetts?

The East India Company selects agents to receive its tea in North America.

Agents are selected to receive the tea on consignment and distribute it for a commission. These coveted positions are few in number; are expected to be quite lucrative; and are filled by the well-connected, causing resentment.

Note: The selection of colonial tea agents would be one of the primary drivers of the protests, as they were seen as being granted special favor at the expense of others.

Sept. 1773 **The British East India Company readies plans to ship 500,000 pounds of surplus tea to the North American colonies.**

In North America, common cause helps unite those merchants in opposition to the Tea Act, as talk of resisting the tea imports continues to grow.

Sept. 1, 1773 **Phillis Wheatley, an African formerly enslaved in Boston, publishes** *Poems on Various Subjects, Religious and Moral.*

Published in London, the book of poetry will make Phyllis Wheatley the most famous African American of the day—both in North America and in Europe.

Note: Believing her poems would not be published in America, in the spring of 1773, Wheatley had traveled to England with Nathaniel Wheatly seeking a publisher.

Debate would swirl at the time over the authenticity of Wheatley's writings, as most White people in England and America were amazed at her command of serious literature. In London's *Critical Review*, a reviewer wrote, "The Negroes of Africa are generally treated as a dull, ignorant, and ignoble race of men, fit only to be slaves, and incapable of any considerable attainments in the liberal arts and sciences. A poet or a poetess amongst them, of any tolerable genius, would be a prodigy in literature. Phillis Wheatley, the author of these poems, is that literary Phaenomenon ... The author appears to be of a serious, and religious turn of mind."

Wheatley's works would be read and commented on by many of the American Founding Fathers, including Thomas Jefferson.

Oct. 9, 1773 **The Shawnee thwart the first White attempt to settle Kentucky lands.**

Daniel Boone leads fifty White settlers and several African slaves overland from North Carolina in hopes of founding a Kentucky frontier settlement, but they are turned back by the Indians one month after their arrival. Considered trespassers by the Shawnee, the Indians manage to capture James Boone and William Russel during an attack and kill the captives after torturing each. Due to Shawnee hostilities and the death of his son, Daniel Boone and the others return to North Carolina.

Oct. 16, 1773 **Philadelphia passes resolutions urging every American to resist consuming tea.**

Philadelphia learns that tea shipments are scheduled to arrive in the city before the year is out. As a result, the campaign to resist the tea imports goes into high gear, hoping to persuade citizens to oppose tea consumption and for the city's tea agents to resign. The Philadelphia resolutions include the following:

- That the disposal of their own property is the inherent right of freemen; that there can be no property in that which another can, of right, take from us without our consent; that the claim of Parliament to tax American is, in other words, a claim of right to levy contributions on us at pleasure.

- That the duty imposed by Parliament upon tea landed in America is a tax on the Americans, or levying contributions on them without their consent.

- That the express purpose for which the tax is levied on the Americans, namely for the support of government, administration of justice, and defense of His Majesty's dominions in America, has a direct tendency to render assemblies useless and to introduce arbitrary government and slavery.

- That a virtuous and strenuous opposition to the ministerial plan of governing America is absolutely necessary to preserve even the shadow of liberty and is a duty every freeman in America owes to his country, to himself, and to his posterity.

- That the resolutions lately entered into by the East India Company to send out their tea to America, subject to payment of duties on its being landed here, is an open attempt to enforce this ministerial plan and a violent attack upon the liberties of America.

- That it is the duty of every American to oppose this attempt.

- That whoever shall directly or indirectly, countenance this attempt or in any wise aid or abet in unloading, receiving, or vending the tea sent or sent out by the East India Company while it remains subject to the payment of a duty here, is an enemy to his country.

- That a committee be immediately chosen to wait on those gentlemen who, it is reported, are appointed by the East India Company to receive and sell said tea and request them, from a regard to their characters and the peace and good order of the city and province, immediately resign their appointment.

Mid Oct. 1773   **In London, the expected East India tea is readied to be shipped.**

Colonial newspapers publish that the East India Company is shipping 600 chests of tea to four American ports: Philadelphia, Boston, New York, and Charles Town.

Nov. 1, 1773   **In Portsmouth, New Hampshire, an unpopular customs officer is tarred and feathered.**

Officer John Malcom haughtily seizes the ship *Brothers* for not having a ship's register, causing the infuriated sailors to tar and feather Malcom and parade him through the streets for an hour before unceremoniously releasing him.

> Note: Malcom was fortunate his tormentors permitted him to wear his clothes while being tarred. Three months later, in Boston, the despised John Malcom would be beaten, abused, and tarred and feathered—this time without his clothing—leading to more severe results.
>
> Though Malcom worked for British customs, he was an American from Boston.

Nov. 2, 1773   **The Sons of Liberty demand the resignations of Boston's tea agents.**

The resignations are to be conducted publicly the following day under the Liberty Tree.

| Nov. 3, 1773 | **The Boston tea agents fail to appear—disappointing a gathered crowd.** |

Nearly 500 people wait at the Liberty Tree, but the agents do not show, and a search party is sent to find them.

| Nov. 18, 1773 | **Fearing for their safety, Boston's tea agents take refuge on Castle Island.** |

In a meeting at Faneuil Hall, citizens demand the tea consignees resign their positions, but they refuse.

| Nov. 28, 1773 | **The first of four tea ships en route to Boston, the *Dartmouth*, arrives in the harbor loaded with 114 chests of tea.** |

Boston is abuzz with news of the *Dartmouth*'s arrival as people wonder how to handle the situation. Led by Sam Adams and other prominent Boston citizens, a call for a town meeting is issued as resistance to the tea's landing begins in earnest.

| Nov. 29, 1773 | **Boston citizens gather to debate a course of action.** |

So many citizens turn out that the meeting must be moved to the Old South Church as the angry crowd demands the *Dartmouth* return to England. Yet Governor Hutchinson is determined to enforce the law and will not permit the ship to leave, creating a political impasse as the people vote to pay no tax and prohibit the tea from being unloaded at all costs. Tensions will simmer in Boston for the next two weeks.

> Note: The tea duty was required to be paid within twenty days of arrival, making December 17 the last day to pay the tax. If not paid—rather than being forced to return to England—the tea would be unloaded by customs and stored beginning December 18.

| Nov. 30, 1773 | **The *Dartmouth* is docked at Griffin's Wharf as Boston's citizens meet again.** |

A message to Boston from the East India Company is read requesting that the tea be unloaded and stored in local warehouses until further instructions can be received. However, the people refuse, for if the tea is unloaded onto land—the required duties will have to be paid.

> Note: The *Dartmouth* would be permitted to unload all its cargo except tea. To ensure this, a *watch committee* was formed to observe the ship at all times.

| Dec. 1773 | **To slow immigration to America, Britain forbids further royal land grants in the colonies.** |

> Note: As relations continued to deteriorate, Britain wished to rein in its growing American colonies and their increasing assertions of rights and self-government. Feeling it was losing control over the Americans, the British Board of Trade did not want people spilling west into the Indian lands recently granted to the influential land companies.

Instructions are given to the royal governors prohibiting new land grants until further notice at the recommendation of the commissioners of the Board of Trade, stating, "the emigration of his Majesty's European subjects ... has for some time past had so great a weight with this Board that it has induced us to deny our concurrence to many proposals of grants of land even in those parts of the continent of America where in all other respects we are of opinion that it consists with the true policy of this kingdom to encourage settlements."

Britain forbids naturalizations of foreign citizens in the American colonies under any conditions and prohibits their purchases of lands.

All royal governors are instructed, "that you do not upon any pretense whatsoever give your assent to any Bill or Bills that you may have been or shall hereafter be passed by the Council and Assembly of the Province under your Government for the naturalization of Aliens … nor for establishing a Title in any Person to Lands, Tenement & real estates in our said Province originally granted to, or purchased by Aliens antecedent to Naturalization." As such, from now on, British naturalization is to be awarded only by the legal statutes of the motherland and not by the various colonial laws regarding the naturalization of foreigners.

Note: This forbiddance is alluded to in grievance seven of the U.S. Declaration of Independence.

Dec. 1, 1773   **At Charles Town, South Carolina, an expected tea shipment arrives from London.**

Arriving aboard the *London*, 257 chests of tea are forced to remain on the ship as the ship's captain and Charles Town's tea consignees ponder the volatile situation. In the meantime, handbills go up around town denouncing the tea and urging citizens to attend a town meeting.

Note: After three days of town meetings, the South Carolina tea consignees were convinced to refuse the tea, but a problem remained. Even though no tea agents would receive it—like Boston—if the duty was not paid by December 20, the tea would be unloaded by customs officers and placed in dockside warehouses.

Dec. 2, 1773   **At Boston, a second tea ship arrives from London.**

The *Eleanor* arrives with 116 chests of tea and is docked at Griffin's Wharf.

Dec. 6, 1773   **A third tea ship approaches Boston but is stopped for quarantine.**

With 112 chests of tea, the *Beaver* stays out of harbor, quarantined for a week at Rainsford Island in the fear that smallpox is on board.

Dec. 11, 1773   **In London, two prominent gentlemen duel over the Hutchinson letters affair.**

After each man falsely accuses the other of forwarding Governor Hutchinson's letters to Boston, John Temple has challenged William Whately to a duel. Born in Boston and currently serving as New Hampshire's lieutenant governor, the hot-headed Temple engages Whately, a wealthy British banker, in a sword duel in Hyde Park. Wounded slightly and temporarily incapacitated, William Whately retires from the fight but both men agree that the duel shall be continued.

Note: Public interest was still keen to find the person responsible for stealing and forwarding the correspondences of Hutchinson and Lieutenant Governor Andrew Oliver to the British Ministry, now being published openly in the colonies.

The real culprit—Benjamin Franklin—would be forced to publicly confess in order to end the unnecessary duel and to finally put the matter to rest.

Dec. 13, 1773   **Boston learns that the tea consignees in Philadelphia and New York have resigned.**

This news makes the Bostonians more determined to force their tea agents to do the same.

Dec. 14, 1773   **Tensions rise in Boston, as demands continue for the tea ships to return to England.**

After sixteen days bobbing in Boston's harbor, time is quickly running out for the *Dartmouth* to either unload her tea cargo and pay the despised tax or simply sail away. Caught in the dilemma, the captains of the *Dartmouth* and *Eleanor* seek permission to leave Boston, taking the tea with them.

Dec. 15, 1773   **In New York, the Sons of Liberty introduce an *Association Agreement* pressuring citizens not to accept the British tea.**

"The following association is signed by a great number of the principal gentlemen of the city, merchants, lawyers, and other inhabitants of all ranks, and it is still carried about the city to give an opportunity to those who have not yet signed, to unite with their fellow citizens, to testify their abhorrence to the diabolical project of enslaving America."

The agreement begins: "It is essential to the freedom and security of a free people, that no taxes be imposed upon them but by their own consent, or their representatives." The resolutions are as follows:

- "1st, *Resolved*, that whoever shall aid or abet, or in any manner assist, in the introduction of tea from any place whatsoever, into this colony, while it is subject, by a British Act of Parliament, to the payment of a duty, for the purpose of raising a revenue in America, he shall be deemed an enemy to the liberties of America.

- 2nd, *Resolved*, that whoever shall be aiding, or assisting, in the landing, or carting of such tea, from any ship, or vessel, or shall hire any house, storehouse, or cellar or any place whatsoever, to deposit the tea, subject to a duty as aforesaid, he shall be deemed an enemy to the liberties of America.

- 3rd, *Resolved*, that whoever shall sell, or buy, or in any manner contribute to the sale, or purchase of tea, subject to a duty as aforesaid, or shall aid, or abet, in transporting such tea, by land or water, from this city, until the 7th George III, chap. 46, commonly called the Revenue Act, shall be totally and clearly repealed, he shall be deemed an enemy to the liberties of America.

- 4th, *Resolved*, that whether the duties on tea, imposed by this Act, be paid in Great Britain or in America, our liberties are equally affected.

- 5th, *Resolved*, that whoever shall transgress any of these resolutions, we will not deal with, or employ, or have any connection with him."

With the *Beaver's* quarantine now lifted, the ship docks at Boston's Griffin's wharf.

Boston now has three ships tied dockside containing a total of 342 crates of tea—the *Dartmouth,* the *Eleanor,* and the *Beaver.*

> Note: Boston's Sons of Liberty were determined that the tea ships would not be unloaded and that they should be forced to return to England.
>
>   A fourth tea ship, the *William,* had wrecked en route to Boston off the coast of Cape Cod. The ship's tea cargo would be salvaged and transported to Fort Castle William where it would be happily consumed by British troops.

Dec. 16, 1773   **Nearly 5,000 citizens gather at Boston's Old South Meeting House.**

In a cold morning meeting, an overflow crowd learns that customs officials have denied permission for the tea ships to depart Boston. With the December 18 deadline looming, the meeting is adjourned until 3 p.m. as the governor is sought out to override the decision and permit the ships to return to London.

Note:	Complicating matters, Governor Hutchinson's sons, Thomas and Elisha Hutchinson, were consignees for the East India Company and were thus financially involved.

Bostonians destroy the East India Company's tea by dumping it into the harbor.

At approximately 6 p.m., after receiving word that Governor Hutchinson has denied permission for the tea ships to depart, Sam Adams rises and loudly declares, "This meeting can do nothing more to save the country," as a group of men and boys dressed loosely as Indians run to the docks shouting, "Boston Harbor a teapot tonight." The following are among the events of the evening:

- The crowd departs the Old South Meeting House to follow the *Indians* and cheers for three hours as the event unfolds.

Note:	Sam Adams and John Hancock—having secretly sent the Sons of Liberty into action—lingered at the meeting house, not wishing to be implicated in the activities and subjected to arrest.

- Three companies—each consisting of fifty to sixty men; mostly young apprentices and artisans in training; their faces blackened by soot and having feathers in their hair—receive word from Adams to board the ships and begin an orderly destruction of the tea cargo.

- The men begin by boarding the two ships tied to the dock—the *Dartmouth* and the *Eleanor*—while others row to the *Beaver* and bring her dockside for the tea destruction to be complete. According to plan, the men are very specific in their deeds. For three hours, the disguised young men work at hacking open the many wooden tea chests and tossing the contents overboard while cheered on by the dockside crowd.

- The British military forces—with no authority to act without the royal governor's permission—watch the scene unfold from a distance while standing ready to intercede if requested by civil authorities.

Note:	Having taken to their country homes, both Governor Thomas Hutchinson and Lieutenant Governor Andrew Oliver were unavailable to give orders to act against the vandals. In addition, British General Thomas Gage was in England at the time.
	For public relations, it was important that only the tea was destroyed. Hoping to establish a moral high ground despite their illegal actions, when finished, the tea-littered vessels were swept clean and a ship's lock broken during the event was replaced.
	Due to a low tide, much of the tea lay heaped in large mounds that rose above the shallow water's surface. Tea leaves would continue to float around the bay for weeks.
	In all, 342 chests of tea—92,000 pounds worth £10,000 at that time—were destroyed.

Dec. 17, 1773   **Bostonians awaken to a tea party hangover: "What have we done?"**

The next morning and throughout the day, curious residents walk the wharves and survey the results of the previous night. The sight of a tea-littered shoreline and three empty ships bobbing at dockside sobers many, who wonder aloud, "What will be next?"

The *Boston Tea Party* has the following effects:

- The king, his ministry, and Parliament view the act as a direct challenge to British authority by the people of Massachusetts and consider it treasonous.

- The lawless action represents a black eye delivered to the British and will serve as a major impediment to any reconciliation with Massachusetts.

- King George III becomes more personally involved in the struggle with the Americans: "We must master them or leave them to themselves."

- The king declares Massachusetts to be in a state of rebellion and decides to make an example of Boston using British might to do it, declaring, "The die is cast, the colonies must either submit or triumph."

> Note: Instead of bringing the colonists to submission, the king's decision would have the opposite effect.

- British General Thomas Gage will be ordered to move his military headquarters from New York to Boston to quell the growing rebellion.

- The event gives Great Britain a moral upper hand as the Bostonians appear little more than gangs of criminals.

- Many in England believe the American public is being brought to agitation by a few radical leaders. These leaders are accused of infecting ordinary people's minds with "100 rights they had never heard of and 100 grievances they had never felt."

- Living in London, Benjamin Franklin initially believes the Americans should pay for the destroyed tea but soon changes his mind after the British government insists on it. Franklin then urges the Americans to hold out and not give in, stating, "Do it for your children and grandchildren."

Dec. 22, 1773   **In Charles Town, South Carolina, the East India tea is unloaded and stored for *safekeeping*.**

After remaining onboard the *London* for three weeks, the deadline has passed for the tea duties to be either paid in full or the cargo shall be confiscated. Therefore, with the tea duties having not been paid, the impasse is broken by a customs officer who orders the tea unloaded and locked in a warehouse for nonpayment of duties.

> Note: An angry crowd would gather and *persuade* the tea agents to resign.
>
> Of the four cities receiving tea shipments, only in Charles Town would the tea be unloaded. The confiscated tea would be stored in a Charles Town warehouse until being sold in September 1776 to raise funds for the American War for Independence.

Dec. 25, 1773   **The East India tea arrives in Philadelphia, Pennsylvania.**

News of the Boston events has reached Philadelphia, and now the despised tea arrives aboard the *Polly*. Captain Ayres is warned of being tarred and feathered if he attempts to unload his cargo, as 697 chests of tea are left aboard the vessel, anchored at nearby Chester.

In England, Benjamin Franklin publicly confesses his involvement in the Hutchinson letters affair.

Franklin writes an editorial for the *London Chronicle* in which he confesses to having forwarded Governor Hutchinson's papers to Massachusetts but denies having taken them. This puts an end to the mystery and stops a second duel between John Temple and William Whately over the matter.

> Note: The news of Franklin's involvement would cause an immediate uproar in the British press and by the public. Accused of having fomented the American rebellion against Great Britain—Franklin's esteemed reputation would forever suffer.

Dec. 28, 1773   **Unable to unload in Philadelphia, the *Polly* sails away with its tea cargo.**

The Pennsylvania tea agents have been persuaded to not accept the tea and the *Polly*'s Captain Ayres returns to England with his cargo as Philadelphia citizens cheer the news.

ACKNOWLEDGEMENTS

I would like to thank the following people for their support in writing this book:

First, my wife Cynthia, without whose love, patience, prodding, and assistance this work would have never been completed.

Second, my copy editor Dan Shutt, who gave the project life by his steady guidance leading to an organized product. As a citizen of the United Kingdom, Dan also provided periodic insight from a British perspective.

Third, my friends Bert Eliason and Nancy McCullum, who provided initial editing contributions.

Fourth, my sister Cyndi Wolfe, who always kept faith in her brother.

In addition, I would like to thank the Eugene Public Library and the various coffee shops that tolerated my presence—particularly the Wandering Goat and 16 Tons Coffee.

Thanks to all.

ABOUT THE AUTHOR

Mr. Ray Brown has spent a lifetime studying American history and a 36-year career in the public schools sharing his love for the subject with students. In 2004, Mr. Brown, in an act of faith, made a decision that would change his life. Perceiving a steady erosion of our nation's civil liberties, Brown—a firm believer in the Constitution—decided to leap the classroom walls and "take it to the streets" dressed in a newly made historical outfit. Calling himself *A Son of Liberty* and armed with copies of the Bill of Rights, Brown began a civic journey that to his surprise would be supported by nearly everyone—no matter one's political persuasion.

That was now nearly 10,000 copies ago.

Retiring from teaching in 2010, Mr. Brown made another monumental decision. In order to further promote the study of American history, the Constitution, and the Bill of Rights, Brown walked across the United States from Florence, Oregon, to Philadelphia's Independence Hall, and on to the Atlantic Ocean while talking to fellow Americans he met along his journey.

That was 3,200 miles ago.

Always a student of American history, before retirement Mr. Brown began composing a detailed timeline of the many events leading to the founding of the United States. This project would become another arduous journey—much longer than his *Walk Across America*. Simply beginning his work by plugging historical events into chronological order, like a jigsaw puzzle, a larger story began to emerge nearly always leading back to England. Now, fifteen years later, *From the Parent Stem: England and the Making of America* is born. It is Mr. Brown's opinion that such a work has never been written and represents a fresh perspective on an old subject.

Truly an epic work.

With degrees from Ohio State and the University of Oregon, Brown lives with his wife Cynthia in Eugene, Oregon.

Web Links

Email contact: sonoflibertywalk@gmail.com

Blog of Brown's *Son of Liberty Walk* across the U.S.: http://sonoflibertywalk.blogspot.com/